W9-CHP-033
5 0508 01921 794 3

This book has been made possible by contributions to the Voice for Great Ideas Campaign (2006 to 2009), whose generous donors include the following individuals and foundations:

Imprimatur Circle
The Ahmanson Foundation
Atkinson Family Foundation
The Stephen Bechtel Fund
The Getty Foundation
The Fletcher Jones Foundation
The Andrew W. Mellon Foundation
National Endowment for the Humanities
The Estate of Joan Palevsky
Barclay & Sharon Simpson

Laureate Circle
The Ralph M. Parsons Foundation
Stephen M. Silberstein
Judy & Bill Timken

Luminary Circle
Harriett & Richard Gold
Leo & Florence Helzel / Helzel Family Foundation
Barbara S. Isgur
Fred M. Levin & Nancy Livingston / The Shenson Foundation
The Estate of David H. Miller
Northern Trust
Eric Papenfuse & Catherine Lawrence
The Rosenthal Family Foundation / Jamie & David Wolf
Roth Family Foundation / Sukey & Gilbert Garcetti
Lisa See & Richard Kendall
Meryl & Robert Selig
Ralph & Shirley Shapiro
Sue Tsao
Peter Booth Wiley & Valerie Barth
Lynne Withey

Publisher's Circle
Anonymous
Jeanne & Michael Adams
EBSCO Publishing
Sonia H. Evers
Carol & John Field
Loren & Frances Rothschild

Literati Circle
William K. Coblentz
Charles R. & Mary Anne Cooper
The John Randolph Haynes & Dora Haynes Foundation / Gilbert Garcetti
Adele M. Hayutin
Raymond Lifchez
Susan McClatchy
Robert & Beverly Middlekauff
James & Carlin Naify
Muriel & Martin Paley
Jennifer Basye Sander
Sidney Stern Memorial Trust

Chairman's Circle
Wendy Ashmore
Clarence & Jacqueline Avant
Gene A. Brucker
Mary-Jo DelVecchio Good & Byron Good
Watson M. & Sita Laetsch
Michael McCone
William & Sheila Nolan
Kenneth & Frances Reid
Michael Sullivan

Director's Circle
Jola & John Anderson
Diana & Ehrhard Bahr
Marilyn Bancel
Robert Borofsky
Beverly Bouwsma
Daniel Boyarin
Joe & Wanda Corn
Liza Dalby
Sam Davis
William Deverell
Frances Dinkelspiel & Gary Wayne
Ross E. Dunn
Phyllis Gebauer
Walter S. Gibson
Jean E. Gold
Jennifer A. González
Daniel Heartz
Prof. & Mrs. D. Kern Holoman
Stephen & Gail Humphreys
Mark Juergensmeyer
Beth & Fred Karren
Lawrence Kramer
Constance Lewallen
David & Sheila Littlejohn
Dianne Sachko Macleod
Doris Cuneo Maslach
Thomas & Barbara Metcalf
Jack & Jacqueline Miles
Fran & Pat Mitchell
Barbara Z. Otto
Dale Peterson
Sheldon Pollock
Lucinda Reinold
Stephen P. Rice
Robert C. Ritchie
Rémy Saisselin
Carolyn See
Ruth A. Solie
Tania W. Stepanian
Patricia Trenton
Roy Wagner
John & Priscilla Walton
Kären Wigen & Martin Lewis
Stanley & Dorothy Wolpert

Patrons
Anonymous (2)
Elizabeth & David Birka-White
Michael Burawoy
Sue & John Diekman
Erich Gruen
Edward J. Kealey
Donald & Jean Lamm
Diane Leslie
Sylvia McLaughlin
Patricia S. Nettleship
Nel Noddings
Georgette O'Connor
Jefferson Parker
Alejandro Portes
Leslie Scalapino & Tom White
Neil Smelser
Sally & Frederic Tubach
J. Samuel Walker
Cynthia W. Woods

Mark Twain

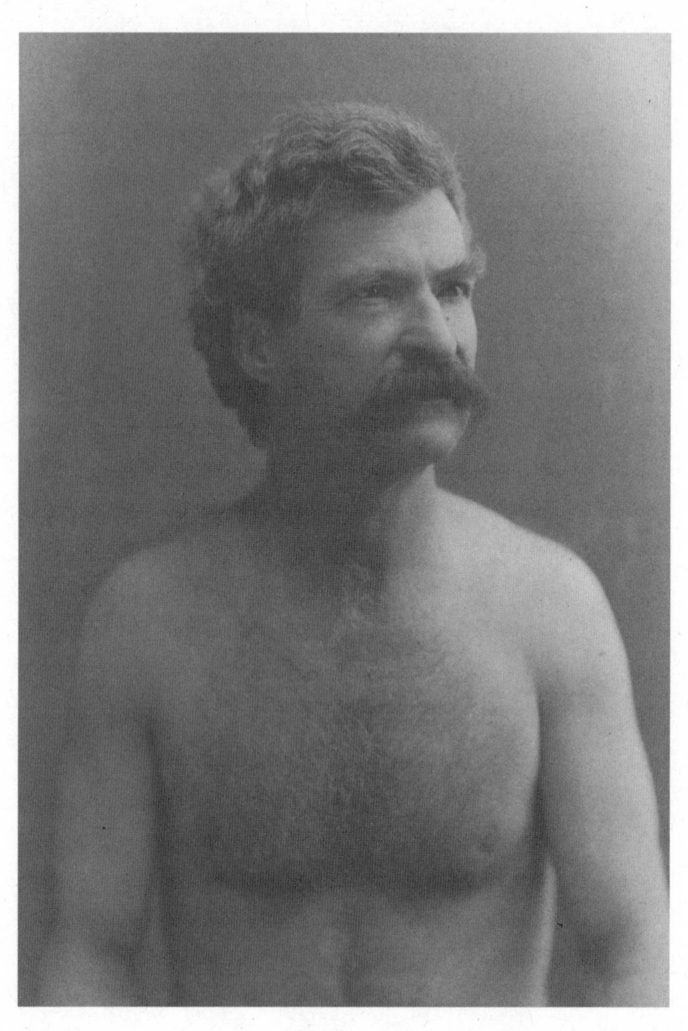

MARK TWAIN

The Adventures of Samuel L. Clemens

JEROME LOVING

UNIVERSITY OF CALIFORNIA PRESS BERKELEY LOS ANGELES LONDON

Frontispiece: Mark Twain shirtless (at about the time of *Huckleberry Finn*). Courtesy of the Mark Twain Papers, The Bancroft Library.

University of California Press, one of the most distinguished university presses in the United States, enriches lives around the world by advancing scholarship in the humanities, social sciences, and natural sciences. Its activities are supported by the UC Press Foundation and by philanthropic contributions from individuals and institutions. For more information, visit www.ucpress.edu.

University of California Press
Berkeley and Los Angeles, California

University of California Press, Ltd.
London, England

Library of Congress Cataloging-in-Publication Data
Loving, Jerome.
Mark Twain : the adventures of Samuel L. Clemens / Jerome Loving.
p. cm.
Includes bibliographical references and index.
ISBN 978-0-520-25257-8 (cloth : alk. paper)
1. Twain, Mark, 1835–1910. 2. Authors, American—19th century—Biography. 3. Humorists, American—19th century—Biography.
I. Title.
PS1331.L68 2010
818'.409—dc22
[B] 2009015366

Manufactured in the United States of America

19 18 17 16 15 14 13 12 11 10
10 9 8 7 6 5 4 3 2 1

This book is printed on Cascades Enviro 100, a 100% post consumer waste, recycled, de-inked fiber. FSC recycled certified and processed chlorine free. It is acid free, Ecologo certified, and manufactured by BioGas energy.

To Cathy, my "Livy"

Contents

II. WRITER IN THE EAST

III. THE ARTIST AND THE BUSINESSMAN

Acknowledgments

As I wrote this biography, certain classics in criticism and biography continued to guide me in my studies of Mark Twain and his work. A few that come directly to mind are by Walter Blair, Van Wyck Brooks, Louis J. Budd, Bernard DeVoto, Justin Kaplan, Albert Bigelow Paine, and Henry Nash Smith, but there are many others, too many to name on a subject more researched and written about than any other figure in American literature. To name one, I owe a permanent debt to James M. Cox's *Mark Twain: The Fate of Humor* (1966).

Without Robert H. Hirst, general editor, and the other editors, namely Victor Fischer and Lin Salamo, at the Mark Twain Project at the University of California at Berkeley, this biography would lack many of the insights born out of definitive editions of letters and texts, as well as the benefit derived from the Project's vast archival holdings. Bob Hirst was extremely helpful in going through my manuscript with his magnifying glass. Another Mark Twain expert who took a turn at my work is Alan Gribben; I thank him for the care with which he read a late draft and made useful suggestions. I would also like to thank Kevin Mac Donnell of Austin, Texas, currently the world's leading Twain collector, for not only reading my biography but also providing many of its unique illustrations, including the dust jacket photo. I owe Kenneth M. Sanderson a favor for allowing me to consult his unpublished paper "The Books of Charles L. Webster & Co." for appendix B. I am grateful to Neda Salem, office manager of the MTP, for her assistance and many courtesies during my several visits to that most important archive.

I owe a long-standing debt to my dear friend Ed Folsom, who has critiqued most of my work in manuscript over the last quarter of a century, including this biography. Another to thank in this regard is M. Jimmie Killingsworth, also a dear friend and colleague, currently head of the English Department at Texas A&M University, where I teach American literature. Louis J. Budd, the reigning dean of Mark Twain studies and my former professor at Duke University in the 1970s, read my manuscript and steadied my hand with regard to both facts and their application. My colleague William Bedford Clark, a poet and a specialist in southern American literature, was always generous with his insights about Mark Twain. I have also been fortunate to have professional advice from Bernard Beranek, Mary Boewe, Paul Christensen, Richard Hauer Costa, Carl Dawson, Susan Goodman, Ezra Greenspan, Cameron L. House, Donald R. House, Jr., David C. Loving, Patricia Loving, Philip McFarland, J. Lawrence Mitchell, Tom Quirk, Stephen Railton, Robert D. Richardson, Barb Schmidt, and Henry Sweets of the Mark Twain Museum in Hannibal. Gary Scharnhorst kindly shared with me the typescript of his now published *Mark Twain: The Complete Interviews* (2006). At the University of California Press, I want to thank Stanley Holwitz, assistant director and acquisitions editor, who has supported my work for more than a decade. He was advised on this book by Frederick Crews and John Seelye. Thanks, too, to Laura Cerruti and Laura Harger, editors at the Press; copyeditor Steven Baker; Lorett Trees, archivist, Bryn Mawr College; Patricia Philippon, collections manager, Mark Twain House & Museum; and Katherine Collett, archivist at Hamilton College.

For assistance in securing a fellowship from the National Endowment for the Humanities that allowed me to complete this biography in time for the centennial of Mark Twain's death, I thank Lawrence Buell and Alan Trachtenberg. I would also like to acknowledge the John Simon Guggenheim Foundation for its support during the early work on this book. At home, this biography was also sponsored by a grant from the College of Liberal Arts at Texas A&M University, where I thank Dean Charles A. Johnson. Two others on my campus to thank are Stephanie Darrow and Stephanie Rivera, my student assistants in 2008–2009.

Permission to publish quotations from letters in multiple collections comes through the MTP (where copies are available) from the following libraries and institutions: Henry W. and Albert A. Berg Collection, New York Public Library; Cornell University Library; Division of Rare Books and Manuscripts, New York Public Library; Franklin D. Roosevelt Library, Hyde Park, New York; Hamilton College Library; Huntington Library; James S. Copley Library, La Jolla, California; Library of Poultney Bigelow, Bigelow Homestead, Malden-on-Hudson, New York; Mark Twain House, Hartford, Connecticut; Mark Twain Museum, Hannibal; Middlebury College Library; Oxford University Library; Pierpont Morgan Library; Princeton University Library; St. John's Seminary, Camarillo, California; University of Illinois Library; University of Louisville Library; University of Southern California Library; Harry Ransom Humanities Research Center, University of Texas Library; University of Virginia Library; University of Wisconsin Library; Vassar University Library; and Yale University Library.

This book is dedicated to my wife, Cathleen C. Loving, my first reader. We are the lucky grandparents of six boys and girls. Sam Clemens very much wanted grandchildren and never lived long enough to see his only granddaughter. I think he would approve of my naming ours in a book about him. So thanks to Mandy, Maya, Jack, Mary, Dave, and Charlie.

Chronology of the Life and Works of Mark Twain

1835: Samuel Langhorne Clemens born two months premature in Florida, Missouri, on the Salt River, November 30, the sixth of seven children.

1839: Clemens family moves to Hannibal, Missouri, on the Mississippi River.

1847: John Marshall Clemens, Sam's father, dies March 24.

1849–1852: Apprenticed to Joseph P. Ament, editor of the Hannibal *Courier,* and subsequently to his older brother Orion Clemens, editor of the *Western Union and Hannibal Journal.* Writes earliest fiction for area newspapers and "The Dandy Frightening the Squatter" for the Boston *Carpet-Bag.*

1853–1854: Leaves home for St. Louis, New York City, and, Philadelphia, where he works as a journeyman printer. Visits Washington, D.C.

1855–1857: Lives and works in Keokuk, Iowa; St. Louis; and Cincinnati. In February of final year he meets Horace Bixby while traveling on the Mississippi River to New Orleans to sail for South America. Bixby agrees to make him an apprentice steamboat pilot for $500.

1858–1861: Serves as a pilot on nineteen or twenty different steamboats operating between St. Louis and New Orleans. Younger brother Henry dies a week after a steamboat accident on June 13, 1858. When Civil War breaks up river commerce in June 1861, Clemens joins the Marion

Rangers, a ragtag state militia that disbands after two weeks. Departs for Nevada Territory July 18 with brother Orion, who has been appointed by the Lincoln administration as secretary to the territorial governor. Arrives in Carson August 14. Becomes a silver and gold prospector.

1862: Joins the staff of the Virginia City *Enterprise* and writes "Petrified Man" and other unsigned items.

1863: Adopts the nom de guerre "Mark Twain," makes his first visit to San Francisco, meets Artemus Ward in Virginia City, and publishes "A Bloody Massacre near Carson," also known as the "Empire City Massacre Hoax."

1864: Elected "Governor of the Third House" by fellow journalists in Carson City, Nevada. Writes hoax suggesting that funds collected for Union soldiers went to a "Miscegenation Society" in the East. Moves permanently to San Francisco to avoid prosecution for challenging an editor from a competing newspaper to a duel resulting from his hoax. Writes for the San Francisco *Morning Call* and the *Californian,* where he meets fellow contributors Bret Harte, Charles Henry Webb, and Charles Warren Stoddard. Writes many of the sketches that would make up his first book, including "Aurelia's Unfortunate Young Man." Following a run-in with the police involving Steve Gillis, he relocates to Jim's Gillis's cabin in the mining town of Jackass Hill.

1865: Returns to San Francisco. Writes "Jim Smiley and His Jumping Frog," first published in the New York *Saturday Press* of November 18, 1865.

1866: Visits Hawaii as a reporter for the Sacramento *Union;* lectures on the Sandwich Islands in California and Nevada; travels to New York via the Nicaragua Isthmus for the San Francisco *Alta California.*

1867: Lectures for the first time in New York City. Publishes *The Celebrated Jumping Frog of Calaveras County, and Other Sketches;* sails on the *Quaker City* for Europe and the Holy Land; returns from cruise in November. Meets Olivia Langdon (Livy) and her parents in New York City.

1868: Visits Livy on New Year's Day. Travels in April to San Francisco to negotiate with the *Alta California* over book rights to the letters he wrote for newspaper publication from Europe and the Holy Land; finishes manuscript for *The Innocents Abroad;* lectures in California; courts Livy in Elmira, New York. Meets the Rev. Joseph H. Twichell, later a lifelong friend and fellow resident in Hartford, Connecticut.

1869: Becomes engaged to Livy Langdon; and purchases with help from his future father-in-law, Jervis Langdon, one-third interest in the Buffalo *Express.* Publishes *The Innocents Abroad.* Meets William Dean Howells in Boston.

1869–1870: Lecture tour with James Redpath Agency between November and January.

1870: Marries Livy February 2 and moves into furnished house in Buffalo purchased by her parents. Jervis Langdon dies of stomach cancer in August. Son Langdon Clemens born prematurely in November.

1871: Publishes *Mark Twain's (Burlesque) Autobiography.* Sells interest in Buffalo *Express,* moves to Hartford's Nook Farm, and rents home from Hooker family.

1872: Publishes *Roughing It* and *Mark Twain's Sketches* (London); lectures in England in the fall. First daughter, Olivia Susan Clemens (Susy), is born March 19. Only son, Langdon, dies June 2.

1873: Publishes *The Gilded Age* with Charles Dudley Warner. Lectures in London in the fall.

1874: *Colonel Sellers,* the play based on a character in *The Gilded Age,* opens in New York City. Publishes "A True Story" in the *Atlantic Monthly.* Publishes *Mark Twain's Sketches* (Hartford). Second daughter, Clara Langdon Clemens, is born June 8. Moves into his newly constructed home in Nook Farm.

1875: Publishes "Old Times of the Mississippi" in the *Atlantic* and *Sketches, New and Old.*

1876: Writes *1601;* writes *Ah Sin* with Bret Harte; publishes *The Adventures of Tom Sawyer.*

1877: Production of *Ah Sin* in Washington, D.C. Visits Bermuda with Joe Twichell. Delivers Whittier Birthday Dinner Speech in Boston. Markets "Mark Twain's Patent Self-Pasting Scrapbook."

1878: Publishes *Punch, Brothers, Punch!*

1878–1879: Lives in Germany, Italy, France, and England.

1880: Publishes *A Tramp Abroad.* Third daughter, Jane Lampton Clemens (Jean), born July 26.

1881: Meets George Washington Cable. Publishes *The Prince and the Pauper.*

1882: Travels down the Mississippi and visits New Orleans; returns upriver, stopping over in Hannibal on his way to St. Paul, and returns to New York and Hartford. Makes initial investment in the Paige Compositor. Writes "The Walt Whitman Controversy."

1883: Publishes *Life on the Mississippi.*

1884: Founds the Charles L. Webster Publishing Company.

1884–1885: Lecture tour with Cable.

1885: Publishes *Adventures of Huckleberry Finn* and *Personal Memoirs of U.S. Grant.*

1888: Publishes *Mark Twain's Library of Humor;* receives honorary master of arts degree from Yale.

1889: Publishes *A Connecticut Yankee in King Arthur's Court.*

1890: Mother Jane Lampton Clemens dies October 27.

1890–1891: Susy Clemens, preferring to use her first name, Olivia, with classmates, attends Bryn Mawr College.

1891: Family closes up Hartford house and sails to Europe. Twain stops further investments in the Paige Compositor. Arranges to write at least six travel letters from Europe for American newspaper publication.

1892: Publishes *Merry Tales* and *The American Claimant.* Family resides in Berlin and later Florence.

1893: Befriended by robber baron Henry Huttleston Rogers, vice president of Standard Oil, Twain makes frequent trips back to United States to look after his interests in his flagging publishing company and the Paige Compositor, in which he still owns many shares.

1894: Charles L. Webster Publishing Company declares bankruptcy. Twain publishes *Pudd'nhead Wilson.*

1895: Abandons his interests in the Paige Typesetter. Publishes "Fenimore Cooper's Literary Offenses." Family returns to the United States and resides for the summer at Quarry Farm in Elmira.

1895–1896: Lecture tour to Australasia, which becomes the basis for *Following the Equator* (1897).

1896: Susy Clemens dies of spinal meningitis August 18. Family establishes residence in England. Jean Clemens diagnosed with epilepsy. Publishes *Personal Recollections of Joan of Arc,* as well as *Tom Sawyer Abroad, Tom Sawyer, Detective, and Other Stories.* Meets William James.

1897: Brother Orion Clemens dies December 11. *Following the Equator* published.

1897–1899: Establishes residence in Vienna so that Clara can study piano. Begins writing "Which Was the Dream?" "The Great Dark," and other dreamscapes.

1898: Pays off all debts related to Webster & Company bankruptcy. Possibly meets Sigmund Freud in Vienna, then still working on *The Interpretation of Dreams.*

1898–1899: Works on the first two "Mysterious Stranger" drafts: "The Chronicle of Young Satan" and "Schoolhouse Hill."

1899: Publishes "Stirring Times in Austria," "Concerning the Jews," and "The Man That Corrupted Hadleyburg."

1900: Moves to England and finally New York City, where the family rents 10 West 10th Street. Publishes *The Man That Corrupted Hadleyburg, and Other Stories and Essays.*

1901: Publishes "To the Person Sitting in Darkness." Summers on Lake Saranac in the Adirondacks. Rents "baronial mansion" at Riverdale-on-the-Hudson.

1902: Visits Hannibal for the last time in conjunction with his going to the University of Missouri to accept an honorary Litt. D. degree. Summers at York Harbor, Maine, where Jean suffers two epileptic attacks. Livy suffers severe asthmatic attack and heart problems that prostrate her for six months. Isabel V. Lyon is hired as secretary. Jean contracts double pneumonia.

1902–1903: Works on "No. 44, The Mysterious Stranger." Summers in Elmira.

1903: Family returns to Riverdale; embarks for Florence in fall.

1904: Livy's health deteriorates. Works on "No. 44, The Mysterious Stranger." Sister-in-law Mollie Clemens dies January 15. Livy dies in Florence June 5. Family returns with body to Elmira. Sister Pamela dies August 31. Twain establishes residence at 21 Fifth Avenue, New York.

1905: Summers in Dublin, New Hampshire. Writes "3,000 Years among the Microbes" and "The War-Prayer." Publishes "King Leopold's Soliloquy."

1906: Publishes *What Is Man?* anonymously. Continues work on "No. 44." Appoints Albert Bigelow Paine as his official biographer.

1907: Visits Bermuda with Joe Twichell. Receives honorary Litt. D. degree from Oxford. Publishes *Christian Science.*

1908: Occupies "Stormfield" home in Redding, Connecticut, designed by John Howells. Nephew Samuel E. Moffett dies suddenly August 1. Suffers first attack of angina pectoris in August.

1909: Writes chapter 33 of "No. 44, The Mysterious Stranger." Publishes *Is Shakespeare Dead?* and *Extract from Captain Stormfield's Visit to Heaven.* Drafts "Letters from the Earth." Henry Rogers dies in May. Clemens suffers second attack of angina in June. Clara Clemens marries Ossip Gabrilowitsch at Stormfield October 6. Visits Bermuda with Paine in November and part of December. At Stormfield, daughter Jean Clemens dies in bathtub after an epileptic seizure on Christmas Eve.

1910: "Death of Jean" published in *Harper's Monthly* in January. Travels to Bermuda, falls ill, and returns in the company of Paine. Dies of heart failure April 21. Nina Clemens Gabrilowitsch, Twain's only grandchild, born August 18.

1936: Ossip Gabrilowitsch dies September 14.

1944: Clara Gabrilowitsch marries Jacques Samossoud May 11.

1962: Clara Clemens Gabrilowitsch Samossoud dies November 19.

1966: Nina Clemens Gabrilowitsch dies January 16.

Prologue

"She was always beautiful," Mark Twain wrote of his mother following her death in 1890. The woman who had given birth to Samuel Langhorne Clemens died in her eighty-eighth year. At the end, even with her mind in the fog of senility, she still knew him perfectly, this third son who had been born two months premature. "But to her disordered fancy I was not a gray-headed man [of almost fifty-five], but a school-boy, and had just arrived from the east on vacation." Actually, to be at her bedside, he had traveled from Hartford, Connecticut, where he had lived with his wife and three daughters for almost two decades, but he was soon to embark on a third decade in European exile. Jane Lampton Clemens had lived with her eldest son, Orion, and his wife in Keokuk, Iowa, on the Mississippi River, since 1883. "I knew her well during the first twenty-five years of my life," he wrote, "but after that I saw her only at wide intervals, for we lived many days' journey apart."

The thing he remembered most about "this first and closest friend" was her abiding interest in "people and the other animals." At one point during his boyhood they shared their home with nineteen cats, undoubtedly nostalgic kin to the felines later found in one or two of his works. "She was the natural ally and friend of the friendless." It was even asserted that his mother would, as a faithful Presbyterian, put in a good word for the devil himself. Prayer often saved a sinner, "but who prays for Satan?" he recalled her asking him. "Who, in eighteen centuries, has had the common humanity to pray for the one sinner that needed it most?"[1] Satan, a staple of Sam's fundamentalist Christian upbringing in

Hannibal, Missouri, would appear in his last long narrative as an innocent youngster who carelessly contributes to the misery of the human condition. In the second of three drafts of what is generally referred to in this biography as "The Mysterious Stranger" stories, Twain sketched, as he noted in an 1897 journal entry, "Satan's boyhood—going around with other boys & surprising them with devilish miracles." This boy devil—one of his last boyhood creations, who is a companion of Huck and Tom—is also the last of such strangers in the fiction and humor of Mark Twain. At the story's end in the most authoritative version, he rushes in Tom Sawyer–like to announce the punch line to the cosmic joke called life—that there is "no God, no universe, no human race, no earthly life, no heaven, no hell."[2]

For most of his career as a writer who became world famous in his thirties, Mark Twain lamented that he was appreciated mainly as a humorist, a sore point shared by most members of his family. Their favorite book was not *Adventures of Huckleberry Finn,* but *The Prince and the Pauper* or, worse, his life of Joan of Arc. Writing anonymously in the latter's serial publication, Samuel Clemens wrote in the standard English of William Dean Howells and Henry James, something he could do quite well. For whenever readers or auditors saw or heard the name "Mark Twain," they expected to laugh. He had a "call," as he told his older brother Orion in 1865, "to literature, of a low order—i.e., humorous." With the publication that year of "Jim Smiley and His Jumping Frog" in the last issue of Henry Clapp's New York *Saturday Press,* the same journal that published the work of another particularly vernacular writer, Walt Whitman, he had turned his "attention to seriously scribbling to excite the laughter of God's creatures."[3] Yet he always insisted, recording it in his autobiographical writings, that humor was only a "fragrance." In any serious literary work, it should never be applied forcibly. Noting the oblivion to which most of the humorists of his day had already been consigned, he wrote that he had lasted for thirty years because humor was merely a by-product of a higher aim. "If the humor came of its own accord," he wrote in his autobiography, "I have allowed it a place in my [work], but I was not writing [it] for the sake of humor."[4]

In fact, the source of Mark Twain's humor was ultimately deadly serious, as indeed it is with the springs of all authentic or lasting humor. In declining to edit a comic periodical for the McClure Syndicate in 1900, he wrote: "For its own interests, humor should take its outings in grave company; its cheerful dress gets heightened color from the proximity of sober hues." Throughout the fiction of Mark Twain, a stranger or an event is usually introduced to pull the rug out from under our expectations. In the famous Jumping Frog story, for example, it is a stranger who fills Jim Smiley's frog with quail shot so that he loses the contest—and the bet. Ultimately, the new guy in town becomes a "mysterious stranger" who turns out to be a close relative of the devil himself. As Bernard De Voto wrote almost eighty years ago: "In Mark Twain's humor, disenchantment, the acknowledgment of defeat, the realization of futility find a mature expression. He laughs and, for the first time, American literature possesses a tragic laughter."[5] We laugh, of course, at the incongruity between illusion and reality, often the tragic rupture between expectation and outcome. Ralph Waldo Emerson, who, ironically, would later be perceived as one of the victims of Twain's humor in the notorious Whittier birthday dinner speech of 1877, observed in the essay "The Comic" that man "is the only joker in nature."[6] This was true, sadly enough, because only humans could see how often life presented itself outside the context of the ideal. Its incongruity was ultimately laughable. In his 1877 speech, Twain had thought it would be "funny" to associate Emerson, Longfellow, and Holmes with drunken miners and to take lines from their best work out of context. It was incongruous and thus funny, but as the more diplomatic Howells recalled years later, he had also "trifled with" great reputations.[7]

Describing his first seven sickly years, living "altogether on expensive allopathic medicines," Twain recalled, no doubt facetiously, that he once asked his mother how she felt about him in those early days. "With an almost pathetic earnestness she said, 'All along at first I was afraid you would die'—a slight reflective pause, then this addition, spoken as if talking to herself—'and after that I was afraid you wouldn't.'"[8] Jane Clemens was surely the wellspring of her son's pointed humor. The stranger in the work of Mark Twain isn't, therefore, simply a person, but always the embodiment of this kind of unexpected twist in the narrative. In his very first truly popular work we find the same kind of grimly ironic humor in the description of Jim Smiley's addiction to gambling: regardless of the consequences, he would selfishly bet on anything, including whether the parson's wife, whose illness was showing improvement, would probably die anyway. Much of Twain's humor is "funny" today simply because it is so serious in what it says about the human condition, or what Twain supposedly called the "Damned Human Race" (this exact phrase never having been found in his collected writings or letters).[9]

Mark Twain (1835–1910) began as a humorist and ended as a pessimist, a determinist who found in both science and biblical fables ironic ways of showing the cruelty and unhappiness of man as the only being on earth who knows the difference between good and evil and yet inevitably chooses evil. At the outset of his writing career, he was satisfied to be regarded by the public as a humorist—an author of the "left hand," as it was said of literary comedians of the Old Southwest—instead of as a serious writer of "literature."[10] Yet during his career, his work underwent a major transformation that reflected the vicissitudes of his life as a printer, Mississippi River pilot, Civil War soldier, western newspaper reporter, travel writer, lecturer, publisher, creator of hymns to childhood, and ultimately, the author of one of America's honored classics. He was also an inventor whose self-pasting scrapbook made him money, and an investor and publisher whose company went bankrupt. Like Whitman, he was an outsider in a genteel literary society whose greatest work was essentially "banned in Boston." Yet as a humorist he was also part of that society and lived the life of a rich man in Hartford for twenty years, and abroad for almost a decade, and finally resided in New York City and Redding, Connecticut. If we count all those trips he made up and down the Mississippi, his trek out west and to Hawaii, and his innumerable trips—sometimes monthly in the 1890s—to Europe, Mark Twain probably traveled more than almost any other American in the nineteenth century. All the while, he was also traveling on the frontier of American literature, making inroads into areas hardly touched by his predecessors.

Mark Twain, the nom de guerre he adopted in 1863, first became famous essentially for telling anew, and in the best tradition of the humor of the Old Southwest, an unoriginal story about a frog. With the success of this and other tales, he became a travel writer, whose formal travel books were *The Innocents Abroad, Roughing It, A Tramp Abroad,* and *Following the Equator.* Yet in a broader sense, all his works were travel books, episodic in their plots. Twain never quite knew where he was going when he started a book, often only with financial gain at the forefront of his mind. Though clearly a literary genius, he was not at the outset a disciplined writer and early in his career seldom spent time on revision. When he "ran out of gas," as he often put it, he would put the work away for months or years. This was repeatedly the case for *Adventures of Huckleberry Finn,* his greatest work, whose unfinished manuscript he threatened to burn at one point. *Huckleberry Finn* was not only his greatest book; it was a travel book that took him furthest into the mystery of existence.

For most of his life this artist considered himself a businessman whose main talent at making money lay not only in authorship and lecturing but also in investments that culminated in a bankrupt publishing company and the loss of many thousands more on the Paige Typesetter—indeed more than four million dollars in today's money. He always wanted to become rich, not particularly because of his humble childhood in Florida and Hannibal, Missouri, but because he was around the impressionable age of thirteen when the California Gold Rush of '49 swept through Hannibal and took a number of its inhabitants out west. He went west himself in 1861 in the company of Orion, who had been appointed secretary to the territorial governor of Nevada. He eventually prospected for gold and silver, but "struck it rich" only when he became a writer, though initially as a newspaper reporter for the Virginia City *Territorial Enterprise.* This opportunity eventually took him to California and other newspaper jobs—in which his great talent lay in reporting his travels, initially in the Hawaiian Islands in 1866—and ultimately to a parallel career as comic lecturer in the tradition of Artemus Ward, who died at an early age in 1867, thus clearing the stage for his friend and protégé.

Twain struggled with the problems of the world more and more as he went through life. He finally became the mysterious stranger he had repeatedly conjured up between "Jim Smiley and His Jumping Frog" and "No. 44, The Mysterious Stranger" (the last of three versions of this posthumously published work). In *A Connecticut Yankee in King Arthur's Court* (1889), for example, an acclaimed work in its own day that is seen by some today as a literary failure, he set out to celebrate the democracy of the common man and ended up condemning humankind. He had briefly found his faith in man in *Huckleberry Finn,* but he had also lost it in the overall process of writing this book. Huck Finn gave way to Hank Morgan, and once that happened, the writer's imagination was doomed to relive childhood Calvinist myths in satires on God and heaven. Especially after the sudden death of his favorite and clearly talented daughter Susy in 1896, he even became a stranger to himself, waking up in a world in which the relationship of God to man is no more than that of a town drunk to one of his microbes. Twain woke up in the twentieth century. Here the essentialist world of God-centered order gave way to a helpless relativism mandated by modern science and its central theory of evolution. In such a brave new world, as Mark Twain wryly noted, God created the monkey just for practice. Then he made man.

Now, one hundred years after his death in 1910, in the "information age" of the still young twenty-first century, it is time to renew our acquaintance with this familiar stranger in our literature and culture. Since the publication of Albert Bigelow Paine's multivolume authorized biography in 1912, more than twenty biographies (not counting juvenile treatments) have been published, most recently Fred Kaplan's and Ron Powers's biographies in 2003 and 2005. Since Justin Kaplan's prize-winning life of the writer in 1966, more than five thousand of Mark Twain's letters have been discovered. Yet there is no truly critical biography of this, America's most famous writer. Even today the most comprehensive treatment is Paine's, still the only source of certain information even though it has become outdated in its research and Victorian principles. More has been written about Mark Twain than about any other American writer; indeed, his biographer comes to realize that there is in fact already a *book* written on nearly every aspect of Twain's life and career, not to mention the hundreds of scholarly and popular articles. What is attempted here is a critical retelling of the life and work, based in part on previously unpublished or little-known archival materials available at the Mark Twain Project at the University of California, Berkeley. Its short chapters, or vignettes, seek to capture the biographical, historical, and to some extent psychological moments of a life that was as long and twisted as the Mississippi River. It was also a segmented or episodic life, much like his greatest fictions, which seems to suit the brief chapters that make up this biography.

On the literary side, Twain's interactions with such writers as James Fenimore Cooper, Ralph Waldo Emerson, and Walt Whitman are explored in new and extended ways. The life of this "family man" is also reexamined to reveal the father of three daughters as not only overly protective but also possibly manipulative. The writer of so-called children's literature never truly wanted his daughters to grow up and referred to them as children even when they were in their twenties. Had she lived a full life, Susy—or Olivia Susan Clemens, as she signed her letters at Bryn Mawr and after—would very possibly have adopted the lifestyle of the Pre-Raphaelites and aesthetes. Finally, this biography strives to celebrate not merely one of America's greatest writers but one of its greatest vernacular writers. It completes what I discovered I was doing only in the process: that is, finishing a trilogy of such major writers of the nineteenth and early twentieth centuries. I began it in 1999 with my life of Walt Whitman, whose *Leaves of Grass* introduced American speech into American poetry. I continued in 2005 with Theodore Dreiser, who was fully formed as a writer in the nineteenth century, breaking out with his first of two masterpieces in 1900, *Sister Carrie.* (Interestingly, that year Harper's rejected Dreiser's first novel around the same time it was becoming Mark Twain's publisher.) With this volume I have tried to demonstrate how yet another literary democrat produced a world literature distinctively homegrown.

PART I Humorist in the West

1 Life on the Salt River

The author's grandfather Samuel B. Clemens died in a house-raising accident at the age of thirty-five. While pushing a log up an incline, Clemens slipped and it crushed him against a stump. His carelessness, Mark Twain later hinted in *The American Claimant* (1892), may have been "induced by over-plus of sour-mash." Clemens and his wife, Pamela Goggin, had been married for eight years when the tragedy struck in 1805. It happened in Mason County, Virginia (now West Virginia), on the banks of the Ohio River, where the couple lived on two tracts of land covering more than a hundred acres. He was the father of five children, including Twain's father, John Marshall Clemens, the eldest, who was named for Virginia's most famous lawyer and the future chief justice of the U.S. Supreme Court, whom his parents may once have had the honor of meeting. His widowed mother, Pamela, moved to Kentucky and kept house for a brother. In 1809 she married Simon Hancock, an earlier suitor. Records preserved by Mark Twain himself show that Hancock quietly placed a lien on Samuel B. Clemens's estate for the cost of raising another man's children. This was in Adair County, just north of the Tennessee state line and near Fentress County and the site of the infamous "Tennessee Land" that would begin the Clemens family weakness for get-rich-quick schemes.[1]

John Marshall Clemens, a sensitive and perhaps unhappy lad, grew up with an emotionally distant stepfather after losing the love of his real one at the age of seven. He gradually replaced the memory of his lost father with the myth of Virginia aristocracy and, as an adult, subscribed to the code of the gentleman who was stiffly dignified in his speech and manner. The type is rather mockingly reflected in a number of Twain's fictional characters, including Colonel Grangerford in *Huckleberry Finn* and Judge York Driscoll and his F.F.V. acquaintances in *Pudd'nhead Wilson,* landed gentlemen who exploit soil and (slave) labor. Twain's disgust with such southern chivalry is amply depicted in *Pudd'nhead Wilson,* in which Roxy tells her miscegenated son that he had no need to feel ashamed of his black blood because it was mixed with that of Colonel Cecil Burleigh Essex, who was of "de highest quality in dis whole town—Ole Virginny stock, Fust Famblies, he was."[2] John Marshall Clemens may or may not have been a warmer man than the type that Mark Twain portrayed in these novels. In *Following the Equator,* Twain remembered him as "a refined and kindly gentleman" who "laid his hand upon me in punishment only twice in his life." Yet an earlier recollection in chapter 18 of *The Innocents Abroad* describes a boyhood fear of "getting thrashed" for playing hooky. His father also cuffed adolescent slaves from time to time. Whereas young Sam was raised as a Presbyterian by his mother, his father "attended no church and never spoke of religious matters." He was "very grave, rather austere" and, probably because of his essentially fatherless youth, a brooder who was one source of Twain's later pessimism.[3] Much of Mark Twain's brilliant sense of humor derived from his mother's side and the spirit of a Kentucky belle named Jane Lampton (a family name sometimes spelled "Lambton"). The daughter of pioneer stock who had followed Daniel Boone into Kentucky and who were improbably related to royalty in England (the Earls of Durham), this vivacious young woman was known for her dancing and horsemanship. Her marriage to Clemens came about almost by accident. She had fallen in love with a young medical student, but because of a misunderstanding and to save face, in 1823 she abruptly married Clemens, then a legal apprentice.[4]

Mark Twain, arguably the most famous literary artist in the English language after Shakespeare and Dickens, ironically evolved from a sequence of male tragedies or at best disappointments. His father lived ten years longer than his grandfather, but he was hardly as successful, ultimately leading his family through an almost hand-to-mouth existence as one opportunity after another turned to little or nothing.

Marshall Clemens and his wife lived their first two years together in Columbia, Kentucky, in Adair County. Shortly before the birth of their first child, Orion, in 1825, they moved directly south to Jackson County, Tennessee. The move was apparently sparked by a concern for Marshall's health, which required the cleaner air of the Tennessee highlands and the Cumberland River. This was in Gainesborough, but they soon moved into Fentress County to a little hamlet called Jamestown, which Marshall, now a shopkeeper, envisioned as a future metropolis. But his vision, like that of Twain's Colonel Sellers in *The Gilded Age,* was almost always fatally blurred. It was about this time that he began to purchase what ultimately amounted to seventy-five thousand acres of nearby land for less than a penny an acre. Nearly worthless then (and today) because of its rugged, hilly terrain, it was located south of the town, in the foothills of the Cumberland Mountains. Like Colonel Sellers, John Marshall Clemens hoped, however, that it would eventually become valuable and make the next generation of his family rich. Mark Twain regularly cursed that land and ultimately gave all his rights to it to Orion, who missed out on the few opportunities to sell it at any profit. In the 1880s, Orion and his mother sold it in bits and pieces to various people in the area for virtually nothing. Its only profit for the family came from the use Twain made of it in his works. In *The Gilded Age,* for example, it is the location for a technical school ("Knobs Industrial University") for ex-slaves that Congress is lobbied to finance.[5]

The Clemens family lived in this general area for the next decade. In 1831 they resided in nearby Three Forks of Wolf River, and soon afterward Clemens kept a store and established a post office at Pall Mall.[6] When they moved to Missouri in 1835, the couple had produced four more children and witnessed the death of one. Pamela Ann Clemens was the only one of Orion's siblings born before Sam who would go on to live a full life. Pleasant Hannibal (both names were ancestral) died in either 1828 or 1829 at the age of three months. Margaret Lampton and Benjamin Lampton, born in 1830 and 1832, both died before the age of ten. Henry, born in Missouri in 1838, would meet a tragic end on the river Mark Twain would make famous. The decision to move to Missouri was based on financial need, as this slave-owning family's number of slaves had been reduced from six to a single girl named Jennie. Everything was sold except the worthless Tennessee Land. The family initially returned to Adair County, where they then took a steamboat down the Ohio River to the Mississippi.

The ultimate destination was Florida, Missouri, some 130 miles northwest of St. Louis. Jane Clemens's father and mother, Benjamin and Margaret Lampton, moved there first along with Jane's younger sister Patsy and her husband, John A. Quarles. Both families purchased government land. Quarles, Sam Clemens's favorite uncle, built a farm four miles outside the town in Monroe County. The Quarles family at the time consisted of eight children and fifteen or twenty slaves, including Aunt Hanner and Uncle Dan'l, the latter one of the prototypes for the slave Jim in *Huckleberry Finn.* Daniel was only three years younger than Quarles, and the two had grown up together in Virginia and Tennessee. Quarles would lose all his slaves and most of his other property in the Civil War, but he freed Uncle Dan'l in 1855.[7]

Very possibly, in the move to Missouri, Marshall and Jane Clemens responded to a letter similar to the one Si and Nancy Hawkins receive in the opening chapter of *The Gilded Age,* which, like the Clemens family relocation, begins in Fentress County and moves to Monroe County: "Come right along to Missouri! Don't wait and worry about a good price but sell out for whatever you can get and come along, or you might be too late." And so this American couple, destined to become the parents of Mark Twain, continued their westward migration, begun initially in Virginia, then passing through Kentucky, and going from Tennessee to the great Mississippi River Valley and the West. The family of now seven briefly considered St. Louis as the place of their next residence, but a cholera epidemic in the city persuaded them to follow their original plan, and so they proceeded higher upriver and considerably inland to the town of Florida, located on a ridge overlooking the north and south forks of the Salt River, which feeds into the Mississippi about ten miles below Hannibal.

Sam Clemens was born in Florida on November 30, 1835. "The village contained a hundred people and I increased the population by 1 per cent," he later joked. "It is more than many of the best men in history could have done for a town. . . . There is no record of a person doing as much—not even Shakespeare."[8] Time, however, has not been kind to Florida. De Lancey Ferguson in his 1943 biography described it as a down-at-the-heel village. Today Clemens could have made an even bigger splash than he did in 1835. Its population has now dwindled to around nine or ten people, a mere crossroads consisting mainly of shacks and trailers. The racial make-up of this former slave-holding community is 100 percent white. Since 1984 the river area has been flooded to produce a series of lakes that form part of Mark Twain State Park. Somewhat ironically for this great chronicler of the Mississippi, a two-room shack in which he was purportedly born is preserved in its visitors' center because the actual spot of ground on which it originally stood is now under water.

But back then, the future for Florida was promising. The Quarles farm, for example, consisted of over 230 acres. Uncle John also ran a general store in town, and John Marshall Clemens became his partner before he purchased his own store from his father-in-law. Clemens also made several purchases of local land to the east and southeast of Florida and smaller purchases to the north of the town—almost 250 acres in all. By 1837, because of his increasing involvement in the civic affairs of the town and, no doubt, because of his Virginia bearing as a learned gentleman on the frontier with a knowledge of the law, he had become a respected member of the Florida community, though not exactly a prosperous one. The town needed more commerce if shopkeepers like him were to thrive as vigorously as their neighbors thirty-five miles to the east in Hannibal. It was a little too soon for the era of the railroad to make a little place like Florida hum, but there was the chance that the Salt River might be dredged and deepened with a series of locks and dams so that traffic from the Mississippi might include the town as a port for something larger than keels and flatboats. With such improvements, it was hoped, Florida, Missouri, could become a thriving commercial center.

Clemens and other town leaders formed the Salt River Navigation Company to raise federal funds for the dredging project. Senator Dilworthy and Colonel Sellers in *The Gilded Age* try the same thing with Congress, to no avail. The similar failure by Florida's delegates reflected the permanent backwater status of the town, as well as the unrealistic aspirations of Mark Twain's father, who had tried, as they used to say in

Missouri, "to row up Salt River."[9] Or in the phrasing of the state's most famous writer, his hopes had been sold *down* the river once again. Mark Twain had not only begun as the son of a failure but also had been born on the wrong river.

The writer therefore spent his earliest years not on the Mississippi exactly, but on the banks of the Salt River, or at least close by it at the Quarles farm. Although he lived in Hannibal during most of the year after 1839, when his father moved the family there to improve his business prospects, from 1843 to 1846 young Sam spent summers with his aunt and uncle—on a farm that he later moved to the "Creation State" of Arkansas as part of the setting for *Huckleberry Finn* and *Tom Sawyer, Detective.* "It was a heavenly place for a boy, that farm of my uncle John's," he fondly recalled in his autobiography. "The house was a double log one, with a spacious floor (roofed in) connecting it with the kitchen. In the summer the table was set in the middle of that shady and breezy floor, and the sumptuous meals—well, it makes me cry to think of them." This is the farm of Silas and Sally Phelps (Sam's Aunt Patsy, who reappears under her own name in *Pudd'nhead Wilson*) in chapter 33 of *Huckleberry Finn.* Tom and Huck have "dinner out in that broad open passage betwixt the house and the kitchen; and there was things enough on that table for seven families."[10]

It was on the Quarles farm that young Sam developed his "strong liking for the [Negro] race," which formed the basis for Huck's conflicted conscience in helping a fugitive slave. "This feeling and this estimate have stood the test of sixty years and more," he wrote in his autobiography. Yet, as he also remembered, "in my schoolboy days I had no aversion to slavery. I was not aware that there was anything wrong about it. No one arraigned it in my hearing; the local papers said nothing against it; the local pulpit taught us that God approved it, that it was a holy thing, and that the doubter need only look in the Bible if he wished to settle his mind." This view was doubtless reinforced for young Sam and his brother Henry by the devoutly religious nature of his mother and Aunt Patsy Quarles and the fact that the families owned slaves. Moreover, he seldom saw a slave abused on the farm or in town, but added keenly that "if the slaves themselves had an aversion to slavery, they were wise and said nothing."[11]

The Quarles place also makes a brief appearance in "The Private History of a Campaign That Failed," Twain's possibly fictional account about his brief career in a Missouri state militia at the start of the Civil War. Although he declined to enlist in the Confederate army after his state militia unit disbanded, two of his cousins—sons of John A. Quarles—served in the military for the South. Benjamin Quarles was a lieutenant in General Sterling Price's bodyguard, and Fred Quarles served as an officer in General Martin Green's command. Green served under Price during the capture of Lexington, Missouri; so the brothers probably served together more or less, and both survived the Civil War.[12]

Missouri was a border state in the American drama of slavery, and in discussing it in his autobiography, Twain reflects the dubious claim that slavery was relatively benign there. In *Adventures of Huckleberry Finn,* Jim achieves manumission and presumably lives happily ever after. Yet Twain may reflect a truer picture of the conditions of slaves in Missouri in *Tom Sawyer's Conspiracy,* written almost twenty years later, at the end of the century when the Jim Crow era came to life and black lynchings in the South were mounting. *Tom Sawyer's Conspiracy* brings Miss Watson back to life, and the Duke and the King return from *Huckleberry Finn* as murderers instead of simply river con men. Jim is still free, but only from slavery, not discrimination. He is on trial for murder partly because of a prank Tom and Huck had pulled on a townspeople worried about a threatened invasion of abolitionists from across the river in Quincy, Illinois. Jim's young lawyer is intimidated by the town hatred for a freed slave. This is dramatically reflected in Tom, who "wouldn't be lawyer for a free nigger himself, unless it was Jim," whom he knows to be innocent.[13] In *Huckleberry Finn,* of course, the white man's secret is that Jim is free.

This literary assessment of the southern attitude toward blacks after the Civil War is complemented by the antebellum tragedy of *Pudd'nhead Wilson,* in which Roxy, whose mixed race allows her to become Twain's only sexually provocative female, is "as white as anybody, but the one-sixteenth of her which was black out-voted the other fifteen parts and made her a negro."[14] Such democracy for the damned in this miscegenated hell guarantees her destiny as a slave in Dawson's Landing. Here Mark Twain looked back to his childhood and saw not the innocent charm of small-town life with Tom Sawyer and Becky Thatcher, but a much darker Hannibal in which even skin color is not always the key to freedom, and getting "engaged," as the two youngsters do in *Tom Sawyer,* leads to more than innocent kissing.

Like the patriarchs in *Pudd'nhead Wilson,* John Quarles and John Marshall Clemens became, despite their conventionally religious wives, freethinkers and Universalists. And while young Sam was somewhat distant from his stolid father, he found his uncle, who was also fond of storytelling, more accessible. "I have not come across a better man than he was," Mark Twain remembered. "I was his guest for two or three months every year, from the fourth year after we removed to Hannibal till I was eleven or twelve years old."[15] The seeds of Mark Twain's fondness for the tall tale as well as his pessimism can probably be traced as far back as Florida, Missouri. Uncle John may have been the first one to tell Sam Clemens the story of the jumping frog. His late-life despair possibly came, then, not only from John Marshall Clemens but also from John Quarles, who also could not reconcile the mystery of human destiny with strict religious dogma. Yet unlike his brother-in-law, Quarles was more successful at submerging this point of view in the gregariousness of town and country life as a shopkeeper, farmer, and even local politico, once serving as a justice of the peace in Monroe County. In *Tom Sawyer, Detective,* however, Twain almost turns Uncle Silas into a murderer.[16] By 1896, when this work was published, the fictional John Quarles has become a brooding, troubled patriarch instead of the sweet part-time preacher who says an extra-long blessing over the vittles. His wife—Sam's Aunt Patsy—had died in 1850 after giving birth. Quarles himself had died in 1875. By the time Twain wrote the dark sequels to *Huckleberry Finn,* the world had changed for him dramatically. With the sudden death of his first daughter, Susy, in 1896, his past came back to him through a glass darkly. Even A. B. Frost's illustrations in *Tom Sawyer, Detective,* unlike E. W. Kemble's in *Huckleberry Finn,* which suggest the innocence of a time gone by, depict Tom and Huck as older than their adolescent conversations would suggest and locate them precariously on the verge of the twentieth century and the dawning of its deterministic philosophy.

2 Window to the West

Mark Twain's fictional name for Hannibal was St. Petersburg. It was possibly a code word for heaven, the home of St. Pete and the site of Sam's childhood happiness. Or, on a more somber note, he may have named his hometown for St. Petersburg—after the city built in the eighteenth century by Peter the Great of Russia. Also set on water, or on pilings driven into the marshes of the Neva River on the Gulf of Finland, in its architecture it looked to the West and to Europe. Until recently, it was called Leningrad, so named in the wake of the Russian Revolution that Twain encouraged; but since the fall of the Soviet Union in 1989, this seaport city through which the famous Neva flows has recovered its original name and perhaps some of that earlier spirit. Twain's interest in the lack of democracy throughout the world fully surfaced in the 1890s, but by the mid-1870s he had become seriously interested in the politics of his own country and possibly was already thinking of czarist Russia and its oppressive royalty when he renamed his own river city.

In 1867 his party on the ship *Quaker City* had stopped in Yalta for an audience with the czar, whose influence over human events, Twain wrote in chapter 37 of *The Innocents Abroad,* was so immense that his sudden death "might shake the thrones of half the world!" (Alexander II was in fact assassinated in 1881.) St. Petersburg in its age of kings, long before the rapid disappearance of aristocracies in the twentieth century, may have suggested with its window to the west the democracy and freedom of youth, certainly the idyll recalled in *Tom Sawyer* if not altogether in *Huckleberry Finn* and the unsuccessful sequels. Later, its sunshine faded into the shadows as Hannibal became the models for Dawson's Landing, Hadleyburg, and the medieval village of Eseldorf. In all cases and in spite of its different manifestations in the fiction, Hannibal was the wellspring of Mark Twain's literary imagination.

The actual town was named for the defeated Carthaginian general. It would eventually signal defeat for John Marshall Clemens, who after four years of storekeeping and farming in Florida as well as petitioning federal authorities in vain for the Salt River improvement, sold his lands in Monroe County and moved to neighboring Marion County and the river town of Hannibal. His departure, however, was due as much to the failure of Florida as to the latest lack of good luck for John Marshall Clemens. Named for the territory of Florida, which had been flourishing ever since its transfer from Spain in 1819, the town of Florida, Missouri, which once foolishly thought itself to be almost as promising, had finally stumbled as a commercial center, not only because of the river commission's inability to get the Salt River dredged all the way up to the town but also because of the Panic of 1837, which swept the country for the next three or more years. Even so, Marshall Clemens was one of the last of the leading citizens to give up and leave, and even then he realized five thousand dollars from the sale of his land in Monroe County.

But this latest new beginning would set his course downward for the rest of his days, even though Hannibal clearly had a more promising future and managed to flourish much more than Florida. Set upon the Mississippi at one of its widest points, the clapboard town was located in a small valley between the bluffs of Holliday's Hill and Lover's Leap. It climbed away from the river in a rather steep incline beginning at Front Street and running up to Fifth and Sixth streets. With a population of three thousand when Sam was a boy, its businesses included a pork-processing plant, a cigar factory, four general stores, three sawmills, three blacksmith shops, two hotels, two schools, two churches, a hemp factory, a tannery, a liquor distillery, and three saloons. In the summer this "white town drowsing," as Twain first described it in "Old Times on the Mississippi," was set against vibrantly green hills. During Twain's boyhood it saw at least two steamboats a day stop at its wharves, one up from St. Louis and the other down from Keokuk, Iowa. Not only was it a regular stop on the Mississippi, but Hannibal was also a port on the way to the Missouri River and its gateway to the West. The village found itself on the circuit for all the river types Twain brought back to life in the pages of *Huckleberry Finn* and his other river writings: town drunks, bogus lecturers, itinerant actors, patent medicine hawkers, minstrels, traveling-circus performers, palm readers, phrenologists, spiritualists, and—that fascination of antebellum America—mesmerists. Once, young Sam went on stage and pretended to be hypnotized.

In Hannibal, Sam's father purchased a series of buildings on the northeast corner of Hill and Main streets for seven thousand dollars. One of these was the Virginia House, a hotel in which he initially housed his family, which by now had grown to five living children, counting Sam and Henry. Margaret, aged nine, had recently died before the family left Florida. Having spent all his cash on real estate, Marshall Clemens borrowed large sums to set himself up in the grocery and dry goods business, but as Huck would say about his own father, "it warn't good judgment." The houses and hotel had been built or financed by Ira Stout, an investor who had somehow persuaded Clemens to co-sign a hefty loan. John Marshall's downfall came either because Stout subsequently declared bankruptcy and (as Twain recalled in a sketch entitled "Villagers of 1840–[5]3") "made a pauper of him" or because his steady decline in business even in Hannibal made it impossible for him to pay his debts. In the words of biographer Dixon Wecter, "With these debts at his back, John M. Clemens opened another in his endless series of general stores—[this one] fronting the muddy thoroughfare of Hannibal, with the great river rolling past the wharf one block below." Eventually, he became Hannibal's justice of the peace and, as his son remembered, "lived on its meager pickings."[1] No wonder this man, who had been virtually cuckolded into marriage, who had been the ward of a man who charged for his upbringing, was remembered by his son as stern and unsmiling. Yet the financial burdens of Marshall Clemens did not daunt young Sam's spirit or stunt his psychological development. For as Twain recalled, he and his comrades never knew they were poor until the California Gold Rush in 1849 sucked out a fair percentage of the town's population. By this time the impressionable youth of Mark Twain had ended. Indeed, Sam Clemens's life—the one that formed the basis of his literary imagination—was over. At the turn of the twentieth century, when Mark Twain had been an international celebrity for thirty years, he told the widow of his best boyhood friend, Will Bowen, that "those were pleasant days; none since have been . . . so well worth living over again. . . . I should greatly like to re-live my youth, & then get drowned. I should like to call back Will Bowen & John Garth & the others, & live the life, & be as we were, & make holiday until 15, then all drown together."[2]

Opportunities for this form of death abounded. There was the river with its islands, including Glasscock and Shucks, which before erosion may have formed the fictional Jackson's Island that Mark Twain moved three miles downriver in *Tom Sawyer* and *Huckleberry Finn.* And there was also Bear Creek, which ran near Broadway south of town. Town legend had it that, from the bluff known as Lover's Leap, about a mile south of town, an Indian and his lover had jumped because the woman's father forbade their marriage and tried to have the brave killed. It jutted out over the low river land and provided a perfect view of the village. Three miles farther south was the cave in which Tom and Becky become trapped and in which the fictional Injun Joe dies of starvation. Just north of town at the end of Third Street stood Holliday's Hill, renamed Cardiff Hill in the novels. Up in that vicinity lived the town gentry.

Yet "money had no place" in this wonderland, Twain emphasized in "Villagers." "To get rich was no one's ambition." In "Old Times on the Mississippi" and *Tom Sawyer,* Twain first re-created the wonderment of his childhood in Hannibal. Tom Sawyer's reading of romances reflects Twain's early reading, in which the primary theme was travel and adventure; hence, the charm of the steamboat. Merchants who traveled to St. Louis were the envy of every boy and girl in town. "When a minor citizen realized the dream of his life," he wrote, "and traveled to St. Louis, he was thrilled to the marrow when he recognized the rank of boats and the spire [of the Catholic Church] and the Planters [House]. . . . He talked St. Louis and nothing but [St. Louis] and its wonders for months and months afterward."[3] When Sam Clemens finally left Hannibal at the age of seventeen, he never came back to stay but literally traveled the world during much of his life. Yet however far and wide his life travels took him from this little town only hundreds of miles from the perilous Indian territories, he never left what Henry Nash Smith has called the Matter of Hannibal and the Matter of the River.[4] Here life had been an idyllic adventure mostly, with its tragic elements kept politely out of sight.

But Hannibal could also be a scary place, especially for an impressionable and imaginative lad such as young Sam. Once, he witnessed a fatal assault on one of its slaves on the city streets. On another occasion, Sam, hiding after playing hooky all day, suddenly realized that he was sitting next to a corpse laid out by the coroner in his father's justice of the peace office.[5] The son of one of the town's three physicians was so demented that he had to be chained to what resembled a doghouse in the family backyard. Believing that his left hand had committed a mortal sin, one day he got hold of a hatchet and chopped it off. Two sisters of one boyhood friend were suspected of prostitution. Invading Yankee abolitionists were sentenced to long prison terms or simply tarred and feathered. And river con men, as Twain ultimately acknowledged in *Tom Sawyer, Detective,* could even be murderers. One slave woman, no doubt the model for Roxy in *Pudd'nhead Wilson,* was sold down the river by a man who had purchased her from Marshall Clemens, who himself had once whipped the woman "for impudence to his wife." Like Roxy, she was seen years later working as a maid on a steamboat. Whether these examples are based on absolute facts or acts of a fading or inventive memory (as parts of Twain's autobiography are), they suggest at least the half-truth of something gone very wrong in the blissful past of Tom Sawyer and Huck Finn. Indeed, the town's murky past may be the source of Twain's lifelong obsession with a guilty conscience, along with his late-life pessimism. Its Calvinism, which failed to include slavery in its condemnations of human behavior, left an indelible mark on this uncertain teller of children's stories.

Most of the principal characters in these so-called boyhood novels are based on family members or Hannibal residents. Aunt Polly, the allopathic matron, is the author's mother. Mary, Tom's cousin, is Sam's older sister, Pamela. Henry, the youngest sibling, and the one who was fated to die in a steamboat explosion, is Sid Sawyer. Tom Sawyer is the combination of three childhood comrades, including Will Bowen. Huck Finn is based on Tom Blankenship, the son of a town drunkard who lived in the alley behind the Clemens home and who fed his family on caught fish and fowl. In the summer of 1847 Tom Blankenship's older brother (by only a year) Bence hid a runaway slave on an island on the Illinois side of the river and brought him food for several weeks. Huck is also a poor white who is sinful enough to help a fugitive slave. The prototype of Huckleberry Finn was "ignorant, unwashed, and insufficiently fed; but he had as good a heart as ever any boy had." And he is the type of underclass boy Sam and his friends were told to avoid. As Twain wrote in *Tom Sawyer,* "Tom was like the rest of the respectable boys, in that he envied Huckleberry his gaudy outcast condition, and was under strict orders not to play with him."[6]

Pap Finn is Jimmy Finn, the *other* town drunk, a position that Twain called "an exceedingly well-defined and unofficial office of those days." Mark Twain's father, as justice of the peace, once tried to reform Jimmy Finn. In *Huckleberry Finn* a new judge tries to do the same. In defense of Judge Clemens, Twain said that his father was only a "spasmodic" reformer. Pap Finn makes a speech and holds out his hand (once "the hand of a hog") to the judge and his wife; then he proceeds to get drunk in their guest room and break his arm in two places. No doubt Judge Clemens felt the same way about Jimmy Finn as the fictional judge did about his ward—that reform for such a lowlife could come only from the end of a shotgun.

Then, as today, almost every small town had at least one drunk, and every one including Hannibal probably had a widow wanting to remarry. This is the Widow Douglas in the novel, in real life Mrs. Richard Holliday. Her brother built the finest mansion in Hannibal for her. Her second husband, Richard Holliday, went broke in 1844. He was one of those who went to California in 1849, where he died. The widow ultimately went insane. Twain remembered her as "old, but anxious to marry," yet actually she was only around forty years of age, though no doubt "aged" to a boy of twelve or thirteen. In chapter 29 of *Tom Sawyer,* Injun Joe plans to mutilate the widow—"slit her nostrils"—in revenge for the fact that her late husband as justice of the peace had ordered him horsewhipped. The half-breed's going "for her looks" could have been Twain's shorthand for an intended rape, still another crime not out of the realm of possibility in the relatively remote river town of Hannibal.[7] Or in Dawson's Landing, where the white crime of miscegenation is openly treated in *Pudd'nhead Wilson*.

This fictional Hannibal is named after one of the real town's teachers, John D. Dawson, who founded a school in 1847 that instructed Sam Clemens and twenty-four of his schoolmates. He appears as Mr. Dobbins in *Tom Sawyer,* the schoolmaster who "had reached middle age with an unsatisfied ambition." His restlessness was probably exorcised two years later when Dobbins suddenly closed the school and joined the California Gold Rush.

It was also in Hannibal that the model for Colonel Sherburn shot down the model for Boggs in chapter 21 of *Huckleberry Finn,* in which Hannibal is called Bricksville. The actors were William Owsley, a proud Kentuckian, and Samuel Smarr, a local cattleman who had insulted him. Justice of the Peace Clemens took twenty-nine depositions for a trial that acquitted Owsley a year later. The murder took place on January 22, 1845, and young Sam Clemens was a witness. Later as the author of *Huckleberry Finn,* he repeated the scene, in the words of Wecter, "almost without a hairsbreadth of variation." As in the novel, the victim, claiming that Owsley had cheated him, drunkenly abused him from the streets. One day Owsley caught Smarr unarmed and shot him point-blank—twice. "The shooting down of poor old Smarr in the main street at noonday," Twain later recalled, "supplied me with some more dreams; and in them I always saw again the grotesque closing picture—the great family Bible spread open on the profane old man's breast by some thoughtful idiot, and rising and sinking to the labored breathings, and adding the torture of its leaden weight to the dying struggles."[8]

In addition to Wecter's biography, there have been several attempts to verify the childhood facts of Hannibal, but the most inspiring one, and generally reliable, can be found in both Twain's autobiographical writings and his hymns to boyhood, especially *Tom Sawyer* and *Huckleberry Finn,* and in the nostalgic parts of *Life on the Mississippi.* Four days after his marriage to Olivia Langdon in 1870, he reminisced from Buffalo, where the couple first lived, to Will Bowen, who, like his brothers, had become a Mississippi pilot before the war. "Your letter [of congratulations] has stirred me to the bottom," he wrote. "The old life has swept before me like a panorama; the old days have trooped by in their old glory again." He spoke fondly of the town drunks and of his first sweetheart, Laura Hawkins, who would make appearances as Becky Thatcher in *Tom Sawyer* and under her real name in *The Gilded Age.* He recalled their play at Holliday's Hill, his jumping off the ferry in the middle of the river on a stormy day in pursuit of his hat (no doubt the seed of the rumor about Huck's drowning in *Huckleberry Finn*), and sadly about a derelict who burned up in the local jail with matches the boys had given him. This was Dennis McDermid, who perished in the Hannibal "calaboose" in 1853.[9]

By the time of his letter to Bowen, Twain had become famous with the Jumping Frog story and, more recently, *The Innocents Abroad,* whose lifetime sales would rival *Uncle Tom's Cabin,* America's first best seller. He was known as a humorist, first in the newspapers and then through subscription publishing, a kind of lowbrow book business that particularly went after readers in hinterlands like Hannibal, where there were no bookstores. He was now part owner of the Buffalo *Express,* a career that would take him nowhere. He thought of himself mainly as a comical travel writer, but also as an investigator and apologist for a rawer American consciousness, a view that stripped away the veneer of European manners. His next book, *Roughing It,* would exploit his experiences in the far west of Nevada, but the basis for his higher art had already developed on the edge of that great territorial expanse—in Missouri and in Hannibal. He may have conversed with murderers and imbibed with prostitutes in the Far West, but he had grown up in a boyland on the banks of the Mississippi that was destined to become not merely a better "Story of a Bad Boy" than Thomas Bailey Aldrich's but also, in *Huckleberry Finn* and other writings, part of the great literature of the United States. For at his apex, Mark Twain did not stand apart from the human melee he reported. Unlike Emerson and Nathaniel Hawthorne, who—in the words of Larzer Ziff—"remained personally apart from what their writings criticized as socially disgraceful," Twain, "who entered enthusiastically into the values of a culture marked by aggressive commercial practice and hungering social aspiration, wrote, correspondingly, in the vernacular of those immersed in the hurly-burly; that is, in the speech of Americans" to achieve the same subtle genius as his New England predecessors.[10]

3 Orion

Hannibal was anything but the sleepy town Mark Twain described in the first installment of "Old Times on the Mississippi," published in the *Atlantic Monthly* in 1875 and later incorporated into *Life on the Mississippi.* It was a busy place even without steamboats, and its activity should have assisted John Marshall Clemens in making a decent living for himself and his family. By the end of the second year in Hannibal, however, the family was forced to sell its last slave and sign over the deeds to most of the property they had purchased from Stout. Jennie was sold first to a "nigger trader" named Beebe, who in turn sold her to a Methodist minister. For all we know, she could ultimately have been sold down the river like Roxy in *Pudd'nhead Wilson.* Later, Mark Twain recalled the visages of other slaves sold in Hannibal; "they had," he wrote, "the saddest faces I have ever seen."[1] To add to the general misery of the Clemens family, it was during this time that they lost two more children, nine-year-old Margaret and ten-year-old Benjamin. These losses were by this point somewhat offset by the birth of Henry in Florida in 1838. With what money he got out of the distress sale of their property, Marshall Clemens was able eventually to build another house for his family on Hill Street, which later became known as "Mark Twain's Boyhood Home."

This purchase was to be the last happy point in his fortunes. John Marshall Clemens died of pneumonia on March 24, 1847, not long after returning from a long journey on horseback to Palmyra, twelve miles to the west, to participate in a legal proceeding against the slave trader Beebe, whose profession was (hypocritically) despised in Hannibal. Ill and dying, Marshall Clemens went to his grave with the mistaken idea that his near-destitute family would be saved by the Tennessee Land. Otherwise emotionless to the last, he embraced only Pamela, his eldest daughter, whom he kissed before sinking back down and asking to die. The last words of the man who never spoke of religion were to express faith in Christ to an attending Presbyterian preacher. "He did not," Mark Twain later recalled stoically, "say good-bye to his wife, or to any but his daughter."[2] Ironically, when John Marshall's father, Sam, had died in the house-raising incident, he neglected that day to kiss his son good-bye. As a second-generation unloved son, Mark Twain would double his efforts to become a loving father.

For more than a year the Clemens family lived in Hannibal without a patriarch. Jane Clemens took in boarders to keep the family afloat. In 1849 Twain's brother Orion, who had been helping the family financially from St. Louis, returned home and established a new paternal authority for the two boys, under which young Sam, at least, would labor with no little resentment.[3] Henry, on the other hand, was already fast becoming the well-behaved lad who would furnish the basis for Sid Sawyer. It wasn't that Sam did not respect Orion, who was his senior by a decade. Like his father, his brother was sincere, truthful, and painfully honest. He was also somewhat reserved and moody like their father. Yet it is not insignificant that Tom Sawyer has no father, or that Huck's father is unable to perform his duties as a parent. The problem with Orion, who may also have shared with his father a form of manic depression, was that his probity and dedication to goodness took him in several, often conflicting, directions at once. As a model, Orion's father had failed him, and for the rest of his life Orion usually found himself starting over in life. His return to Hannibal in 1849 in effect extended the Clemens patriarchal tradition of failure begun by his grandfather and father. In Samuel B. Clemens's case, failure had been brought about by an early death. In Marshall Clemens's case, it had been simply financial failure. In Orion's, the central problem may have been a preoccupation with too many conflicting ideas.

Orion's first work experience was as a clerk in his father's general store in Florida and later Hannibal, but at about age eighteen he left

Hannibal for St. Louis and worked as an apprentice and later journeyman printer. In his search for a new model, he found the example of Benjamin Franklin, America's First Printer. When Franklin had worked at the trade as a young man in London, he had been known as the "water American" because of his teetotalism among workers who drank pints of beer throughout the day instead of water, thinking it gave them strength. Franklin's example of temperance may have been resented among his English fellow workers. Apparently Orion followed Franklin's example in drink, as well, for his nickname in the St. Louis print shop was "Parson Snivel."[4]

The national crusade against demon rum in the 1840s was very big, and as a reform-minded person, Orion was hardly alone in his point of view. Temperance was seen as vitally necessary to the development of America's fledgling democracy. It went hand in hand with the American Dream that Franklin conveyed in his autobiography. This was the dream of success, destined for anyone (male, of course, in those days) who was both moral and industrious. This Jeffersonian ideal, now transported to the frontier, said that one could rise or fall in the social hierarchy based on virtue and talent, instead of being assigned a place based on property and birthright. This concept of a "natural aristocracy" was somewhat out of keeping not only with his father's myth of a Virginia aristocracy but also with his own faith in the Tennessee Land. Yet for Orion as well as his father, dreams of success and honor often clouded his judgment of the immediate present.

Another problem Sam had with Orion was that his elder brother may have returned to Hannibal with anti-slavery sympathies. In the northern part of a border state like Missouri, having such views wouldn't have been uncommon even though the town supported what it viewed as a benign form of black slavery. Orion could have picked up these ideas from his mentor in St. Louis, a lawyer named Edward Bates, destined to become Lincoln's first attorney general. Although Mark Twain would make probably one of the strongest post–Civil War arguments against slavery in *Huckleberry Finn,* in the 1850s young Sam was a racist and a pro-slavery advocate. Like most southerners—indeed most Americans—of that day, he could not abide blacks who were not (as he would discover on his first trip north in 1853) automatically subservient to whites.[5]

Bates, a former slaveholder himself, represented the conservative wing of the coming Republican, or old Whig, Party, which would favor Free Soil over abolition in the 1850s. It was an important distinction, as Free Soil advocates opposed not slavery per se (in the southern states where it already existed) but the expansion of the institution into the western territories. Bates, who was older than Orion's father, had also come from Virginia, where he had been the son of a planter and merchant. As a young man he had studied law in St. Louis and subsequently had become involved in city and state politics. He occupied several local offices before being elected to Congress in 1826, but his opposition to Andrew Jackson in 1828 cost him his re-election.[6] No doubt Orion came to see the elder Bates as a surrogate father figure resembling Franklin, though Orion must have seemed to Bates something of a lost soul. But he became the young man's mentor, nevertheless. When Bates finally gave up his own presidential aspirations and got behind Lincoln in 1860, Orion may have helped his mentor by campaigning for the candidate in Hannibal and possibly other rural spots in the state.

While still in St. Louis, Orion showed the clearest signs of his lifelong lack of tenacity and frequent indecisiveness. He remained a printer in the city mainly because his father demanded it. As he reveals in what remains of his otherwise lost autobiography, Orion had hoped to become an orator, the fastest way to fame in the nineteenth century. "My life would have been full of bliss," Orion wrote of that fleeting possibility.[7] But then, under Bates's influence, he thought he would like to be a lawyer like his father, a profession not altogether distinct from a career in oratory. Orion studied law in Bates's law offices while continuing to work as a printer. Later he considered becoming a minister. Yet he never followed through on or finished anything. This scattershot vision would also—in a much happier application—be Mark Twain's problem, curiously enough, as a writer who throughout his life usually had on hand a number of unfinished works in different genres waiting for completion, including *Huckleberry Finn,* which was written over a period of eight years.

"Parson Snivel" undoubtedly experienced ridicule in Hannibal as well as in St. Louis. He had his father's bearing. He was quiet, even somewhat brooding, but he lacked the full weight of his father's aristocratic pretensions as a member of the supposed Virginia gentry. And rather than hold back as a freethinker, Orion changed religions almost as frequently as others changed horses. Twain observed years later in a letter to Howells that Orion had "belonged to as many as five different religious denominations."[8] As a result of his uneven temperament and spasmodic efforts to move ahead in the world, Orion inadvertently became one of the major sources, though not the primary one, for Mark Twain's great sense of humor. He became the boy's straight man in some respects, the one whom the younger brother was always trying to outmaneuver. Sam's genius for irreverence was probably honed on Orion's indignant sense of reform and general lack of humor.

Indeed, it is not at all surprising that Sam Clemens grew up to become a writer of boy's books, for he was formally constrained as a child for a longer period than most—first by his somber father, then by his rather awkward elder brother. Even though he began to work at a young age, it was under the supervision of this brother and surrogate father, who was essentially responsible for Sam's adolescent attitude, which extended into adulthood. Orion as an authority figure presented something of a buffoon—at least to a smart-aleck younger brother like Sam, now entering his teens. Early on under Orion's eye, Sam began to develop the mentality of a Tom Sawyer who cons his friends to whitewash the most famous fence in American fiction. The truth is that Mark Twain was virtually a "kid" all his life, not only to his own children but also to the America that came to cherish him. (His final years, following the death of his wife, find him in almost a second childhood, the idol of the press and a public always ready to chortle over whatever quip of his they read or heard about.) This delayed adolescence derived from his campaigns to undermine Orion's authority and from a teenage upbringing in which he bridled at his brother's authority as a stand-in for the father he had really never come to know well. Ironically, early in his career as a writer, he sought out such authority figures, as we shall see.

He did not, of course, rebel from these people exactly, as he had from Orion, but he continued in the same role he had played under his brother, that of the unpredictable and occasionally gauche individual in civilized society—"God's fool," as he described himself after the scandalous Whittier birthday dinner speech he made in 1877 in Boston, the most civilized society in nineteenth-century America. As the humorist's first straight man, Orion gave Sam his sense of comic contrast. He would callously ridicule his brother's behavior in letters to his mother and to William Dean Howells, his closest literary ally. In what is perhaps an exaggeration, he recalled in his autobiography an incident that made his brother sound like a bumbling idiot. While Orion was still living in St. Louis, he once returned to Hannibal unannounced and found himself in a most embarrassing situation. His family had moved locally without telling him, and so he entered the wrong house, quietly because he wanted to surprise his family the next morning. He retired into a bedroom then occupied by two "ripe old-maid sisters," the daughters of a local physician. Undressing in the dark and slipping into bed with them, thinking it occupied by one of his brothers, he was jolted out of both the bed and the house, where he found himself barely dressed and threatened by a butcher knife wielded by the irate father.[9]

Like his father, Orion was always dreaming but never fully succeeding in any worthwhile endeavor. When he died in 1897, he was found sitting at a table in the early morning, having jotted down his next idea for either new employment or another invention, the latter a penchant Sam also shared. Only once in Orion's life did he come close to success, and that was in the Nevada territory in the 1860s. With one recent exception, however, biographers have not given Orion adequate credit for the performance of his duties as territorial secretary of state, probably because of the sport his brother took with him in letters to Howells and others. Philip Ashley Fanning unfortunately tears down Twain in order to reconstruct Orion, but he also offers an important corrective to the "Damned Fool" view of Orion perpetuated in the Paine biography.

By 1853 Orion's attempt at editing a commercially successful newspaper in Hannibal had gone persistently downhill. He had a faulty business sense, another trait his younger brother would share. The Hannibal *Journal* failed mainly because of flagging subscriptions and a general lack of advertising revenue. Orion's politics, though never very consistent, may have been part of the problem. Even a whiff of abolitionism would have sent many Hannibal readers away. Slaves were still an important source of labor, as well as revenue for local and state governments because they were taxed like land.[10] Talk of temperance, while politely endorsed by the town's families, also wouldn't have been welcomed by its politically powerful saloon and distillery owners. Although Orion worked long and hard, writing editorials late into the night and choosing literary selections and stories from exchange newspapers, which was the way the press reported the national and international news before the days of the wire services, he failed to generate enough revenue to survive, much less to pay Sam or their brother Henry, who was learning printing on the job. Not only was Sam unhappy at the lack of wages, but he had to work ever harder to make up for his brother Henry's typesetting mistakes.

One day, desperate for money, Orion set out much like his father on a journey intended to reverse his ailing fortunes. He traveled to Tennessee in yet another attempt to sell that worthless land, which would eventually be seen as a curse their father had put on the family. But the family curse lay mainly with Orion, whose principle of the moment always prevented a sale of any kind. This particular failure probably involved scruples over temperance or the welfare of immigrants—or both. On at least two occasions, the stumbling block had been temperance. This time it may have involved a vintner who, Orion thought, intended to bring in European labor that might be mistreated, homesick, and consequently unhappy in "those far eastern Tennessee mountains."[11]

Whatever the case, Orion returned to Hannibal empty-handed. In the words of Albert Bigelow Paine, it was "a journey without financial results; yet it bore fruit, for it marked the beginning of Mark Twain's literary career."[12] Already exposed to the printed word as a printer's apprentice for five years, Sam now got a chance to serve Orion's paper unofficially as "assistant editor," though the post was unpaid. While Orion was away, he had been put in charge of a newspaper that badly needed material to compete with the other papers. Although Orion had taken Franklin as his model, Sam, whose wit and outlook on life much more sharply resembled the First American's, took him as a model in another way—and got Orion in some hot water.

4 Southwest Humorist

At almost the same age as Twain, Benjamin Franklin had written as "Silence Dogood" in a parody of Puritan piety in his brother's newspaper, the New England *Courant.* Sam Clemens wrote under several pseudonyms in his brother Orion's newspaper and began a writing career that Walter Blair has called the culmination of the humor of the Old Southwest.[1] Blair's pioneering work on the subject has recently been deepened by James H. Justus in *Fetching the Old Southwest* (2004). In this penetrating history of southwestern humor before Mark Twain, Justus reminds us of how serious the humor could become in the hands of its culminator. While mysterious strangers easily mixed with a steamboat of strangers, in towns like Hannibal they were easily spotted as agents of mischief and deceit, or made the object of a prank or ostracized because of their dandyness. The image of the stranger in southwestern American humor, Justus writes, "figures prominently in the critical juncture between settler and migrant."[2] Often the local was the practical joker and the stranger was the con artist.

William T. Porter's *Spirit of the Times,* a New York weekly that had been publishing tales of the Old Southwest since the 1830s, saw the South and the West as mines of material rich in strange dialects and stranger behavior. The stories of these regions were written by circuit judges and swamp doctors, educators and journalists—educated professionals who were out to interpret their part of the backcountry and were always careful to frame their dialect stories with the standard English of a stranger to the action, often the initial auditor. It was a form of realism that attempted to paint life as it was, "without the artificial embellishments of romance."[3]

These writers who preceded the rise of Mark Twain included William Tappan Thompson, Augustus Baldwin Longstreet, Joseph G. Baldwin, Johnson J. Hooper, Madison Tensas, Thomas Bangs Thorpe, George W. Harris, and later on, Twain's early sponsor Artemus Ward. Most of these writers of the "Left Hand" used pseudonyms to further insulate themselves from the crudity of their fictional characters based on real life. Such "humorous" writings go all the way back to the beginning of American literature, certainly to the beginning of American drama with *The Contrast* by Royall Tyler in 1787. This is an upstairs-downstairs social comedy in which the crudity of the basically honest American is contrasted with the elegance of the corrupted Englishman. Its incongruities are initially funny but ultimately become the basis for defining the American as the epitome of candor and courage. With the scene shift to the South and the West, the British fop or, later, congressman is replaced by the American Yankee—or, more generally, the Stranger. "Although at first the West had applauded the eastern Yankee as a symbol of American ascendancy," writes Edgar Marquess Branch, "it soon developed its own ideal types."[4]

Sam's first apprenticeship as a printer was not with his brother's paper but with Joseph P. Ament's Missouri *Courier,* a position he took up about a year after his father's death in 1847. Dixon Wecter theorizes that a reliable marker for Sam's change to his brother's paper, the weekly Hannibal *Western Union,* eventually converted into the Hannibal *Journal,* is the publication of Twain's first story on January 16, 1851.[5] The story essentially makes fun of the slow-witted Jim Wolfe, a printer's devil in Orion's print shop. Sam's range of comical targets could be wide. The parameters of humor have shrunken in our time, so that no one except the objects of ridicule themselves can with impunity make fun of women, blacks, Jews, gays, or just about any other minority except representatives of Congress, rednecks, or possibly Catholics these days. In *Huckleberry Finn,* the "hare lip" drives Huck "up a stump" with her prying questions about his fictional background as a domestic in England. Yet in another real way, humor hasn't changed at all, for its object is often a stranger to the culture, the outsider. Once that stranger becomes an accepted part of our community, we can no longer make fun of him or her.

On January 9 a fire broke out in the establishment next door to Orion's newspaper. It was discovered by Wolfe, whose actions young Sam described in one of the earliest examples of the wit that would glitter through the best work of Mark Twain:

> Our gallant *devil,* seeing us somewhat excited, concluded he would perform a noble deed, and immediately gathered the broom, an old mallet, the wash-pan and a dirty towel, and in a fit of patriotic excitement, rushed out of the office and deposited his precious burden some ten squares off, out of danger. Being of a *snailish* disposition, even in his quickest moments, the fire had been extinguished during his absence. He returned in the course of an hour, nearly out of breath, and thinking he had immortalized himself, threw his giant frame in a tragic attitude, and exclaimed, with an eloquent expression: "If that thar fire hadn't bin put out, thar'd a' bin the greatest *confirmation* of the age!"[6]

This is the Jim Wolfe on whom Sam and Henry played practical jokes. He was eighteen when the fire occurred, three years older than Sam. His shyness around girls became the subject of Twain's "Jim Wolfe and the Cats" in 1867. Once, they loaded his bedclothes with wasps, for which Sam was pummeled by Jim. Later, Twain expressed regret over his conduct with Wolfe, saying his tricks had been "all cruel and all barren of wit."[7] But the practical joke was part of small-town life. Huck and Tom place garter snakes in Aunt Sally's sewing basket, and young Sam probably did the same to his mother.

If Sam learned anything from being a small-town practical joker, it was an appreciation for the basic incongruity of any humorous situation. The printer's devil is anything but "gallant." The least valuable items in the newspaper office are the broom, a wash bowl, and a dirty towel. There is no reason to remove these worthless items ten blocks away from the fire. This "snailish" individual is out of breath after taking an hour to return. The anecdote is topped off with malapropism in a play on the word "conflagration." This is basic humor, but it is also the foundation for the much more subtle humor of *Huckleberry Finn* and *Pudd'nhead Wilson.* Sam Clemens was barely sixteen when he wrote this sketch, his first known publication. Yet he already sensed the raucous absurdity of the human race's demand for self-approval in the face of outright failure. Orion's sense of self-importance as a reformer had most likely been his first lesson.

Very possibly Sam published other such short pieces in Orion's newspaper and perhaps elsewhere, but nothing of his has been identified until "The Dandy Frightening the Squatter," which appeared in the Boston *Carpet-Bag*—like *The Spirit of the Times,* another repository for American humor. As with "A Gallant Fireman," Twain wrote in standard English, not yet introducing much vernacular. Later he would regret that he hadn't written *Tom Sawyer* in the first person. "The Dandy" was published on May 1, 1852. Typical of the newspaper humor of that day in which the country type outwits the city slicker, it featured "a spruce young dandy" and a "brawny woodsman." A steamboat has just landed in Hannibal, and the dandy attempts to frighten a town rough in order to impress the ladies on board. He pretends to have found this fellow after a long search and, confronting him with a bowie knife in his belt and a "large horse pistol in each hand," is dispatched by the "squatter" with a deft blow that sends its victim into the muddy Mississippi.

The story has the exaggeration of the tall tale. The dandy warns the woodsman to say his prayers. Pointing his pistols at his intended victim, he says, "You'll make a capital barn door, and I shall drill the key-hole myself!" Following the easterner's quick defeat, the woodsman refers to the keyhole metaphor in a comic dismissal of the poseur. Tales of raftsmen in this literary tradition featured braggarts who would, in their efforts to frighten their opponents without actually fighting, compare themselves and their efforts to events of cosmic proportion. In the raft scene that Twain borrowed from the yet unfinished *Huckleberry Finn* manuscript and placed in chapter 3 of *Life on the Mississippi* to pad his book, the little guy, a third party to an impending quarrel between two raftsmen, handily defeats the loudmouthed pretenders.

A week after "The Dandy" appeared, Sam Clemens placed a sketch about Hannibal in the Philadelphia *American Courier.* It was remarkably polished for the sixteen-year-old school dropout, indeed for any person of that tender age. Entitled simply "Hannibal, Missouri" in the May 8 issue, it contains the seeds of the most famous Hannibal stories such as *Tom Sawyer* and *Huckleberry Finn,* including a description of the town's cave he would make famous. "Your Eastern people seem to think this country is a barren, uncultivated region, with a population consisting of heathens," the future chronicler of the Mississippi wrote in defense of his region. (Young Sam may indeed have also been defending slavery in the South, which had come under increased scrutiny following the newly strengthened fugitive slave law of 1850.) He speaks of the first houses being built in Hannibal around the time of his birth, as if Hannibal is itself indistinguishable from the writer who is already introducing himself to the world at large, or to the East, where in 1877 he would satirize the works of three of its literary saints in the notorious Whittier birthday speech. He speaks of the "children of the forest" now gone from their canoes, replaced by the steamboat. Later, in *Roughing It,* he would become clearer about his disdain for the eastern myth of the Indian. Finally, there is an allusion to the *Arabian Nights,* from which he would draw inspiration for his own approximation of the thousand and one stories that originated in the river town of his childhood.[8]

"Hannibal, Missouri" was sent as a letter to the editor and signed "S.L.C." Among other firsts in the career of Samuel Langhorne Clemens, it began his efforts as a travel writer who was describing the events to the folks back home. In this case, of course, he was describing home to the folks far away, but the genre was begun with "A Family Muss," appearing in his brother's newspaper for September 9, 1852. Here he adopted his first nom de plume, "W. Epaminondas Adrastus Perkins." Otherwise, the piece is largely unremarkable as a literary effort. The object of his satirical scorn is a collection of immigrant Catholic families of German, Irish, and Scottish origin in Hannibal—"a small house, occupied by an indefinite number of very large families" on the other side of Holliday's Hill. Raised as a Presbyterian fundamentalist, Clemens often expressed anti-Catholic sentiments in his early thinking and writing. Here alcoholism and domestic violence are the subjects of humor, the anecdote spiced at the end with comic Irish dialect.

Shortly after "A Family Muss," Orion made his trip east to the Tennessee Land, and Sam got the newspaper into a feud, an episode not unlike

Franklin's mischief on his brother's newspaper. It was another case of the printer wanting to become the writer. The local papers had commented about barking dogs. In the nineteenth century, such untended or roaming animals were routinely shot without protest. The details of this story are conflicting, but young Sam decided to ridicule a rival editor, a "newcomer" from Illinois named J. T. Hinton, who ran the Hannibal *Triweekly Messenger* and whose politics were Whig. On August 24, 1852, he had defended the dogs and sarcastically criticized Orion for complaining about their barking in the night.

Sam retaliated on September 16 by publishing a sketch he had carved himself on a printer's block—something he would do later for the *Galaxy* in his parody of military maps of the siege of Paris during the Franco-Prussian War. He had heard the town rumor that Hinton as a disappointed suitor had attempted suicide in Hannibal's Bear Creek but changed his mind and quickly waded ashore. The sketch was entitled "'Local' Resolves to Commit Suicide." Its caption indicated that Hinton had attempted suicide because he had not heard from Orion in response to his attack in which he had labeled Orion "A Dog-Be-Deviled Citizen." It portrayed Hinton with a dog's head and a bottle of liquor as his suicide "pistol" as he descends into a local creek. "Fearing, however, that he may get out of his depth," the legend continued, "*he sounds the stream with his walking-stick.*" "Mark Twain," as he would later call himself, made his first sounding in water that was somewhere between "safe" and "dangerous" for steamboats and humorists. He would do it again many times and did it first as a journalist. He closed with a pun, "Peace to his *re*-manes," and signed it "A DOG-BE-DEVILED CITIZEN."[9] Clemens followed this up the next week with a second piece, also illustrated, called "'Pictur' Department." These naturally caused ill will toward Orion, whom Hinton assumed to be its author, but upon his return Orion was able to bring the exchange to a close by publicly dismissing it as a farce.

In the same issue of the paper, under the name now of W. Epaminondas Adrastus Blab, Clemens printed three more features: "Editorial Agility," "Blabbing Government Secrets!" and "Historical Exhibition—A No. 1 Ruse," which anticipates Twain's future use of history as the basis of satire and humor. It also anticipates the crowd-baiting used by the Duke and the Dauphin in their "Royal Nonesuch" production in chapter 23 of *Huckleberry Finn.* In "Historical Exhibition," a Jim C is duped into paying to see an exhibit titled "Napoleon Crossing the Rhine," which turns out to be the "bony part" of a hog's leg being passed over a piece of hog's rind. The victim is subsequently encouraged to respond like the townsfolk of Bricksville, who hide their disappointment until all of their neighbors have been duped by the same scheme. According to the editors of the early sketches, the piece contains the phallic humor of the country with the play on the word "bony" for "boner," but Twain was probably not relying on this aspect to draw laughter. He was known to the public throughout his career as a "clean" humorist, and aside from the off-color humor of the privately published *1601,* a few other pieces not published during his lifetime, and possibly the mildly scatological "Royal Nonesuch" in *Huckleberry Finn,* he seldom depended on that effect.[10]

The next week, with Orion probably still out of town, Adrastus Blab announced that he was leaving for a "furrin" tour of Glasscock's Island, and this name—a variation on Sam's first literary pseudonym—was permanently retired. For the rest of 1852 and until he left Hannibal the following June, there are in all thus far thirteen extant pieces that can probably be attributed to him. In "'Connubial Bliss'" he may have returned to the impoverished inebriates at the foot of Holliday's Hill. The piece is included in Twain's collected works because of the last sentence, which forms a pun involving the *change* in the existence of the drunk's wife from the earliest blissful days of her marriage before she realized she had wed an alcoholic, and what little spare *change* there is to be found in the pockets of printers. This was on November 4 in Orion's newspaper, and it may have been a muted complaint about the absence of a salary for Sam, who was about to turn seventeen and getting restless.

By the following spring we find a couple of poems and letters written by "Rambler." It is doubtful that "The Heart's Lament," a straightforward imitation of one of Thomas Moore's love ballads, published in Orion's journal on May 5, is the work of the young Sam Clemens. Yet it may have given him the idea for the poem and letters that immediately followed in the Hannibal *Daily Journal.* Called "Love Concealed," it was subtitled

"To Miss Katie of H—l," meaning "Hannibal" but leaving open the other possibility. The actual printing shows that the title was too long for the column, thus requiring the elided final word, though Twain in another of his *Galaxy* articles in 1871 claimed it was an intentional "thunderbolt of humor."[11] The poem draws the response of the "Grumbler," who expresses his opinion that damning a former girlfriend to hell is "carrying the matter too far." This is followed up by other exchanges whose humor has not survived the nineteenth century.

One of Sam's last clearly identifiable contributions to his brother's sagging newspaper is "The Burial of Sir Abner Gilstrap, Editor of the Bloomington 'Republican,'" published on May 23, 1853. It reminds us again of Ben Franklin, who published a premature obituary of one of his competitors in retaliation for continuing to use a journal title that Franklin had purchased from him. The humor of Sam's "Burial" not only outlives its century but also anticipates Twain's famous parody of poetry, or doggerel, in chapter 17 of *Huckleberry Finn.* The incident originated in a competition between Hannibal and Bloomington, Missouri, then the county seat of neighboring Macon County, over the route of what became the Hannibal and St. Joseph Railroad. As editor of one of Bloomington's newspapers and also an aspiring politico, Gilstrap had accused certain Hannibal businesses of bribery in winning the railroad route.[12] The issue was discussed by a number of area newspapers in a time when editors regularly assailed each other in print. But this editor became the object of one of Mark Twain's hilarious parodies of poetry, a literary genre he never truly appreciated but nevertheless used to good effect.

His poetic talent here would culminate with Emmeline Grangerford's "Ode to Stephen Dowling Bots, Dec'd," in which the beloved Stephen does not die from whooping cough or measles "drear, with spots." Rather, "His soul did from this cold world fly, / By falling down a well." In the case of Abner Gilstrap:

Not a sound was heard, nor a funeral note,
  As his carcass through town we hurried;
Not e'en an obituary we wrote,
  In respect for the rascal we buried.

. . . .

No useless coffin confined his breast,
  Nor in sheet nor in shirt we bound him;
But he lay like an Editor taking his rest
  With a Hannibal Journal around him.[13]

Sam Clemens was eighteen years old and already possessed of the satirical glee that would first make him famous. But his real-life Hannibal days, the experience that would become the basis for his most memorable work, were now over.

5 Tramp Printer

"I disappeared one night and fled to St. Louis," Twain recalled in his autobiography. This was probably sometime in the first two weeks of June 1853. "There I worked in the composing-room of the *Evening News* for a time and then started on my travels to see the world." His first stop was New York City, but it is remotely possible that by the time he resided there, he had already decided to travel to South America and profit in coca (possibly the first of a lifetime series of get-rich schemes or inventions), and not simply after he returned to the Mississippi Valley almost a year later. New York would have been as convenient a port of departure as New Orleans.

He spent the summer in St. Louis working for the *News* and staying with his sister Pamela. She was by now married to William A. Moffett, whom Twain described later as "a merchant, Virginian—a fine man in every way." Sam made only eight or nine dollars a week, somewhat below what the average compositor could command, but he evidently saved his money, having promised his mother never to drink or throw a card. On August 19 he began an arduous six-day journey by steamboat, rail, and stagecoach to New York, where one of the attractions was the first World's Fair, being held at the Crystal Palace, a huge dome of glass and iron on Fifth Avenue behind the Croton Reservoir, today the site of the New York Public Library. Back in Hannibal, he had very possibly read about the grand exhibit. On May 26 in Orion's newspaper, a report stated that between fifteen and twenty thousand people came to it every day.[1]

Although the city was overrun with printers, it could still absorb a sober applicant who hadn't found anything upriver in St. Louis. He landed a position at John A. Gray's book and job printing house (coincidentally, the printers of *The Celebrated Jumping Frog of Calaveras County* in 1867) at 95–97 Cliff Street near the East River, next to Harper and Brothers publishing house. "I work in the fifth story," he told his mother, "and from one window I have a pretty good view of the city, while another commands a view of the shipping beyond the Battery; and the 'forest of masts,' with all sorts of flags flying." There were at the time, unfortunately, two competing printers' unions in the city, which drove down the pay to as low as twenty-three cents per one thousand ems, the rate seventeen-year-old Sam received. But, as he told his mother on August 31, he was lucky to get the job, which was permanent as long as he wanted it. He boarded ten blocks away near Broadway on Duane Street, where he missed southern home cooking.[2]

Walt Whitman claimed to have known young Clemens during Sam's first time in New York. Now a former newspaper editor, Whitman was working away on the first edition of *Leaves of Grass* while running a bookstore in Brooklyn. He would still have made frequent visits to printers' row where Sam worked. "I have met Clemens," the poet later told his Boswell, Horace Traubel, "met him many years ago, before he was rich and famous. Like all humorists he was very sober: inclined to talk of the latest things in politics, men, books, a man after old-fashioned models, slow to move, liking to stop and chat—the sort of fellow one is quietly drawn to."[3]

Parts of Sam's letter to his mother and other letters were published by Orion, first in Hannibal and then in Muscatine, Iowa, where he had briefly relocated with another newspaper. Although Twain began his career as a travel writer, he was actually traveling for the first time. Hardly three months earlier he had never been far from Hannibal. Now, here he was in one of the biggest and most populous cities in America. "I was going to leave New York, every day for the last two weeks," he wrote his sister in St. Louis. "I have taken a liking to the abominable place, and every time I get ready to leave, I put it off a day or so, from some unaccountable cause." By the third week of October, he had relocated to

Philadelphia. He went by steamboat to South Amboy, New Jersey, and then by train to Camden and over the Delaware River by ferry to what he described as a city "rich in Revolutionary associations."

Travel by rail was still dangerous in this era and throughout the nineteenth century because most trains, dependent on telegraph dispatchers sometimes either asleep or drunk on the job, ran on a single track going in opposite directions. Sam told Orion that he had traveled on the same line on which a deadly collision had occurred the previous August. He never thought of the danger, he said, until the train stopped "'all of a sudden,' and then began to go backwards like blazes. Then ran back half a mile, and switched off on another track, and stopped; and the next moment a large passenger train came round a bend in the road, and whistled past us like lightning!"[4] Perhaps he later saw the experience as an omen for his brother Henry's death on a steamboat, yet another very dangerous mode of transportation in the rapidly expanding nation.

In the meantime he worried about the changes at home. Having read somewhere that Orion had given up the *Journal*, he supposed that the family had joined Pamela in St. Louis, where his brother had previously made a living wage as a printer. He liked Philadelphia better than New York. It was, of course, the city of Franklin, Orion's one-time model. "The grave of Franklin," he told his brother in that era of grave robbers, "is in Christ Church-yard, cor. of Fifth and Arch streets. They keep the gates locked, and one can only see the flat slab that lies over his remains and that of his wife." He visited Fairmont Park and the famous cable suspension bridge over the Schuylkill River that ran down the western side of the city. He saw steamboats with signs indicating they were headed for Germantown and Wissahickon Creek and vowed to visit the area as soon as possible. He had read about it in George Lippard's *Legends of the American Revolution* (1847). Remembered by his fellow printers as a dedicated reader, young Sam may have even read this book in the Printers' Free Library in New York.[5]

Clemens remained in Philadelphia until the winter of 1854. He worked, as he later recalled, on the Philadelphia *Inquirer* and the *Public Ledger*, but only as a substitute printer. He didn't worry, however, as he was still in the glow of happiness at having gotten away from Hannibal and seeing the wide world. (Despite its charm today as the home of Mark Twain, a visitor to that small river town will quickly realize why Sam Clemens yearned to spread his wings.) He told Orion of a printers' annual ball that raised a thousand dollars toward the erection of a statue of Franklin. But the patriotic Clemens was annoyed by the many Irish ("foreigners") in the city and among the ranks of the printers, "who hate everything American." Two days before his eighteenth birthday, he still maintained his bias toward the Irish, northern blacks who didn't know how to behave themselves around whites, and abolitionists. "I reckon I had better black my face," he had told his mother while still in New York, "for in these Eastern States niggers are considerably better than white people."[6]

All the same, he was now living in the city of the Quakers, who had led the movement to draw freed and fugitive slaves north. Along with Boston, Philadelphia was a haven for such activity and sympathy. New York, on the other hand, was known to be hostile to passengers on the Underground Railroad. By now Orion, his mother, and Henry had moved to the Free Soil state of Iowa, and Sam asked his brother how he liked the change from Missouri. "I would like amazingly to see a good, old-fashioned negro," he closed, meaning a black person beyond the politics of the anti-slavery movement that was heating up in the North. Ever since the Wilmot Proviso (introduced by a Pennsylvania congressman, no less) had been defeated in 1847, the differences between the North and the South had been sharpened. It had called for outlawing slavery in the new territories, and states like Iowa and Missouri whose western borders faced the territories were on the cusp of the controversy.

This was Mark Twain's first visit to the distant North, the land of the abolitionists that Hannibal residents increasingly feared, as he would later suggest in *Tom Sawyer's Conspiracy*. He also hailed from a southern town that was remote in terms of the fever pitch that the national debate over slavery had reached since the strengthened fugitive slave law of 1850. The closest metropolis that embraced the politics of abolition was forty miles away, across the river in Quincy, Illinois. The nearest big city was St. Louis, more than a hundred miles downriver, and it was still pro-southern on the question of slavery. The institution was also thoroughly supported in the pulpits in Hannibal, and Clemens had probably had little or no access to northern newspapers that called it into question. It would take some time in the West for this southerner to ever feel at home in the North.

In fact, vestiges of his divided feelings toward blacks can be found as late as the turn of the century, long after his celebration of racial sympathy in *Huckleberry Finn*. Even when he was excitedly planning a book on lynching in 1901, to be based on an article he planned to submit to the *North American Review* entitled "The United States of Lyncherdom," he recalled in the précis for his intended publisher the case of a black man who *had* deserved punishment (lawful retribution, not lynching). He had raped a girl and clubbed "her & her younger brother to death." The crime had taken place near Hannibal in 1849. "I remember all about it," he told Frank Bliss. "It came out that his owner smuggled him out of Virginia because he had raped 3 white women there & his commercial value was deteriorating."[7]

Faithful to the promise he had made to his mother, he told Orion while still in Philadelphia, "I believe I am the only person in the Inquirer office that does not drink." That would have pleased Orion, who had tried to set the same example as a printer in St. Louis. But printers were rather notorious drunkards whose lifestyles in general were not typically healthy. "One young fellow makes $18 for a few weeks," he wrote Orion, "and gets on a grand 'bender' and spends every cent of it." He told his sister Pamela that he had hoped to return to St. Louis before the Mississippi froze over that winter and closed the river to steamboat traffic. Instead he stayed on and contributed two more letters to the Muscatine *Journal*. Once again, as he had in the Hannibal *Journal* before leaving town, he called upon his talent for mocking sentimental poetry.

"The people here," he wrote in the Muscatine *Journal* of February 3, 1854, "seem very fond of tacking a bit of poetry (?) to the notices of the death of friends, published in the Ledger." He cited as an example of this "most villainous doggerel" the following:

Ah! dry your tears, and shed no more.
Because your child, husband, and brother has gone before;
In love he lived, in peace he died,
His life was asked, but was denied.

"What do you think of that?" he asked his Iowa readers. "Will not Byron lose some of his popularity now?"[8] Even though he did not know any Muscatine readers personally, he could address them with the same intimacy he might have written to Hannibal readers because they were not from the East and would have appreciated his mockery of supposedly highbrow culture.

Not long after writing this letter, Sam made what he later remembered as a "flying trip" to Washington, D.C. In fact, it was on February 17 that he stood in the snow before the unfinished Capitol dome. As snow fell heavily on his shoulders, he sank "ankle deep" in the unpaved street of mud and snow. Possibly he felt more comfortable in Washington than he had in Philadelphia with regard to slavery, for the District of Columbia still allowed it. He stood proudly before a recently constructed equestrian statue of Andrew Jackson near the White House. He thought the public buildings "fine specimens of architecture," which would more readily embellish New York City. "Here they are sadly out of place looking like so many palaces in a Hottentot village." He was consciously writing now to the Muscatine readers. "The streets," he told them, "indeed are fine—wide, straight, and level as a floor. But the buildings, almost invariably, are very poor—two and three story brick houses, and strewed about in clusters."

He ventured into the chambers of the Senate and the House of Representatives and lamented that the halls of the Capitol were no longer peopled with greats like Clay, Webster, or Calhoun. At the time he visited one session of Congress, debate was beginning on the proposed Kansas-Nebraska Act, which when passed the following year, would void the Missouri Compromise of 1820 and help to create John Brown's firestorm in Kansas. This visit may have marked the beginning of what would become his lifelong practice of making fun of congressmen. But even more interesting than Congress to this future inventor of a self-pasting scrapbook and self-adjusting suspenders was the U.S. Patent Office. Also, as the largest future investor in the doomed Paige typesetting machine, he admired the printing press used by Franklin a hundred years earlier, remarking, "What vast progress has been made in the art of printing!"[9]

One would think that Sam Clemens would have spent more than a weekend in Washington to take in the sights, including the Washington Monument, under construction since 1848, but it was probably no more than a weekend that he actually spent there, four or five days at the most, before he returned to work again as a printer in Philadelphia. In terms of surviving letters, the rest of 1854 and the first part of 1855 constitute a blank. His authorized biographer states that Clemens, after working a while in Philadelphia, returned for a brief visit to New York before heading west again in the spring or summer of 1854.

He went to St. Louis, but he probably didn't stay there very long, mainly because he wanted to see his mother, who with fourteen-year-old Henry was living with Orion in Muscatine. In chapter 57 of *Life on the Mississippi,* while discussing the upper river towns, he describes Muscatine's beautiful sunsets. He called them "summer sunsets," which suggests that he spent only the summer in the Iowa town, working perhaps in his brother's newspaper office before returning to St. Louis to resume his printing job on the *Evening News.* He had made little money as a printer in St. Louis on his first try, and this situation may have persisted in the winter of 1855. In 1908 Anthony Kennedy, a printer who had worked alongside Clemens then, claimed that the young printer "could not have set up an advertisement in acceptable form to save his life." The testimony is a little suspect since Orion had expressed an admiration for Sam's abilities as a printer in Hannibal. By 1908 Clemens, of course, had become the world-famous Mark Twain, while Kennedy had remained a relative nobody. Yet Kennedy's description does conform to those of others suggesting that the small-boned, red-headed Clemens, who stood around five feet eight and a half inches, was never "one of the boys." "He was a silent chap, who attended to his own business and didn't mingle with the wild fellows who worked with him."[10]

In December 1854 Orion married Mary Eleanor Stotts, or "Mollie," as she was called. He met her in Keokuk, and her homesickness soon prodded them to move from Muscatine to Keokuk, less than a hundred miles downriver, the following June. Almost exactly nine months to the day after their marriage, Mollie gave birth to their only child, named Jennie. Sam made a visit from St. Louis in June and returned that fall to work for the Muscatine *Journal,* to which he had already contributed from St. Louis. During that summer he briefly visited Hannibal and—for the last time in his life—Florida, Missouri.

In one of his letters to the Muscatine *Journal,* dated February 16, 1855, he alluded somewhat approvingly to the case of a free black woman from Ohio who had been arrested in St. Louis for entering Missouri without permission. State law at the time forbade a free black from entering the state "unless in the service of a white man, or for the purpose of passing through." Yet at the same time, he took the point of view of a passive observer, noting that she had avoided the price of a license to save money and would "doubtless be more careful in the future." He was heading, it seems, in several directions at once in life during this period, taking in events and scenes that would later crop up in his fiction, such as in Pap Finn's tirade against the free black man from Ohio in chapter 6 of *Huckleberry Finn.* He was, as his earliest known journal shows, studying phrenology, that forerunner of self-help psychology. He also began the study of the French language in 1855, possibly because he hoped soon—or someday soon—to visit New Orleans. This too would come back to serve him well in his famous jokes about the French.[11]

It probably wasn't until some months after Orion had re-established himself in Keokuk that Sam left St. Louis to live there and work for him. Orion had taken possession of the Ben Franklin Book and Job Office, located on the third floor of 52 Main Street. Henry also worked in the office, where both he and Sam slept at night. Orion and Mollie, now with a new infant, moved in with her father, William Stotts, on Timea Street. Fred W. Lorch writes that this period in Keokuk was one of the happiest in Sam's early career because he was now old enough to both work for Orion and be independent of him. Orion, too, was now preoccupied not only with a new business but with a new baby as well. Well known for his pranks in Hannibal, Sam lived up to the same reputation in Keokuk. He also began to develop the public personality of a humorist, which would throughout his life overshadow the literary talent we celebrate today.

In fact, he delivered his first public speech at a banquet in Keokuk given by the printers' association on the 150th birthday of Ben Franklin.

The event took place at the Ivins House on January 17, 1856. After the planned portion of the program had been completed, including a speech by Orion, there was a boisterous call for Sam Clemens to speak. He responded with an informal talk, enhanced by the slow drawl he had inherited from his mother and "replete with wit and humor, being interrupted by long and continued bursts of applause." These are the words of Orion, who had been elected secretary for the occasion. He wrote an article in the Keokuk *Gate City* that described the banquet in detail. Later, J.C. Fry, who had sat next to Clemens at the Keokuk banquet, recalled his performance.

"Blushing and slowly getting upon his feet, stammering in the start," Fry wrote in the *Gate City* of January 17, 1885, "he finally rallied his powers, and when he sat down, his speech was pronounced by all present a remarkable production of pathos and wit, the latter however predominating, convulsing his hearers with round after round of applause."[12] This description appears to anticipate Twain's mature lectures, when "the trouble" began with him playing the part of the reluctant lecturer. Then he would appear on stage without anyone to introduce him, seem not to know what he was about during a silence that could last up to five minutes, and then unfurl his wings of irony and wit.

Clemens no doubt remained in Keokuk for most of the next year, but in October 1856 he moved to Cincinnati to work. He may have first visited his mother, who was now back with Pamela in St. Louis. It is not altogether clear just why he made this move so far away, almost as if he were heading back east again. The move was later romanticized in a late-life memoir entitled "The Turning Point of My Life," which shares with his autobiography some of the tendency for simplification. Paine uses the story in his biography. Sam found a fifty-dollar bill on the street in Keokuk and took the discovery as a good omen for his plan to go to the Amazon, having read an account of its exploration.[13]

Otherwise, Cincinnati is a biographical blind spot. It was from here that he wrote the Thomas Jefferson Snodgrass letters to the Keokuk *Daily Post*. As Paine remarks, the comedic effort was crude and seemed to echo in both its vernacular and dramatic situations the work of Petroleum V. Nasby and Artemus Ward. But it was more than a start. In two short years he had taken two important steps. He had made his first public speech. And for the first time since his early efforts in Hannibal, he was trying his hand again directly at writing humorous journalism. In Cincinnati he worked for the T. Wrightson Printing Company. He may have met a Scot by the name of Macfarlane, who was eccentric enough in this Ohio river town to be well read and an agnostic. According to Paine, this individual gave Sam Clemens his first glimpse of the philosophical determinism that would gain ascendancy in his final years.[14] But soon—by February 1857—another mentor would change his immediate plans, though not his philosophy. He would be the most important man that Mark Twain would ever meet on the Mississippi River.

6 Cub Pilot

The name of Horace E. Bixby is one of the more notable landmarks in the life of Mark Twain. Bixby was a New Yorker who had spent more than a third of his life in the South on the Mississippi River. Yet he would have no qualms about serving as a Union pilot when the war broke out almost exactly four years after first meeting Clemens. Bixby may well be the "pilot mate" in "The Private History of a Campaign That Failed" who was "strong for the Union" when the war brought steamboat traffic to a virtual halt in the spring of 1861. Thirty-one in 1857 when he met Clemens, who was then supposedly on his way to the Amazon, this Bixby would not allow the younger pilot, already divided in his allegiances to North and South, to declare himself a Unionist. In the senior pilot's eyes, Mark Twain's loyalty "was smirched . . . because my father had owned slaves." It did not matter that Sam's father, according to his "Private History," had thought slavery wrong and would have freed his slaves if it had been economically feasible.

The Bixby Mark Twain recalled in his "war story," or tall tale, became for a brief time a rebel sympathizer when "the secession atmosphere had considerably thickened on the Lower Mississippi." Yet he also objected to Clemens's doing his share of rebel shouting, because he had come "of bad stock—of a father who had been willing to set slaves free."[1] Bixby is never named in "The Private History," in which he is depicted as something of a hypocrite. The essay appeared in the May 1885 issue of *Century* magazine, in its "Battles and Leaders" series. In his river essays in "Old Times on the Mississippi" in the *Atlantic* and in *Life on the Mississippi,* Twain had already memorialized Bixby by name as an irascible but lovable mentor who diverted him from a voyage to the Amazon, where he would get rich on coca, to a career on the river. (This was before the discovery of the process of isolating cocaine from coca leaves, which were at the time chewed or otherwise consumed for medicinal purposes.)

With these particular Mississippi chapters, Twain preempted his master, who never wrote his own memoirs of his sixty-six years on the river, and who was still active in 1882 as a skipper even after that commerce had been almost completely replaced by the railroad. He was literally hijacked by his protégé's fame as Mark Twain, who nevertheless insisted that if he had his choice in life (even after the advent of his world fame), he would have remained on the river as a steamboat pilot. When Twain, then famous for *The Innocents Abroad* and "Old Times on the Mississippi," returned to the river in the spring of 1882 with the idea of expanding the *Atlantic* chapters into a book, Horace Bixby was in New Orleans to greet him and to testify to his piloting talent. He reconfirmed this positive judgment in 1907 or 1908 to Albert Bigelow Paine. Clemens was not merely a pilot on the Mississippi, he told Paine, "but a good one." Paine adds that Bixby acknowledged, "It is the fashion to-day to disparage Sam's piloting."[2]

In fact, there was indeed in that day a tradition among pilots and river men in the Lower Mississippi Valley to denigrate Mark Twain's ability as a pilot. In his 1968 dissertation on Twain's river days, Allan Bates quotes several pilots who challenged Twain's record on the river. "'Mark Twain hell!' they bark sharply when questioned," according to Marquis Childs in 1926. "'He didn't know anything about the river.'" This dissenting consensus even goes so far as to suggest that Twain was never trusted to take the wheel of a steamboat alone. In fact, he is known to have done so on more than one boat. The best that can be safely said is that Clemens was an average pilot who thought he was better than average. As late as the 1960s, one river man rhetorically asked Bates, "He could write, all right, but he sure didn't know much about the river, did he?"[3] Even Bixby himself, who had grown tired of living in Mark Twain's shadow, recanted once his "cub" was dead. Shortly before the writer's death, in

1908, Bixby had exclaimed to a reporter, "I wish Clemens was dead, then maybe you fellows would leave me alone." When Twain did die, Bixby told the river editor for the Memphis *Commercial Appeal* in the spring of 1912: "Sam was never a good pilot. He knew the Mississippi River like a book, but he lacked confidence. This developed soon after he came on my boat. It never left him. . . . No sir, Sam Clemens knew the river, but being a coward he was a failure as a pilot."[4]

Bixby died a couple of months later at age eighty-six while still actively working on the river. After so many years as Mark Twain's false witness, he seemingly freed himself before going to his grave. This judgment ought to ring true to anyone reading Twain's description of his piloting days in *Life on the Mississippi.* Before the war there were no official nautical charts of the thousand-mile stretch between St. Louis and New Orleans, the route that Clemens traveled for four years. Safe navigation depended on a crude form of what is still called "piloting" in the United States Navy: the establishment of two or more angular fixes upon land sites in order to determine latitude and longitude of a vessel at sea. In Bixby and Clemens's day (and night) on the river, one had to depend on the location of woodpiles and farmhouses on a constantly shifting river, and it took nerve that Clemens, who ran the *Alonzo Child* aground in 1860, evidently lacked to some degree.[5]

Twain himself confesses his lack of nerve while a cub pilot in chapter 13 of *Life on the Mississippi,* material that came from the original "Old Times" pieces of 1875. One day during his two-year training, Bixby pretended to have gone below decks after turning over the helm to Clemens at Island 66, somewhere between Cairo and New Orleans. It was at a deepwater crossing that posed no danger whatever of hitting a shoal. Sam knew the depth, but his confidence was shaken when he heard—as part of Bixby's prank and test of his apprentice—"the leadsman's sepulchral cry" of "mark twain!" This indicated a depth of twelve feet or two fathoms—water barely safe for even a shallow-draft steamboat. "I was helpless," Twain later wrote in *Life.* "I did not know what in the world to do. I was quaking from head to foot." When confronted by his teacher, who suddenly reappeared from behind a smokestack, Clemens admitted that he had *known* the real depth of the water, that it had "no bottom" at that particular crossing, but he had simply lost his nerve. Steamboats regularly ran aground, and it therefore took more than simply skill to make a pilot successful. In fact, Bixby himself was one of the pilots on the *Colonel Crossman* in 1858 that blew a boiler in an explosion that killed fourteen people.[6]

During his four-year career as an apprentice and licensed pilot, Sam Clemens served on nineteen or twenty different steamboats, mostly packets that followed regular routes and worked in conjunction with the encroaching railroad. His professional life on the river started on one or two tramp vessels, which roved wherever there was cargo to transport.[7] He initially boarded the *Paul Jones* at Cincinnati on February 16, 1857. The boat was from Pittsburgh, and it made only occasional trips to the Crescent City, at least until Sam's time on the river. Though he was headed for New Orleans to sail to South America, once aboard the *Paul Jones,* Clemens's boyhood love of the river was stirred, and he asked Bixby if he would train him as a pilot. They purportedly agreed on a total tuition of $500, $100 of which was to be paid at the outset of his training, $150 over the next twelve months, and the balance out of his early wages as a pilot.[8]

Just when the two men made this agreement is not completely clear. In his autobiography Twain recalled that he had gotten to know Bixby on the way down to New Orleans and had even done some steering for him because the pilot had a sore foot. When he got to New Orleans and discovered that no ships were scheduled to leave for South America—that "there probably wouldn't be any during that century"—he went to Bixby and asked him to make him a cub pilot. Whatever the case, Clemens left New Orleans on the *Colonel Crossman* sometime between March 4 and 15 as a new cub. Arriving at St. Louis on May 9, he borrowed the down payment of $100 from his brother-in-law. Ultimately, Twain probably did not pay Bixby more than $350, because the senior pilot placed him in the care of other pilots several times during his two-year training period, while he worked on the Missouri River for slightly higher wages than on the Mississippi.[9]

In St. Louis, Sam and Horace shifted over to the *Crescent City,* which left St. Louis on April 29 and arrived in New Orleans five days later.

While there, Sam wrote a letter to Annie Taylor, an acquaintance from Keokuk. Nothing is known of the degree of intimacy he enjoyed with this young woman, who was now attending Iowa Wesleyan College in nearby Mount Pleasant, but the two must have enjoyed a certain level of intellectual exchange.[10] No doubt the twenty-one-year-old Clemens was lonely for something other than the company of the prostitutes who frequented the ballrooms of steamboats and the streets of New Orleans.

He scolded Annie lightly for not writing him in Cincinnati, saying that her one letter to him since leaving Keokuk had "rather 'set me up.'" He told her enthusiastically about the French Market, comparing it with the one in Keokuk. "The place," he told her, "was crowded (as most places in New Orleans are) with men, women and children of every age, color and nation. . . . Italians, French, Dutch, Irish, Spaniards, Indians, Chinese, Americans, English, and the Lord knows how many more different kinds of people, selling all kinds of articles." He had also visited one of the cemeteries, where the dead were buried above ground. As he had back in Philadelphia while writing to Orion's Muscatine *Journal,* he poked fun at the sentimental verse he now found in the inscriptions on the tombstones. One was in French, a language he had been studying on his own off and on for the past two years. "The inscription . . ." Sam wrote, "said the occupant was a girl of 17, and finished by a wish from the mother that the stranger would drop a tear there. . . . They say that the flowers upon many of these tombs are replaced every day by fresh ones. These were fresh, and the poor girl had been dead *five years.*" Such sentimentality would become the subject of humor in *Huckleberry Finn* with Emmeline Grangerford's obituary verse, but by the time of "The Mysterious Stranger" manuscripts, it would turn to pathos. In that later story, when young Satan, or "No. 44," runs the world backwards, the narrator encounters a young mother who has lost her child and subsequently "cried her life away." Even though this tragedy occurred five thousand years ago, it still moves him to pity because "such things never grow old, but remain always new."[11]

As another Mississippi Valley writer, Tennessee Williams, would say, life—or death in this case—depended on "the kindness of strangers." The narrator of "The Mysterious Stranger" variations is never a stranger to tragedy, and neither was Mark Twain. Yet in his world, there were other kinds of strangers—all from the river—who furnished prototypes for every kind of personality he would meet. "When I find a well-drawn character in fiction or biography," he tells us in chapter 18 of *Life on the Mississippi,* "I generally take a warm personal interest in him, for the reason that I have known him before—met him on the river." Clemens may not have been the best pilot, but he knew the river intimately, not only its geography but also its innumerable types. After Bixby took his cub to the *Rufus J. Lackland* in July, he left Clemens there in order to pilot temporarily on the Missouri River. In August and September of 1857 Clemens studied his profession on the *John J. Roe* under pilots Zeb Leavenworth and Sobiesky "Beck" Jolly. The majority of the steamboats carried passengers housed in large cabins and staterooms. The *Roe,* however, carried mainly freight and as a result was less formal and had a less hierarchical crew. As Allan Bates has remarked, this was the steamboat that Twain remembered most fondly. In 1906 he recalled the intimacy of the boat's crew with relatively few passengers to care for—and he thought the boat itself more resembled a farm than a steamboat, where all mixed freely with the captain and participated in "moonlight dancing and daylight frolics." The *Roe* was also one of the slowest boats on the river: "Up-stream she couldn't even beat an island; down-stream she was never able to overtake the current."[12]

After a brief turn again under Bixby on the *William M. Morrison* in October, Clemens was assigned to the *Pennsylvania* under pilot William Brown. This boat was much more passenger-oriented and formal in its relationships. In this environment, a young apprentice was expected not to mingle with the passengers or his superiors in the ship's crew. This was especially true in the case of Brown, whom Twain described in chapter 18 of *Life on the Mississippi* as a "horse-faced, ignorant, stingy, malicious, snarling, fault-hunting, mote-magnifying tyrant." This relationship unfortunately involved one of the three or four great tragedies in Mark Twain's life and will be discussed in the following chapter. Twain served twice under Brown on the *Pennsylvania*—in November and part of December 1857 and from the following February until June 1858.

That summer, following a month off the river, he teamed up with one and then another of the Bowen brothers, all childhood friends, on the *Alfred T. Lacy* and the *John H. Dickey.* In October he followed pilot Sam

Bowen on the *White Cloud* for a week, and then was back again under Bixby on the *New Falls City* until almost Christmas. Clemens finished up his pilot training under Bixby on the *Aleck Scott* in the winter and spring. He earned his pilot's license in St. Louis on April 9, 1859, and began steering for other pilots at a princely salary of approximately $250 a month, supposedly more than the vice president of the United States earned.[13] He enjoyed these wages off and on for two years.

Once out from under the tyrannous eye of Bixby or the other master pilots he had trained under, Twain found time to contribute at least one satirical letter to the New Orleans *Crescent*. Dated from Vicksburg on May 8, 1859, it was probably written a few days later in New Orleans, where it was hand delivered to the editor of the *Crescent*'s "River Intelligence" column, shortly before publication on May 17. It burlesqued the river letters of Captain Isaiah Sellers, from whom he later claimed, in chapter 50 of *Life on the Mississippi,* to have stolen his pen name "Mark Twain." There is, however, some question as to just how many river letters Sellers actually wrote. One of the oldest and most experienced pilots on the river, he annoyed younger pilots with reminiscences that belittled any newly made records by implying that they were somehow inferior to feats of earlier days. Under "River Intelligence" published in the New Orleans *Daily Crescent* of May 17, Clemens burlesqued the old pilot by redubbing him the oldest *cub* pilot on the river and by making fun of a piece from Sellers that had appeared in the *True Delta* of March 22.

There also remains considerable doubt that Sellers ever used the pseudonym "Mark Twain" or that Clemens stole it from him in 1863, though he repeated this claim at least once more, in an interview in the Milwaukee *Evening Wisconsin* of January 29, 1885. Twain signed his lampoon "Sergeant Fathom," and Ernest Leisy was probably correct long ago in guessing that Clemens's "choice of the name 'Fathom' gave rise in his mind to the term used for the water sounding, Mark Twain, and that only in this remote, indirect way was he indebted to the redoubtable Isaiah Sellers." The idea of Sellers as the oldest "cub" pilot may have also stemmed from or reinforced Sam's own sense of professional immaturity even as a licensed pilot.[14]

He was on the *Alfred T. Lacey* with Bart Bowen when he wrote this letter. He shifted to the *J.C. Swon* on June 25, 1859, and a month or so later he was back with Bart (now as captain) on the *Edward J. Gay,* where he remained until October 1859. He worked on the *A.B. Chambers* from then until February 1860. He appears to have sought out the company of friends who were more accomplished pilots or captains, either Bixby or one of the three Bowen brothers from Hannibal. The next month (March 1860) he was a pilot on the *City of Memphis,* possibly the most glamorous job he enjoyed during his four years on the river. The St. Louis *Evening News* of April 24, 1857, described the boat as "the largest and finest steamer ever at the St. Louis wharf." Unlike some of the tramp boats he had worked on, service on the *City of Memphis,* as he told Orion, would give him a reputation on the river that would ensure continuous and profitable employment.[15] For really the first time, he was on his own as a pilot of a major steamboat.

This assignment lasted only for three months, however, or until the beginning of July. We don't know the circumstances of his departure, but the next month the best he could do was the *Arago,* a tramp steamer hardly a third the size of the *City of Memphis.* The *Arago* sank on September 9, but Clemens had already left the ship. Ten days later he boarded the last boat on which he would ever serve. It was the *Alonzo Child,* and he was steaming again with old friends—not only his mentor Bixby but Will Bowen, who with Sam Brown were copilots of the boat. The future of the *Alonzo Child,* however, was as threatened as Clemens's piloting career by the coming war. Built primarily for the Missouri River trade, the boat was destroyed by Confederate forces in 1863 to prevent its capture by the Union army. Its engines were refitted for the Confederate ironclad *Tennessee.* When Louisiana seceded from the Union in January 1861, Sam Clemens, after having his prospects first boosted by a position on the magnificent *City of Memphis* and then dampened by his demotion to the *Arago,* faced not only the end of his piloting career but also one of the most serious dilemmas of his lifetime and career as a writer. His initial softness on the matter of slavery and his ultimate avoidance of the Civil War would have an abiding influence upon his literary achievement.

7 Death on the Mississippi

"HENRY DIED THIS MORNING," said the telegram, "leave tomorrow with THE CORPSE." So wrote a tearful Sam Clemens to his sister Pamela and her husband, Will Moffett, in St. Louis on June 21, 1858. Henry, very likely the model for Sid in *Tom Sawyer* and possibly a lingering image in Twain's 1870 *Galaxy* sketch entitled "The Story of the Good Little Boy Who Did Not Prosper," was fatally injured in the explosion of the *Pennsylvania* on June 13.[1] Three days before sending the telegram, Sam had written Mollie Clemens, Orion's wife, predicting his younger brother's imminent death: "Long before this reaches you, my poor Henry,—my pride, my glory, my *all*, will have finished his blameless career, and the light of my life will have gone out in utter darkness. O, God! this is hard to bear."[2] Henry's violent death on the Mississippi is conceivably the reason Twain waited until the 1870s to use the matters of Hannibal and the River in his work. Indeed, the tragedy actively haunted him as late as 1872, when he visited a spiritual medium in New York City to inquire about his lost brother. In chapter 48 of *Life on the Mississippi*, he pretended that he had seen the spiritualist about a dead uncle, but the manuscript for this notebook entry reveals that the object of his visit was Henry.[3]

Mark Twain told the story of the fight with William Brown and the explosion of the *Pennsylvania* in chapters 18 to 20 of *Life on the Mississippi*. During Sam's second hitch as a cub under Brown on the fated steamboat, Henry Clemens came aboard at St. Louis as third or "mud" clerk on February 17. For bed and board, he ran errands and performed odd jobs.

When Brown threatened him with a ten-pound piece of coal on June 3 as the steamboat neared Vicksburg on the way south, Sam allegedly hit the pilot over the head with a heavy stool and continued pummeling him while the steamboat went unmanned. As a result, Sam was barred from returning from New Orleans to St. Louis on the *Pennsylvania* when it departed on June 9, and Henry made the trip on the boat without him. Henry was completing his sixth round-trip between St. Louis and New Orleans when the explosion occurred at the foot of Bordeaux's Chute, about sixty miles south of Memphis. (A chute is a passage between a river island and the main shore that is preferable to the open river because its current is weaker and the distance is shorter.) Sam Clemens was following the *Pennsylvania* by two days on the *Alfred T. Lacey,* which was itself destroyed by fire two years later. This similarity of fates gives us some idea of the danger on the river and adds a deeper hue to the significance of Huck's telling Aunt Sally that he was delayed because his steamboat had blown a cylinder head.

Mark Twain blamed himself for this death, as he would blame himself for other deaths in his family. If he had not hit Brown with a stool in the pilot house on June 3, his brother would not have been without him on the *Pennsylvania* when the explosion occurred. But, of course, Henry would still have been on the boat when it blew up, just with his older brother, who might have somehow saved him, assuming he could have saved himself. The boat's entire superstructure, from the side wheels forward, was destroyed by an explosion that sent most of its one-hundred-plus fatalities into the air, after which they landed on the boilers. The explosion was probably caused by damage to the boat sustained when the *Pennsylvania* ran aground during a race with the *Duke* on June 9. It was later speculated during a formal investigation of the tragedy that the grounding might have led to a separation of the parts of the steamer that supported the five boilers (not eight, as Twain reports in *Life on the Mississippi*). The accident became even more deadly about a half hour after the explosion, when the boat's cargo, which included barrels of turpentine, caught fire.

Hot steam alone was enough to kill anybody. Henry, after evidently inhaling some of it, allegedly dived into the river to make his escape to safety. He "believed he was not hurt (what an unaccountable error!)," Twain wrote in chapter 20 of *Life,* "and therefore [swam] back to the boat [to] help save the wounded." In fact, Henry may have been so seriously injured that he never even left the scene of the explosion on his own or tried to save anybody. In his detailed study of the tragedy, Edgar Marquess Branch cites a statement Clemens later made in June or July 1859 in an unidentified newspaper (and recorded in one of Twain's scrapbooks at the MTP) which suggests that in 1883 Twain was writing more river fiction. The clipping indicates that the location where Henry was sleeping (the explosion took place on a Sunday morning) was directly over the boilers. Henry was evidently thrown skyward, then landed on the exploded boilers with a piece of the superstructure also falling on him. Not yet dead, he was not only burned by the steam but suffered a concussion from the falling debris that rendered him senseless.

The notion that Henry was heroic in his last moments probably originated in Twain's imagination from a discussion about steamboat disasters the two brothers had had on the wharf in New Orleans the night before the departure of the *Pennsylvania.* "We doubted if persons not clothed with authority were of much use in cases of disaster and attendant panic," Twain wrote in chapter 20 of *Life.* "Still, they might be of *some* use; so we decided that if a disaster ever fell within our experience we would at least stick to the boat, and give such minor service as chance might throw in the way. Henry remembered this, afterward, when the disaster came, and acted accordingly." In reality, Henry was probably among the wounded and dying removed in boats before the wreck burst into flames.

The rescue vessels consisted of the steamboat's yawl (or lifeboat) and a wood flat brought out to the scene by George Harrison along with his father and two others. The yawl was of relatively little help, but the wood flat accommodated some two hundred persons (out of nearly four hundred on board the steamboat that morning), many of them finding only standing room. Among this suffering human mass was Henry Clemens, who—Twain later wrote in the scrapbook material—"lay exposed (with a hundred others) to the wind and the scorching rays of a Southern sun, for eight hours."[4] As the flaming steamboat drifted downriver away from the large flatboat, Harrison was unable for a long time to bring the flatboat to land because of heavy flooding of the shore area on both sides of the river. The weight of the flat's load also made it unmanageable, but it was finally rendered stationary. The injured baked in the sun until midmorning, when a skiff from the Arkansas shore arrived bearing linseed oil and liniment, which was applied to the victims' burns with cotton taken from quilts.

In early afternoon, they were also assisted by the *Imperial,* which was headed downriver. For the next two hours this boat lay at Austin, Mississippi, waiting for a northern-bound boat to take the wounded to Memphis. When the *Kate Frisbee* arrived to take the injured and dying there, the pilot, William Brown, was not among them. Blown into the river, he was found by a coal boat pilot who had been returning home on the *Pennsylvania.* Brown's last words were "My poor wife and children." Twain reported in chapter 20 of *Life* that his nemesis was "never seen or heard of after the explosion." But Brown and Bixby would live forever as the Bad Boy and Good Boy of Mississippi piloting in the works of Mark Twain.

Sam arrived in Memphis two days after Henry. Henry got to Memphis at three in the morning of June 14. He was among thirty-two victims taken to the Memphis Exchange, where mattresses were spread out and the patients attended to by doctors and nurses. In the scrapbook clipping, Sam wrote that Henry "lingered in fearful agony seven days and a half, during which time he had full possession of his senses, only at long intervals, and then but for a few moments at a time. His brain was injured by the concussion, and from that moment his great intellect was a ruin. We were not sorry his wounds proved fatal, for if he had lived he would have been but the wreck of his former self." Sam wasn't doing so well himself. His niece Annie Moffett remembered that he had to be accompanied back to St. Louis (he was eventually coming home to Hannibal with the body). He "was so overcome with grief," she remembered, "that they were afraid he would go insane." She added that her uncle was "shadowed for years" by the loss.[5]

This tragedy, only the first in a series of calamities to rain down upon this otherwise singularly successful American life, had a long-lasting impact on Sam Clemens and Mark Twain. Not only did Twain wait to use his river background in his fiction, but Clemens never returned to the river as a pilot after 1861. He often said that he had wanted to return and that piloting for him would have been the most satisfying career in the world, but he no more wanted to return to the river as a pilot than he wanted to return to Hannibal to live—as an adult. The Hannibal he remembered was gone forever because it was the Hannibal of his boyhood. As he later told Will Bowen's widow (see chapter 2), he would have liked to relive his youth and then get drowned with his comrades.

He probably could have returned to the river as a pilot after the war (since Bixby continued in the profession, curtailed though it was by the ascent of the railroad). Few would have known that he had served briefly in a Missouri state militia unit that could—had it survived—have become part of the Confederate army. When the war ended in the spring of 1865, his future as a reporter and certainly as a writer was not altogether bright. Although he had been lauded in the San Francisco *Golden Era* as the "Washoe Giant" as early as 1863 (while still in Virginia City, Nevada), he did not publish the Jumping Frog story until November 1865 and didn't become fully aware of his newly won fame until he had traveled to New York in January 1867.[6] Living at Angel's Camp and then in San Francisco on the edge of poverty in 1864 and 1865, he might then—with the war coming to a close—have returned to the river. But he didn't.

8 Fetching Grant

We come now to the question of Sam Clemens's military activities during the Civil War and specifically whether he was in fact a deserter from the Confederate army. In spite of the numerous biographies and extensive studies of this writer, one of the most remarkable areas of neglect is exactly what he did in the Civil War and why. All we have, it seems, is "The Private History of a Campaign That Failed," along with a few other primary sources that contain sometimes conflicting information.[1] They suggest only that Clemens served briefly in a state militia informally called the Marion Rangers (so named for Hannibal's main county) and that the unit disbanded after two or three weeks in June 1861 because of a lack of leadership and the soldiers' wavering commitment to a wartime experience. As the war raged between North and South, Sam Clemens lived safely outside the war zone, in the territory of Nevada and the state of California, which was as isolated as any territory before the completion of the transcontinental railroad. His letters back home during this period suggest that he tried to forget the war, seldom mentioning it in his extant correspondence.[2]

While Walt Whitman, for example, fretted about his soldier-brother after the Battle of Antietam in 1862, Sam Clemens—perhaps having heeded the stories in the St. Louis newspapers about mining discoveries in Nevada—was prospecting for silver in Esmeralda County. By the time of the Battle of Gettysburg, almost a year later, when Whitman in his role as "wound dresser" in Washington was tending to the flood of casualties coming in from the Pennsylvania farmlands, Twain was soon to be dazzled by the serene beauty of Lake Tahoe, then called Bigler. At least six of Twain's letters are missing from the time of Gettysburg, between June 4 and July 18, 1863, but in the letter of July 18 the subject is not the Union victory in Pennsylvania or even Grant's at Vicksburg the same week, but his own behavior in San Francisco, where he promises his mother that he is drinking nothing "stronger than claret or lager beer."[3] Otherwise, the subject is his hope for another silver mine claim, this one outside Virginia City.

Missouri was a slave state, and if its governor had had his way at the outset of the war, it would have seceded and fought for the South; yet this border state was quickly neutralized, and Twain in his "Private History" essay claims that he was in the final analysis "strong for the Union," or at least not totally invested "in the cause of the Southern Confederacy." In other words, he was possibly on the "right" side during most of the war, not simply after it, when the winners and losers were known. This is a credible assertion given his brother Orion's early allegiance to the Republican Party and Lincoln. A recent study has made a probable case for Orion's influence over his younger brother at least through the 1860s and perhaps until the publication of *Roughing It*—for which Orion provided valuable recollections of the journey from Hannibal to Carson City in 1861. Yet one has to wonder exactly where young Sam Clemens stood on the issues in 1860, though we surely know of his later position on the awful institution of slavery from "A True Story" (1874) and the ironic denunciation of it in *Adventures of Huckleberry Finn*. Unlike Orion, Sam did not vote for Lincoln in 1860 but supported instead the pro-slavery ticket of John Bell and Edward Everett, or the Constitutional Party, which was nevertheless dedicated to keeping the Union intact.[4]

It is entirely possible that his two-week enlistment was based solely on personal opposition to the Yankee invasion of his state rather than on the States' Rights issue of the legality of slavery. Along with pilots Absalom Grimes and Sam Bowen, he was taken by federal officers to St. Louis in May 1861 and confronted by a Union colonel. The three Mississippi pilots were about to be inducted into Union service on the Missouri River. But when the officer was distracted by a visit of prominent ladies, they slipped away and returned to Hannibal to help form the

Marion Rangers. Clemens states in the "Campaign That Failed" that he and his military comrades were sworn "on the Bible to be faithful to the State of Missouri and drive all invaders from her soil, no matter whence they might come or under what flag they might march." Another recent study contends that Clemens did not swear allegiance to the Confederate government, but Twain does state in his military memoir that it was quite clear that they "had been invested . . . in the cause of the Southern Confederacy."[5]

Almost a quarter century later Twain became the publisher of Grant's memoirs, a business deal that made both author and publisher a great deal of money. This former military deserter—if that is indeed an accurate description of Samuel Clemens in 1861—was even a featured speaker at the gathering of Union officers in honor of Grant's return from his world tour in 1879, a six-hour orgy of speeches and whiskey that went long into the night. His reports to friends and family of that evening in Chicago are simply ecstatic. There is no evidence of any tinge of guilt for not having served in the war and avoiding most of it, nor any embarrassment whatever about occupying a public stage with these famous military titans of the Union.[6]

Six years later he could even make light of his conduct in the war in "The Private History of a Campaign That Failed." It is as if the mantle of humorist somehow relieved him of the responsibility he had accepted as a Marion Ranger while also bestowing upon him the privilege of sitting shoulder to shoulder with such military idols as Sherman, Sheridan, and Pope, along with the iron man Grant. Twain's anti-heroic account of his brief military service appeared in *Century* magazine's "Battles and Leaders" series in December 1885, a publication that otherwise celebrated military courage and leadership and that to this day is considered one of the outstanding sources for Civil War historians. (Twain's contribution was omitted from the subsequently published four-volume edition of the series.) The *Century* editors enlisted not only accounts from the victors such as Grant and McClellan but from Confederate generals such as Beauregard and Longstreet.[7] This was the context for Twain's essential confession of his confusion and fear in the face of the enemy, an admission relieved only in the fictional killing of a mysterious stranger—not the first of such ironic intruders in the writings of Mark Twain. Here he merely embellished an event in which nervous, trigger-happy Marion Rangers open fire in the blackness of night on tall grass or mullein stalks blowing in the wind. There is no such traumatic killing in the Putnam Phalanx Dinner Speech, an earlier version of the "Private Campaign" given in Hartford in 1877.[8] There he depicted himself and his compatriots as buffoons in constant retreat from the enemy and focused mainly on the unmilitary behavior of a character called Ben Tupper.

Perhaps in 1885 Twain felt compelled to publish a more dignified version of the speech, following the death of Grant on July 23 and the deathbed publication of his *Personal Memoirs.* Now Twain's military desertion is presented as primarily a reaction to the killing of strangers, war or no war. Justin Kaplan suggests that Twain was intoxicated with Grant's military courage and saw their friendship as a surrogate for his own lack of valor. (In fact, much of Clemens's experience as a soldier was too embarrassing to reflect upon accurately: throughout his unit's skirmishing with a phantom enemy, he suffered from a boil on his backside, was chased by a woman whose husband was fighting for the Union, fell out of a barn onto rocks ten feet below while sleeping and sprained his ankle, and was accidentally set afire by a blaze in the barn.)[9]

For someone who didn't want to be known solely as a humorist throughout most of his career, humor became his suit of armor—not only in the "Campaign That Failed" but also that night in Chicago. Grant, he told both his wife and brother, had sat "like a graven image" through fourteen speeches that evening, "but I fetched him!"[10] The speech was "The Babies," and like the one on women that he had given to a Washington press club years before and was asked to give on this occasion, it toyed with the eminence of its subject without belittling it.

Rather astonishingly in light of the great reverence then given Civil War veterans, "The Private History of a Campaign That Failed" purports to speak for the thousands of soldiers who "got just a taste" of the war and "stepped out again permanently." For the future author of *Personal Recollections of Joan of Arc* (1896), the theme of this essay—at least where it introduces the accidental shooting of a stranger—reads more like his

"The War Prayer" (1905), in which war is seen as a paradox about right and wrong. Joan, "the Maid of Orleans," of course, claims that she never killed anyone while leading the French through a series of bloody victories over the English. In the "Campaign That Failed," Twain is likewise confronted with the paradox of war, or legal homicide.

In his 1885 essay, Twain makes fun of the general confusion over slavery, especially in the state of Missouri. But it was not funny in 1861. This border state faced a double bind. Not only was it divided to some extent on the question of slavery, but it was also literally divided up—physically scattered—by the war. Once Missouri was neutralized by Federal troops early in the war, many of the state's battalions followed their chosen leaders south. Indeed, in one of the few references Twain made to the war while living in Nevada, he alludes in 1862 to Northern troops chasing Missouri irregulars all the way to Arkansas before defeating them. He also expresses some regret that he was not among the defenders of his state.[11] No doubt he was forgetting that when he *was* in the war, he and his ragged band of Marion Rangers had made a virtue of retreating while under the impression that they were being chased by Federal troops. In drenching rain and lightning, the experience had taken "all the romance out of the campaign and turned our dreams of glory into a repulsive nightmare."

"In time," Twain claimed, as he had not that night in Chicago, "I came to know that [the] Union colonel whose coming frightened me out of the war and crippled the Southern cause . . . [was] Grant." Actually, this connection was also an exaggeration, for Twain had already left for Nevada with Orion by the time Grant's troops reached Florida, Missouri. Yet Twain had tentatively entitled his *Century* article "My Campaign against Grant" and insisted in this war story, or tall-tale version of the truth, that he had come "within a few hours of seeing him when he was an unknown as I was myself; at a time when anybody could have said, 'Grant?—Ulysses S Grant? I do not remember hearing the name before.'" The man who, as he said of himself in the essay, was better fitted for "a child's nurse" than a soldier falsely claimed to have crossed the path of Lincoln's fiercest general.[12]

Mark Twain's response to the Civil War and his actual role in it would come to reflect his life as a literary person and a humorist. Just as Huck and Jim inadvertently go south in search of freedom, Twain ultimately went north—both literally and psychologically—in search of a clear conscience. He first went west, of course, and it was in Nevada and California that he stumbled upon his great talent as a writer. This success gave him the humorist's cover under which to return to "the States" as "Wild Humorist of the Pacific Slope" instead of Confederate Deserter. Following his tour of the Sandwich Islands and his beginning as a lecturer in San Francisco, he went east to become the kind of funny man the nation sorely needed after a long war and a presidential assassination. It was time to laugh again, and so he began his fame as both a lecturer and a humorous travel writer, most significantly in *The Innocents Abroad.* Interestingly, one of the most prominent passengers expected on the *Quaker City* cruise that was the basis for his first travel book was to be none other than General William Tecumseh Sherman (who ultimately did not sail with the ship). Twain's timing couldn't have been better—from failed soldier to America's wittiest writer in a mere six or seven years, famous initially for a jumping frog. Never mind the fact that he also became one of the country's most gifted writers, evidenced almost immediately in those beautiful passages in *The Innocents Abroad.* That fame as a serious author was always destined to be posthumous, because in the long shadow of the Civil War he required the cover of the clown. It was this necessity, possibly more than anything else, that kept him trapped in the anti-hero's costume during his lifetime. As Clara Clemens wrote in her memoir of her father, ironically invoking battle imagery: "He had fought his way on the battlefield with the fire of a soldier, but his weapons had been that wit and humor which is born of profound human understanding."[13] In other words, his literary handicap became the agency of his brilliance as one of America's greatest writers, humor notwithstanding.

As noted, Twain conceded in the "Campaign That Failed" that he was not cut out to be a military combatant. Even Whitman in one of his lighter-headed moments claimed he was prepared for actual combat.[14] Yet he was too old at forty-three, whereas Twain was only twenty-six, though he claimed to be two years younger in the essay whose *Century* illustrations by E. W. Kemble tended to portray his military experience as a Tom Sawyer episode. Many years ago the literary historian Fred Lewis Pattee pointedly asked, "What of Mark Twain during this Gethsemane [Civil War] of his nation, when hundreds of thousands of his generation were dead upon the battlefields of the South that had been his home?" The neo-Confederate poet Edgar Lee Masters charged Twain with the equivalent of draft evasion: "There is no vestige of conviction in anything that he did in facing the war."[15]

Yet in spite of Whitman's brief boast, the poet never volunteered for military duty, while Twain did enlist. It is also important to note that Twain knew about his brother's appointment as secretary of the territory of Nevada long before he joined the Marion Rangers in a war he thought, like everybody else, would last no longer than three months. News of the Nevada appointment reached Orion in St. Louis by March 27, 1861, when Twain was still in the city, taking time out to earn the apprentice and master degrees in the Masons. By now he was out of work as a Mississippi River pilot because of the war. In other words, it is clearly possible that after almost being drafted into Union forces, Twain initially *chose* combat in Missouri over silver mining in Nevada, at least to defend his home state from invaders if not fight for the losing cause of the South. According to Albert Bigelow Paine, Orion agreed to overlook his brother's defection to the South and make him his "secretary" in Nevada if Sam paid for their overland journey.[16] But this information certainly does not rule out earlier discussions between the two brothers on the subject of Nevada. Whatever the case, Mark Twain, it appears, paid a high price for his war record, and publishing Grant's *Memoirs* therefore became a holy cause to him. Fortunately for American literature, Sam Clemens did not pay the ultimate price in war by meeting then-colonel Grant on the field of battle. Instead, he "fetched" the former general and U.S. president on the speaker's platform fourteen years after the war. In doing so, he made amends—in his own mind, at least—for his ineptitude as a soldier.

9 Lighting Out

The day Sam and Orion departed from "the States" at St. Joseph, Missouri, was exhilarating. It was July 26, 1861, "a superb summer morning, and all the landscape was brilliant with sunshine." The two brothers felt, as Twain recorded in chapter 2 of *Roughing It,* a "sense of emancipation from all sorts of cares and responsibilities." The relief that Sam felt in getting away from the war was *his* main source of exhilaration. Orion, on the other hand, was now traveling for the Union, to a job as secretary of Nevada Territory, which would pay him a salary of eighteen hundred dollars a year. For all Sam knew, he was a wanted man after lighting out from that colonel's office in St. Louis and then serving in a military unit that was, ostensibly, dedicated to the Confederacy. Sam Bowen would be arrested that fall as a Southern sympathizer. At first, Clemens's escape hadn't run very smoothly. Before boarding the Overland Stage at St. Joseph for Carson City, he and Orion had to travel for six days on the Missouri River. Its shallow bottom and frequent shoals made it necessary to run the boat deliberately over the many snags and reefs and sandbars. "In fact," Twain recalled in the first chapter of *Roughing It,* "the boat might almost as well have gone to St. Joe by land, for she was walking most of the time, anyhow." Otherwise, that first leg of their trip west was so uneventful that he could recall little else about it.

After two years of prosperity as a pilot on a bigger river, Sam Clemens's prospects for the future didn't appear rosy. Like Ulysses S Grant at the beginning of the war, it may have seemed to Samuel Langhorne Clemens that his success in life was already largely finished.

But the war was already well on its way to elevating Grant (whose troops would soon sweep through the Hannibal area), whereas it had dashed Clemens's livelihood on the river and was now dispatching him out west to a job that had no established salary. It was in a way like returning to his brother's employ in Hannibal as an unpaid assistant editor. To make matters worse, because of Orion's general state of poverty, Sam was paying the four-hundred-dollar stagecoach fare for both of them.

In fact, memory of the entire trip to Nevada was so difficult to retrieve nine years later when he was writing *Roughing It* that he had to ask Orion for his recollection of the particulars of the journey. "Do you remember any of the scenes, names, incidents or adventures of the coach trip?" he inquired rather desperately as he began his "600-page book." "I remember next to *nothing* about the matter."[1] He didn't remember because he was probably preoccupied during the whole of the trip with what he would do once he got to Carson City. He had heard, of course, of the silver-mining fame of the Comstock Lode. Perhaps this would get him going again. Relying on Orion's specific record of the trip for the "facts," the first twenty chapters of *Roughing It* are a quasi-fictional work by an accomplished artist whose second book, *The Innocents Abroad,* had become a surprising success. This professional travel writer knew how to fill in the interstices of an itinerary, not with the philosophical digressions of a Henry David Thoreau in *A Week on the Concord and Merrimack Rivers* (1849), but with the miscellany of travel books. Yet the western philosophy of Mark Twain comes through as well as his humor.

On day two of their journey out of St. Joseph, July 27, they entered the Nebraska territory and saw their first jackrabbit. On the third day they reached Fort Kearney on the Platte River. They were still in the age of the short-lived pony express mail carrier, prior to the telegraph and railroad connections that made this vast land more familiar to Americans. There were many novel sights in those days—prairie dogs, coyotes, and Indians. Twain saw resemblances in the last two, noting that the coyote "will eat anything in the world that his first cousins, the desert-frequenting tribes of Indians will."[2] These Native Americans were still dangerous to white settlers and travelers, and it would take Twain several decades to get over his bias against the "red man." Sam and Orion's stagecoach averaged about 125 miles a day, traveling just over five miles per hour seven days a week. Journeying out west then was like going abroad today in the sense that one had to travel lightly. In St. Joseph they had been forced to send back home most of their luggage. A pony express letter traveled twice as fast, but it cost two dollars an ounce to mail, like the featherlike envelopes sent to and from the United States to Europe before the advent of e-mail.

Noah Brooks, the editor of the San Francisco *Alta* when Twain went abroad for that newspaper on the *Quaker City* in 1867, had made a similar journey across the Great Plains that he later described in an article about Twain. "Imagine," he wrote at the end of the century, "a long caravan of emigrants stretched over the vast and comparatively unknown region lying between Missouri and the Pacific Ocean, numbering many thousands, but broken into innumerable bands and companies . . . while passing through the haunts of hostile and predatory Indians, but often passing and repassing one another when some travel-worn party would be camped by the trail for rest and recuperation. . . . Here and there, at exceedingly rare intervals, we found the deserted cabin of some vanished explorer or trapper, in which were posted the rude bulletins of those who had preceded us."[3] This historical moment paralleled the impressions of Orion and Sam as they pushed into the wilder regions of the North American continent.

They passed Fort Laramie on the night of July 31 and found themselves the next morning in the Black Hills of the Dakota territory. Here they were definitely in hostile Indian country. It is at this point in the narrative of *Roughing It* that Twain introduced the saga of the notorious Jack Slade, the murderer who met the future Mark Twain. Or at least this is what Twain claimed in his book. It was on the ninth day of their journey. Sam was having breakfast at the Rocky Ridge station when he froze as he heard someone address a stranger as Slade. "Here, right by my side," he wrote in *Roughing It,* "was the actual ogre who, in fights and brawls and various ways, *had taken the lives of twenty-six human beings,* or all men lied about him!" The coffee supply ran down to one cup. Slade, who suffered intervals of civility, politely offered it to Sam, who just as politely declined because he was afraid Slade "had not killed anybody that morning."[4]

Just beyond South Pass City, they encountered "banks of snow in dead summer time." They were now high in the Rocky Mountains where the low clouds gave them "a sense of a hidden great deep of mountains and plains." He described the mountains as "Sultans" turbaned in clouds. On the afternoon of August 4 they reached Fort Bridger, where they were told that its troops "had fired upon three hundred or four hundred Indians, whom they supposed gathered together for no good purpose." By the next day, they stopped for two days at the Mountain Dell station at Salt Lake City. The first night, Bemis, their fellow passenger, got so drunk on "valley tan," a Mormon whiskey, that some of his words "had more hiccups than syllables" in them.[5]

Since Orion was now secretary of the neighboring territory of Nevada, they met the acting governor, who introduced them, as Twain noted, to the other "Gentiles." He wasn't a Mormon, and neither was his successor in September, Frank Fuller, who would become a lifelong friend of Sam's. The acting governor and the governor were both secessionists who had refused to serve in Lincoln's administration. One had already left for the South, and the other would shortly, when Fuller arrived the next month. In *Roughing It,* Twain misremembers that it was Fuller whom they met in Salt Lake City.[6] These officials were only the first of many secessionists Sam would encounter in the Union territories, especially Nevada. Even though Virginia City was predominantly Union in its support, Southern support abounded out there, including even Sam, who would instigate a miscegenation hoax against the U.S. Sanitary Commission in the *Territorial Enterprise* in 1864, as we shall see.

Sam and Orion did meet the famed Brigham Young. This was on August 7, 1861. Young talked state business with Orion and the acting governor, but he completely ignored the secretary to the secretary in spite of his several attempts to "draw him out." "He merely looked around at me, at distant intervals," Twain wrote in *Roughing It,* "something as I have seen a benignant old cat look around to see which kitten was meddling with her tail." This perceived snub may in some way be the catalyst for Twain's disdain of Mormons in his book, expressed not just in his inclusion of a condemnatory account of the Mountain Meadows Massacre in appendix B but also in his general joking around about their polygamous habits. About their first day in Salt Lake City, for example, Twain wrote, "We felt a curiosity to ask every child how many mothers it had, and if it could tell them apart."[7]

Most likely this appendix and another on Mormon history were intended as chapters 13 and 14 of his book. His publisher Elisha Bliss may have thought they formed a digression in the narrative or were perhaps too acerbic; they were probably reinstated as appendices when Clemens had trouble reaching the six-hundred-page minimum demanded of subscription books in an era in which readers felt that anything less did not give them their money's worth. (How times change!) Chapters 15 and 16, on the polygamy of the Mormons and their bible, struck a balance between satire and outright criticism. In the first the typical polygamist is described as "some portly old frog of an elder . . . [who] marries a girl—likes her, marries her sister—likes her, marries another sister—likes her, takes another—likes her, marries her mother—likes her, marries her father, grandfather, great grandfather, and then comes back hungry and asks for more." The chapter on the Mormon bible, however, reveals the author's Protestant objection and bias. There is nothing "vicious" in the Mormon creed as stated in their bible, only that its stories are structured like the Old Testament and its language is also "smouched" from the New Testament without giving any credit.[8]

With six hundred miles still left between them and Carson City, they crossed the Great Salt Lake Desert and the Ruby Mountains in Nevada. Two hundred and fifty miles along that stretch, they entered Rocky Canyon and came across the Goshute Indians, a tribe of five hundred "braves" whom Twain derided as bushmen "manifestly descended from the self-same gorilla, or kangaroo, or Norway rat, whichever animal-Adam the Darwinians trace them to." As already noted, he was still in the early stages of his Indian hating, exemplified as much by his direct attacks here on the Goshutes as in his mockery of the idealized image of the Indian in the works of James Fenimore Cooper. While he never got over Cooper's excesses and would much later in life satirize them, he softened on his view of American aborigines as he learned more about their treatment by the U.S. government.[9] He never went as far, however, in his humanitarian view of Indians as he did with his sympathetic portrayal of blacks and the Chinese workers he encountered in the West. In the 1890s he came to satirize Cooper's cigar store Indians as unrealistic. Earlier, in the unfinished "Huck Finn and Tom Sawyer among the Indians," written in 1885, Tom learns a cruel lesson about the difference between Cooper's "book" Indians and the real ones, who prove to be stone-age savages who kidnap—and rape, it is clearly implied—the heroine of the story and murder her parents.

On August 13 Sam's traveling party crossed its last no-man's-land before Carson City. This was Forty Mile Desert, covered with "bottomless sand" into which their wagon wheels sank as deep as a foot in places. "The desert," Twain wrote in chapter 20, "was one prodigious graveyard" of the breakdowns of previous travelers' wagons. But by the next morning they had finally reached the territorial capital of Nevada, a beehive of activity that sat at the base of the beautiful Sierra Nevada. Twain described Carson City as a "wooden" town with a population of two thousand. "The main street consisted of four or five blocks of little white frame stores," he wrote in *Roughing It*. Named for the Indian scout Kit Carson, it had begun as a stage coach stop in 1851. With the discovery of the Comstock Lode in 1859, it had lost much of its business to nearby Virginia City. Yet Carson City remained the territorial capital and thus was Mark Twain's first destination in Washoe, the nickname given to Nevada because of the native Washoe Indians.

Before he knew it, he began a third career as a silver miner, since there was no set pay in being Orion's secretary and hardly any compensation when he clerked that fall in the territorial government's first assembly. His future and Orion's fortune lay in the mines, he thought, but he was already honing his skill as a writer of wit and originality in letters home. In October 1861, he told his mother that the country was "fabulously rich in gold, silver, copper, lead, coal, iron, quicksilver, marble, granite, chalk, plaster of Paris, (gypsum,) thieves, murderers, desperadoes, . . . poets, preachers, and jackass rabbits."[10]

There was no fanfare over Orion's arrival in the city. The two brothers quietly took up residence in the front bedroom of the Ormsby House, which doubled as Orion's office during the daytime. The territorial governor was James W. Nye, an experienced politico who had been a district attorney and judge in New York City as well as the first president of that city's metropolitan police board. He saw the territorial governorship merely as a stepping stone to a Senate seat when Nevada became a state. As a result, he would be absent from the state for much of the time that Orion was in office, so that Orion often served as the acting governor.[11]

Nye, Orion, Sam, and other members of the government mission all ate at Margaret Murphy's boardinghouse. Around its table, as Effie Mona Mack observes, Sam "found his future companions in play, in work, and in adventure."[12] That adventure may have included girls of dubious status, the sort he had no doubt encountered during his steamboat days, even as he wrote letters to marriageable women. This activity, interestingly enough, was not exactly treated as confidential. Bachelorhood had privileges in the Clemens clan that were nothing to be ashamed of—at least among married adults, and as long as marriage itself was regarded as sacredly monogamous. In January 1862 he told his sister-in-law Mollie, whose sister Belle Stotts he had flirted with before her marriage, that he didn't "mind sleeping with female servants as long as I am a bachelor—by *no* means—but *after* I marry, that sort of thing will be 'played out,' you know." He closed by urging his sister-in-law not "to *hint* this depravity to the girls."[13] But bachelors needed money, and the silver mines of Nevada beckoned.

10 A Millionaire for Ten Days

Two years after "Silverado"—the silver rush to Washoe—Sam Clemens entered the still-promising field. Henry Tompkins Paige Comstock had put his name on the Lode in 1859, but as with so many turns of fate in the mining business, his "discovery" had originally been the property of someone else, in this case two unlucky brothers from Pennsylvania, Ethan Allen and Hosea Ballou Grosh, sons of a Universalist minister. Following the accidental death of Hosea, his brother set out in November 1857 to cross the Sierra. He put his cabin in the charge of Comstock, a Canadian. Ethan Grosh left in the company of another Canadian, Richard Maurice Bucke. A storm overtook them on their journey, and the two became lost in the mountains. Grosh died of frostbite, and Bucke lost most of one foot and part of another to amputation. Before he died, Grosh hid the map to his silver mines in a tree that was never found, but Comstock eventually figured out their location in what became known as Gold Hill, adjacent to Virginia City, and the rest is history.[1] Bucke returned to Canada, studied medicine, and ultimately became superintendent of an insane asylum in London, Ontario. He also became a good friend of Walt Whitman, whose biography he wrote in 1883.

By that time Mark Twain would already be more famous than the Good Gray Poet, but in 1861 the prospects for even moderate success for Sam were remote. He thought of returning home in two or three months because "I was private secretary to his majesty the Secretary and there was not yet writing enough for two of us."[2] The Nevada silver mines seemed his only chance while he still had some of his piloting savings left. Before going there, however, he set out in September with John D. Kinney, an Ohio native who had arrived in Virginia City about the same time as the Clemens brothers reached Carson City, to see the beauty of Lake Bigler, poised in a piney forest more than six thousand feet above sea level. It sat on the California border and was named for one of the state's governors, John Bigler. During the war it reverted to its Indian name of Tahoe because of Bigler's secessionist sympathies. While there Clemens and Kinney got the idea of staking out a timber claim on its surrounding banks. One could do that in those days by simply chopping down a few trees to indicate the location of a claim. Unfortunately they set fire to the woods with a campfire that ignited the pine needles around it, and—even though they may have staked out a second claim—never got rich in lumber.[3]

Opportunities to get rich quick seemed to abound in Nevada at the time. Besides his temporary "day job" earning forty dollars a week as Orion's legislative clerk during the territorial government's first assembly that fall (a salary that would cease with the close of the session in January or February), Sam purchased five hundred "feet" (or shares) of a silver mine near the town of Aurora in the Esmeralda mining district, located some 125 miles southeast of Carson City. It sat in the Sierra foothills on the still disputed border between California and Nevada (ultimately adjudged to be part of Nevada in 1863). The shares were valued at ten dollars a foot, but Clemens probably did not have to pay the full price at the time of purchase because most shares were sold on margin. The immediate expense lay in the actual mining of the claim, but more often, as he soon learned, the "real secret" was not to mine the claims at all but to merely pretend to work them and sell the ledges off for a quick profit. Here it took an entrepreneur, and Sam twice urged his uncle James Lampton (the model for Colonel Sellers in *The Gilded Age*) to come out and help them get rich. "Orion and I," he told his sister and mother in a letter of October 25, 1861, "have confidence enough in this country . . . if the war will let us alone." As he acknowledged in *Roughing It*, "By and by I was smitten with the silver fever."[4]

The talk was hot with stories of even common loafers getting rich overnight. And according to Twain in *Roughing It*, news of fresh mine fields was heard "every few days." After making a brief visit to Esmeralda in September, he focused again on the Humboldt region, which was beginning to "shriek for attention."[5] Around 175 miles northeast of Carson City, in a territory crisscrossed with toll roads, this mining district was near the town of Unionville. In December, Sam and William E. Clagett, a lawyer he had known as a student in Keokuk, set out for the Humboldt mining fields. Clagett's wife would accompany Mollie Clemens when the two women rejoined their husbands in Nevada in the fall of 1862.

In 1869, in declining an invitation to speak before the California Pioneers of New York City, he wrote: "I entered upon an affluent career in Virginia City, and . . . became the owner of about all the worthless wildcat mines there were in that part of the country." He called up the exaggeration of the tall tale in saying, "I ran tunnels till I tapped the Arctic ocean, and I sunk shafts till I broke through the roof of perdition."[6] Much of the excitement had been the result of earlier tall tales about the potential of alleged discoveries, many of which were "salted" with melted half dollars and little else. Later as a reporter for the *Enterprise,* Twain himself occasionally picked up shares by "lying about somebody's mine."[7]

Clemens described his trip to Humboldt in chapters 27–33 of *Roughing It.* While there, he wrote in chapter 30, "I met men at every turn who owned from one thousand to thirty thousand 'feet' in undeveloped silver mines, every single foot of which they believed would shortly be worth from fifty to a thousand dollars—and as often as any other way they were men who had not twenty-five dollars in the world." Sam spent seven weeks or so on his unsuccessful excursion to Humboldt, where he had no more good luck than the others he described. It required an arduous trip across the alkali wastes of Forty Mile Desert in the winter cold. His trip back to Carson City in February 1862 wasn't any easier. He and his companions endured rainstorms, flooded streams, and finally a snowstorm. Here, however, Twain struck literary gold a decade later in *Roughing It* by turning the snowstorm incident into one of his most humorous anecdotes about the hypocrisy of reformers.

The anecdote foreshadows his brilliant masterpieces of human folly and fraud in the characterizations of Pap Finn, Tom Driscoll of

Pudd'nhead Wilson, and the nineteen families in "The Man That Corrupted Hadleyburg." The narrator, along with characters named Ballou and Ollendorff, becomes snowbound and lost. After failing to build a fire, they bundle themselves up and prepare to freeze to death. "Poor Ollendorff" breaks down and cries. He swears that "whether he lived or died" he would never touch another drop of whiskey. Ballou throws away his pack of greasy playing cards and swears never to gamble again. As for the narrator, "I threw away my pipe, and in doing it felt that at last I was free of a hated vice and one that had ridden me like a tyrant all my days." (Actually, to please his wife, Twain had quit smoking—once and only once—as he began *Roughing It* in 1870.) When the three reformers wake up the following morning and find that they are only "fifteen steps" from one of the frame buildings of a stagecoach stop, "the joy in our hearts at our deliverance," Twain wrote, "was poisoned. . . . We presently began to grow pettish by degrees." Like Pap Finn, they soon tire of reform. "At last I lit the pipe," he wrote, "and no human being can feel meaner and baser than I did." Ollendorff returns to his bottle, and Ballou falls deeply into a game of solitaire. "We shook hands and agreed to say no more about 'reform' and 'examples to the rising generation.'" Twain himself soon went back to his three hundred cigars a month in order to finish his book.[8]

Twain probably deserved a good smoke for the work he was doing then, but back in 1862 he was becoming discouraged and swore he would return to Missouri by July. "Don't you know," he told his mother and sister, "that I have expended money in this country but have made none myself? Don't you know that I have never held in my hands a gold or silver bar that belonged to me?" By now it was probably only the war that kept him out there. Grant was on the move against the South. "They have taken Fort Henry, and Fort Donelson, and the half of Tennessee," he told his friend Clagett in February, "and the stars and stripes wave over the Capitol at Nashville." Back in Carson City, he attended the proceedings of the great landslide case, a hoax that snubbed a "stranger" from the East, Benjamin E. Bunker, who was the new United States attorney for Nevada.[9] In April he returned to Aurora in the Esmeralda district with John Nye, the territorial governor's entrepreneurial brother.

There the two took up various claims, digging mine shafts and tunnels, but failed to finish any of them. "We were always hunting up new claims and doing a little work on them and then waiting for a buyer—who never came," he stated in *Roughing It*. Soon he was reduced to milling, or doing the work of a common laborer. This left him little time for anything else. "It is a pity that Adam could not have gone straight out of Eden into a quartz mill," he would quip in his book, "in order to understand the full force of his doom to 'earn his bread by the sweat of his brow.'"[10] This was not the last of Twain's many Adam jokes. In chapter 53 of *The Innocents Abroad*, at "the tomb of Adam," he lamented that the old man had not lived to see his kin. In 1880 he even half seriously proposed the erection of a statue to Adam in Elmira.[11]

Esmeralda wasn't a very healthy place to be, mainly because of a running battle south of Aurora between cattlemen and the so-called Digger Indians. Although he said he remained in the milling business one week, he actually stayed there until July, juggling mining claims and going deeper into debt. "Last summer," he told Bill Clagett, who had remained in the Humboldt area and settled in Unionville, "Orion paid $50 for 15 feet in a claim here. Yesterday one of the owners came and offered me 25 feet more for $50, with 30 days time on half the amount. He said he hated to part with it, but then he wanted me to have a good 'stake.' I told him I appreciated his kindness to me, but that I was 'on the sell' myself."[12] Sam had also begun to submit his "Josh" letters (now lost) to the *Enterprise*, where they were published probably without any payment. The letters nonetheless became his financial salvation when the newspaper offered him a job as a reporter in July.

While in Esmeralda, he quarreled with John Nye, who was himself laid up with an attack of inflammatory rheumatism. In *Roughing It*, he next travels with Calvin Higbie across the California border to the area of Lake Mono in search of the mythical Whiteman cement mine. A miner named Gideon F. Whiteman had described the existence of a wonderful vein of gold supposedly as thick as a curbstone, running through cement, somewhere in the vicinity of Mono. It was rumored that every pound of the cement was worth two hundred dollars.

But their visit to the lake in fact happened after the "blind-lead episode" described in chapter 40.[13] According to the account in *Roughing It,* Clemens and Higbie discovered that the Wild West Mining Company's claim near Aurora, a rich silver mine, was (unbeknownst to the owners) connected to an equally rich ledge still in the public domain, the so-called blind lead. With a third partner, they made a claim on it that required them to begin excavation within ten days. But Clemens was called away to nurse Nye. He left Higbie a note to start the excavation on his own, but Higbie was already off again to Lake Mono still in search of the cement mine. Their crossed signals resulted in the jumping of their claim and the dedication of *Roughing It* to Higbie: "In Memory of the Curious Time When We Two Were Millionaires for Ten Days."

Later, Higbie blamed Twain for the loss of their fortune. Bitter at having endured a life of relative poverty and perhaps angry when his old friend declined to make him a sizable loan and did not encourage his literary endeavors, he testified that Twain was physically lazy. But he had to admit his delight in the humorous stories Twain told. "In that humorous drawl of his, that made him a favorite with practically everyone he met, he would spin yarns by the hour."[14] It was his genius as a storyteller, of course, that made Mark Twain a millionaire for at least ten years. But as with his prospecting for silver, he was destined to stumble continually over fool's gold, or Whiteman's mythical cement, in his pursuit of wealth beyond his writing. He was about to partially realize that talent in literature, though for now it would be confined to journalism.

11 "Mark Twain"

Mark Twain told his authorized biographer that when he gave up mining for journalism, he walked the 125 miles from Esmeralda County to Virginia City. "It was the afternoon of a hot, dusty August day," Paine dutifully wrote, "when a worn, travel-stained pilgrim drifted laggingly into the office of the Virginia City *Enterprise,* then in its new building on C Street, and, loosening a heavy roll of blankets from his shoulders, dropped wearily into a chair." Actually, it was late September, not August, because Clemens was still in Esmeralda on September 9, 1862, and his earliest known writing for the *Enterprise* did not appear until October 1. It is also doubtful that Sam made the journey entirely on foot. For one thing, it would have been dangerous in terms not only of the hostile "Digger" Indians in the Aurora area but also of highwaymen who lurked along those desert roads. There was also ample transportation between mining towns in those days, and Carson City, the territorial capital, was on the road between Aurora and Virginia City.[1] Later—with Joe Twichell, first in New England and then in Europe—Twain would become notorious for beginning such walking tours and quickly switching to train or stagecoach.

Virginia City was located on the eastern slope of Mount Davidson, and C Street ran the gamut of this mountainside town and served as its Main Street on which merchants paid thousands for fifty-foot frontages.[2] This was near ground zero for Gold Hill and the Comstock Lode, and prices ran high in the early 1860s. The *Enterprise* was the oldest newspaper in the territory, having been founded in 1858, a year before the discovery of silver in Nevada. Its material was regularly copied into other Nevada and California newspapers and occasionally by eastern and even foreign papers. When Clemens arrived on the staff, the paper's coeditor along with Rollin M. Daggett was Joseph T. Goodman, who was also part owner of the paper with Denis E. McCarthy. Sam was hired at twenty-five dollars a week as a replacement for Dan De Quille, whose real name was William Wright. De Quille later wrote a history of the Comstock Lode and, with Clemens's help, published it through the same subscription publisher that issued *Roughing It.*

Wright was taking a nine-month sabbatical to visit his family in Iowa, but before leaving, he showed Clemens the ropes, and upon his return they became roommates and close friends. As a contributor to other newspapers as well, Dan De Quille cast an important early influence upon the work of Mark Twain. His solar-armor story may have planted a very early seed for the image in *A Connecticut Yankee in King Arthur's Court* of Hank Morgan's frustrated confinement in the armor of the knights of Camelot. Dan's tale concerned an inventor of an India rubber suit equipped with a compressor to keep himself cool in the three-digit heat of Death Valley. Unable to turn off the compressor one day, he turned up dead in the desert by freezing to death. Another friend who would figure more significantly in the development of Twain's fame was Steve Gillis, a printer on the *Enterprise.* A southerner (from Mississippi) like Clemens, he was three years younger than the future author of "Jim Smiley and His Jumping Frog," which might not ever have been written without Gillis and his brothers Jim and Bill. Another close friend wrote for the newspaper's competition in Virginia City, Clement T. Rice of the *Union.* Twain dubbed him "the Unreliable" in dueling newspaper accounts the two wrote from Carson City when the territorial legislature was in session. They would become close friends and drinking companions but almost certainly not homosexual lovers, as one biography has suggested.[3]

Besides mining news, murders, Indian trouble, and saloon brawls, there was little else to report in Virginia City. Of course, the legislature was a news item when in session, and one of its biggest debates was over the growing presence of toll roads in Nevada. Often these writers, many of whom had an eye toward a national market, would write stories that turned out to be hoaxes, hoping they would be circulated around the country. This kind of newspaper literature apparently matched the Wild West mood of Virginia City, where there was heavy drinking and the back-slapping camaraderie that calls for endless jokes and guffaws. It was generally a man's town, with the requisite vulgarity. Virginia City's population of two thousand was more than 90 percent male. According to an 1860 census, around one hundred of the women were accompanying husbands.[4] Most of the rest—those with whom a single man like Sam would come in contact—were either prostitutes or saloon ladies who sold dances. In a way, this segment of the town's female society mirrored the floating palaces Clemens had experienced as a steamboat pilot.

As we shall see, Mark Twain actually started out writing rather vulgar material, but even here we can detect emerging genius. There are examples, of course, of the low state of his humor that make us wonder how he ever managed to succeed in the general marketplace. Not until the publication of *The Innocents Abroad,* almost ten years later, did he fully cleanse himself of the backroom humor of both the river and the West. By that time, he had become a writer whose humor was always appropriate for the "evening lamp" of the family circle. His obituaries would attest to that, and the literary world would have to wait another decade for Van Wyck Brooks to suggest, sometimes in exaggerated or distorted terms, the other personality, the one partly shaped by the steamboats and mining camps that always lurked below the surface in his plots and themes.[5]

Unlike Walt Whitman and Theodore Dreiser, two other major American writers whose democratic themes challenged the order of Victorian standards of morality in literature, Mark Twain ultimately entered the forum as a "safe" (if also subversive) writer, one who would eventually be embraced and championed by Howells, the "dean" and arbiter of American literature in his day.

There is no complete file of the *Territorial Enterprise,* but perhaps 20 percent of Sam's pieces survived in his brother's scrapbooks or were reprinted in newspapers whose files were not destroyed. One of the first hoaxes he wrote for the paper was entitled "Petrified Man." Widely reprinted in other papers, it first appeared in the *Enterprise* on October 4,

1862, when he had been on the job for only a couple of weeks. Usually, one of the unwritten rules of any hoax was that it had to contain enough erroneous information to alert local readers and ensure that its story didn't cause civil alarm. In the case of "Petrified Man," the geography was the main giveaway, along with the mention of a justice of the peace by the name of "Sewell or Sowell." This was Judge G. T. Sewall of Humboldt County, the target of this hoax and satire. We do not know why Clemens, as he told his brother Orion, "got it up to worry Sewall."[6] The judge had been active in mining around Aurora, and he and Sam may have disagreed over a claim.

But the true reason for the hoax was probably not so much to bother Judge Sewell, though Twain claimed to have sent him "exchanges" reprinting the squib for another year. He was trying to shine on the *Enterprise* and probably emulating Dan De Quille, who was also known for scientific tall tales. In "Petrified Man," Clemens described a recently discovered "mummy" in hilarious detail, all the way down to the fact that it was thumbing its nose. Every "limb and feature," he said, was perfect, including a petrified wooden leg. The body was found in the nearby mountains "in a sitting posture . . . the attitude was pensive, the right thumb resting against the side of the nose; the left thumb partially supported the chin, the fore-finger pressing the inner corner of the left eye and drawing it partly open; the right eye was closed, and the fingers of the right hand spread apart." We learn that Judge Sewell "at once proceeded to the spot and held an inquest on the body" of a man described earlier as "defunct" for almost a century.[7]

Clemens, after all, never forgot that officially he was simply filling in for De Quille, and no doubt thought he had to try to match him in such matters. And that meant he was hired more for satire than straight reporting. In fact, De Quille was still in Virginia City when "Petrified Man" appeared, and wouldn't leave for the Midwest until December 27. The pressure was on from the outset for this substitute reporter to measure up. No doubt Sam became an apprentice to Dan during the first two months of writing for the *Enterprise.* "Old Dan is gone," Sam was finally able to say in the newspaper one day in December; "that good old soul, we ne'er shall see him more—for some time."[8] But it would be time enough for Clemens to establish his own identity as a humorist and win the lifelong friendship of *Enterprise* owner and editor Joe Goodman.

Goodman and Clemens, especially after De Quille's departure, frequently dined together in a local French restaurant and drank at a nearby saloon.[9] Looking for material to keep alive his job on the *Enterprise,* he asked Goodman to send him to Carson City to cover the second meeting of the territorial legislature, which was being managed by his brother Orion. He went there in late November and stayed with Orion and Mollie through the middle of January. It was from Carson City on February 3, 1863, during a return visit, that he may have used for the first time in print the nom de guerre "Mark Twain." The letter in all probability was sent from Carson City on January 31. Although its content suggests to some that Twain had used the name in an earlier *Enterprise* article (now lost), it would be nice to imagine that we of posterity have caught the great man in the very act of donning his public name for the first time. Indeed, Henry Nash Smith, possibly the most insightful critic of Mark Twain, in an obvious attempt to celebrate that point, even printed in 1957 a misleading illustration of the letter: a facsimile of the actual newspaper clipping from the *Enterprise,* but reproducing only the beginning and ending of the letter, including "Yours, dreamily, Mark Twain," without the intervening text.[10]

When exactly was Mark Twain first born? The answer is probably not February 3, 1863, of course, but that is a very close estimate of the day on which the humorist Mark Twain was born. That other, deeper, much greater writer was born later, and he probably outlived the humorist in his grim readings of the human condition following the publications of *A Connecticut Yankee* and *Pudd'nhead Wilson.* The humorist was born—and not prematurely this time, as Sam Clemens had been in 1835—in the literary wilderness of Nevada Territory.

By February 1863 his salary had been raised to almost forty dollars a week. With his room, board, and laundry costing him only seventy-five a month, he had plenty of drinking and dining money.[11] He continued to purchase shares in silver mines as well. This would be the beginning of his lifelong losing streak as an investor, culminating in the Paige typesetting machine in the 1890s. Along the way, he would decline to invest in Alexander Graham Bell's telephone. But his reputation as a local reporter in the West and on the Pacific Coast was taking off. In May and June he took another working leave, accompanied by Clement Rice, to San Francisco, where he was fast becoming known as the "Wild Humorist of the Pacific Slope." The two writers ate and drank their way through the city for weeks, making important literary connections along the way. "I suppose I know at least a thousand people here," he told his mother and sister in June. "We dine out, & we lunch out, and we eat, drink and are happy—as it were. After breakfast, I don't often see the hotel again until midnight—or after."[12]

He was back in San Francisco for another visit in September, this time by himself. Now he was writing for both the San Francisco *Call* and the *Golden Era* in addition to his regular duties on the *Enterprise.* Dan De Quille returned to Virginia City that month. Evidently, his renewed presence stirred up Clemens's sense of competition, for on October 28, 1863, he published an upsetting hoax entitled "A Bloody Massacre near Carson," in which a forty-two-year-old man named Hopkins was reported to have scalped his wife and killed all of his nine children as well as himself because he had invested and lost "an immense amount in the Spring Valley Water Company of San Francisco." Sam included the usual clues to warn local readers, but the story was so despicably bloody that it shocked the *Enterprise* readership in general and threatened the newspaper's reputation for veracity, even in a market in which hoaxes were not uncommon. Clemens published a retraction the very next day, but "I Take It All Back" failed to satisfy or quiet his critics, who maintained a negative if low-key drumbeat for almost another year.

He claimed that the purpose of the hoax was "to get the fact into the San Francisco papers[, which immediately picked up the story] that the Spring Valley Water company was 'cooking' dividends by borrowing money to declare them on for its stockholders." But one has to agree with Ivan Benson that the piece is simply hard to explain. Even Effie Mona Mack's discovery that it was also a ploy to embarrass a local official named Pete Hopkins, or politicians who met regularly at Hopkins's Magnolia Saloon in Carson City, where the killer allegedly dies of self-inflicted wounds, does not lessen the horror of Sam's hoax. Although later he would also regret (for a time at least) a hoax he delivered at the seventieth-birthday dinner of John Greenleaf Whittier, here he was truly guilty of a bizarre act.[13]

He offered his resignation to Goodman, but Joe stood by him and tried—unlike a later editor friend at the Whittier speech—to persuade him that he had done little or no harm to either his reputation or that of the newspaper he worked for.[14] Mark Twain, as he was now known in the West, survived the scandal and continued to grow in reputation as the "Washoe Giant." He would soon have the firm and enthusiastic support of Artemus Ward (Charles Farrar Browne), though this influential humorist would not live long enough to savor the fame of his Nevada apprentice.

12 Governor of the Third House

By the end of October 1863, Sam was back in Carson City to report on the territory's constitutional convention, in which statehood was rejected because the vote called for a property tax on mines, not simply on their output. The negative vote delayed statehood for another nine months, and western secessionist presses hailed it as a victory for anti-Union sentiment in the territories.[1] Clemens either remained through the New Year or returned there from Virginia City, to cover the third territorial legislature, which eventually redesigned the state constitution to limit the tax on mines. In spite of the recent setback to his reputation as a journalist as a result of "A Bloody Massacre near Carson," he had developed into a credible political reporter who had inside influence through such well-placed friends as Jack Simmons, speaker of the house of representatives, and Billy Clagett, who was also a delegate to the legislature. With James Nye, the governor, out of town most of the time lobbying for Nevada (and for himself as one of its first two senators upon statehood), Orion was frequently the chief politico in the Territory.

Indeed, Sam Clemens was so popular with the political press that he was named "Governor of the Third House," perhaps to complement Orion's de facto status. While Orion conducted the business of the third legislature, his younger brother addressed a mock legislature of reporters in Carson City on January 27, 1864. The text of his speech is not extant. It is thought that the target of this humorous address was the elusive Governor Nye, with whom he would have a future not entirely congenial. Orion ultimately botched his chances of becoming part of the territory's political hierarchy when Nevada became the nation's thirty-sixth state on October 31, 1864. In fact, his fortunes began to slide shortly before that. The death of Jennie, his only child, on February 1 of that year may have permanently dampened the spirits of the often moody Orion. Although he was respected for his honesty as a politician, he lost his bid to become the first secretary of state of Nevada essentially because of his anti-whiskey stand. Twain later called it a "spasm of virtue," but we should remember that Orion had been a confirmed teetotaler since his days as a printer's apprentice in St. Louis. The territorial secretary would ultimately find himself out of work in the new state and forced to sell his house in Carson City at a financial loss. He and Mollie eventually moved back to her beloved Keokuk, where he began the second and final act of a life of persistent failure, his career as a statesman in Nevada its intermission and only bright spot.

As Orion's future pointed downward, his brother's began what became a rather swift ascent to a long series of literary successes and, for the most part, financial stability. He was already a celebrity in Virginia City when the notorious Adah Isaacs Menken came to town on February 24 to perform for four nights at Maguire's Opera House. Among her acts was what became her "Lady Godiva" performance, in which she appeared in the title role of *Mazeppa,* based on one of Byron's poems. Her entire costume consisted of tights that simulated nudity. The "great unadorned" or "bare" caught the attention of all the journalists, including Twain, who was described by the *Golden Era* as having fallen "under [Menken's] spell." This report may have been exaggerated. In fact, the rising humorist might have been more interested in meeting her current husband, whom Menken was rumored to have abandoned for another man but who had nevertheless traveled with her to Virginia City. This was Robert Henry Newell, poet and author of the ongoing Orpheus C. Kerr Papers (1862–68).[2]

Indeed, his head may still have been spinning from the visit to Virginia City in December and January by the more famous humorist Artemus Ward. For three weeks Ward drank the bars dry with Joe Goodman, Dan De Quille, and Mark Twain (as he was now definitely becoming known not only in Nevada but also in California). A favorite on President Lincoln's list of humorists, Ward had come to lecture, but stayed to play. He was at the pinnacle of a career that would be cut short by death in 1867. In the words of Bernard De Voto, this literary comedian "made men glow."[3] Nights of oyster dinners and roof walking in this hilly city were the routine. During those weeks of comradeship and high spirits, Sam came to know Ward, who advised him on his career. It was at Ward's encouragement that Sam set his sights higher than that of western journalist (the career that Dan De Quille would have to settle for). Ward promised to tell the editors of the New York *Sunday Mercury* about Sam's work. He even suggested that Sam eventually relocate to New York, where he himself was headed.[4]

This was a period of hard drinking for a man who during most of his life abused tobacco but not liquor. Had Twain been a twentieth-century American writer like such alcoholics as Faulkner, Fitzgerald, or Hemingway, he would have extended his binges well beyond the nightspots of Virginia City and San Francisco. But he resembled most writers of that era in that he adhered to the national image of the "gentleman," who did not go to bed every night drunk or indeed very high on alcohol. Bret Harte was the kind of self-destructive drunk that Sam Clemens, whose standard of morality made him eligible for a cameo role in a Howells novel, certainly strove to avoid. But he was in fact high on more than life on the evening of May 16, 1864, when he playfully wrote a report intimating that funds raised for the United States Sanitary Commission by the ladies of Carson City were to be donated to "a Miscegenation Society somewhere in the East."[5]

The Sanitary Commission was a government bureaucracy that eventually became the Red Cross. Rather than a hands-on medical agency like the Christian Commission, which Walt Whitman much preferred during his years as "Wound Dresser" in Washington's wartime hospitals, the Sanitary Commission too often made enemies of common soldiers, who rarely saw the real fruits of its efforts, which were organizational and financial rather than directly humanitarian. Furthermore, the former Confederate soldier may have looked askance on any organization that favored Union soldiers over those from the South. In any event, as Clemens confessed to Mollie Clemens, one of the Carson City ladies who had organized the fund-raising campaign, he had written the piece involving a miscegenation society one night after having drunk too much with Dan De Quille. Definitely a Union supporter, De Quille had told Sam that evening in no uncertain terms that he would be offended if such a joke were ever published. Sam, whose mind must have been somewhat muddled with liquor, hastily assured his senior associate at the *Enterprise* that he hadn't meant it, but tossed the manuscript by mistake on the editing table. The printing foreman, Sam told his sister-in-law, "prospecting for copy [the next morning], found it, & seeing that it was in my handwriting, thought it was to be published, & carried it off."[6] At least this is the account he later gave.

The Carson City sponsors of the Sanitary Commission fund-raiser sent a letter of protest to the *Enterprise,* which refused to print it. The *Union,* always eager to do battle with its local competition, published the letter as a public notice, three days running, under the headline of "The 'Enterprise' Libel of the Ladies of Carson." Even though Sam's authorship was generally assumed, the letter demanded the name of the author of such a lie, published at a time when so many were dying for the Union. Naturally, the subjects of race or slavery never entered the discussion. The matter was further complicated by an editorial that appeared in the *Union* before the letter from the ladies of Carson City was published; it assailed the *Enterprise* for insinuating that the printers for the *Union* as well as others on the staff did not pay the money they had publicly pledged to the Sanitary Fund campaign. That insinuation had been made in Sam's "How Is It?" published on May 18, the day after his "libel" of the ladies of Carson City. He answered the editorial with one of his own, and it was in turn replied to with a letter signed "Printer" and another editorial escalating the war of words.[7]

The *Union* editorials were not signed, but Clemens singled out James L. Laird, co-owner and editor of the newspaper, as the responsible party. In a letter of May 21, he demanded a public retraction. When Laird ludicrously replied that the *Union* author of the insults was not he but a printer on the paper, Clemens challenged Laird to a duel. Calling him a "cowardly sneak," he wrote, "I now *peremptorily* demand of you the satisfaction due to a gentleman—without alternative." This was followed up the very same day with a letter expressing Clemens's astonishment that Laird would "endeavor to shield your craven carcass behind the person of an individual who in spite of *your* introduction is entirely unknown to me, and upon whose shoulders you *cannot* throw the whole responsibility." On May 24 Clemens published the entire correspondence between himself and Laird, denouncing him for refusing to fight and calling him an "unmitigated liar."[8]

Looking back on this episode in the life of Mark Twain, one cannot help but conjure up the absurdity of the Code Duello and its ramifications in the Grangerford and Sherburn-Boggs chapters of *Huckleberry Finn,* along with their implicit criticism of the rigid but romantic ideology of Sir Walter Scott. Whether Sam would have gone through with the challenge to Laird is not altogether clear. Steve Gillis, who was designated Sam's second in the duel, later told Albert Bigelow Paine that Clemens and Laird actually met on the field of honor, but that Laird was scared off when Gillis shot the head off a bird and attributed the act to Clemens, who wasn't known for his straight shooting. Yet in a helpful corrective to this myth, Henry Nash Smith theorizes that there was never even this much of a duel. Twain claimed in his autobiography that he and Gillis were fearful of a new Nevada law against dueling, which carried a penalty of two years in jail. But it was not a new law, and it was not strictly enforced in the "Wild West." Joe Goodman himself had been involved in a duel with a *Union* editor a year earlier. The main threat Sam faced—in the words of Smith—"was the danger of being ridiculous and ridiculed."[9]

Once again, as with Orion and his Hannibal newspaper, Sam had gotten a paper in trouble while the editor was away. But as in the case of "A Bloody Massacre near Carson," Goodman fully supported the hoaxer. Just what Orion thought of the incident has gone unrecorded, but soon thereafter Sam asked him for a loan of two hundred dollars to get out of town and thus avoid arrest for dueling in Nevada. By the end of the month, he and Steve Gillis had left for San Francisco. "I have never had anything to do with duels since," he wrote in his autobiography. "I thoroughly disapprove of duels. I consider them unwise, and I know they are dangerous." Mark Twain's true weapon, of course, was humor, which nothing could ultimately withstand. His headstrong personality occasionally took him beyond his physical abilities. (Indeed, one wonders whether, in *Life on the Mississippi,* he exaggerated his pummeling of the pilot Brown.) His war service suggests that he could not abide the perils and discomforts of combat. As he wrote in "The Private History of a Campaign That Failed," he had "entered the war, got just a taste of it, and then stepped out again permanently." But it wasn't the first time he had retreated in the face of danger. While living in St. Louis in 1854, he had joined a local militia to quell a riot in which members of the Know-Nothing Party were plundering the rooming houses of immigrants. In a private dress rehearsal for his conduct in the Civil War, he decided to opt out when violence actually threatened. Just before his company made contact with the rioters, he asked a fellow militiaman to hold his weapon, according to an account in chapter 51 of *Life on the Mississippi,* "while I dropped out and got a drink. Then I branched off and went home."[10] Prudence and comedy were the tactics he preferred.

13 The Jumping Frog

Sam Clemens's permanent removal to San Francisco in 1864 marked an important stage in his career as Mark Twain, for he began to publish sketches, hundreds of them, that would not only lead to but also enhance his initial fame as the author of the Jumping Frog story in 1865. Most were written after he made his last move to the Bay City, and twenty-six of them went essentially unchanged (the editing in most cases amounting to selective cutting) into his first book along with "Jim Smiley and His Jumping Frog," retitled "The Celebrated Jumping Frog of Calaveras County." His first job in San Francisco was on the *Morning Call,* but he also wrote sketches for the *Californian* and, starting about mid-1865, sent letters to the *Enterprise* back in Virginia City. He probably landed the *Call* job through Joe Goodman, who had worked in San Francisco before he conducted the *Enterprise* and was respected as a journalist there. Sam worked at the *Call* from June to October, but the job didn't allow him the artistic freedom or leisure he had enjoyed at the *Enterprise.* His starting salary was reasonably good at forty dollars a week, but the work was "killingly monotonous" with its daily sessions in police court and a beat that included reporting on the endless squabbles involving either the city's Irish or Chinese residents, the latter brutalized by the police and not even counted in the official census. The "fearful drudgery" of this tedious routine persuaded Clemens to take a twenty-dollar pay cut during his final month on the paper in return for a shorter workday.

He got discouraged about his situation and about the progress of his career as a writer, restricted as it was to the world of journalism. Forty years later he still remembered feeling his "deep shame in being situated as I was—slave of such a journal as the *Morning Call*."[1] Although the job required straight reporting, he was occasionally allowed the editorial freedom to engage his imagination. In "No Earthquake," published on August 23, he reflected the edginess of the city that, only a generation or two later, would experience its big bang of 1906. "In consequence of the warm, close atmosphere, . . ." he wrote, "everybody expected to be shaken out of their boots by an earthquake before night, but up to the hour of our going to press the supernatural boot-jack had not arrived yet." Aside from these flights of wit, however, his heart simply wasn't in the job of gathering the news. He was, as it was tactfully put, willingly "retired" by his employer, George E. Barnes, that fall.[2]

Clemens also wrote occasionally for the *Golden Era* and the *Californian*, where he met at least three contributors who would play a part in his future: Bret Harte, Charles Henry Webb, and Charles Warren Stoddard. Harte was working for the San Francisco Mint and contributing to the *Californian*, which he would later edit for a time with Webb. Webb, an established humorist who would edit and publish Clemens's first book in 1867, was the founding editor of the *Californian*. And Stoddard, a minor essayist, poet, and closeted homosexual who would soon be writing exotic letters from Hawaii to Walt Whitman, became Sam's private secretary when he lived and lectured in London in 1872 and 1873.[3] Another associate, with whom he had a more distant relationship, was Ambrose Bierce, who also contributed to the *Golden Era*.

He continued living with Steve Gillis in a succession of rooming houses following their brief residence in the lavish Occidental Hotel ("Heaven on the half shell") and surviving (barely) on the commissions he got from the *Californian, Golden Era,* and *Enterprise*. His residence in San Francisco was abruptly suspended in late 1864 when his roommate got into a barroom brawl with a bully who was a friend of the police chief. Steve had knocked his adversary unconscious with a beer pitcher. As another of the Gillis boys, Billy, remembered the episode, it became "the fight that made Mark Twain famous."[4] Steve was arrested and later bailed out by Sam on a "straw bond" (fifty dollars on a five-hundred-dollar bond). When Steve promptly jumped bail and returned to his printer's job in Virginia City, Sam was in danger of arrest himself by the angry police chief, because he would immediately owe the entire amount of the bond once Steve turned up missing in court. Sam would have to flee himself. At this point, Jim Gillis, yet another of the Gillis brood from Mississippi, intervened to invite Sam to hide out at his cabin in the Tuolumne Hills until the trouble cleared. Arriving at the Gillis mining shack on Jackass Hill near Tuttleton and Sonora on December 4, Mark Twain came upon his opportunity for fame that Steve had effectively ordained in that barroom brawl in San Francisco.[5] For it was during the subsequent three-month sojourn near the Mother Lode that he first heard the story of the Jumping Frog and subsequently wrote it up in his own fashion, thus securing American humor as a key component of American literature.

Before turning to the toad named Daniel Webster, however, it is useful to glance at some of the stories that led up to the success of the Jumping Frog, earlier sketches that helped make up the other twenty-six pieces in *The Celebrated Jumping Frog of Calaveras County, and Other Sketches.* These stories are representative of the countless ones he wrote during his sudden climb to fame in the 1860s. They also represent, to some extent, those he considered most worth preserving and reprinting, in 1867 and again in 1875, with *Sketches New and Old.*

Twain was already nationally known both for the frog story when the book appeared and for several sketches that had earlier been reprinted from the *Californian* in the East. As the New York *Times* and other reviewers of the 1867 collection noted, several in the volume "were nearly equal to it in merit." They were probably not referring to the earliest one included, "Curing a Cold," which had first appeared as "How to Cure a Cold" in the *Golden Era* of September 20, 1863, or to "Information for the Million," first published as "Washoe—'Information Wanted,'" in the *Enterprise* in early May (issue not extant) and reprinted in the *Golden Era* on May 22, 1864. The first was a spoof on home remedies, and the second satirized the shameless land-promotion schemes in Nevada, usually for worthless mines. But a third, originally called "Whereas" in the *Californian* of October 22, 1864, probably struck as much literary gold in terms of this humorist's development as "Jim Smiley and His Jumping Frog."

For the book it was retitled "Aurelia's Unfortunate Young Man," and it is still hilarious today, whereas one needs to know something about the traditions of American humor to fully appreciate the lead story in Twain's first book. With "Aurelia's Unfortunate Young Man," whose public readings (Twain later told William Dean Howells) convulsed audiences with laughter, we don't need any history to appreciate its humor.[6] The first half of the original sketch mimicked classical writers such as Goldsmith and Irving on the travails of love. In Twain's version, this "Palace of Cupid," as the editors of the *Early Tales* note, is now called "Love's Bakery." It proves to be "peculiarly fitting" as an introduction to a story as riotously laughable as the fantasies of Emmeline Grangerford in *Huckleberry Finn.*

Aurelia Maria has written the author of a self-help column about a particularly troublesome fiancé whose clumsiness causes him to lose body parts. (Edgar Allan Poe's "The Man That Was Used Up" may have given Twain the basic idea for his plot.) Williamson Breckinridge Caruthers of New Jersey first becomes infected with smallpox, "and when he recovered from his illness, his face was pitted like a waffle-mould." Not long after Aurelia has accepted these facial distortions, Mr. Caruthers, "watching the flight of a balloon," walks—like Stephen Dowling Bots of Emmeline Grangeford's sentimental poem—into a well and fractures one of his legs, which has to be amputated at the knee. "Again," Twain writes, "Aurelia was moved to break off the engagement, but again love triumphed," and she resolved to give him "another chance to reform." Caruthers then suffers the loss of an arm "by the premature discharge of a Fourth-of-July cannon" and soon afterward the accidental loss of the other. "Deeply grieved to see her lover passing from her by piecemeal," she nevertheless resigns herself to remain faithful at least a little longer. But "shortly before the time set for the nuptials," and loss of an eye and the other leg, the final disaster occurs: "There was but one man scalped by the Owens River Indians last year. That man was Williamson Breckinridge Caruthers, of New-Jersey."

Sam Clemens had been mocking sentimentality at least since his days in the graveyards of Philadelphia and New Orleans. The perfect dupe or butt of the humor, of course, was conveniently a Yankee from New

Jersey, somebody whose pretentious trinomial suggests that he should know enough to come in out of the rain. American humor began by making fun of the British gentleman in all his puffery; then, as it emerged in the American South, the target became the stranger from the North, or the Yankee, and then finally the stranger from anywhere. The columnist's final advice to poor Aurelia is to reconstruct this Yankee fool, who by now consists of only two-thirds of himself:

> How would it do to build him? If Aurelia can afford the expense, let her furnish her mutilated lover with wooden arms and wooden legs, and a glass eye and a wig, and give him another show; give him ninety days, without grace, and if he does not break his neck in the meantime, marry him and take chances.[7]

Twain would eventually make an even better joke with a wooden leg in *Huckleberry Finn.*

Sentimentality, or any kind of posed emotion or nostalgia, was always the target of Twain's satire. In "A Touching Story of George Washington's Boyhood," the next sketch he wrote that went into his book (*Californian,* October 29, 1864), the narrator doesn't get to his point until the very end of the tale, but by then he has already forgotten his subject, the lie about the president who could never tell one. Mark Twain would put this national myth to better use in the conclusion of *Tom Sawyer,* where Judge Thatcher lugubriously insists that Tom's lie to save the magistrate's daughter Becky from a whipping by the schoolmaster "was worthy to hold up its head and march down through history breast to breast with George Washington's lauded Truth about the hatchet." The story also anticipates "The Story of the Old Ram" in chapter 53 of *Roughing It,* in which a drunken narrator goes through one compulsive digression after another, never getting to the point of his story. Twain was earning only twelve dollars or so for these early pieces, but it was ideal on-the-job training for what he would soon become.[8]

In "The Killing of Julius Caesar 'Localized'" (*Californian,* November 12, 1864), he made fun of the kind of sensational news stories he had been encouraged to write for the *Call.* Interestingly, in "Lucretia Smith's Soldier" (*Californian,* December 3, 1864) his target was again

Clockwise from top left: Figure 1. Jane Lampton Clemens, Sam's mother, 1870. Courtesy of the Mark Twain Papers, The Bancroft Library. *Figure 2.* Orion Clemens, Sam's brother, early 1860s. Nevada Historical Society. *Figure 3.* Mary E. ("Mollie") Clemens, Orion's wife, 1866. Nevada Historical Society.

Figure 4. Olivia ("Livy") Langdon Clemens, Sam's wife, 1895, Melbourne, Australia. The Mark Twain House & Museum, Hartford, CT.

Figure 5, left. Daughter Olivia Susan ("Susy") Clemens, Florence, Italy, 1892. Courtesy of the Mark Twain Papers, The Bancroft Library. *Figure 6, right.* Daughter Jean Clemens, 1909. Courtesy of the Mark Twain Papers, The Bancroft Library.

Figure 7. Bret Harte. Gary Scharnhorst.

Figure 8. The Hartford house.
The Mark Twain House & Museum, Hartford, CT.

Figure 9. Elisha Bliss, president of the American Publishing Company. Courtesy of the Mark Twain Papers, The Bancroft Library.

Figure 10. Mary Ann Cord ("A True Story").
Special Collections, University of Maryland Libraries.

Figure 11. Charles L. Webster, 1884. Special Collections, Vassar College Libraries. *Figure 12.* Annie Moffett Webster, early 1870s. Special Collections, Vassar College Libraries.

Figure 13. Nina Gabrilowitsch, Sam's only grandchild, 1930. Courtesy of the Mark Twain Papers, The Bancroft Library.

Figure 14. Virginia City, Nevada, 1860s. Nevada Historical Society.

Figure 15. Twain on his thirty-ninth birthday.
The Mark Twain House & Museum, Hartford, CT.

Figure 16. Normandy Hotel, Paris, France, 1879.
Courtesy of the Mark Twain Papers, The Bancroft Library.

Figure 17. Henry Raymond ("Colonel Sellers") and Twain, 1875.
Kevin Mac Donnell.

Figure 18. Twain and George Washington Cable, 1884.
Kevin Mac Donnell.

Figure 19. Twain in a series of four poses about the time of *Huckleberry Finn.* The Mark Twain House & Museum, Hartford, CT.

Figure 20. The "Uncle Silas" prank in *Huckleberry Finn*. University of Virginia Library.

Figure 21. The Paige Compositor, 1880s. Courtesy of the Mark Twain Papers, The Bancroft Library.

Figure 22. Left: Roxy, 1894. Right: Roxy, 1899.
Both images, University of Virginia Library.

Kemble.
92.

Figure 23. Mark Twain during the overland part of his world tour, 1895. The Mark Twain House & Museum, Hartford, CT.

Figure 24. Clara, Livy, and Twain at Dollis Hill estate outside London, 1900. The Mark Twain House & Museum, Hartford, CT.

Figure 25. Mark Twain, London, October 1899, by Henry Walter Barnett. Kevin Mac Donnell.

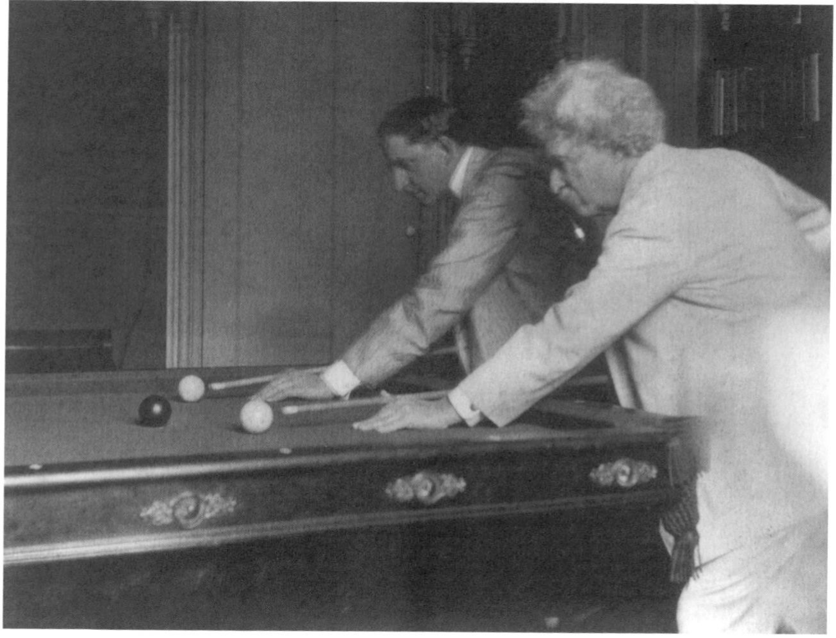

Figure 26, top. Twain and Henry Huttleston Rogers, 1908. Courtesy of the Mark Twain Papers, The Bancroft Library. *Figure 27, bottom.* Albert Bigelow Paine and Twain playing billiards, 1908. Courtesy of the Mark Twain Papers, The Bancroft Library.

Figure 28. Isabel V. Lyon, Ralph Ashcroft, and Twain at Stormfield in 1908. Courtesy of the Mark Twain Papers, The Bancroft Library.

Figure 29. Twain sitting on the terrace at Stormfield, 1908.
Kevin Mac Donnell.

Figure 30. Stormfield. Kevin Mac Donnell.

Figure 31. Twain and "Angel-fish" Irene Gerken, Bermuda, 1908. Courtesy of the Mark Twain Papers, The Bancroft Library.

Figure 32. William Dean Howells and Twain, 1909.
Courtesy of the Mark Twain Papers, The Bancroft Library.

Figure 33. Wedding of Clara and Ossip Gabrilowitsch, October 6, 1909. (*Right to left:* MT, Jervis Langdon II, Jean Clemens, Gabrilowitsch, Clara, and the Reverend Joseph Twichell.) The Mark Twain House & Museum, Hartford, CT.

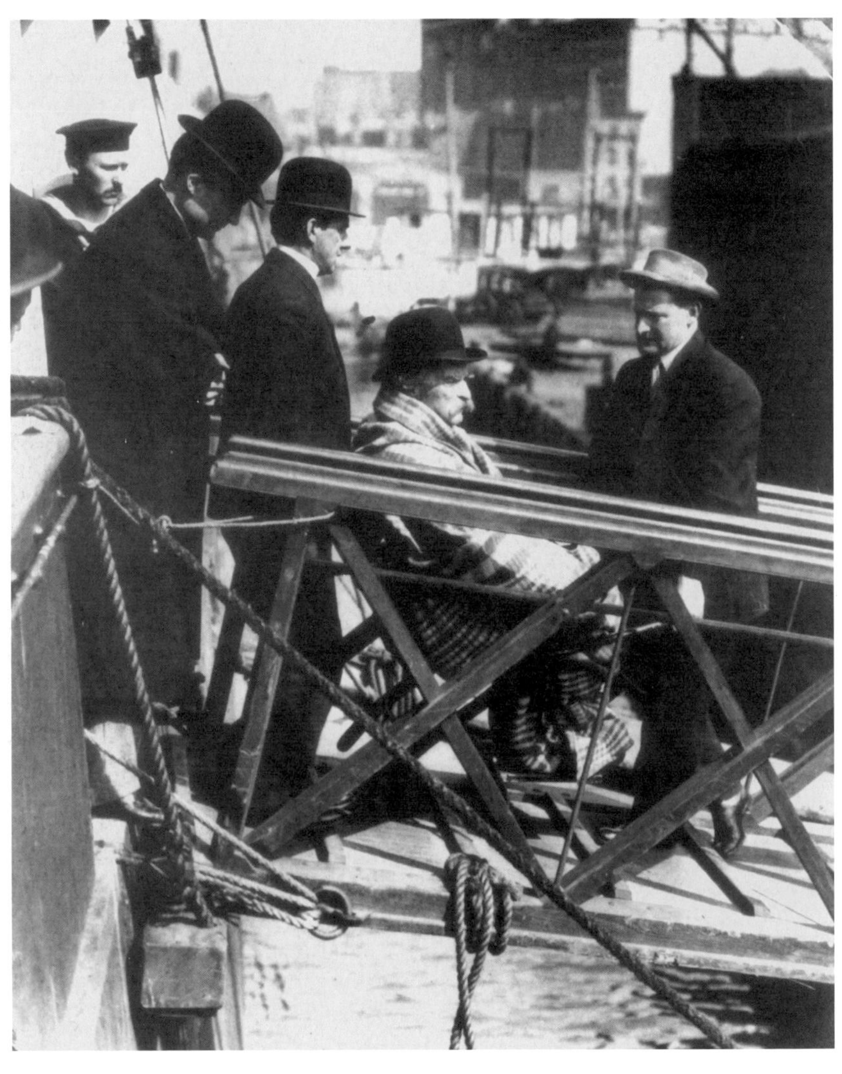

Figure 34. Mark Twain returning from Bermuda, 1910. Courtesy of the Mark Twain Papers, The Bancroft Library.

Figure 35. Funeral cortege, April 24, 1910.
Courtesy of the Mark Twain Papers, The Bancroft Library.

Figure 36. Mark Twain as icon on Ogden's Guinea Gold Cigarettes. Kevin Mac Donnell.

the news media, but this time he aimed at their maudlin stories about the war (the one that was still raging then in Grant's final campaign against the Southern capital of Richmond). It didn't seem to matter that he himself was arguably a fugitive from the war, probably because so many like him were hiding out in Nevada Territory. *Harper's Weekly* was known for its melodramatic war stories, or tales about the home front in which young women refuse to marry their boyfriends unless they help them "make a sacrifice" for their country by enlisting. "Lucretia Smith's Soldier" was Twain's version of one of those "sickly war stories." Lucretia sits at the bedside of her wounded lover, who is wrapped in bandages covering most of his face, only to discover when the dressing is removed that she has been "slobbering over the wrong soldier!"[9]

The best that can be said for "Literature in the Dry Diggings" (originally "An Unbiased Criticism," *Californian,* March 18, 1865) is that it is another feat of elaborate digressing that mentions Ben Coon, the real-life person who first told the Jumping Frog story to Sam and his friends at Angels Camp, not far from the Gillis cabin. Ben Coon became the loquacious Simon Wheeler in Twain's frog story, but not before making his debut as the author of "He Done His Level Best" in the *Californian* on June 17, 1865 (made part of "Answers to Correspondents" in his book, which melded together several installments of "Answers").

By the summer and fall of 1865, Sam Clemens was placing items wherever he could merely to stay afloat—among them "Advice for Good Little Girls" in the San Francisco *Youth's Companion* and the fourth installment of "Answers to Correspondents" in the *Californian,* both initially published on June 24, before they were spliced into the book. Each was largely magazine filler, but in the second he pokes fun at motherhood and those women who declare that a "baby is a thing of beauty and a joy forever!" Much later, H. L. Mencken, one of the earliest champions of *Huckleberry Finn* as great literature, may have been inspired by this sketch to ghost-write a baby book for a Baltimore pediatrician which argued that a "mother should not make a slave of herself waiting on the child, but clothe it in some comfortable manner and let it fight out its own troubles."[10]

In "An Item Which the Editor Himself Could Not Understand," part of "The Facts," first published in the *Californian* of August 26, we have more of the discursive narrative that would culminate in "The Story of the Old Ram" in *Roughing It.* Sam must have felt, with well more than a hundred sketches to his credit, that he was going somewhere as a literary person, certainly as a humorist. That fall he told Orion and Mollie that he had "a 'call' to literature, of a low order." That his readers thought he wrote exclusively in this "low order" would never cease to bother him, but for now it was enough to sustain his ego. He warned his brother to burn his letter to them to avoid the publication of any "literary remains" until after he was "planted," a caveat he would have to issue several times during his career as his fame grew. Also that fall, the San Francisco *Dramatic Chronicle* had compared his literary style favorably with that of John Phoenix.[11] A day earlier the same journal issued his "Earthquake Almanac," which made its way into the book as "A Page from a California Almanac." Like "No Earthquake" in the *Call,* it made fun of weather reports indicating the possibility of the big one.

"The Launch of the Steamer Capital" ("'Mark Twain' on the Launch of the Steamer 'Capital,'" *Californian,* November 18, 1865) is another exercise in digression, but by now, as the original title indicates, "Mark Twain" carried immediate name recognition, at least on the West Coast. Indeed, Webb took many of his texts for the 1867 book from reprints in the prestigious *Californian,* which by now under Bret Harte's editorship counted Clemens as an important commodity. After a hand-to-mouth existence in San Francisco following his return from Jackass Hill and his pocket-mining buddies, he was starting to see the vistas in his literary landscape. That terrain widened significantly following the publication of "Jim Smiley and His Jumping Frog"—also on November 18, but on the opposite coast. It made its debut in the famed and newly revived New York *Saturday Press,* edited by Henry Clapp, one of Whitman's drinking companions at Pfaff's on Broadway and the first publisher, back in 1859, of "Out of the Cradle Endlessly Rocking."

Yet, not long after the Jumping Frog sketch had been hailed as remarkable and widely reprinted, Clemens told his mother and sister Pamela: "To think that after writing many an article a man might be excused for thinking tolerably good, those New York people should single out a villainous backwoods sketch to compliment me on!" He dismissed it as "a squib that would never have been written but to please Artemus Ward."[12] Ward and Clemens had been friends since Ward's visit to Virginia City two years earlier. The humorist had written Twain in November 1864 inviting him to contribute one of his sketches to what in 1865 became *Artemus Ward: His Travels.* When he finally sent the jumping frog sketch in October, however, it was too late for the book. Ward's publisher gave it to Clapp, who needed material to rejuvenate his journal.

Mark Twain's low opinion of the sketch would change as compliments poured in from all across the country, including one from James Russell Lowell, who allegedly called it "the finest piece of humorous writing ever produced in America."[13] At the time, Lowell was America's leading humorist, but his material now is dated and resonates almost solely in the context of the antiwar sentiment of many of the country's northeastern intellectuals during the Mexican War.

In writing the sketch, Twain was actually trying to work up a humorous description of his experiences in the California mining camps. The original draft, which he started about September 1, 1865, and didn't complete until the third week of October, was called "The Only Reliable Account of the Celebrated Jumping Frog of Calaveras County, Together with Some Reference to the Decaying City of Boomerang. . . ." Boomerang was his name for Angels Camp, and the first two parts of the sketch, never published in Twain's lifetime, discuss the largely abandoned mining town and its constable named Bilgewater, a favorite name that would later perform a greater literary service to the author in *Huckleberry Finn.* Besides offering a brief demonstration of the digressive narrator, the material is largely without merit. Only when he gets to Simon Wheeler does the narrative congeal into the frog story.

The story was not original with Twain; only his "account" was, as he acknowledged in his initial title. The tale had first appeared as "The Toad Story" in the Sonora *Herald* in 1853 and again in a slightly different version in the San Andreas *Independent* in 1858. Although it did not single-handedly launch Twain's career as America's greatest humorist (a number of his writings of this era were hitting their mark in western publications recopied in the East), it does give us one of the earliest important glimpses of his use of the stranger who upsets normal expectations, a theme that one way or another increasingly, or at least ultimately, characterizes the fiction of Mark Twain all the way to "The Mysterious Stranger" manuscripts. In the Jumping Frog tale, however, the stranger is not in any way sinister, but merely a better hustler—a stock figure in the Bret Harte tradition—who can take advantage of Jim Smiley's addiction to gambling. Smiley's willingness to bet on anything, even on the death of a minister's wife, provides one of the funniest and most grotesque passages in the story.

> If there was a dog-fight he'd bet on it; if there was a cat-fight, he bet on it; if there was a chicken-fight, he'd bet on it; why if there was two birds setting on a fence, he would bet you which one would fly first . . . it never made no difference to *him*—he would bet on *anything*. . . . Parson Walker's wife laid very sick, once, for a good while, and it seemed as if they warn't going to save her; but one morning he come in and Smiley asked him how she was, and he said she was considerable better—thank the Lord for his inf'nit mercy—and coming on so smart that with the blessing of Providence she'd get well yet—and Smiley, before he thought, says, "Well, I'll resk two-and-a-half that she don't, anyway."[14]

Jim Smiley's helplessness in the face of temptation will always be funny because it goes to the heart of human darkness in a world that Darwin had recently explained. Smiley, we learn in the climax of the tale, bets on "rat-terriers, and chicken cocks, and tom-cats." One day he catches a frog, which he "learns" to jump farther than any other frog. "You never see a frog so modest and straightfor'ard as he was, for all he was so gifted," Simon Wheeler, the interior narrator of this frame story, observes. The frog is no prouder than Smiley himself, who is now set up for a confidence man, a stranger in town, who doesn't "see no p'ints about that frog that's any better'n any other frog." Smiley bets the stranger forty dollars and leaves to find the stranger a frog with which to race "Dan'l Webster." While he "slopped around in the mud," the stranger fills Smiley's frog with quail shot. Clemens wrote the tale in his own words after hearing it in a barroom. It captures the local color of California mining camps of that day, and Twain's version is particularly full of precious comic stuff, such as the image of the adulterated frog, now filled with lead, trying to jump but succeeding only in hoisting its shoulders "like a Frenchman."

Earlier in the story we learn of Smiley's "small bull pup" whose main advantage in a fight was his ability to seize his opponent's hind legs "and freeze to it—not chaw, you understand, but only jest grip and hang on till they throwed up the sponge, if it was a year." Smiley always won with him "till he harnessed a dog once that didn't have no hind legs, because they'd been sawed off in a circular saw." Afterward, his dog "gave Smiley a look, as much as to say his heart was broke, and it was *his* fault, for putting up a dog that hadn't no hind legs for him to take holt of, which was his main dependence in a fight, and then he limped off a piece, and laid down and died." In the cases of both the debased frog and frustrated dog, Twain gives these animals human aspects that reflect the hubris of their owner, whose ego is inflated beyond all sense of reality. The story's humor is miraculously amplified when it is read aloud in Twain's accent (southerners have the advantage here).

In 1906, looking over a pirated edition of his anthology of humorists of the past forty years (*Mark Twain's Library of Humor*), Twain called the book a cemetery. "In this mortuary volume I find Nasby, Artemus Ward, Yawcob Strauss, Derby, Burdette, Eli Perkins, the 'Danbury News Man,' Orpheus C. Kerr, Smith O'Brien, Josh Billings, and a score of others, maybe two score, whose writings . . . are now heard of no more and are no longer mentioned." "A number of these names," he wrote, "were as familiar as George Ade and Dooley today"—excluding Twain's, names of famous writers at the turn of the nineteenth century that have long vanished from the public memory of our day.[15] He credited his own survival to the fact that humor was only a part of the "sermon"—a mere fragrance coming from something eternally relevant to readers in every age. The other part, however, contained the pathos embedded in every lasting joke. "Jim Smiley and His Jumping Frog" lives on today, not merely because of its service to the national literature in 1865 or the fact that it was written by Mark Twain. It survives because it touches upon the springs of humor, which is surely pathos.

14 Vandal Abroad

Mark Twain's next adventure in the West would be a sojourn to the Sandwich Islands. Of the six sketches published after the *Saturday Press* issue of the Jumping Frog story but before his Hawaii sketches, and also printed in *The Celebrated Jumping Frog,* probably only one is significant for his development as a writer. This was "The Story of the Bad Little Boy That Bore a Charmed Life," which appeared in the *Californian* on December 23, 1865. Its title in *Jumping Frog* became "The Story of the Bad Little Boy Who Didn't Come to Grief."[1] It marks both the first time Twain took up the theme of the bad little boy before writing *The Adventures of Tom Sawyer* and the first clear foreshadowing of his late-life satires on heaven. Interestingly, the bad little boy's name is Jim, but it could have just as easily been Tom, as both are favorite names of boys in Twain's world. "Most bad boys in the Sunday books are named James," he wrote, "and have sick mothers, who teach them to say, 'Now I lay me down,' etc., and sing them to sleep with sweet plaintive voices, and then kiss them good-night, and kneel down by the bedside and weep. But it was different with this fellow."

Contrary to the teachings of the Good Book, bad behavior is not always punished. Indeed, it is often rewarded. Sam himself, as legend has it, was a "bad boy" like Huck and Tom Sawyer. His brother Henry was the good boy in the family; he died young. Having been brought up in the Calvinist tradition of hellfire and brimstone as the "reward" for the sinner, Sam Clemens was beginning to see that humor had a wider range than he supposed. But it still couldn't wander into profanity and off-color stories. That kind of writing disappeared, almost without exception, from his public repertoire after a very early sketch that punned on "bony part" for Bonaparte. Twain was hailed in all his obituaries as a "clean" humorist. In fact, traditional religious belief was also off-limits as a subject for humor during the entirety of the nineteenth century. Novels in the Victorian age were supposed to support moral and conventional behavior. Those that did not—such as Kate Chopin's *The Awakening* or Theodore Dreiser's *Sister Carrie,* both appearing at the very end of the century—paid the price of bad reviews and suppression in the marketplace.

The bad boy who never comes to grief eats all the jam and refills the container with tar. He steals the teacher's penknife and plants it on one of the good little boys. He steals his father's gun and goes hunting on Sunday. Even murder can't get him arrested. In the still rippling wake of the violence of "A Bloody Massacre near Carson," Jim raises a large family "and brain[s] them all with an ax one night." When we last see this villain, he "is universally respected, and belongs to the Legislature." But Jim is clearly fiction because this is American humor, not American realism. It's all just a joke and is not important in the scheme of things. Such was the fate of the humorist as well. But we get ahead of our story.

After "Jim Smiley and His Jumping Frog" struck the national funny bone in the fall of 1865, the attention prompted the Sacramento *Union* to send its author, also respected for his letters back to the *Enterprise* in 1865 and 1866, to the Sandwich Islands in the winter of 1866—to "write up the sugar interest," as he later remembered the assignment. The series turned out to be much more than promoting sugar, for during the stint, Twain became a full-fledged travel writer blissfully ignorant of Emerson's caveat that "traveling is a fool's paradise." The beautiful Hawaiian Islands were indeed a paradise, at least until American missionaries, as he wrote, made the natives "permanently miserable by telling them how beautiful and how blissful a place heaven is, and how nearly impossible it is to get there."[2] He sailed from San Francisco on the *Ajax* on March 6 for what was supposed to be a month's visit during which he would write "twenty or thirty" letters back to the *Union.* As it turned out, the trip lasted five months and produced twenty-five letters. Essentially, they became Mark Twain's first travel book, a trial run for *The Innocents Abroad.*

Twain used four of the pieces he wrote about Hawaii in his Jumping Frog book. "Honored as a Curiosity in Honolulu" came from his fifth letter to the *Union,* published on April 20, 1866, and given the subheading "Etiquette." Here he made fun of the excessive use of titles in Honolulu, including captains, reverends, and "First Gentleman of the Bedchamber." "The Steed 'Oahu'" came from letter six, where it appeared under the same title (a subheading), published on April 21. Its comical description of Clemens's rental of a horse that tries to "climb over a stone wall five or six feet high" and leaves its rider "literally dripping with perspiration and profanity" would be repeated in *Roughing It,* where he reused some of these Hawaiian sketches in the later chapters.

"A Strange Dream" in the book was first published under the same title in the New York *Saturday Press* of June 2, where he had placed "Jim Smiley and His Jumping Frog" the previous November. It allegedly describes a dream the author experienced while visiting the Volcano House, located on the crater of Kilauea on the big island of Hawaii. It was his first experiment with the fiction of dreams that culminated at the end of his career with "Which Was the Dream?" In the latter, the narrator can't tell whether or not the dream is the reality. Here he is satisfied to conclude that "you can not bet any thing on dreams." "Short and Singular Rations" was first published as "The Last Ration!" a subheading in letter fifteen to the Sacramento *Union,* published on July 19, 1866. This letter was devoted to the sinking of the clipper *Hornet* and the forty-three-day ordeal of its survivors, who reached Oahu in an open boat while Twain was there. Three others that went into the 1867 book were published after his return to California.[3] These are largely insignificant, especially when one considers veins of superior material in the *Union* letters.

The voyage to Hawaii would mark the first of many seagoing adventures in Mark Twain's life. Later he crossed the Atlantic almost as regularly as one might today by air. And then such voyages were rigorous and often dangerous. In his first letter to the *Union,* he described the journey as "very rough for several days and nights, and the vessel rolled and pitched heavily. All but six or eight of us took their meals in bed constantly, and remained shut up in the staterooms day and night. The saloons and decks looked deserted and lonesome." Clemens probably thrived on such travel because he seldom became seasick. The Hawaii letters mark the first time that the writer engaged in the beautiful descriptive prose that so distinguishes *The Innocents Abroad* and other works. These passages, however, didn't always escape the criticism of his imaginary traveling companion, Mr. Brown, who at one point (in letter four) exploded: "You can go on writing that slop about balmy breezes and fragrant flowers, and all that sort of truck, but you're not going to leave out them centipedes and things for want of being reminded of it, you know."[4]

During his four months in the islands, he visited three of them, Oahu, Maui, and Hawaii. He had intended to visit Kauai, but this plan was abandoned when in Oahu he met Anson Burlingame, who was returning to China as the U.S. ambassador. A month after Sam's arrival in Honolulu, he sailed on an interisland schooner to Maui, passing by the newly established leper colony on Molokai (lying "like a homely sway-backed whale on the water"), which operated into the next century. Descriptions of its horrors would have to await the pens of Jack London and Robert Louis Stevenson, and later James A. Michener and W.S. Merwin. Clemens remained on Maui for five weeks, returning to Oahu on May 22. Four days later he sailed for Hawaii, where he visited the volcano Kilauea. He returned to Oahu on June 16 and remained on Waikiki until sailing for San Francisco.

Although he later remembered going to the islands mainly to write about the sugar industry, he didn't get to that subject until his twenty-third letter, in which he dutifully quoted facts about the production from the various islands. In comparing it with the sugar industry in Louisiana, however, he appears to have been ahead of his time in suggesting the benefits of today's outsourcing. "The hire of each laborer [in Hawaii] is $100 a year," he wrote when the ink was hardly dry on the United States' decision to end slavery, if not on the Emancipation Proclamation itself—"just about what it used to cost to board and clothe and doctor a

Negro—but there is no original outlay of $500 to $1,000 for the purchase of the laborer, or $50 to $100 annual interest to be paid on the sum so laid out."[5] After five years in the West, he still remained something of a southerner in terms of his sensitivity to the recent crime of slavery.

There was also a need to satisfy his Sacramento readers, whose numbers no doubt included a healthy minority of copperheads. Otherwise, Mark Twain, whose nom de guerre was about to become permanently famous, provided a colorful overview of the islands, now in their last years of the Kamehameha dynasty. Hawaii was still the center of whaling, a central focus in the letters, which argued for that industry's relocation to San Francisco. He criticized the "Kanakas" (not then a pejorative for Hawaiians) for their general dishonesty as vendors and their poor treatment of horses, much as he would Arabs during his visit to the Holy Land a year later. He spoke mirthfully of the history of the Hawaiians and their human sacrifices of grandmothers in honor of their kings and queens. Even the semisecular legislature did not escape unscathed, although he saw no difference between that one and any other. He recalled the case of the Wisconsin legislature that had debated a penalty for the crime of arson. A clueless legislator had risen to suggest "that when a man committed the damning crime of arson they ought either to hang him or make him marry the girl!"[6]

The letters contain a reasonably strong hint (at least to the modern reader) that Twain was enjoying casual sexual relations with native women. In fact, the recent biographer who argues for Clemens's homosexual tryst with Rice also thinks that he may have contracted a case of venereal disease there, or more likely earlier in either Virginia City or San Francisco. This suggestion is based on a diary entry written during the visit to Hawaii in which the writer complains of having the "mumps," adding, "I suppose I am to take a new disease to the Islands & depopulate them, as all white men have done heretofore." Twain also notes that it is "a damned disease that children have," but adults can and still do contract it. The allusion to depopulating the islands may simply be a reference to the fact that whites did indeed bring venereal disease to the South Sea islands (Melville's relatively poorer Marquesas, for example), and nothing more. Practically the only marriageable women in Nevada when he was there were already married, like Orion's Mollie and the other ladies of Carson City. In 1862, as we have seen, Sam confessed to his sister-in-law that he didn't "mind sleeping with female servants" as long as he remained a bachelor.[7] Apparently, there was nothing wrong with somebody of his social background and standing engaging in such conduct as long as he was not married. Nothing in the rough-and-tumble environment of the mining towns of Nevada and California occasioned the indirect mention of casual sex, and certainly not with prostitutes, but the still largely unknown Sandwich Islands, where visitors considered the hula dance obscene, did invite such allusions. The women there were not lily-white Victorian women but lightly clad olive-skinned teenagers who could be described in a suggestive context.

In his *Union* letters he speaks of these pretty young women with their "splendid black eyes and heavy masses of long black hair." Mention of a female's abundant thick black hair was shorthand in the nineteenth century for a sexually liberated woman. These "long-haired, saddle-colored Sandwich Island maidens" caught his eye time and again during his travels there. While on the big island, he described "these creatures" as "bathing about half their time. If a man were to see a nude woman bathing at noonday in the States, he would be apt to think she was very little better than she ought to be. . . . [Such women] are only particular about getting undressed safely, and in this science they all follow the same fashion. They stoop down, snatch the single garment over the head, and spring in. They will do this with great confidence within thirty steps of a man." Apparently, these women were available to foreigners who might somehow enrich their husbands or fathers. He describes the Hawaiians as a "strange race," "amazingly unselfish and hospitable. To the wayfarer who visits them they freely offer their houses, food, beds, and often their wives and daughters."[8]

No wonder he stayed longer than a month and almost went broke doing it. He doubtless enjoyed more freedom to satisfy himself in this way on the less populated islands. It was on his return to Oahu from Hawaii on June 16 that he met Ambassador Burlingame. A highly cultured man who had served three terms in Congress, he took an interest in Mark Twain and may have been the first cultivating force in his life, preceding the influences of Mary Fairbanks, his wife, and Howells. Burlingame encouraged Sam to turn his writing talent to more serious subjects. When the survivors of the *Hornet* sinking arrived in Honolulu, the ambassador and his son (who later became the first editor of *Scribner's Magazine*) got Clemens out of a sickbed to interview them and subsequently break the horrifying story to the world. The account first appeared as letter fifteen to the *Union,* which otherwise made little fanfare over Twain's letters. This in turn led to an adaptation that appeared in the national press.[9]

When Burlingame arrived in the islands, he sent word to Twain, who was recovering from saddle boils caused by riding mules on the big island, that he and his son would like to call on him. During their first meeting, Clemens told his mother, Edward Burlingame "said he could tell that frog story as well as anybody." Both were highly interested in the writer. "At his request," he remembered, "I have loaned Mr Burlingame pretty much everything I ever wrote."[10] As a diplomat, Burlingame was an idealist and a democrat who opposed privileges for foreigners in China; earlier, as Lincoln's minister to Austria, he had been in favor of the Hungarian Revolution. His policies of noninterference in foreign affairs probably influenced Twain's later anti-imperialist politics. In *Roughing It* where Twain criticizes the American treatment of Chinese immigrants in Nevada and California, he cites Burlingame's support for China's "bitter opposition to railroads [since] a road could not be built anywhere in the empire without disturbing the graves of their ancestors or friends."[11]

Twain remembered that he had "made Honolulu howl" in the company of this diplomat, as well as the ambassador to Japan, who was traveling with the Burlingame party on returning to his own post. They all attended a ball on the Fourth of July and stayed up talking until three the next morning. "I only got tight once, though," he told Will Bowen in a letter the next month. "I know better than to get tight oftener than once in 3 months. It sets a man back in the esteem of people whose good opinions are worth having."[12] He left Hawaii something of a changed man, one who was clearly struggling to put the experience of at least the last eight years into clearer perspective. This new vision surveyed the river, the West, the coast, and now the Sandwich Islands, where some of his rough edges were starting to be smoothed away. He sailed on the *Smyrniote* on July 19 and arrived in San Francisco on August 13. He went to Sacramento to collect his pay, which amounted to twenty dollars a week plus one hundred for the *Hornet* letter. "They paid me a great deal more than they promised me," he told his mother and Pamela. "I suppose that means that I gave satisfaction, but they did not say so."[13]

15 Wild Humorist of the Pacific Slope

Evidently, it was Ambassador Burlingame who gave Twain the idea of lecturing by suggesting that he do it in the Far East. He had talked publicly before, of course, long ago in Keokuk at that printer apprentices' dinner and more recently as the burlesque Governor of the Third House in Carson City. Yet it would take some seed money and a newspaper sponsor to get such a project off the ground. Thanks to Emerson's success in what was still considered the West (mainly Ohio and adjacent states), the public lecture was becoming popular. As Paul Fatout remarks, by the end of the Civil War, "almost every town of any size had a young men's literary society, which arranged a course of six or eight lectures by visiting speakers."[1] This tradition had grown out of the lyceum movement in New England, where Emerson had first tried to apply the ideas of the European romantic movement to the United States and its Puritan origins.

Transcendentalism, as it was called, was pretty much exhausted by the end of the war, and the American public was hungry for something lighter and perhaps exotic. What better than an informative lecture about some lovely islands more than two thousand miles southwest of San Francisco ("why they were put away out there in the middle of the Pacific . . . is no business of ours") that was also funny? In chapter 78 of *Roughing It,* Twain described himself as returning to San Francisco "without means and without employment. I tortured my brain for a saving scheme of some kind, and at last a public lecture occurred to me!"[2] He suggests that he was rather isolated from the rest of the city, discouraged by friends to whom he showed a draft of his lecture, and not encouraged by the newspapers. But the facts from stories in the papers suggest that Mark Twain's first great success on the lecturer's platform originated in a conspiracy.

The first clue is that the Sandwich Islands lecture of October 2, 1866, wasn't that funny. Actually, it is difficult to tell whether it was funny, because, Paine's assertion aside, we do not have a verbatim account of the initial delivery of a talk that Twain gave more than forty times with variations as to audience and place. Certainly, aspects of it are still amusing, but the speech itself is rather long on information and short on humor. In a few subsequent performances of it—for example, in Petaluma—the local paper thought that Mark Twain as a lecturer had fallen "below mediocrity." Yet this criticism may have been provoked by the lecturer's failure to provide complimentary tickets to the press.[3]

It may have been Twain's delivery or the way he conducted himself onstage that made funny what today seems rather drab. Many testified that he could tell a story better than he could write one. Incredibly for someone who died as late as 1910 and made several recordings with Edison, apparently no recordings of his voice have survived. The closest we have is a 2.45-minute imitation of Twain reading from his Jumping Frog tale done by his former friend and neighbor William H. Gillette before a Harvard English literature class in 1934. It suggests that the tale told with his Missouri drawl was funnier than it is today in cold print. It was not only his accent that worked in his favor but also the informal way he lounged about the stage with his hands in his pockets, acting as if the audience wasn't even present. One auditor recalled that he had sat "simmering in laughter" through what he misperceived as merely Twain's introductory remarks, only to discover that he had been so amused for almost the entire lecture.[4]

Twain's humor was readily suggested by a handbill advertising the lecture at Maguire's Academy of Music, where potential auditors were told that the doors opened at seven and the "Trouble" was to begin at eight. The advertisement referred first to the informational part of the lecture on American missionaries, "the absurd Customs and Characteristics of the natives," and the volcano Kilauea. Beneath this announcement, partially in capital letters, were the following inducements:

A SPLENDID ORCHESTRA
Is in town, but has not been engaged
ALSO
A DEN OF FEROCIOUS WILD BEASTS
Will be on Exhibition in the next Block.

And so on.

The ad clearly assumed the success of the lecture, perhaps because Twain had the newspapers almost unanimously on his side. John McComb, one of the managers of the *Alta,* had come forward in full support of the lecturing idea. Probably encouraged by Twain's letters from Hawaii, he got Twain to approach Tom Maguire, whom the humorist had known in Virginia City, for the use of the hall at half price.[5] McComb's support put the *Alta* on Twain's side, and it and other like-minded newspapers published predictions for a large audience and a successful lecture. Hence, the fear of failure Twain described in *Roughing It* was probably an exaggeration to dramatize his initial struggles as a lecturer, an activity he was once again engaged in as that book came on the market in 1872. As the *Call* observed on September 30, "the various city papers have been busy congratulating their readers during the past week, that this keen observer and facile writer has consented to gratify the public with a *viva voce* description of the life and manners of the Hawaiian Islanders."

The same newspapers followed the lecture with high praise for the performance. It is true that the house was sold out in advance, leaving a few latecomers to the event out in the cold. But its success was probably not in its humor, if any of the texts that still exist are reliable, but in its entertaining way of conveying information about an exotic place. Although the typical California audience had largely emigrated from "the States," most Americans before the Civil War never traveled far from the place of their birth. Indeed, it was the war that got people, as soldiers, moving around the country and created an interest in other parts of the nation and the world. This national predisposal to the travel lecture helped, but his friends in the press guaranteed success. Only the *Golden Era* failed to join the effort of celebrating one of their own. "Mark made a number of very good hits, and then he made some passes which were not hits at all," the paper commented on October 7. It also suggested that the uniformity of praise was due more to fear than honesty: "They are all afraid of you, Mark; afraid of your pen."

Twain's reputation for retaliation in the press certainly followed him from Virginia City, but by 1866 he had many more friends than enemies in the Fourth Estate. Whatever the case, he netted four hundred dollars from this initial lecture and quickly made plans to take his show on the road. Between October 2 and December 15, 1866, when he left for the East Coast, he gave his Sandwich Islands lecture seventeen times.[6] His next stop was the Metropolitan Theater in Sacramento, where he was known for his Hawaii letters, which were in fact still coming out in the *Union.* Following appearances in a number of mining towns in California, he crossed over to Nevada and stood on October 31 before a full house in Virginia City. But he hesitated to give the lecture in Carson City on November 3 because of the miscegenation hoax he had played on its first ladies back in 1864. These fears were quickly allayed by a public invitation in the *Enterprise.* In his response, also published in the *Enterprise,* he thanked Carson City for its toleration "of one who has shamefully deserted the high office of Governor of the Third House of Nevada and gone into the Missionary business."[7]

Sam Clemens's return to Nevada as Mark Twain was marred only by a fake holdup played on him and Denis McCarthy, a one-time coproprietor of the *Enterprise* and Twain's lecture agent, who was in fact in on the hoax. Everybody thought that Twain, known in Virginia City as a practical joker, got what he deserved, but the hoaxee in this case was in fact somewhat angry—as the pranksters had brandished actual guns, causing the rising star to fear for his life. The two men were returning after dark from Gold Hill, where Twain had lectured on November 10, to Virginia City, a distance of around five miles. It marked Sam Clemens's final departure from that vast silver land of Nevada—to which he would return only vicariously to exploit his experiences in *Roughing It.*

Twain finished his tour of the Pacific slope where he had begun it—in

San Francisco, this time in Congress Hall on December 10. Although the hall wasn't filled to capacity, the lecture was well attended. This time he added an impromptu address to the audience, which no doubt contained many of his journalistic friends. By now he had made an agreement with the *Alta* to write letters about his trip back east. The idea, as earlier suggested, may have come from Burlingame, who thought he ought to travel to Asia. His plans were to return home to his family, then in St. Louis, via New York and then, after a well-earned reunion, to find a way to begin his new travels. Standing on the stage that night, he didn't quite know where he was headed ultimately or how. He just knew he had launched himself as both a lecturer and a travel writer and thought he would never again have to worry about a steady income. Little did he know what riches awaited him.

Acknowledging his kind treatment by the city (leading to the fame of the Jumping Frog), he thanked his "ancient comrades" and "brethren of the Press." He told them he was going home but added that he dreaded the changes he was bound to find there. As he would early demonstrate in the cave scene in *Tom Sawyer* in which Injun Joe dies and in the opening chapter of *Life on the Mississippi,* Mark Twain was ever fascinated with time and its ravages. "I shall share the fate of many another longing exile," he told his audience, "who wanders back to his early home to find gray hairs where he expected youth, graves where he looked for firesides, grief where he had pictured joy—everywhere change!"[8] The theme of death curiously hovered in the consciousness of this rising American humorist as he embarked on a voyage that would nearly kill him.

Travel across the Great Plains was not easy in 1866, though it would become far less arduous after the completion of the transcontinental railroad just three years later. An easier and not much longer way in terms of time to cross the continent was to take a ship down to either Panama or the Nicaragua Isthmus and cross by land and inland water to the Atlantic and take another ship north to New York. Having made the overland journey from Missouri to Nevada in 1861, Sam was not eager to revisit those hardships and dangers. He sailed on the steamship *America,* captained by the fifty-year-old Ned Wakeman, a most colorful character who would make a strong impression on Sam and appear in a number of his later fictions, including "Captain Stormfield's Visit to Heaven." The *America* sailed in "opposition" to the more established Pacific Steamship Company's Panama route. It may have attracted Sam because it was cheaper, though his pockets were presumably heavy with lecture receipts. Yet he might have had to stretch what he had. Thrift may also have been the reason a blushing unmarried couple took the same passage, to the shock of the other passengers. They planned to marry in New Jersey, they said, but Wakeman married them onboard five days out of San Francisco in a ceremony full of nautical metaphors. ("The world's got little enough fair weather in it as it is," Twain quoted the old salt in his second letter to the *Alta.* "Splice and make the most of it. Sail in company and help one another.")[9]

Yet the ceremony was one of the last delights on a journey that involved many deaths. On December 24 a young child died aboard the ship. Brought together in artificial ways as a ship's passengers often are, especially in times of danger, the *America*'s passengers and crew acted as if "they were related by blood to the child." On Christmas night, Twain told the *Alta,* the first officer and the boatswain's mate "held the canvassed corpse with its head resting on their shoulders and its feet upon the taffrail—at the conclusion [of the ceremony] there was a breathless pause; . . . a sharp plunge of the weighted body into the sea, a shudder from the startled passengers, a wild shriek from the young mother (a mere girl), and all was over."[10] Mark Twain was already traveling well beyond his now established reputation as a humorist.

When the *America* reached the port of San Juan del Sur on the Pacific on December 28, the passengers got their first hint that cholera awaited them on the other ocean. They heard a report that the deadly disease had broken out among six hundred passengers, many of them soldiers, coming from the East Coast. In fact, the sick had sailed on the very ship that Twain's group was to take up to New York. To get to Greytown on the east coast of Nicaragua, however, Twain's party had to travel by carriage and boat. During the first twelve-mile leg of a nearly four-hour journey through the Nicaraguan jungles, Twain, as he had in Hawaii, showed an interest in the native girls—"raven-haired, splendid-eyed

Nicaragua damsels standing in attitudes of careless grace." "They are virtuous according to their lights," he told his *Alta* readers, "but I guess their lights are a little dim."[11]

Once reaching Virgin Bay and the shores of Lake Nicaragua, they boarded a steamer to Fort San Carlos on the San Juan River. After a nearly all-day and overnight passage, they had to go ashore at Castillo to get around the rapids and change to another stern-wheeler, which brought them to Greytown on New Year's Eve. The following day the traveling party, enduring heavy surfs and drenching rain, boarded the *San Francisco* for New York. The first two cases of cholera on board became evident the very next day, and the death toll throughout this leg of Twain's trip from San Francisco would climb to seven. He himself feared for his life on January 5, after three had died, including a minister who had conducted two burials at sea. By now the ship was a floating hospital without medicine, and the dead were being thrown overboard within an hour of their last moments to ward off the spread of infection.[12] To make matters even worse, the ship's engine kept breaking down as it steamed around Cuba.

Its immediate destination was Key West, but the captain feared the ship would be quarantined, thereby trapping the healthy with the sick. This fear was not realized, as the port of Key West was more interested in making money than halting the disease. The port doctor called the sickness "malignant diarrhea" and, Twain told his readers back in San Francisco, "cheerfully let us land and spend $3,000 or $4,000" there. The sick quickly departed, as did others fearful of continuing the journey to New York. The cholera victims were also quickly forgotten by the *Alta* reporter, who was consumed with disgust at the greedy Key Westers who lived off the government by selling whiskey to the soldiers at Fort Taylor and running an expensive customhouse. On the other hand, he was pleased to be back in "the States" again after almost six years. Two more passengers died on the way up to New York, but as the ship moved out of the warm climate of the Gulf Stream, the January temperatures began to drop rapidly along with "all the fright about the disease."[13]

By the morning of January 12, 1867, the *San Francisco* was passing the snow-covered houses on Staten Island and returning Sam Clemens to the East to expand upon his new career as Mark Twain. He immediately recognized the Castle Garden, which he had visited thirteen years earlier as a teenage journeyman printer. Naturally, the vast city with its palisades and "its hundred steeples" had changed since his first visit. It now ran far beyond Union Square and past what would become known in the twentieth century as Times Square. He lodged on East 16th Street, but even from here it was difficult to get around the city except by walking. The omnibuses were so packed with passengers that a belated rider had to stand perilously on the open platforms. Sam was back in the States, if not yet home again in St. Louis.

PART II Writer in the East

16 Westerner in the East

The "Wild Humorist of the Pacific Slope" had finally come to Manhattan, by then beginning to rival Boston as the publishing center of the American universe. With hardly more than a year since his Jumping Frog story had appeared in the New York *Saturday Press,* there was a buzz about its author, this new funny man on the horizon called Mark Twain, perhaps because of the news of Charles Henry Webb's imminent publication of *The Celebrated Jumping Frog of Calaveras County, and Other Sketches.* In recycling the story for the *Californian* in the July 16, 1865, issue, the word "Celebrated" had been added to the title of Jim Smiley's story. Now with the tale's publication as a lead story in a book, that change seemed to underscore Sam's national literary debut. For at least the month of January 1867, he stayed at the Metropolitan Hotel at the corner of Broadway just below Houston Street, one of the "great caravan hotels" popular among Californians, with a capacity for six hundred guests. Because of postwar inflation, prices for a hotel room in New York City had more than doubled since his visit in 1853. He soon moved to cheaper accommodations above Union Square. "I room in East Sixteenth street, and I walk," he told his *Alta* readers in a letter dated February 2. "It is a mighty honest walk from there to anywhere else, and very destructive to legs, but then the omnibuses are too slow during this mixed rainy, snowy, slushy and hard-frozen weather, and the [street]cars too full." He added that the city "is all changed since I was here thirteen years ago, when I was a pure and sinless sprout."[1]

Twain had changed, too. His clean-shaven, still-boyish look at eighteen, in dress slightly rumpled, had transformed into that of a rather polished gentleman of thirty-one, still with a thick head of red hair but now sporting a heavy moustache, the face slightly leaner, but the eyes just as piercing. Only when he spoke in the same drawl of the Mississippi Valley did he betray his origins, speaking so slowly that easterners occasionally suspected that he was drunk. In fact, having long given up his promise made back in 1853 to his mother about not drinking, he spent some leisure hours at Pfaff's celebrated subterranean tavern on Broadway near Bleecker. For one thing, it was the hangout for Henry Clapp, the editor of the now defunct *Saturday Press.* Pfaff's was a well-known watering hole for New York literati of a bohemian persuasion.[2] Earlier in the decade, Twain's future best literary friend, William Dean Howells, was rumored to have shaken hands there with Walt Whitman, another regular in times past.

Symbolically, the meeting of Howells and Whitman, if indeed it truly occurred, was the age of Social Darwinism, with its hedges on the full meaning of evolution, coming up against the kind of gritty realism that would lead almost directly to determinism. Twain would walk the line between them throughout his literary career. For now, he was just a humorist with a book in press. *The Celebrated Jumping Frog of Calaveras County* would appear on April 30, 1867. Despite its dedication to John Smith ("It is said that the man to whom a volume is dedicated, always buys a copy"), he never personally made a dime on the book, though his publisher did. Twain also had another manuscript in hand at this time, a version of his Sandwich Island letters, parts of which eventually appeared in chapters 62 through 77 of *Roughing It.* He even submitted the manuscript to a New York publisher but eventually withdrew it, probably because the publishing house wasn't showing much interest.[3] Even the Jumping Frog book had been turned down by another publisher before Webb took it on, and Twain wasn't yet sure that he had a true book in him.

In the meantime he would make his living by writing for the newspapers and, soon thereafter, with a resumption of his lectures. He was still planning to travel around the world, but how to do it didn't become clear until sometime in February when he heard that members of the

Reverend Henry Ward Beecher's Brooklyn congregation were going on one of the country's first tourist cruises to Europe and the Holy Land. Tourism before the war had been restricted mainly to the North American landscape, a testament to the impact of the work of Frederick Church, Winslow Homer, and Thomas Moran, whose paintings, respectively, of Niagara Falls (shown at the Paris Exposition of 1867, when Twain would visit the city), the Catskills, and Yosemite, among other scenic wonders, helped focus Americans on the beauty of their own country. Now that interest expanded to the Old World, resulting in an invasion that Europeans would forever condescend to parody (though perhaps not so easily after the publication of *The Innocents Abroad*). In a letter dated only a day before his departure for St. Louis and a long-awaited reunion with his family, Twain wrote to his *Alta* readers that the passenger list of the *Quaker City* was filling up fast: "The ship is to have ample accommodations for 150 cabin passengers, but in order that there may be no crowding, she will only carry 110. The steamer fare is fixed at $1,250," but passengers were advised to bring an additional $500 in gold for extra expenses away from the ship.[4]

Beecher himself, the country's most famous clergyman and then minister of Brooklyn's Plymouth Congregational Church, was the main draw, but it was also rumored that General Sherman would join the cruise. Mark Twain soon got the *Alta* to pay his own fare in partial return for his travel letters chronicling the trip. Subsequently, both Beecher and Sherman failed to book passage on the steamer, prompting a number of the minister's congregation to withdraw from the passenger list, but at this point the ship's captain and organizer, Charles C. Duncan, could still be picky about the clientele. Potential passengers had to satisfy a committee as to their social standing. Duncan and Twain would clash in the newspapers in the next decade, but the seeds of their mutual dislike probably began to germinate even before the ship departed. Clemens, in the company of Edward H. House, a drama critic for the New York *Tribune* whom he had met for the first time in January at Webb's office, went down to the ship's offices to see Duncan about arranging his passage.

Perhaps after the two had made a visit to Pfaff's, House introduced

Clemens to Duncan as the "Rev. Mark Twain," who had been a missionary to the Sandwich Islands. Moreover, he was further introduced as a Baptist minister who wished to take part in the religious services on board. Beecher was a religious liberal, a Congregationalist who would have been uncomfortable with the fundamentalism of the Reverend Twain's faith. No matter, said Duncan, however reluctantly, and soon discovered that he had been the victim of a hoax. This story went to the *Alta* readers. The bad blood was initially on Duncan's side as the object of House and Clemens's trick, but ultimately it was Clemens who seethed over the captain's behavior, especially after he endured what he considered Duncan's phony religiosity during the cruise. When Twain attacked him in the newspapers in 1877 for another perceived offense, Duncan claimed that Mark Twain had been drunk the day they met (and in reply Twain admitted as much).[5] Prior to all that acrimony, however, Twain was securely on the passenger list of the *Quaker City*, and—as it turned out, following the loss of Beecher and Sherman—its most famous passenger.

But first he would have that reunion with his family in St. Louis. Mark Twain told his *Alta* readers in a letter dated March 15 that he left New York on the New Jersey Central on March 3 in the middle of a snowstorm. The sleeping car was full the first night, and this Civil War dropout sat up all night listening to the war stories of a young beardless veteran who had fought some of the bloodiest battles, including Second Bull Run and Antietam. Interestingly, Twain doesn't spell out for his western audience (which contained many former copperheads) which side the "handsome, modest, honest, good-hearted boy of twenty-three" fought for. Traveling twenty-five miles per hour, the train reached smoky Pittsburgh the next afternoon and St. Louis at midnight on March 5. "I went straight home," he wrote, "and sat up till breakfast time, talking and telling other lies."[6]

Like New York, St. Louis had changed, though not as much. It had added 50,000 more residents, bringing the 1867 count up to 250,000. During his visit, perhaps as a way of publicizing his forthcoming Jumping Frog collection, he told the title tale to a local Sunday school gathering, and its success led to a series of five Sandwich Islands lectures in the area, two in St. Louis and one each in Hannibal, Keokuk, and Quincy, Illinois. Following the first one, to an overflow audience at the Mercantile Library Hall on March 25, the St. Louis *Republican* noted that Twain had "succeeded in doing what we have seen Emerson and other literary magnates fail in attempting. He interested and amused a large and promiscuous audience." Ralph Waldo Emerson had been speaking in the area as late as February, giving a lecture entitled "The Man of the World" in Keokuk and Quincy.[7] Twain quoted the *Republican*'s review in his *Alta* letter of March 25, perhaps firing the first shot of a volley that would eventually be heard around the world of literary Boston exactly ten years later, in the form of his Whittier birthday dinner speech.

By this time Emerson had been invited back to Harvard. A year earlier, in 1866, the college (and its Brahmin literary community) had forgiven him for his heretical "Divinity School" lecture of 1838 and awarded him an honorary doctorate. (By then, New England Congregationalism had absorbed most of the nuances of Unitarianism, which undercut or compromised the distinction between Christ and the first self-reliant man, or transcendentalist.) Emerson was now an institution to be cherished, not feared by the establishment. He had even published the poem "Terminus," in which he announced, "It is time to be old." In the West, they would have agreed. On February 28, two days after Emerson lectured in Quincy, the editors of the Quincy *Herald* entitled their review "Another Bore." "The Man of the World" (not to be confused with his "Napoleon: The Man of the World," which had appeared in *Representative Men* in 1850) taught the Emersonian doctrine that the individual of action is also he who "knows the joys of the imagination."[8] But this was postwar America, in which action and the social animal ruled; it was the beginning of what Twain and Charles Dudley Warner would in the next decade christen "The Gilded Age."

While in St. Louis, Sam stayed with his sister Pamela and her two children, Annie and Sammy, at 1312 Chestnut Street. Clemens's mother, Jane, was living there as well. Pamela's husband, William Moffett, had died in 1865. Twain returned to New York in the middle of April. With the prospect of future employment on the *Quaker City* cruise, he registered first at the Metropolitan and then a few days later at the Westminster, which he described as "a hundred times better hotel." He was feeling on top of things after his successful lectures.[9]

As his ship wouldn't sail until June 8, he needed to make some more money lecturing. The exposure would also help to advertise the forthcoming Jumping Frog collection. He recalled in his autobiography that Frank Fuller, his old friend and the former governor of Utah Territory, had instigated his very first lecture in New York at Cooper Union on May 6. Now in business in New York, Fuller, Twain later remembered, was a "magnified and ennobled Col. Sellers," the garrulous illusionist of *The Gilded Age* (1874). Fuller "had one enthusiasm per day, and it was always a storm. He said I must take the biggest hall in New York and deliver that lecture of mine on the Sandwich Islands—said that people would be wild to hear me." Paine confirmed this version, but a year after Twain's death Fuller remembered it differently. "Frank," he said Twain told him, "I want to preach right here in New York, and it must be in the biggest hall to be found. I find it is the Cooper union." Twain, however, had the last word in a document written in 1895. There he wrote, "There are two private versions of the matter. . . . One of them is not true. I have always had more confidence in mine, because although he was older than I, he had not had as much practice in telling the truth."[10]

Fuller organized the Pacific slope people then in the city to attend the lecture in order to fill out the audience. Then he got James W. Nye, the territorial governor of Nevada when Twain was living there, to agree to introduce Twain at Cooper Union. In fact, Fuller paid for both the hiring of the hall and the advertising. As it turned out, though, the other governor out of Sam's past, Jim Nye, never showed up on the night of the lecture (later allegedly calling Sam "a damned Secessionist").[11] But Nye's unexpected absence contributed to Mark Twain's success, because it was that night he began the practice of introducing himself. Fuller had also papered the house with free tickets, certainly insurance against the stiff New York City competition of other events planned for the same evening.

"Mark Twain will deliver a Serio-Humorous Lecture Concerning Kanakadom, or the Sandwich Islands," the flyers said. In terms of the suspense and uncertainty, it was a reenactment of his first lecture in San

Francisco, when the "trouble" began at eight. Now it was "the Wisdom will begin to flow at 8." It was the same lecture, but it wasn't the same lecturer. For now Clemens had stepped more confidently into the role of Mark Twain, as not only an experienced lecturer but also (by now) the author of a just-published book. Once onstage and clearly abandoned by Nye, he lampooned the missing governor to all the fellow westerners in the audience. Nye had also gone missing as governor of Nevada, often leaving Orion Clemens to do all the heavy lifting. Nye, as noted, had most likely taken the job only to be available for one of the first senatorial spots once Nevada achieved statehood. Twain's allusion to Nye was a little payback for Orion, who had been exploited by this slick politico.

The Cooper Union lecture marked a new high in the career of Mark Twain as he prepared to embark on the *Quaker City*. "I was happy, and I was excited beyond expression," he remembered. "I poured the Sandwich Islands out on to those people with a free hand, and they laughed and shouted to my entire content. For an hour and fifteen minutes I was in Paradise."[12] If the Jumping Frog book failed (which it did, at least in the sense that it sold far fewer copies than he expected and he received no royalties from Webb) and if the travel writing fizzled, Twain was still assured of regular employment on the lecture circuit, even though he would come to despise its stress and discomfort. On the success of Cooper Union, he was invited to give the same lecture at the Brooklyn Athenaeum on May 22 and back in New York at Irving Hall on May 23.

With lecture fees in his pocket and his fare on the *Quaker City* paid, he could now turn his attention fully to the cruise, which was still somewhat in doubt because of the loss of the Beecher congregation, Beecher himself, and now General Sherman, who said he had to go out west to hunt Indians. "If the ship sails," Sam told the folks in St. Louis, "I sail in her—but I make no calculations, have bought no cigars, no seagoing clothing,—have made no preparations whatever—shall not pack my trunk till the morning we sail." The ship would sail with slightly more than half of the proposed quota of 110 passengers. Moses Beach, editor of the New York *Sun* and a long-standing member of Plymouth Church, more or less filled in for Beecher, his Brooklyn neighbor, as the nominal elder of the cruise. Two days before the ship sailed, he held a get-acquainted reception for the passengers at his home. "Yes, we are to meet at Mr Beach's next Thursday night," Sam told his mother; "& I suppose we shall have to be gotten up regardless of expense, in swallow-tails, white kids & everything *en régle.*" What he didn't tell his mother is that the night before sailing he got drunk with friends, including his new shipboard roommate Dan Slote, a Brooklyn businessman who smoked as much as Clemens. Slote's shipboard luggage included, Sam noted approvingly, three thousand cigars.[13]

17 Pilgrims on the Loose

Dan Slote and Mark Twain would have a future together, but their relationship would rupture in the end over a business deal gone sour. The humorist made few enemies during his lifetime, but anybody who wronged him, who betrayed his confidence, crossed the Rubicon. A pot-bellied merchant in his late thirties, Slote was one of Twain's innermost circle of friends on the trip. He could well afford a cruise that was six or seven times more expensive than the average round-trip crossing to Paris on a Cunard liner. In fact, he left the ship in Egypt and remained abroad for a few more months. By contrast, of course, Twain was earning his way by providing the *Alta* with fifty letters at twenty dollars apiece.

He and Slote occupied No. 10 on the *Quaker City*, the double cabin originally reserved for General Sherman and his daughter Minnie. Slote was also his closest male companion. Others included Abraham Reeves Jackson of Philadelphia, officially the ship's surgeon and unofficially the "guide-persecuting 'Doctor'" when the American pilgrims reached Europe. A little later in the cruise, Twain's first circle included Julius Moulton ("Moult") of St. Louis. About ten years younger than Twain, Moulton was also writing travel letters for a newspaper, even though his most recent job had been chief engineer on a railroad. Another member of this group, Jack Van Nostrand of New Jersey, didn't make the best first impression on Twain, but he soon warmed to the "good-hearted and always well-meaning" twenty-year-old, who may have gone to sea for his health. He died of tuberculosis about ten years later. He is referred to as the Interrogation Point in *The Innocents Abroad*.

There were seventeen women among the passengers. The most prominent as far as Mark Twain was concerned was Mary Mason Fairbanks, the thirty-nine-year-old wife of Abel Fairbanks, the part owner of the Cleveland *Herald*. She was also contributing letters to the newspaper. In her second of twenty-eight letters, she described Twain as "perfectly mirth-provoking" as he sat "lazily" at the ship's table "scarcely genteel in his appearance" but nevertheless interesting and attractive. "I saw to-day at dinner," she wrote, "venerable divines and sage looking men, convulsed with laughter at his drolleries and quaint original manners."[1] Mary Fairbanks would become "Mother" Fairbanks to Twain, and, in the letters he wrote not only to the *Alta* but also to the New York *Tribune* (signed) and *Herald* (unsigned), she would be the one who always tried to adjust his quaint manners.

Another who was struck by the humorist's folksy manners was young Charles Langdon, the seventeen-year-old son of Jervis Langdon of Elmira, New York, owner of coal and lumber interests in New York and Pennsylvania. The senior Langdon had made a fortune during the Civil War and, before that, had befriended Frederick Douglass, whose abolitionist campaign he quietly supported. He had sent his son abroad mainly to keep him away from the local taverns. What better place for him than on a cruise full of rich Christians? He had an older sister, Olivia Louise Langdon, who was twenty-one. Mention of the western humorist in letters home sparked an interest in Olivia that her younger brother immediately tried to discourage.

Langdon liked all the passengers, he told his mother on their second day at sea (actually the side-wheeler with sail was still in the New York lower harbor because of stormy weather), "but I am afraid we have some hard cases with us." On July 11, he wrote in response to questions about Twain that his sister had conveyed through their mother, "Now let me see what Libbie says & answer her questions. . . . I would say . . . that in regard to Mark Twain she is very much misstaken. He is one of the hardest characters we have with us." He added that Sam (and implicitly his companions) "drink a great deal." In a letter of August 21–22 he wrote that Twain's "moral character" was "anything but good." Charlie would soon change his opinion (though never completely) about his future brother-in-law. By September he had even shown Twain a picture of his sister and was urging his mother to get the back numbers of the *Alta* to read his letters.[2]

The other passengers, to name only a few, were colorfully interesting: William Gibson of Jamestown, Pennsylvania, a physician who, with an overblown sense of self-importance, carried with him a letter of introduction from the Department of Agriculture addressed "To the United States Ministers & Consuls in Europe, Asia & Africa"; the self-appointed poet Bloodgood Haviland Cutter of Long Island, called the "Poet-Lariat" in *The Innocents Abroad,* who provided rhymes for almost every occasion; Frederick H. Greer ("young Wm. Blucher"), who was constantly distracted by the change of ship's time as it sailed east; and Colonel William R. Denny of Winchester, Virginia, who kept, next to Twain's, one of the fullest records of the trip.[3]

Denny, as he described himself, was someone about whom "not much of good can be said . . . except that he tries to do right and finds himself in the wrong very often." Apparently something of a moralist, he described Twain in terms similar to Charlie Langdon's first impressions: "Saml L Clemens of Sanfrancisco California a wicked fellow that will take the name of the Lord in vain, that is no respector of persons, yet he is liberal, kind and obliging, and if he were only a christian would make his mark."[4] One can well imagine how shocking, initially at least, Twain's liberal use of "damn," "goddamn," and "hell" would have been to these overly saturated Christians. The origin of his behavior was the West of Nevada and California, not the "South" of Missouri and the Mississippi Valley, where manners sometimes disguised immorality. Twain was like a man just back from a war zone in terms of polite society.

Yet he was relatively famous. Twenty-seven-year-old Emily Severance, traveling with her banker husband, was fascinated with Twain and became something of a confidante. Another female passenger, Julia Newell, the most outgoing of the women and another newspaper travel writer, from Janesville, Wisconsin, would make one of the ship's side trips (through Spain) with Twain and some of his circle. On June 22 she described him to the Janesville *Gazette* as "a rather handsome fellow, but talks to you with an abominable drawl that is exasperating." She added, "Whether he intends to be funny for the amusement of the party, I have not yet ascertained."[5] Miss Newell also became friends with Dr. Jackson and, after his wife died, married him in 1871. Emma Beach was another of the female cohorts, the seventeen-year-old daughter of Moses Beach. Young Emma was one of Twain's favorites, and he may have had for her more than an avuncular attraction.

The voyage of the *Quaker City* began on June 8 (the vessel actually leaving the harbor on June 10 because of the storm) and concluded on November 19, 1867. During those nearly six months, the ship stopped in various European ports, skirted Russia, and allowed side visits through the Holy Land and elsewhere. By the last week of June the ship had reached Gibraltar, and Twain with a party of seven took a steamer to Tangier. The *Quaker City* docked in Marseille on July 4; here Twain, Dr. Jackson, and Slote took the train for Paris. Unfortunately, Twain lost the original letter he apparently wrote about this leg of their European tour, and so the reader of *The Innocents Abroad* is consequently disappointed at the treatment of France by one of the world's great Francophobes.

By the middle of July, the ship had stopped in Genoa, from which the same trio took a train for Milan and Como, and then went by steamer to Bellagio on Lake Como. The *Quaker City* docked in Naples for the first eleven days in August, seven of which it was quarantined. On August 7 Twain and his friends left the ship for Ischia, Mount Vesuvius, and Capri. On August 14 he and three companions violated the Athens quarantine and hiked to the Acropolis. The ship docked at Constantinople on August 17. By the end of the month, the ship's party had seen Sevastopol, Odessa, Yalta, and (for the second time) Constantinople. It was from Smyrna on September 6 that most of the passengers took a train to Ephesus. Four days later, the *Quaker City* reached Beirut. Twain and seven other passengers set out the next day on an overland journey through the Holy Land. They rejoined the ship in Jaffa early in October. By the end of that first week, Twain's party arrived at Alexandria and took a train to Cairo and the pyramids at Giza, returning to the ship two days later. By mid-October, the ship was headed home, with only two extended stops at Gibraltar and Bermuda. From Gibraltar, Twain traveled through Spain. The stop in Bermuda was the first of eight visits he made during his lifetime, the last indeed only weeks before his death.[6]

In going abroad for the first time aside from his visit to Hawaii, Mark Twain had something of what we today would call an "attitude." Many before him had worshipped at the shrine of Europe and the Old World. One of them was Henry Wadsworth Longfellow, as good a versifier as Poe, but also a poet whose work was often undercut by the love of things European. Longfellow, as we shall see, would become another of those three drunks in Twain's Whittier birthday speech ten years hence. Following the example of Washington Irving's dreamy recollection of England in *The Sketch-Book* (1819–20), Longfellow, after spending more than three years in Europe, wrote *Outre-Mer: A Pilgrimage Beyond the Sea* (1833–34), which overflowed with German romanticism and American deference to the Old World.

The New Pilgrim's Progress, as Twain originally titled it (he was persuaded to use this as the subtitle for *The Innocents Abroad*) rejected not only the typical guidebooks of the day, which told Americans what to admire and how to behave, but also the dictum that European culture was superior to American culture. "What is there in Rome," he would ask in chapter 26 of America's first honest travel book, "for me to see that others have not seen before me? . . . What is there for me to feel, to learn, to hear, to know, that shall thrill me before it pass to others?" In other words, what could this civilization that represented what Emerson had once called "the dry bones of the past" really teach him? But if he were Roman, what wonders would he discover by going to America? He would say upon his return: "I saw there a country which has no overshadowing Mother Church, and yet the people survive. I saw a government which never was protected by foreign soldiers at a cost greater than that required to carry on the government itself. I saw common men and common women who could read."

This was the New World idealism of Cotton Mather, who wrote in *The Wonders of the Invisible World* (1692) of an Englishman returning from the Puritan settlement and declaring before Parliament: "I have been seven years in a country where I never saw one man drunk, or heard one oath sworn, or beheld one beggar in the streets all the while." Twain was writing a new, albeit secular pilgrim's progress, one about an America that had survived a terrible quarrel with itself to become truly whole as a nation—at least in terms of its foreign policies and overall government. It mirrored Twain's own quarrel with himself—that individual who would soon be learning to combine his various skills into one unity of purpose. This southerner-turned-westerner-turned-easterner, as his makeup would ultimately develop, had not come east to sit at the feet of New England culture, the way his future friend and literary confidant William Dean Howells had done. Indeed, his European trip was merely a dress rehearsal for his invasion of New England culture as a modern-day Brother Jonathan, whose shrewdness was not to be confused with any European sense of refinement.

In his epistles to the *Alta* and elsewhere, he lambasted many of these traditions and cultural sanctities. The critiques would soften when the travel letters were turned into a book. In fact, he was terrified when the *Alta* later threatened to make a book out of the original letters. It was bad enough that the newspaper was still publishing them well into 1868 when he was at work on the book version of these critiques. "My publishers want me to write the book all over new, & not mind what the *Alta* does—but *that* won't do," he told Mary Fairbanks.[7] Based as it ultimately was on the *Alta* letters, the book—indeed Mark Twain's literary debut as the author of a real *book*—was irreverent enough to be funny to the masses. Even the use of the term "poet-lariat," which he applied to the doggerel-spouting Cutter, was an offhand critique of the world of English poetry and its poet laureates such as Wordsworth. Notre Dame, that most famous of European churches, was described as a "brown old Gothic pile." "The handsomest women we have seen in France," he would remark in chapter 15, "were born and reared in America."

In Italy, he even went after great art (reminding us of Van Wyck Brooks's famous remark that Mark Twain was an artist who hated art).[8] "Anyone who is acquainted with the old masters," he says in chapter 19, "will comprehend how much 'The Last Supper' is damaged when I say that the spectator cannot really tell whether the disciples are Hebrews or Italians." Later (in chapter 27) he decries the excess of Michelangelo and the other painters of old who "fairly swarm" the Vatican and radiate outward through Italy by saying: "I do not want Michelangelo for breakfast—for luncheon—for dinner—for tea—for supper—for between meals." He and the other Old Masters "painted Virgins enough and popes enough and saintly scarecrows enough to people paradise almost, and these things are all they did paint." Finally, "I have never felt so fervently thankful, so soothed, so tranquil, so filled with a blessed peace as I did yesterday when I learned that Michelangelo was dead."

Religion, of course, comes in for a sanitary ribbing. Before the American Publishing Company would agree to publish *The Innocents Abroad* in 1869, Elisha Bliss had to overrule his board of directors by threatening to issue the book himself.[9] This was because of the irreverent nature of the book's comments on religion, which were still tame, especially when compared to several of Twain's late-life (and unpublished until after his death) satires on heaven and the Bible. When the firm published *The Innocents Abroad,* for example, it also issued J. E. Stebbins's *Illustrated History of the Bible; Its Origins, Truth, and Divinity.* In Twain's book (chapter 27), his insouciant group of "incorrigible pilgrims," who readily pilfer sacred artifacts, ask whether a mummy is dead, while addressing their foreign guide as "Ferguson." The Sea of Galilee (chapter 48) is best seen in the pitch black of night; its beauty, Twain implies, is merely the extension of religious ideologies about the Holy Land. In chapter 53 these simpleminded religionists weep at the tomb of Adam.

Yet *The Innocents Abroad* is replete with many evocative passages that reveal profound sentiment. In Damascus (chapter 45), Twain writes, it feels strange, not lugubriously sad as it is at Adam's grave, "to be standing on ground that was once actually pressed by the feet of the Saviour." "I cannot comprehend this," he concludes, because "the gods of my understanding have been always hidden in clouds and very far away." Christ, he remarks two chapters later, remains to him "a mysterious stranger." Sam Clemens was reared with the Bible and was thoroughly familiar with it by the age of ten. Hence, even in his blossoming agnosticism (which he would soon have to curb in order to marry), he was respectful of the biblical fact of Christ. "One of the most astonishing things that have yet fallen under our observation," he wrote about Syria and the Holy Land, "is the exceedingly small portion of the earth from which sprang the now flourishing plant of Christianity." The longest journey Christ ever made was barely more than a hundred miles: "he spent his life, preached his gospel, and performed his miracles within a compass no larger than an ordinary county in the United States."

18 Love in a Locket

While Mark Twain was still traveling in Spain, he sent a letter back to his old friend and former boss Joe Goodman, who published parts of it in the Virginia City *Enterprise.* "Between you and I," he wrote, "this pleasure party of ours is composed of the damnedest, rustiest, ignorant, vulgar, slimy, psalm-singing cattle that could be scraped up in seventeen States." He prefaced this remark by saying that he hadn't let it out yet, "but am going to." The next day this cat with nine lives was already out of the bag. While the *Quaker City* was docked in Cadiz, Spain, for refueling, the ship's mail delivery contained a copy of Twain's letter to the New York *Tribune* of September 19, in which he disparaged many of the passengers while extolling the social talents of Mary Fairbanks during their meeting with the czar of Russia in Yalta. By the time the ship reached New York on November 19, Clemens was in hot water with any number of the passengers. Their wrath was further fueled by an article he then published in the New York *Herald* entitled "The Quaker City Pilgrimage," a piece unsigned but of obvious authorship, which the *Herald* later confirmed. It even listed the actual names of the passengers.[1]

The article complained that the voyage was anything but a pleasure cruise because of the puritanical nature of many of the passengers. Instead, he wrote, "the pleasure ship was a synagogue, and the pleasure trip was a funeral excursion without a corpse," adding that there is "nothing exhilarating about a funeral excursion without a corpse." (No doubt, Jane Clemens, who enjoyed any and all funeral processions in her old age, would have agreed.) The article, in its way, was another trial balloon for *The Innocents Abroad.* About their excursion to Paris, he wrote there and in his book that the French simply stared when the pilgrims spoke French: "We never did succeed in making those idiots understand their own language." As to the rest of the cruise, "Well, we were at home in Palestine. It was easy to see that that was the grand feature of the expedition. We had cared nothing much about Europe. We galloped through the Louvre, the Pitti, the Ufizzi, the Vatican. . . . We examined modern and ancient statuary with a critical eye in Florence, Rome or anywhere we found it, and praised it if we saw fit, and if we didn't we said we preferred the wooden Indians in front of the cigar stores of America."[2]

Many of the passengers were "howling" about the *Herald* article, but Mrs. Fairbanks tried to lighten the mood by arguing for Mark Twain's future as a respectable writer. "'Mark Twain,'" she wrote in her last letter to the Cleveland *Herald,* "may have ridiculed our prayer-meetings and our psalm-singing—that is his profession—and his newspapers expected it of him; but the better man, Samuel L. Clemens, I believe in his heart reverences the sacred mission of prayer, and will, I am sure, often recall with satisfaction the evening hours when his voice blended with others in the hymns of the 'Plymouth Collection.'"[3] Sam appreciated the protection Mrs. Fairbanks offered him and her other "cubs," who included young Charlie Langdon. It is probably fair to say that this rough humorist from the West would never have successfully wooed the genteel Olivia Louise Langdon without "Mother" Fairbanks's belief in and support for Mark Twain's potential as a "cultivated" writer. This mother of two children of her own and one step-daughter had married the widowed Abel Fairbanks in 1852 and raised their three children. She would become the western reserve of the Clemens-Langdon union.

Back home, Twain hit the ground running. Two days after the arrival of the *Quaker City* in New York, he shifted to Washington, D.C., taking up a job as private secretary to one of the senators from the new state of Nevada, William M. Stewart. This position wasn't any more stable or remunerative than the one he had had with Orion in Nevada. And the relationship apparently was not strong either. In 1908 Stewart described the arrival of Clemens at 224 F Street North, where the two men planned to live: "I was seated at my window one morning when a very disreputable-looking person slouched into the room. He was arrayed in a seedy suit, which hung upon his lean frame in bunches with no style worth mentioning. A sheaf of scraggy black hair leaked out of a battered old slouch hat, like stuffing from an ancient Colonial sofa, and an evil-smelling cigar butt, very much frazzled, protruded from the corner of his mouth. He had a very sinister appearance. He was a man I had known around the Nevada mining camps several years before."[4] This portrait, while perhaps having some semblance of truth, was also an ill-spirited exaggeration, payback for the illustration of a one-eyed Stewart in a slouch hat that Clemens had inserted at the last moment in *Roughing It*.

Twain used his position as senatorial secretary for the next two months as a base from which to write letters for at least three different newspapers and to entertain invitations to lecture. He told his family on November 25 that he had received eighteen invitations to lecture at one hundred dollars apiece, but he told Frank Fuller that he didn't want to "start in the provinces."[5] By now, however, he was well enough known to get another kind of invitation. In a letter dated November 21, 1867, Elisha Bliss, secretary and later president of the American Publishing Company in Hartford, Connecticut, inquired as to whether Clemens would like to revise and collect his *Quaker City* letters in a book. Bliss, a clever and sometimes devious businessman, would become Mark Twain's publisher for more than a decade. "We are perhaps," he told Sam, "the oldest subscription house in the country." This was lowbrow publishing, scorned by most established and eastern writers, in which sales agents went into the towns and hinterlands of America to gather subscriptions before the first copy was printed. They took along a so-called prospectus, bound copies of sample chapters (and illustrations), and recorded the orders in the back pages, which were lined for the names and addresses of customers.

The American Publishing Company had been successful in using this approach with Albert Deane Richardson's memoir as a wartime journalist and Confederate prisoner, and it was now set to publish his *Beyond the Mississippi* (1867) and *Personal History of Ulysses S Grant* (1868), two titles that proved to be prescient indications of Twain's future as a writer and later as a publisher. (In fact, Richardson's biography of Grant may have marked the beginning of Twain's lifelong fascination with the conquering general, whom he met for the first time in early 1868.) Twain probably lied when he told Bliss that he had "other propositions for a book," but this response would not have discouraged the cagey Bliss, who ultimately had to stare down his company board to publish the irreverent *Innocents.* Sam told Bliss he knew of Richardson's first book, *The Secret Service, The Field, The Dungeon, and the Escape* (1865) and knew something about "the subscription plan of publishing."[6] Richardson, a flamboyant reporter for the New York *Tribune,* was gaining (before his untimely death in 1869 at the hands of a jealous ex-husband) the very kind of popularity that Twain craved. Twain was definitely interested, especially since *The Celebrated Jumping Frog of Calaveras County,* while published in the traditional way, had failed him financially. Richardson's own first book, on the other hand, was still flourishing in the wake of the Civil War and would sell more than a hundred thousand copies.

As Christmas approached, Twain stayed on in Washington, writing his letters, visiting at least one session of Congress as Stewart's secretary, and also trying to secure a place for his brother Orion in the Department of the Interior. Walt Whitman had recently been fired from his position as a third-class clerk in that department on the grounds that he was the author of a "dirty book," and we might wonder whether Sam Clemens, or Mark Twain, would have been more acceptable (even as a source of reference for his brother, a former federal employee) to Interior Secretary James Harlan, a former professor of mental and moral science from Iowa. Whatever the case, Orion continued to flounder in Keokuk, Iowa. Twain also kept up his familiar epistolary conversations with "Mother" Fairbanks. He told her that he had received a letter from Charlie Langdon. In fact, though he didn't know it yet, he would soon meet Charlie's parents and—most important—his sister. He had already seen her picture in a miniature back in September while still on the cruise. "A good wife," he told Mrs. Fairbanks, "would be a perpetual incentive to progress," but then he joked away the idea by saying that he wanted "a good wife—I want a couple of them if they are particularly good." Then he turned serious again, promising lifelong fidelity because the girl he married would have to be above him socially, would have to uplift him. "I wouldn't expect to be 'worthy' of her," he told his maternal friend. "I wouldn't *have* a girl that *I* was worthy of. *She* wouldn't do. She wouldn't be respectable enough."[7] It is fairly obvious that he already had a particular woman, or at least a type, in mind. Indeed, his association with this class of American female for five months on the *Quaker City* had stimulated such an interest, embodied mainly in the character of Mary Fairbanks.

Olivia Langdon had grown up in Elmira, New York, then a thriving community served by the New York and Erie Railroad, in a palatial home in the center of town (today the site of a small shopping center), but also exactly one mile from one of the worst prisoner-of-war camps in the North. It had been dubbed "Hellmira" for its treatment of Confederate prisoners, three thousand of whom perished there from starvation and disease. During her teenage years she had been mysteriously paralyzed by what we now think was a case of neurasthenia, then particularly common among women of child-bearing age. Whether or not her illness was psychosomatic, it would continue to manifest itself annually, Twain would recall in a letter twenty-nine years after their marriage, in "a hard and wasting dysentery."[8] Olivia lay in a shuttered bedroom for two years until a faith healer came and ordered her to stand and walk. She had just turned twenty-two when she met Clemens, and in one or another of the photographs of her that he first saw in Charlie Langdon's stateroom on the *Quaker City,* she bears a slight resemblance to Sam's mother, Jane Clemens. And, as her brother's ignored caveat about Twain's questionable moral character (quoted in the previous chapter) may suggest, she was ready to meet Mark Twain and perhaps to fall in love with him.

One puzzler in the life of this mysterious stranger is how Olivia's father, this coal and lumber baron who hobnobbed with national leaders, ever allowed his daughter to become involved with a man of the slightest questionable character. Ample documentation from the autobiography and elsewhere shows that Jervis Langdon asked for letters of reference when Sam announced his serious intentions and that Langdon received discouraging responses (that Twain, for example, while in the West got drunk "oftener than was necessary"). Clearly, it was a case of love at first sight that could not be reversed. Livy, as she was familiarly addressed, was a sensitive young woman, well educated for her time but with a history of physical and mental fragility. Her future mate was a man desperate for a woman he could not only respect but also worship, someone whose angelic, girl-like tenderness made her utterly desirable in the nineteenth century. No Victorian-era father sensitive enough to become a champion for fugitive slaves, as Langdon had been, was going to miss the point here. Their union was simply inevitable. It had been only four years since she recovered from her illness, triggered by a fall on the ice, and as Twain later wrote in his autobiography, "she was never strong again while her life lasted."[9] He would become her protector.

Returning to New York on Christmas Day, Twain stayed at Dan Slote's place in Manhattan and saw some of his closest allies on the *Quaker City*. On New Year's Day, as he told his mother, recalling the point later in his autobiography almost exactly, he started out to make a number of social calls but was stopped in his tracks at the home of a Mrs. Thomas S. Berry on West 44th Street, where he encountered Olivia Langdon. She was there that day to help her friend receive holiday guests. "Charlie Langdon's sister was there (beautiful girl,) & Miss Alice Hooker, another beautiful girl, a niece of Henry Ward Beecher's," he wrote on January 8, 1868. "We sent the old folks home early, with instructions not to send the carriage till midnight, & then I just staid there & deviled the life out of those girls." In fact, he had first met his future wife the night before, on New Year's Eve. After a night of drinking during Christmas week with the "Quaker City night-hawks," including Charlie Langdon, he called on the "cub" at the St. Nicholas Hotel, where the young man was staying with his parents and sister, whom Sam later remembered as "a sweet & timid & lovely young girl." The Langdons had obviously heard much about the humorist and invited him to dine with them that evening, after which the party heard Charles Dickens, a favorite writer of Sam's, on his second and last tour of America, read from *David Copperfield* at Steinway Hall.[10]

After New Year's Day, Twain would not see Olivia for another eight months, when he finally visited her in Elmira. He did, however, visit

Alice Hooker, the other pretty girl he had met, daughter of John and Isabella Hooker, in Hartford. She lived with her parents in the Nook Farm community to the west of town. Hartford was also the home of the American Publishing Company and Elisha Bliss. During the next two months Twain visited the publisher and perhaps developed an early interest in Nook Farm, which was the home of such writers as Harriet Beecher Stowe (related to the Hookers) and Charles Dudley Warner, co-owner of the prominent Hartford *Courant* and future co-author with Twain of *The Gilded Age.* The reason he didn't visit Livy sooner is that he would leave for San Francisco on March 11 and not return east until the beginning of August. He also kept up a correspondence with young Emma Beach, so we have to wonder just how committed he was to Livy at this point. It appears, however, that he was simply biding his time, ratcheting up his name and reputation, so to speak, through the book and other activities before making his intentions known in Elmira.

Back in Washington on January 11, he had given a late-night toast to "Woman" at the second annual banquet of the local newspaper correspondents' club. It suggests the state of his mind about the so-called weaker sex and the institution of marriage. What follows is part of an actual newspaper stenographer's record; it also tells us something about the idea of women in America in 1868: women were an institution that kept the opposite sex safely away from its inner animal.

> Human intelligence cannot estimate what we owe to woman, sir. She sews on our buttons, [laughter,] she mends our clothes, [laughter,] she ropes us in at the church fairs. . . . Wheresoever you place woman, sir—in whatsoever position or estate—she is an ornament to that place she occupies, and a treasure to the world. [Here Mr. Twain paused, looked inquiringly at his hearers and remarked that the applause should come in at this point. It came in. Mr. Twain resumed his eulogy.]

He then catalogued the names of the noblest women in history: Cleopatra, Desdemona, Florence Nightingale, Joan of Arc, even the naked Mother Eve, who "was ornamental, sir—particularly before the fashions changed," and the mother of George Washington, who "raised a boy that could not lie."[11] Twain, of course, had already made fun of that legend before in the West.

As this speech suggests and as his courtship letters confirm, Sam Clemens envisioned woman as his savior and marriage as his salvation. Woman—and in this case, Livy—was the ornament to his claim of civilization. He would soon promise almost everything to gain her hand. He would even try to become a Christian again (doubly difficult after the *Quaker City* experience), and, in the biggest challenge of all, he would give up smoking (for a time).

19 The Innocent at Home

If Twain was indeed committed to Livy only a few months into the relationship, he wasn't telling anybody about it. In a recently recovered letter to his sister-in-law in Keokuk on February 21, 1868, he sounds as though he is playing the field and enjoying the recent acclaim stemming from his postvoyage letters in the *Tribune* and *Herald.* "I must answer some letters of 'Quaker City' ladies," he told Mollie. "They are indefatigable correspondents, & exceedingly pleasant withal. I give them a paragraph from the book, now & then, just to hear them howl." Earlier in the letter he speaks of receiving "a dainty little letter" from Lou Conrad, a neighbor of the Clemenses in St. Louis. "But what worries me," he continued, "is that I have received no letter from my sweetheart in New York for three days. This won't do. I shall have to run up there & see what the mischief is the matter. I will break that girl's heart. I am getting too venerable now to put up with nonsense from children."[1]

Mollie may have known the identity of the second woman, who remains a mystery woman in the life of Mark Twain, but the allusion is probably not to Olivia Langdon. For Twain, Olivia never left her pedestal, and his tone here may suggest someone flirtatious and naively clever. The reference does establish Twain's emotional state as he entered the laborious and often frustrating process of writing and revising his second book.

The first obstacle was the *Alta,* which, in an unusual step for any newspaper, had copyrighted Twain's letters and now threatened to make a book of them itself, denying him the right to do so. Bliss suggested that he simply rewrite the letters, but that was out of the question. He would, he knew, have to make serious revisions in the *Alta* letters for a book, mainly toning down the religious and cultural irreverence and cleaning up his use of slang. Yet, whatever the changes, the *Alta* letters and *The Innocents Abroad* would obviously tell the same story. So on March 11 he left Washington behind and sailed on the *Henry Chauncey* out of New York, essentially reversing his arduous journey of a year before. He was more worried about the damage that the *Alta*'s planned publication might cause his newly won literary reputation in the East than he was about not being able to use the material for his own book. "If the *Alta*'s book were to come out with those wretched, slangy letters unrevised," he told Mary Fairbanks, "I should be utterly ruined."[2]

He arrived in San Francisco on April 2 and immediately began his negotiations with the *Alta.* He also lectured at least twenty times between his arrival in San Francisco and return to New York in late July, including two shipboard performances. In one of the more intriguing intersections in American literary history, he spoke in his first San Francisco appearance on April 6 before a "'Literary Society' recently formed by the younger members of Rev. Dr. Charles Wadsworth's church." That Reverend Wadsworth would be Emily Dickinson's "dearest earthly friend," who had led the Calvary Presbyterian Church in the city since 1862, following a ministerial stint in Philadelphia, where the subsequently reclusive poet met him. Wadsworth's national reputation as a clergyman was second only to Henry Ward Beecher's, but unlike Beecher (and like Dickinson) he was apparently a shy individual, who never greeted his congregation after services. At least according to the Dickinson legend, Wadsworth had broken the belle of Amherst's heart when he moved west. Twain had known of Wadsworth since at least March 4, 1866, when he attended one of the clergyman's sermons. In a section of his *Enterprise* letter titled "Reflections on the Sabbath" and published that year about March 5 or 6, he had praised Wadsworth's style of sermonizing, which included jokes delivered in a deadpan manner and criticism of Sunday school books, points of view that accorded well with Clemens's own.[3]

It is not altogether clear how Twain convinced the *Alta* editors to drop their plans for a book and give him full permission to use his letters elsewhere. By early May he told Mary Fairbanks that the matter had been settled in his favor. At first they had wanted to give him a 10 percent royalty on their book, but Twain argued that such a book would not reach his eastern audience and thus would cost him a fortune in lost royalties there. It was probably the goodwill he had established through his reputation as a humorist in San Francisco as well as his having staunch friends on the newspaper staff (he was praised by the *Alta* while he was in the city) that persuaded the editors to drop their claim, including even their request that the paper be thanked in the preface to *The Innocents Abroad.* The book's future author spent the rest of his western visit lecturing again, both before and after his confrontation with the *Alta,* in California and Nevada. The highlight of the 1868 tour came on April 14, when Clemens spoke at Platt's Hall, the house packed with an audience of sixteen hundred. He had given a lecture called "The Frozen Truth" on January 9 in Washington but now revised the title to "Pilgrim Life, Being a Sketch of His Notorious Voyage to Europe, Palestine, Etc., on Board the Steamship Quaker City."[4]

These lectures helped advertise the future book, and they also no doubt assisted Twain in the process of revising his *Alta* letters for it. The claim that he was revising mainly for a different audience in the East is probably exaggerated. American humor of the West and Southwest had long been familiar to New York readers of *The Spirit of the Times,* which published the best of what was being written before the Civil War.[5] But a book was surely different from a series of newspaper articles because it required context and transitions that weekly letters did not. Clemens, as we have noted, also had to modify his expressions, purifying coarse passages and avoiding the charge of blasphemy. Generally, the story gets funnier with the revisions, but occasionally his changes backfire. The famous weeping-at-the-tomb-of-Adam scene in chapter 53, for example, is perhaps more richly humorous in the newspaper version, where Twain says he "shed some tender tears over poor old Adam" because he had lost so much by dying "young": "He had not seen the telegraph, or the locomotive, or the steamboat; he did not even see the flood. He missed the Paris Exposition." In the revision, also raucously funny, the narrator simply "burst into tears" because the "noble old man" didn't live long enough to see his "blood relation," having died "six thousand brief summers before I was born."[6]

Generally in the revision, he was kinder about the piety of his fellow passengers than he had been in either the *Alta* or the two New York papers. He also reduced the vulgarity of the fictional Mr. Brown, who had accompanied him on his travels since Hawaii. He completed much of this revision while still in San Francisco. As the editors of the scholarly edition of Twain's letters note, more than half of the manuscript consisted of revised printed letters from the *Alta* and New York *Tribune* and *Herald*. He also persuaded Bret Harte to read his work, and he responded gratefully to Harte's recommended cuts in the material—possibly a total of sixty-five pages of manuscript.[7]

When he got back to New York, Twain was eager to bring his latest copy up to Bliss in Hartford, but the publisher put him off because he was busy with Richardson's book on Grant. The two may have met in New York in very early August, but Twain also visited Bliss in Hartford for a week starting on August 7. By that time the American Publishing Company had possession of the manuscript and was in the process of providing extensive illustrations for it. Ten days later, he told "Mother" Fairbanks—who was vexed about something, possibly the fact that her "son" hadn't visited her in Cleveland before making his recent trip to California (the last in his life, it would turn out)—that he planned to return to New York the next day and, shortly thereafter, travel to Elmira, ostensibly to visit Charlie Langdon.[8] The two *Quaker City* friends also planned to visit Mary Fairbanks in Cleveland in September.

In his authorized biography, which came out under the watchful eye of Clemens's daughter Clara in 1912, just two years after Twain's death, Paine describes in fairy-tale fashion the way the rising humorist fell in love with the delicate damsel. Charley picked Twain up at the train station in nearby Waverly (mainly because the visitor had taken the slower train from New York and didn't reach Elmira till nearly midnight) and got him settled in for the night without meeting any other family members. "A gay and happy week followed," the biographer tells us, "a week during which Samuel Clemens realized more fully than ever that in his heart there was room for only one woman in all the world."[9] Livy, too, Paine adds, realized a thing or two.

During the visit, extended into the first week of September because of a minor carriage accident the injuries from which Twain exaggerated, he proposed marriage. The next we know, according to the first of more than a hundred courtship letters over the next eighteen months (she kept most of his, but we have only one of hers during this period), he was addressing her as his "Honored Sister." By this time he had returned to St. Louis to visit his mother again. Livy had, according to the decorum of the day, already refused his first proposal and agreed to carry on a correspondence with him only if they treated each other as "brother" and "sister." He thanked her on September 21 for letting him down "so gently when you could have wounded so deeply," but he confided his frustration to close friends in New York, saying that he was in love with a beautiful girl who was unfortunately rich.[10] He very much resented the label of "fortune hunter" and was determined even before the success of *The Innocents Abroad* to support his wife on his own earnings, something he wasn't always able to do in later years.

When she finally said yes in November and her parents gave their conditional approval pending appropriate character references from the West, he was about to begin a winter lecture tour performing "The American Vandal Abroad" under the auspices of the American Literary Bureau. His original schedule of ten lectures ultimately grew to forty-three in nine different states from New York to Iowa between November 17 in Cleveland and March 20, 1869, in Sharon, Pennsylvania. The third lecture in this exhausting series took place at the opera house in Elmira on November 23, around the time his engagement to Livy was fixed. "Mr. & Mrs. L. have yielded a *conditional* consent," he told Mary Fairbanks. "Livy has said, over & over again, the word which is so hard for a maiden to say. . . . She isn't my sister any more—but some time in the future she is going to be my wife."[11]

That day wouldn't come for more than a year, during which time the Langdon family had to come to terms with its shock. Charlie, despite his friendship with Sam, initially and somewhat adamantly opposed their marriage. The family members gradually gave up their fears about

Mark Twain's dubious past and convinced themselves—without favorable letters of reference, as it turned out—that he was a *changing* man. Olivia Lewis Langdon, the bride-to-be's mother, wrote Mary Fairbanks in December 1868 to inquire just "what the kind of man he *has been,* and what the man [*sic*] he now is, or is to become." Mary Fairbanks answered evidently that the better half of Mark Twain, the gentleman called Samuel Langhorne Clemens, was taking charge. "I touch no more spirituous liquors after this day," Sam had told Mrs. Fairbanks on Thanksgiving Day. "I shall do no act which you or Livy might be pained to hear of—I shall seek the society of the good—I shall be a *Christian.* . . . Have no fears, my mother. I shall be *worthy*—yet."[12]

Becoming a Christian was the most important part of her parents' terms in approving the marriage, he told his sister Pamela. Livy had offered to pray for him, and during their long courtship she sent him synopses of the weekly printed sermons of Henry Ward Beecher, half-brother not only to the famous novelist Harriet Beecher Stowe but the Reverend Thomas K. Beecher, who was a Congregationalist minister in Elmira and a close friend of Jervis Langdon's. Twain, soon to go on record in his forthcoming book about the ugliness of the Sea of Galilee, told Livy that he had been praying since September to accept Christ into his heart, "& that *now* I began clearly to comprehend that one *must* seek Jesus for himself alone, & uninfluenced by selfish motives."[13]

Considering also his later satires about the Garden of Eden ("Niagara Falls Park") and heaven, as well as his past as an essentially lapsed Christian, it is not easy to tell how sincere Sam was about returning to Christianity. Certainly he was earnest in his desire for Livy. At any rate, he engaged her in numerous discussions about the difficulty he was having in coming to terms with the idea of Jesus as the son of God. He grappled with Beecher's statement, in a sermon entitled "The Duty of Using One's Life for Others," that it was not enough simply to be a good person; one had to be a Christian in order to be a "fruit-bearer. A moral man is a vine that does not bear fruit." "That is me, exactly," he told Livy after reading the synopsis of the sermon she had sent; "*I* do not swear, I do not steal, I do not murder, I do not drink. [Yet] my 'whole life is *not.*' I am '*not* all over.'" He confessed that he may have lacked "the *chief* ingredient of piety"—that "inner sense" that allows one to live primarily for Christ. But he would keep trying, he told her: "I *can* be a Christian—I *shall* be a Christian."[14]

He was living on the cusp of Darwinism, which would lead to the replacement of essentialism with relativism. He never engaged publicly in such blasphemy, knowing well enough that he would lose the greater part of his American (i.e., Christian) readership, but we know from his posthumous writings how much private fun he had with these ideas. Years later, under his influence even Livy would lose her faith in Christianity.

They were officially engaged on February 4, 1869, and married almost exactly a year later, on February 2. By the time of the engagement, he could boast to his love, "I *devour* religious literature, now, with a genuine interest & pleasure that I am *so* glad to see growing—& I hope it may *always* grow—& I believe it will."[15]

After so many months on the road during the 1868–69 lecture tour, while also going back and forth with Bliss over details of publication, he came to hate both lecturing *and* Bliss, about whom he would later, in his autobiography, become downright nasty, noting a quarter century after the publisher's death that he felt "only compassion for him and if I could send him a fan I would."[16] He stayed with both, however, lecturing for one more season and writing for Bliss for more than ten years. He believed (before the immense success of *The Innocents Abroad*) that he could not make a decent living at either lecturing or authorship, certainly not enough to support a wife and family. Furthermore, lecturing took him away from Livy, something that, she soon made clear, especially after their wedding, she would not easily abide. The best idea, he thought, was to return to journalism. And here his initially skeptical future father-in-law came to his rescue with a sizable loan.

The difficulty Mark Twain encountered in buying into a newspaper underscores the fact that he was still not entirely "respectable" in literary and elite journalistic circles. He first tried to buy into the Hartford *Courant*, one of whose owners was the future co-author of *The Gilded Age*. As Twain described this effort to Livy after their marriage, the *Courant* ultimately sought out his participation as a partner in the wake of the success of *The Innocents Abroad.* ("Twelve thousand copies of the book sold *this month,*" he told his wife in December 1869. "Nothing like it since Uncle Tom's Cabin, I guess.") But his original interest in joining the *Courant* had been met with "insultingly contemptuous indifference." Next he looked into Samuel Bowles's Springfield *Republican,* telling this abrasive editor, who was both friend of Emily Dickinson and foe of Walt Whitman: "I am simply in search of a home. I must come to anchor." Bowles not only ignored his offer but warned Warner and his co-owner against their taking Twain as a partner on the *Courant.*[17]

He confided to Mary Fairbanks his interest in the *Courant,* and she may somehow have encouraged him to consider buying into her husband's paper, the Cleveland *Herald.* Clemens had earlier thought of Cleveland as a place to make his home with Livy. But Abel Fairbanks and his partners at the *Herald* apparently were no more anxious to become formally associated with Mark Twain than the others. Sam told his sister Pamela that Jervis Langdon would probably put up $60,000 to buy a third interest in the paper for his future son-in-law. But, no doubt as an evasive tactic, Fairbanks raised the price by offering his wife's friend only one-fourth of the business at the cost of $50,000.[18]

This feint came after much back-and-forth, and by then, in August 1869, Sam was on the verge of buying into the Buffalo *Express.* (A decade later the Fairbankses would fall on hard times, and Mary would borrow a thousand dollars from the successful—and now "respectable"—Mark Twain.) He told Bliss that he "had just got mad with the Cleveland Herald folks & broken off all further negotiations for a purchase. . . . I have bought one-third of the Buffalo 'Express.'" The full price was $25,000. Jervis Langdon, with his generous loan of half of that sum to help Sam make the down payment of $15,000, had effectively arranged to keep his daughter within reach, since Buffalo was an easy train ride from Elmira. Livy had earlier expressed her fears of "ever leaving this home of mine." Twain, who had been essentially homeless for the last sixteen years, was himself a bit mystified at this latest juncture in his rootless life. He now had Livy *and* a way to support her. Yet in the larger sense, as he told Mary Fairbanks, in a diplomatic effort to explain why he had declined the *Herald*'s latest offer, this next chapter in his life was just another beginning—"*another* apprenticeship . . . to be tacked on to the tail end of a foolish life *made up* of apprenticeships. I believe I have been apprentice to pretty much everything."[19] This apprenticeship as a newspaper editor turned out to be a wrong turn, though it would provide some grist for his next book. He would begin again and again in a life that eventually took him back in his literary imagination to Hannibal and the Mississippi River.

20 False Start in Buffalo

Sam Clemens sealed two lifelong friendships in 1868, not only the deep affection of Olivia Langdon but also the unwavering loyalty of the Reverend Joseph Hopkins Twichell. It seems a fair surmise that Clemens remained relatively quiet about his own Civil War service for almost a quarter century, in part because he was intimidated by the war stories of the Reverend Joe, who had been a chaplain in the Army of the Potomac. In that Union force under the successive commands of Generals John Pope and Ambrose Burnside, as Lincoln continued to search for a killer named Grant, Twichell had witnessed such terrible campaigns as the Union defeats at Second Bull Run and Fredericksburg in 1862. Two years later at the bloody but successful Union encounter with the Confederates at Gettysburg, essentially the South's last stand, he helped restrain General Dan Sickles while a combat surgeon amputated his right leg without anesthesia. Before the war, the notorious Sickles had been acquitted, on a plea of insanity, of killing his wife's lover. And the sanity of his military movements at the Battle of Gettysburg was questioned for years after the war. Twichell finished his three-year term in the Seventy-first New York Regiment of Volunteers on schedule in July 1864, as Grant moved inexorably through the Wilderness toward Richmond and Union victory.

After his war years, Twichell eventually became the minister of the Asylum Hill Congregational Church in Hartford. It was in October 1868, while Twain was visiting Bliss, whose house stood across the street from the church, that he first met Twichell. The two men hit it off immediately, even after Twain suggested that this upscale church in the upscale literary community of Nook Farm, west of Hartford, might be called the "Church of the Holy Speculators." He told Livy that month, "I have made a friend. It is the Rev. J. H. Twichell. I have only known him a week, & yet I believe I think almost as much of him as I do of Charlie. I could hardly find words strong enough to tell how much I *do* think of that man."[1] The feeling would soon be mutual and lasting: Twain would travel to Bermuda and Germany with Twichell and write him into several of his works. The Reverend Twichell would officiate at Mark Twain's wedding and speak at his funeral.

Albert Bigelow Paine tells us that clergymen just loved Mark Twain, but it is something of a puzzle to figure out what drew Twichell to him, at least at the outset of their relationship. Twichell had seen three years of combat serving as moral and religious mentor to the tough Irish Catholic laborers who formed the regiment that originated under Sickles as the Excelsior Brigade in Lower Manhattan. After describing to his father the awful results of an early battle in which eighty-three men in a nearby regiment had been killed, he told him: "If I had no faith in God, and did not feel that the plan, the *plan,* is unfolding in ways of His appointment, I should go crazy."[2] Like many Americans on both sides, he had believed in the war as a holy cause, while his new friend had fled from it as a bad idea. Twichell had been pastor of Asylum Hill Church since 1865, and would soon become known as "Mark Twain's pastor." There seems little doubt that most of Twichell's war experience spilled out of him as these two became fast friends, especially after Twain moved to Hartford (as he did shortly) and they began taking long Saturday morning walks together. Hearing the horror of the pastor's war memories may have ultimately tilted Twain toward his antiwar frame of mind in the anti-imperialist essays at the end of the century and earlier in his own essentially antiwar story "The Private History of a Campaign That Failed," in which such sentiment is camouflaged as humor.

One of the factors that surely brought this polished advocate of "Muscular Christianity" together with the often carelessly dressed, twang-tongued agnostic out of the West was Clemens's need to become a Christian in order to please both Livy and her parents. A graduate of Yale College and the Union Theological Seminary, Twichell stood for personal morality and integrity over the more pietistic doctrines of Christian orthodoxy. All his ideas were bound up with anti-slavery and the Republican Party, which after the war ran roughshod over the defeated South. As a man of the cloth, he may initially have seen Mark Twain as his biggest challenge, but the relationship soon settled into a lasting friendship, apparently unthreatened by their obvious disagreement on the subject of Christianity.[3]

In November 1868 Mark Twain began his first lecture tour with James Redpath's Speakers' Bureau in Boston; it would take him to the Midwest and back with approximately forty-three engagements in 123 days, Christmas included, ending on March 20, 1869. By this time Redpath—a vocal abolitionist, reporter in the Kansas territory from 1854 to 1859, and author of panegyrics that helped make the name of John Brown a shibboleth for the anti-slavery cause—had become with the war's outcome a respectable businessman with a stable of some of the most renowned speakers in the country. These included Anna E. Dickinson, staunch advocate for both abolition and women's rights, and Petroleum V. Nasby, who championed the same causes by appearing to oppose them. Both earned well above the one-hundred-dollar lecture fee that Twain then received.

By that August 1869, Twain was settled into a rooming house in Buffalo only a few doors down East Swan Street from the *Express* and ready to take on his new duties as editor alongside Josephus N. Larned, the political editor (who, said Twain in his newspaper "Salutatory" of August 21, "is already excellent, and only needs to serve a term in the penitentiary in order to be perfect").[4] Larned and his associates were delighted to have Mark Twain on their editorial staff and even more pleased the following year when he gave the regional newspaper a national touch by agreeing to write a regular column for the *Galaxy*. This prominent literary monthly had already taken the risk of publishing not only John Burroughs's defense of the unorthodox *Leaves of Grass* but also Whitman's own essay "Personalism" and some of his poems. (Whitman's essay had been about his version of Emersonian self-reliance, but Twain's wit—or some of it—in the *Galaxy* reflected the self-reliance of the lowbrow interpreter of the human condition.)

The *Express* was a Republican newspaper that at the very outset of Twain's association with it assailed Democrats as a joke. Its editorial of August 19 on that subject, "Inspired Humor," went unsigned, but a clipping of it with penciled correction by Sam survives in the MTP. An editorial on the following day entitled "The 'Monopoly' Speaks" attempted to calm the waters with regard to Jervis Langdon's high coal prices in Buffalo. Internal evidence from Sam's letter to Livy on August 19 suggests that he wrote or seriously influenced that editorial, which asked readers to consider the arguments of John D. Slee that the high prices were the result of the "unreasonable demands of the miners." Slee was an agent of the coal association representing Langdon's interests.[5] Twain obviously felt obligated to defend his future father-in-law, despite any sympathy he may have had for the miners. He must have been in a "close place," as he would have Huck say about his troubled conscience over Jim in *Huckleberry Finn.* He was not only helping to divert unflattering attention away from Jervis Langdon, to whom he was deeply grateful, but was also pleasing Langdon's daughter and his future wife. Up to this time the *Express* had been sympathetic to citizens' complaints about the price of coal, but Larned, who operated the "political crank," now sat at a desk directly facing the one occupied by Editor Clemens.

One issue on which the *Express* was not shy was the so-called Byron scandal, at least not in defending Harriet Beecher Stowe. The famous author of *Uncle Tom's Cabin* had recently asserted in the *Atlantic Monthly* that the poet Lord Byron's widow had told her years earlier that Byron had committed incest with his half-sister. The defense by the *Express* was probably a courageous act, for the *Atlantic* itself lost a great many subscribers over Stowe's article, which was considered to have been in poor taste. As a matter of fact, Stowe's reputation itself suffered permanent damage. The paper, and Twain, may have been pressured to help by the Reverend Thomas Beecher, her half-brother, who had recently come to her defense in an Elmira paper. Already, Twain was regretting that he and Livy could not live (or so they then thought) in the Nook Farm community of Hartford, where the Beecher clan owned or controlled most of the land for sale. (Twain would initially rent the home of Isabella Beecher Hooker, Stowe's half-sister, when his family moved to Hartford.) Furthermore, he was hopeful that sales of *The Innocents Abroad* would put him in the same financial ballpark as Mrs. Stowe (a goal the book may have reached after several years but certainly not with its initial sales). "To some, who cherish an ancient political grudge against the author of 'Uncle Tom's Cabin,'" he wrote in an unsigned editorial of August 24, "there seems to be a sufficient reason for savagely denouncing the story in the fact that it comes from Mrs. Stowe, whom they improve the occasion to abuse."[6]

Twain soon started an "Around the World" series for the *Express* in which Professor Darius R. Ford of Elmira College would travel and write "the newspaper account of his (our) trip." Twain would stay in Buffalo and embellish Ford's letters as they arrived. Ford already had a traveling companion in young Charlie Langdon, whose father now sent him on another "cruise" to keep him away from his Elmira drinking companions. The series was planned for forty or fifty letters, but only ten were ultimately published between October 16, 1869, and January 29, 1870, most of them written solely by Mark Twain. In fact, Professor Ford, perhaps himself an imbiber, produced only two of the letters.[7]

The scheme, however, gave Twain the idea in 1870 of having Bliss bankroll an old journalist friend and drinking pal from California to travel to South Africa in search of diamonds. John Henry Riley would be allowed to keep all the diamonds he found there and had only to save up his memories of the venture for Twain's later embellishment into a book. But by the time Riley returned the same year (without any diamonds), Twain was too busy with other matters and kept putting him off. Before Twain could give Riley his full attention, the unfortunate journalist died of blood poisoning after accidentally stabbing himself with a fork.[8] The book was never written, of course, and the contract for it with the American Publishing Company was fulfilled only in 1876 with the publication of *The Adventures of Tom Sawyer.*

The ill-fated Riley would live again in chapter 59 of *Roughing It* as "Blucher," an eccentric newspaper reporter in San Francisco. In fact, Twain wrote about him in the *Galaxy* for November 1870 and had it reprinted in the *Express*.[9] The idea for African diamonds would be only the first of a series of harebrained schemes, investments, and inventions that regularly distracted Mark Twain from his work as a writer. When he did get away long enough to succeed in literature, often accomplished by frenzied spurts of writing, the outcome was usually an accident, a fortuitous collision of genius and serendipity.

Twain took long weekends off during the waning days of his bachelorhood in Buffalo in order to visit Livy in Elmira. Afterwards, when the two settled there in a furnished home on Delaware Avenue that her parents had paid for, he spent even less time at "the office." The Buffalo period was nevertheless an important time in Mark Twain's development as a writer.[10] He soon realized that he had forgotten just what drudgery journalism involved, and writing monthly for a national magazine was almost as bad. Furthermore, writing for the *Galaxy* tended to overexpose him and thus threatened the sales of his future books. But in the *Express* and the *Galaxy* he wrote pieces that he would later reuse in such works as *Roughing It* and *Sketches, New and Old* (1875). There were, for example, the sketch about Lake Mono in California in the former book and "Journalism in Tennessee" in the latter. Furthermore, most of the "Around the World" letters focused on western memories and went, revised, into *Roughing It*. He was learning to turn the oral traditions of the Old Southwest and West into literary performances that were viable and lasting.

When the assassin of his friend Albert D. Richardson was acquitted on an insanity plea in a sensational trial in New York City in the spring of 1870, Twain went on record, probably for the first time, not only against that kind of legal tactic but also against the jury system itself. Richardson, star *Tribune* journalist and successful fellow writer for the American Publishing Company, had been shot by the ex-husband of a woman he had recently married. In "Our Precious Lunatic," the *Express* editor belittled the jury's decision by observing that the murderer's great-grandfather (a Tammany henchman and drunk by the name of Daniel McFarland) had also been "tainted with insanity, and frequently killed people who were distasteful to him." In reference to the defendant's alcoholism, Twain wrote that the younger McFarland "had to submit to the inconvenience of having his wife [Abby Sage Richardson, who would later dramatize *The Prince and the Pauper*] give public readings for the family support; and at times, when he handed these shameful earnings to the barkeeper, his haughty soul was so torn with anguish that he could hardly stand without leaning up against something."[11]

By this time, Sam had been married in Elmira, a wedding attended by his sister Pamela and her daughter Annie, but for unknown reasons not his mother, who remained in St. Louis. Instead, his other "mother," Mary Fairbanks, came all the way from Cleveland to attend the ceremony. The bride's side of the family included, along with her parents, Mrs. Theodore W. Crane (Susan, Livy's foster sister) and a number of other relatives. Charlie, who was still making his world tour with the professor, was also missing—in person, if not now in his approval of the marriage. Other guests to the ceremony presided over by Thomas K. Beecher and friend Joe Twichell included acquaintances from Elmira and associates of Jervis Langdon, as well as Larned of the *Express*.

It is well known to Mark Twain scholars that his literary return to Hannibal was sparked by his conversation in 1874 with Twichell about piloting and the resulting articles in the *Atlantic*. But his marriage also evoked ghosts of the past. In a letter four days after the wedding, on February 2, 1870, to Will Bowen, who had settled in St. Louis following his involuntary service for the Union as a river pilot, Sam thanked him for his letter of congratulations and told him that it had brought their childhood past back to him "like a panorama." Saying that the "old days have trooped by in their old glory again," he recalled Jimmy Finn, the town drunkard; "that one-legged nigger, Higgins"; his childhood sweetheart Laura Hawkins (Becky Thatcher in *Tom Sawyer*); and the time "I jumped overboard from the ferry boat in the middle of the river that stormy day to get my hat, & swam two or three miles after it (& *got* it)."[12] Now he had taken yet another plunge into the Mississippi River, and its muddy waters would leave an aftertaste that was not soon forgotten.

He had finished his second winter lecture tour the month before and was now basking in the glow of his honeymoon at home and avoiding the *Express* office altogether. By the spring and summer of 1870 he not only was engaged in producing the monthly *Galaxy* articles but also had signed a contract to produce "another 600-page" book for the American Publishing Company, this one to be called *Roughing It.* He wouldn't actually begin its composition right away, however, because of terrible misfortunes that emerged in the wake of his happy marriage. First, Jervis Langdon was diagnosed with stomach cancer and died at age sixty on August 6. The long ordeal of his dying exhausted the family, especially Livy, who sat for hours every day at his side, taking her turn with other family members, including Sam. Jervis left an estate valued at over one million dollars, to be equally divided among his wife, daughter, son, and foster daughter. (Part of Susan Crane's inheritance included Quarry Farm, which became the family's summer hillside getaway, about three miles outside Elmira overlooking the Chemung River. It would come to play a major role in the literary career of Mark Twain.)[13] Livy came close to suffering an emotional breakdown over the sudden loss of her father, and she nearly lost the baby she was then carrying. The next month Emma Nye, a childhood friend, made a previously scheduled visit to the Clemens's Buffalo home and almost immediately contracted typhoid fever; she died in their bedroom on September 29, further exacerbating Livy's fragile emotional state.

Incredibly, Sam kept right on working on promised projects, both the book and the *Galaxy* pieces. He suffered along with the rest of the family, fretting deeply over his wife's condition, but he nevertheless managed to write. It is hard to imagine, even today, how he functioned as a humorist, but the *Galaxy* is hard evidence of his success. Admittedly, most of the best pieces were written before these crises, which culminated with the premature birth and ill health of their first child, Langdon, on November 7, 1872. Twain's *Galaxy* writings featured such prominent works in the Twain canon as "The Facts in the Case of the Great Beef Contract" and "The Story of the Good Little Boy Who Did Not Prosper." The latter is not as funny as "The Story of the Bad Little Boy Who Didn't Come to Grief," first published in the *Californian* in 1865 as "The Christmas Fireside" and reprinted with the longer title in the 1867 *Jumping Frog* collection. That is probably because it is not as optimistic. While the Bad Little Boy can outmaneuver fate and even the goody-goody scenarios of boyhood behavior promoted by the pulpit, the Good Little Boy has to live after the Fall of Man. In his world (and that of the rest of humanity) "there was a screw loose somewhere." The 1870 sequel may faintly anticipate Twain's later pessimism. It also belonged to the genre of the benign attacks on the model boy, exemplified in Thomas Bailey Aldrich's *The Story of a Bad Boy* (1869).[14] Yet Twain's "The Christmas Fireside" had in fact made this attack four years before Aldrich's book.

In the June number the quality of Twain's *Galaxy* work fell off somewhat, but, significantly, in a series of recollections, he referred to his *Enterprise* hoaxes, including "A Bloody Massacre near Carson." It seems that he was still apologizing for it, or defending himself about it. "The idea that anybody could ever take my massacre for a genuine occurrence," he told his *Galaxy* readers, "never once suggested itself to me, hedged about as it was by all those tell-tale absurdities."[15]

One of his cruder but still amusing pieces of this period (at least from the distance of more than a century) never made it into the *Galaxy,* probably because it did not meet the prevailing Victorian standard of literary taste. As a matter of fact, when Twain completed his stint with that magazine, the *Nation,* which had been monitoring his performances in the *Galaxy,* remarked in the April 1871 issue that the humorist "was sometimes rather vulgar and low." When the Franco-Prussian War in the spring of 1870 led quickly to a siege of Paris and reduced the French to eating the animals out of their own zoo at the Jardin des Plantes, Twain described the menu of a famous Parisian restaurant, Trois Frères, as offering "giraffe cutlets, rhinoceros steaks, and ragout of kangaroo." "Less pretentious dishes," he continued, "fell to the commonality. The latter had to content themselves with such ordinary *plats* as horse, mule, donkey, cats, dogs, and rats," or a bill of fare offering "horse soup" and "minced cat."[16]

"War and 'Wittles'" appeared in the *Express* of December 16, 1870. His humor here came at the expense of human suffering and reflected his current mood, which was somewhat dark. Buffalo had never pleased him. He had always wanted to live in Hartford, since his first visit there. Young Langdon wasn't strong and would soon struggle against the very same disease that had killed Emma Nye only months before in the same house. Livy, still mourning for her dead father and quite ill herself, was unable to care for the child and had to rely on a wet nurse. Servants in the Buffalo house had also become an unpleasant distraction, what with rivalries among them and their failure to perform satisfactorily. It was time for a change. By March, Sam had put up both his house and his share of the newspaper for sale (ultimately taking a loss on both) and taken the first step away from Buffalo for good. "We are packing up, to-night," he told Bliss on March 17, 1871, "& tomorrow I shall take my wife to Elmira on a mattress—for she can neither sit up nor stand. . . . I had rather die twice over than repeat the last six months of my life."[17] Livy was not prostrated merely by her grief. A month before, she too had come down with typhoid fever.

21 Back on the Lecture Circuit

What began as a dream just a year ago had now turned into a nightmare. Abandoning the scene of that dream, the Buffalo house that Livy's parents bought and furnished for them—a genuine surprise for Sam, who was duped into thinking they were to occupy rented rooms—the couple retreated with their sick child to Elmira, where both mother and son slowly recovered from typhoid fever. One of the few bright notes at this time of continued crisis was the growing success of *The Innocents Abroad.* By this time it was clear that the book would probably make him rich, or at least pay all his debts. In its first year it sold 69,500 copies, netting its author $14,000. Now in early 1871, sales continued to boom. Moreover, as he told Bliss, he was "flooded with lecture invitations, & one periodical offers me $6,000 cash for 12 articles"—offers he did not accept. Then there was the $2,000 annually he was paid for writing his *Galaxy* pieces. Whatever he derived in the way of salary from the *Express* is not known, but it was very likely little or nothing. When he had first assumed his one-third ownership of that paper, he had expressed a concern about the newspaper's day-to-day profitability. Yet with the other streams of income, he could afford to ignore this issue. "I hate business," he told the business-astute Bliss, who had cut corners on the production of *Roughing It,* something Twain learned about only because Orion Clemens was now working for Bliss.[1]

Before retreating to Elmira, Sam had tried to cash in on his *Innocents Abroad* fame with a booklet called *Mark Twain's (Burlesque) Autobiography and First Romance* (1871), but it failed to make him any serious money. He knew he needed to remain focused on writing *Roughing It,* but that was becoming deucedly difficult. He had already received help from Orion's notebook about their journey across the plains in 1861, for which he paid his brother a thousand dollars and got him the job with Bliss editing a new promotional magazine called *The American Publisher.* Joe Goodman, another player out of the same past, soon came to Elmira and read his friend's manuscript, making valuable suggestions and praising the work as one of the best things Sam had ever written. He stayed with the Clemens family for a couple of months.[2] Goodman steadied his friend as he pushed forward amidst persistent family problems, especially the continually precarious state of young Langdon's health.

After Sam completed most of *Roughing It,* the Clemens family moved to Hartford in the first week of October, taking possession of the house they had rented. A few days later the legendary Chicago fire began, and J. Langdon & Company, which had coal and lumber offices in the city, suffered an estimated loss of fifty thousand dollars. ("There is literally no Chicago *here,"* Twain told his wife when he visited the city that December. "I recognize *nothing* here, that I ever saw before.") With his family barely installed in the Hooker house and Livy six months pregnant, Twain had to leave for another lecture tour, again managed by the Redpath agency. It would be exhausting, of course, with seventy-seven engagements in almost as many cities in more than fifteen states between October 16, 1872, and the following February 27. He began in Bethlehem, Pennsylvania, with a lecture awkwardly titled "Reminiscences of Some un-Commonplace Characters I Have Chanced to Meet." It failed him almost immediately, but quickly morphed into "Artemus Ward, Humorist," which hardly fared much better. He was reluctant to share the bad news with Livy. After delivering the talk to mixed reviews in Boston in November, he told her: "It was a bad night, but we had a packed house, & if the papers say any disparaging things, don't you believe a single *word* of it, for I never saw a lecture go off so *magnificently* before."[3]

Mark Twain was fatigued even before he began this tour, having gone through so much emotional adversity at home. In December, after switching back and forth between lectures, he gave up the one on Artemus

Ward and started reading selections from the proofs of *Roughing It.* This choice would carry him through the spring phase of the lecture tour and also serve to advertise his new book. Redpath featured the new success in the January number of his *Lyceum Circular.* Its quotations from several Chicago newspapers following two performances the week before Christmas provide us with a special window on the past. One described the speaker as "lank, lantern-jawed, and impudent" and added three inches to his actual height of five feet, eight and a half inches. "For something like a minute," it continued, "he says not a word, but rubs his hands awkwardly and . . . begins in a slow drawl." The first performance in Chicago was such a success that Twain agreed to give the second in a church, something he usually tried to avoid because he said people were reluctant to laugh in church. "While truly eloquent in his glowing descriptions of California scenery," the Chicago *Tribune* observed, "he was infinitely droll in his yarns of life on the Pacific slope." Unfortunately, the *Tribune* reproduced large patches of the lecture verbatim, thereby undermining its freshness in nearby cities and towns. This became an ongoing problem throughout the tour.[4]

Twain hadn't started this tour with readings from his forthcoming book because he had still not completed it in late 1871. Instead, he had actually intended to begin with—but never gave—a lecture entitled "An Appeal in Behalf of Extending the Suffrage to Boys," another of the early germs for *Tom Sawyer.* The way his lecture for the 1871–72 season evolved from one topic to the next is a good example of how Mark Twain's genius worked: rather than focusing on one coherent idea, he often plunged in and creatively moved from one thing to another until everything somehow coalesced into a particular story. The "Reminiscences" lecture with which he actually began the season may have initially featured Artemus Ward, Dick Baker the quartz miner, Riley the journalist, and other "unCommonplace Characters" he had encountered in the West and Hawaii. It was mainly, however, about Ward, whose life and sayings ultimately took over the lecture and turned it into "Artemus Ward, Humorist."

There were, however, two problems with that talk. First, some audiences found it in poor taste to speak mirthfully about the dead. (Ward had died of tuberculosis in England in 1867.) Second, Ward wasn't that funny any longer, certainly not as funny as Mark Twain. As Twain kept patching up his lecture on the road, he told his wife that he was "trying to weed Artemus out of it & work myself *in.* What *I* say, *fetches* 'em—but what *he* says—*don't.*" There was also the problem that Ward's sayings were already familiar, especially in the East. For her part, Livy, living in the age of Victoria, was somewhat uncomfortable with her husband's reputation as a mere humorist as against a "serious" author. This bias would be handed down to their children, beginning with Olivia Susan (Susy) Clemens, who was born in 1872. Livy also hated her husband's long absences. After he lectured in Hartford in November and quickly departed, Livy told him: "I do hope that this will be the last season that it will be necessary for you to lecture. It is not the way for a husband and wife to live if they can possibly avoid it, is it? Separation comes soon enough." She was still feeling like a bride in spite of all the tragedy that had followed their wedding almost immediately. "I answered all your letters today," she told him, referring to business letters Clemens could not reply to on the road. "It was a pleasure to be writing letters for you, it is a pleasure to do *any* thing for you." She was so devoted to him that her traditional religious moorings were already weakening. "Do you pray for me Youth?" she asked the same month. "Pray for me as you used to do—I am not prayerful as of old but I believe my heart prays."[5] Part of this newly questioning state of mind arose from the pent-up anger over the death of her father, who had been a giant presence in her life.

Sam hadn't seen *his* only living parent for more than a year. He finally did so when he performed his *Roughing It* lecture on December 8 in Fredonia, New York. Fortunately, he had still sworn off drinking liquor (to please Livy), for Fredonia, where the first meeting of the Woman's Christian Temperance Union would be held in 1873, was no doubt dry. Shortly after his marriage and residence in Buffalo, he had persuaded his mother and sister Pamela to move to this small town on Lake Erie. He called his mother his "first and closest friend," but he always knew that she preferred her firstborn, Orion, whose bumbling life he would later ridicule in his letters to her. These would often contain money, which he also gave Orion in one way or another for the rest of his life. In the lecture season of 1871–72, he averaged just under $130 a performance (one or two going as high as $250), or $9,890 less Redpath's 10 percent commission.[6]

Usually on the road alone, Twain had much time to think—and reminisce. After he lectured in Steubenville, Ohio, on January 9, he marveled in a letter to Livy that the nearby Ohio River had once been alive with steamboats. "Where be the pilots?" he asked rhetorically. "They were the starchy boys, in my time, & greatly envied by the youth of the West." Part of this daydreaming came as a result of his boredom with lecturing. "At last I am through with the most detestable campaign that ever was—a campaign which was one eternal worry with contriving new lectures & being dissatisfied with them," he told Mary Fairbanks in February when he had only two more lectures to give. He swore that he would never embark on such an ordeal again—"unless I get in debt again."[7] He had paid too much for his share of the Buffalo *Express,* but he had now made up that loss, and he had repaid the Langdon estate for the $12,500 he had borrowed from his late father-in-law. Sam had been home only once since November, and Susy would be born the next month.

His final two performances of the season were dismally reviewed. The Danbury (Connecticut) *News* called the February 21 lecture "a failure and a disappointment." "Mr. Twain is not a beautiful man," it continued. "His hair is carroty, his gait is shambling." This wasn't good press only fifty miles from Hartford, where his heart longed to be. Neither was the review of his last lecture in Amherst, Massachusetts, on February 27. The Amherst *Student* solemnly observed: "We do not know whether the audience had expected too much of the funny Mark Twain from reading his funny book, or whether two hours of nonsense is more than people care for at once, or not, but true it is that they had heard enough of him when he was done." The Amherst *Record* was much more appreciative of Twain's socializing at a reception at the Amherst House. Its remarks suggest that Mark Twain was already generating the first thoughts about one of his best-known books, then still more than a decade in the future. "He kept the company in the best of humor," the *Record* observed, "by narrating some of his experiences in piloting on the Mississippi."[8]

No doubt he was in better humor now that the ordeal of lecturing had finally come to an end for the season, and he thus enjoyed the society of this college town that hid away another great American writer. Emily Dickinson had not bothered to go next door to her brother's house to meet Emerson when he came to Amherst to lecture in 1857 (he too had disappointed his Amherst auditors, according to another local paper). By 1872 the reclusive poet never left her father's house. Ordinarily, Twain didn't enjoy this kind of socializing either. He had long ago found that his various lecture hosts kept him up too late or infringed on his quiet time before performances. Staying with town leaders was even worse, and sometimes he even registered at hotels under a false name, or under his real one (that is, Samuel Clemens instead of Mark Twain), to avoid having to deal with anxious hosts. Lecturing in nineteenth-century America was no picnic. There were long and tedious train rides, notoriously uncomfortable hotels, and often harsh wintry weather to contend with. It is remarkable that Emerson did it for so many years—out of financial necessity, no doubt—but Mark Twain was getting richer by the week, and this would be his last season of lecturing for some time to come. In the first three months of publication, *Roughing It*, published in February, would earn him royalties of more than $10,000. And Olivia's share of her father's estate amounted to more than $237,000 in 1872.[9]

Sam was back home for the birth of his first daughter on March 19. She was born a healthy child, but eighteen-month-old Langdon was running out of time. He died on the second day of June—"quietly in his mother's arms," according to a witness. Reading the autobiographical account of this tragedy, one is shocked at Sam Clemens's admissions, which were greatly exaggerated. "I was the cause of the child's illness," he confessed. "I took him [for] a drive in an open barouche for an airing. It was a raw, cold morning, but he was well wrapped about with furs. . . . But I soon dropped into a reverie and forgot all about my charge." By the time he noticed that "the child's furs had fallen loose," he continued, "it was too late. The child was almost frozen." Whatever truth there was in this confession, it is important to note that the incident obviously happened in the winter, and Langdon died of diphtheria in June.[10] His autobiography is often notoriously (and typically) unreliable. Furthermore, Sam Clemens felt guilty about several deaths in his life, not only his brother Henry's death on the Mississippi but also other premature departures that would profoundly shape his late ideas about the world. Some writers, Dreiser for example, never seemed to feel guilty about anything. Whitman saw everything as part of the grand scheme of nature that reflected the benign presence of God. But Mark Twain, who despised Conscience and held it responsible for so much evil in the world, initially took himself to task and then ultimately blamed everything on an insensitive God.

22 Home in Hartford

Mark Twain and his family rented the Hooker house for two and half years before occupying the Hartford mansion on Farmington Avenue, which is today the main shrine to the author of "The Celebrated Jumping Frog of Calaveras County" and *Adventures of Huckleberry Finn.* Living "next door" was young William Hooker Gillette, the son of one of the two founders of the suburban development that had turned the Nook Farm woodland into an upper-class neighborhood by the time Twain lived there. As Gillette told a speech class at Harvard College in the 1930s, he knew the voice of his famous neighbor intimately. Although there is now a familiar three-minute motion picture clip of Mark Twain filmed in the early part of the twentieth century, no audio recording of him is extant, even though Thomas Edison's company made both the film and several recordings. There is even a recording of Walt Whitman reading his poem entitled "America," but nothing of America's other great vernacular writer. We know the sound of Twain's voice largely through contemporary descriptions, usually in the form of newspaper reviews of his lectures.

Anyone who visits Hannibal will find a Mark Twain imitator or two either performing at bed-and-breakfasts or simply crossing the streets of a town whose economic life now depends almost solely on the memory of Mark Twain's boyhood and its dramatization in *Tom Sawyer* and *Huckleberry Finn.* Otherwise, one may listen to a recording of Hal Holbrook performing in *Mark Twain Tonight* or, at this writing, even *see* the actor, now well over the age of Twain at his death, impersonate him. We have, however, something almost as close to the real thing as the Whitman recording: we can almost hear Mark Twain's "voice" in a recording Will Gillette made before that speech class in the 1930s. Gillette had been an actor noted for his portrayal of Sherlock Holmes. Twain helped pay for part of his acting education and later helped him win parts, including a role in the Hartford production of *The Gilded Age* in 1875.[1] Holbrook relied in part on Gillette's imitation in preparation for his own performances.

Besides the slight New England accent that Twain would barely have picked up by the 1870s and 1880s, while he lived in Hartford, there is in Gillette's impression a certain whine in the voice, especially at points of emphasis. The recording is of the first few lines of the Jumping Frog story, and it recalls the tale's brilliance as an exemplar of the oral tradition in American literature. Gillette told the speech class the day he made the recording that Mark Twain had been "a close friend." His general recollection of the story is inexact but nevertheless accurate in its description of Jim Smiley as a man who was "always *betting* on anything that turned up you ever see, if he could get anybody to bet on the other *side,* and if he couldn't he'd *change* sides." (My italics indicate emphasis or elongated vowels, which each time maximize the whining sound of Simon Wheeler's voice.) "Any *way* that suited the other man would suit *him,*" the story continues, "if there was a *dog* fight, he'd bet on it; if there was a *cat* fight, he bet on it . . . why if there was two birds [a-settin'] on a fence, he would bet on which one would fly first . . . if he even see a straddle-bug *start* to go anywheres, he would bet you how long it would take him." According to legend, Twain is supposed to have told Gillette more than once that his impression of him was the most accurate he had ever heard.

Thus we possess, at least, the mediated sound of the voice of Mark Twain in the early years of his life in this upscale community of such New England saints and sinners as Harriet Beecher Stowe and Isabelle Beecher Hooker—both sisters of Henry Ward Beecher. It is important to imagine the contrast of sounds and sense between this rough character from the hinterlands of Missouri and Nevada and these solemn New England advocates of abolition and women's rights. Just his way of *say-*

ing something, making an observation from his point of view with his unique vocalization, must have been its own wellspring of humor. No doubt as a newcomer to the Nook Farm community, he had to stifle his wickedly observant thoughts from time to time, if only for the sake of his Victorian wife. It was a community of established professionals, such as essayist and newspaper editor Charles Dudley Warner and preacher Joe Twichell, both now long forgotten except for their connection to this new outsider and stranger to New England culture. Livy, of course, wanted him to *write* like them—someday.

When Kenneth R. Andrews published his groundbreaking study of the Nook Farm literary community in 1950, Mark Twain's eight-thousand-square-foot Hartford mansion of nineteen rooms and seven bathrooms (with flushing toilets) had already been sold several times and finally reduced to the quarters of the Mark Twain branch of the town library on the ground floor and residential apartments on the upper floors. In the words of Wilson H. Faude, curator of the Mark Twain Memorial Committee, which oversaw the house's full restoration on the centenary of its initial construction in 1874: "Where Thomas Nast, Edwin Booth, William Dean Howells, Generals Sheridan and Sherman, and Sir Henry Morton Stanley had dined, strangers checked out books." Before it was a library, the grand house at 351 Farmington Avenue had even served as a boys' school. The then shabby building may suggest what *could* have happened to Mark Twain's genius after he moved into upper-middle-class Hartford and lived there for almost twenty years. At it turned out, of course, he didn't fade away with the house over the next hundred years, but neither did Mark Twain the humorist sell Samuel Langhorne Clemens down the river of American literature, contrary to Van Wyck Brooks's argument in 1920. Mark Twain coexisted with Sam Clemens in Hartford, but wrote mostly during the summer months in a hilltop study at his sister-in-law's Quarry Farm estate outside Elmira.[2]

His neighbors and social intimates at Nook Farm, where the unlocked doors permitted unannounced visits from one house to another, included John Hooker, a direct descendant of the founder of Hartford, and his brother-in-law Francis Gillette, a renowned abolitionist and temperance advocate. Together they had purchased the Nook Farm tract of one hundred acres about three miles west of downtown Hartford, then one of the most prosperous towns in America. Hartford was the home of the country's first insurance companies and the Colt Fire Arms Manufactory, among other thriving businesses, including the American Publishing Company. Harriet Beecher Stowe and her husband, Calvin, a retired theology professor, had resided in the Nook Farm community since 1862, and by this time she was weathering the tarnishing of her reputation that began with her 1869 *Atlantic Monthly* essay about Byron's incestuous affair with his half-sister.[3] Also living in the community were her sister Isabella Hooker and Isabella's eldest daughter, Mary Hooker Burton. Isabella's reputation would also suffer (at least in the eyes of Twain and other Nook Farmers) for her support of fellow feminist Victoria Woodhull's 1872 denunciation of Henry Ward Beecher as an adulterer. Twichell, as we know, lived nearby, and so did Charles Dudley Warner and his wife, Susan. Warner, who ran the *Courant* with Joseph R. Hawley, a recent governor of the state, was known generally for graceful travel letters that he would first publish in the *Courant* before gathering them into books. Just before Twain moved into the neighborhood, Warner was enjoying the success of a collection of nature sketches published as a book, *My Summer in a Garden,* in 1871. In his younger days as a bachelor, he had been a railroad surveyor out west, and those experiences would soon be put to use in his collaboration with Twain, *The Gilded Age.* In sum, Twain's neighbors were literary and clerical professionals as well as stolid Republicans who were growing a little uncomfortable with the radicals in the party, now that the war was over and slavery seemingly abolished.

One of those Republicans was William Dean Howells of the *Atlantic.* He didn't live in Nook Farm, but once he and Twain became close friends (and literary allies, Howells always writing glowing reviews of Twain's books, Twain writing for the *Atlantic*) in the 1870s, Twain tried to get him to move there from his home just outside Boston in Cambridge. They first met in Boston in late 1869 after Howells had reviewed *The Innocents Abroad.* The review was unsigned, but everyone knew who was writing the reports for the magazine's review section. Twain had gone to its editorial offices at 124 Tremont Street to thank James T. Fields, who in 1869 was still the chief editor of the *Atlantic;* Fields introduced him to Howells. Howells, later known as the "Dean of American Literature" (who memorably would call Twain the "Lincoln of our literature"), became the John Updike of his era, a realist whose novels captured the details of everyday life in dramas about current pressing social and psychological issues. He was also nearly as prolific as Updike, publishing more than sixty novels, travel books, and collections of essays. As his reward for writing one of the campaign biographies of Lincoln, he served as U.S. consul in Venice during the war. (Significantly, both Howells and Twain managed to sidestep the fratricide of their times.) His earliest books were travel essays—*Venetian Life* (1866) and *Italian Journeys* (1867). Both he and his new friend would labor on almost the same schedule with similar distractions before their ultimate achievements—*The Rise of Silas Lapham* and *Adventures of Huckleberry Finn.*[4]

Another Boston literary friend who would visit the Twain mansion in Hartford, with his wife, Lilian, was Thomas Bailey Aldrich. As DeLancey Ferguson observes, Mark Twain was never fully accepted by the New England literati. Even Howells had his doubts, perhaps ultimately seeing Twain as great mainly as a humorist whose material never mocked "any good or really fine thing," unlike the humorists who preceded him who were "on the side of slavery, of drunkenness, and of irreligion." But it was chiefly he and Aldrich, both Bostonians by adoption, who accepted Sam as their friend and literary compatriot. Yet Twain's relationship with Aldrich, who had recently published the prototypical *A Story of a Bad Boy,* almost got off on the wrong foot. When Aldrich brought Twain home for dinner unannounced one night in the winter of 1872, his wife had no idea who her guest was and also suspected, from his manner and slow speech, that he was intoxicated. As a result, she kept putting off the expected dinner until Sam got the message that he wasn't wanted as Mrs. Aldrich's guest and departed. When she discovered from her husband that she had mistaken his drawl and southwestern vernacular for the slurred speech of a drunk, she was naturally embarrassed. Twain never forgot the slight, even though the Aldriches became regular social acquaintances. He may indeed have been slightly intoxicated that evening, for while the imperfect speech was explained, nothing (in Lilian

Aldrich's own account of this incident) was offered to explain away Twain's "marked inability to stand perpendicular."[5]

A third literary ally who made at least two visits to Mark Twain in Hartford and regularly drank to excess was his old literary companion and adviser from San Francisco, Bret Harte. In 1871 Harte had come east in a far more triumphant fashion than Mark Twain had in 1867 (or 1868), and he landed a lavish contract with the *Atlantic* to provide ten stories, for ten thousand dollars, on a par with those he had already published in *The Luck of Roaring Camp, and Other Sketches* (1870). There is at least a remote possibility that this deal was at the root of their notoriously troubled relationship. Twain seems not to have made totally public his dislike for Harte until he was on his international lecture campaign in 1895 (the tour that would result in *Following the Equator*). Harte, as Twain gratefully admitted to Aldrich in 1871, had read the *Innocents Abroad* manuscript for him, and had (then and earlier) "trimmed & trained & schooled me patiently until he changed me from an awkward utterer of coarse grotesqueness to a writer of paragraphs & chapters that have found a certain favor in the eyes of even some of the very decentest people in the land."

Yet Harte's character, especially his lack of integrity, came to annoy Twain mightily. "In the early days," he recorded in his autobiography, "I liked Bret Harte, and so also did the others, but by and by I got over it; so did the others." Among other things, Harte had been "an incorrigible borrower of money." In June 1872 Harte visited Twain in Hartford and borrowed $250, which was never repaid. One Christmas season in 1876 Harte was guest at the newly completed "Steamboat Gothic" mansion. He was working on a story but in the process managed to consume at least two bottles of whiskey, staying up all night. During the same visit the two began cowriting a play to be called *Ah Sin*, based on Harte's then famous poem "Plain Language from Truthful James" (better known as "The Heathen Chinee"). The "last feather" came when, toward the end of his visit of several weeks, he included Mrs. Clemens in his "smart and bright criticisms leveled at everything" in the house.[6] Their play's failure to become a hit, along with Harte's failure, at least in Twain's view, to do his share of the work in seeing to the play's successful production, would end their once promising friendship at a time when Harte's descent was already well under way.

The house in which Harte made his deadliest mistake with Twain no doubt helped to precipitate the impolite remarks, for it was a monument to Twain's towering success, far greater by then than that of his mentor in the West. It cost around sixty thousand dollars to build then—not counting the several acres on which it stood. Today the Twain house no longer overlooks a branch of the Park River, long since piped underground because of persistent flooding, but instead a parking lot for the Mark Twain Visitors Center, completed in 2003. In general, the Victorian structures remaining (except for Stowe's Victorian cottage, her carriage house, and Twain's) have been either demolished or retrofitted as apartments in economically depressed Hartford. The Hooker house, which the Clemenses rented in Nook Farm, is now an apartment complex partially concealed from the street by another apartment building.

Twain was adjusting to the fact of his rising wealth, but the question nevertheless remains why he and Livy built such an expensive and indeed curious house. He could afford to do so at this point only with his wife's inheritance, but earlier, during the courtship, he had emphasized to his mother and sister Pamela that he did not want to depend on Livy's money for their support.[7] (Ultimately, he did and lost much of it in bad investments.) Perhaps his description of Hartford during his very first visit explains why he built his castle there. In a letter to the *Alta* of January 25, 1868, written just after he signed a contract with Elisha Bliss for *The Innocents Abroad,* he sang the city's praises, calling it "the best built and the handsomest town" he had ever seen. "The dwelling houses," he continued, "are the amplest in size, and the shapeliest, and have the most capacious ornamental grounds about them. . . . This is the centre of Connecticut wealth." He noted that the city's population was forty thousand, "and the most of them ride in sleighs. That is a sign of prosperity, and a knowledge of how to live—isn't it?"[8] Having married a wealthy woman and becoming rich himself, he sought to make a positive, though still particular, impression on the Nook Farm community. Instead, he created a curiosity that ironically reflected the fact that this writer capable of "word paintings" was still basically a humorist whose job it was to startle people out of their own sense of what to expect. This unintended image of the Writer vying with the Humorist would be a problem for the rest of his career.

As Justin Kaplan astutely wrote of the house, this "stately mansion was a classic American success story, a reminder that it was possible to be born in a two-room clapboard house in Florida, Missouri, . . . and to become world-famous, . . . and live a life of domestic bliss in a house that was the marvel of Hartford." And marvel it was—though marveled at mainly (according to the local newspaper) as "one of the oddest looking buildings in the State." The exterior featured three turrets, none of which was the same size as the other, five balconies, a porch that wound around the house to the left of the main entrance, brickwork both painted and, in places, set in vertical rows. The designer was Edward Tuckerman Potter, of New York, a writer and musician in addition to an architect, mainly known for designing churches and college buildings. He had designed Charles Dudley Warner's house, and Twain's would be one of his last before he retired as an architect and turned to other career challenges.[9]

The interior was signature Victorian in its deliberate exclusion of sunlight. The first of three floors featured an entrance hall, a guest room, a drawing room, a dining room, a library, a conservatory, and a kitchen wing with a pantry and servants' hall and entry. In the last, Patrick McAleer, the coachman who had been with the family since Buffalo, and housekeeper Katy Leary, whom Livy hired in 1880 from Elmira, where Leary's sister worked for the Charles Langdon family, labored along with several other servants, preparing meals with vegetables and meats fresh from the local markets. An ornate carved wooden staircase in the entry hall led to five bedrooms and a servants' wing on the second floor. One of the bedrooms was intended for Sam's study, but was turned into a schoolroom for the children. There was an additional guest room where Livy's mother stayed when visiting from Elmira, a bedroom for Clara and ultimately Jean (born respectively in 1874 and 1880), one for Susy, and one for Sam and Livy, which was eventually dominated by a large, intricately carved wooden bedstead that the Clemenses would buy in Venice in 1878. The third floor offered yet another guest room, an additional servants' room, and a large billiard room that doubled as

Sam's study. It opened onto a deck that he sometimes occupied when he wanted his butler, George Griffin (a former slave who came one day "to wash some windows, & remained half a generation"), to say he had "stepped out" without telling an actual lie to unwanted guests—an example, perhaps, of the moral hairsplitting required in that Social Darwinist era of upper-class America. The McAleer family, with seven children, lived on the second floor of the adjoining carriage house, or stable. During 1883, when all seven of the McAleer children one after another came down with scarlet fever within a period of six months, "there was," Twain told Mrs. Fairbanks, "no communication between the house and the stable except by speaking tubes."[10]

Mark Twain had arrived. Less than a decade after the Civil War and the end of the Southern cause he had essentially abandoned, he found himself in the lap of Yankee luxury. In fact, it was just ten years and two months between the time he and his fellow Marion Rangers had skedaddled and the time when he occupied the Beecher house in Nook Farm. The house he built there would be home to the family of Samuel Langhorne Clemens for most of the next (and best) two decades of his life, a stretch of singular happiness punctuated by two family trips abroad in the seventies and summers in Elmira at Quarry Farm, owned by Theodore and Susan Crane, Livy's adopted sister. Here in Hartford the three children would grow up—receive home schooling—and even put on plays based on their father's novel about a prince and a pauper, which resembles in certain aspects that now famous black and white twosome in *Adventures of Huckleberry Finn.* He was composing *The Prince and the Pauper* at the same time, but *Huckleberry Finn* would never be dramatized in his home because the family generally wanted Mark Twain to write as Samuel Clemens. In an unfinished biography of her father that Susy began writing in 1885 (at the age of thirteen), she even apologized for his perceived lowbrow literature (though later she came to better appreciate her father's true genius). But then, in this house Mark Twain *did* live as Samuel Clemens, the American "phunny phellow" who could write with the best of the Victorian bores. That kind of writing came later in the life of the house, of course. For now, if only to pay the mounting bills this audacious house generated, he had to continue writing as Mark Twain.

23 Sequel to a Success

Roughing It became Mark Twain's first major effort as a professional writer, planned as such at the very outset. His previous books, *The Celebrated Jumping Frog* and *The Innocents,* had evolved almost entirely out of his short magazine pieces and newspaper letters. It was a major step up as a professional writer. Even before he had withdrawn the Hawaii book of travel letters, he fell into the chance to travel on the *Quaker City* to Europe and the Near East, after originally not knowing how he was going to pursue Anson Burlingame's idea of writing from Asia. If Elisha Bliss hadn't approached him about collecting those *Quaker City* letters into a book, he might not ever have written *The Innocents Abroad,* especially after the financial failure of the Jumping Frog and his inability to get his Hawaii letters published in 1867 (about half of them would go into *Roughing It*). After the grand financial success of *The Innocents Abroad,* with its format of travel letters that allowed the embedding of slices of American humor, he naturally wanted to try to repeat the success and so ultimately chose his experiences as a silver and gold prospector in Nevada and California. It was the right move, for *Roughing It* eventually sold almost as many copies as *The Innocents Abroad.*

Henry Nash Smith notes that in this new book he showed for the first time "a marked advance toward the structural firmness of fiction" in a long narrative, and also that "the first half of *Roughing It* is a striking demonstration of Mark Twain's ability to recognize the representative aspects of his own experience." But after getting his narrator across the plains and through the "greenhorn" stages of life in the West, Twain "ran out of gas," though he didn't stop writing, as he would learn to do with future books. He remained at work on the book by relying on scrapbooks and thus falling into the same inconsistencies in the characterization of the narrator found in *The Innocents Abroad,* for which many notebooks and journalistic letters were also employed.[1] To fill out the approximately 350 remaining pages of this second travel book, he imported material from his writings in the *Enterprise,* the California newspapers, even the Buffalo *Express* and the *Galaxy.* In fact, six of the letters he wrote for the *Express*'s "Around the World" series focused on his adventures in the West and may have been the earliest germ for *Roughing It.* Originally, he had planned, at Bliss's urging, another trip for adventures to fill yet another travel book, but this time he couldn't get away. He had just been married and his father-in-law was fatally ill. Other domestic distractions, as we have seen, made such travel abroad impossible for the foreseeable future.[2]

Both travel books—*The Innocents Abroad* and *Roughing It*—remain eminently readable today, at least by those who still read and appreciate the historical value of travel experiences either in the new world of American tourism or the Wild West of the nineteenth century. The personality of the storyteller comes right to the fore in *Roughing It.* He employs a "Prefatory" the same way he would later in *Huckleberry Finn,* warning off any high expectations while at the same time encouraging them. "This book," the author writes, "is merely a personal narrative, and not a pretentious history or a philosophical dissertation." The market was already flooded with narratives of recent travel in the West, so that Twain had to carve out his particular approach. "It is a record," he continues, "of several years of variegated vagabondizing, and its object is rather to help the resting reader while away an idle hour than afflict him with metaphysics, or goad him with science."[3] It is this easygoing narrator, who is obviously not as straightforward as he seems, who makes this western tale unique even today. Like the *Innocents,* this book was plentifully illustrated, and it is indeed something of an injustice to publish Twain's writings today without the original illustrations. He was after the masses, as he once said, and the illustrations were a key part of his content.

In *The Green Hills of Africa* (1935), written in the same loose-narrative tradition of *Roughing It,* Ernest Hemingway included the now often quoted statement that American literature begins with one book. He was talking not about *Roughing It,* of course, but about *Huckleberry Finn,* where he found the origins of the American vernacular in fiction. This biographer once asked Mary Hemingway about the so-called Hemingway Code, in which human beings are seen as having only one life to live and so must live it bravely. It was at one of those faculty receptions, given for Mrs. Hemingway, who had come to campus to speak on her book about her experiences (not *his,* as my class discovered) in World War II, *How It Was* (1976). "My dear boy," she answered, "Ernie wasn't concerned with philosophical meanings; he just wrote stories." It can be said, of course, that all classical writing, including American writing, starts out as something other than "Literature." Emerson's essays are secularized sermons. Melville's *Moby-Dick* is, on one level at least, a maniacal travel account of his whaling experiences, something he had avoided in his tales of the sea up to its publication. Hawthorne's *The Scarlet Letter* may depend in part on the author's ancestral history with incest in the symbolic rendering of Hester as lover and mother. These works become American classics, as Professor Smith says of *Roughing It,* when the universality of their experiences is demonstrated and dramatized.

The classic quality in *Roughing It* is more clearly seen in the first half, but it may be unfair to deem the rest of the book inferior simply because it falls back on the anecdotal nature of American humor that is imported piecemeal from earlier publications. The reason is that his newspaper journalism is here sculpted into literature in which many of the episodes go deeper into the folly and the fatality of the human condition. In chapter 48, for example, we encounter Twain's dislike of the jury system, which, he had earlier hinted in the *Express,* was to blame for the acquittal by reason of insanity of the murderer of Albert D. Richardson. Arguing that only ignoramuses could qualify for jury duty, he said of one murder trial he allegedly witnessed in Virginia City, "It actually came out afterward, that one of these latter [jury members] thought that incest and arson were the same thing" (321). This line is the recycling of the comment in the Hawaii letters about the Wisconsin state legislator who confused arson with illicit sex and thought the legal system ought "either to hang him or make him marry the girl!"[4] It is clear that for Twain jurors and congressmen were first cousins.

Some of Twain's most memorable and humorous stories and sketches first appeared in the latter part of *Roughing It.* "Somebody has said that in order to know a community, one must observe the style of its funerals," he wrote in chapter 47 of what would become known in the Mark Twain canon as "Buck Fanshaw's Funeral." Its point of departure is the death in a gunfight of a well-known Virginia City figure called by the fictional name Buck Fanshaw. (Its real-life elements may come from a story about the demise of a gunfighter in the San Francisco *Call* of February 3, 1866.) After taking another jab at juries for failing to determine the obvious cause of Buck's death, Twain gives his readers a virtuoso performance of the slang in Silverland that is equal to the finest examples of the tall-tale brag of the Old Southwest. In preparing a local minister (a "fledgling from an eastern theological seminary") to give the "Obs'quies," Buck's friend Scotty Briggs describes Buck as "one of the whitest men that was ever in the mines. . . . He warn't a Catholic. Scasely. He was down on 'em. . . . He was the bulliest man in the mountains, pard! He could run faster, jump higher, hit harder, and hold more tangle-foot whisky without spilling it than any man in seventeen counties."

This story provides today's reader with not only some rough humor but also something like an ethnographic treatise on the 1860s slang of the Nevada Territory. Meanwhile, "The Story of the Old Ram" (chapter 53 of *Roughing It,* also known informally as "My Grandfather's Ram") not only resurrects Twain's digression tale but also employs (contrary to Howells's claim in *My Mark Twain*) intemperance as the basis for humor. In later years it became one of Twain's more popular platform pieces, this in spite of continuing temperance campaigns after the Civil War. Jim Blaine, the tale's narrator, reminds us of Jim Smiley of the Jumping Frog story. He is the interior narrator who talks in the vernacular, while the outside narrator—in the tradition of American humor—speaks in standard English. And like the opening narrator of the Jumping Frog story, this one is tricked by "the boys" into asking Blaine to tell his pointless story.

It is pointless because Blaine is drunk—"tranquilly, serenely, symmetrically drunk"; in other words, "a stalwart miner of the period." At last the boys sitting around Jim Blaine's cabin are told: "Sh—! Don't speak—he's going to commence." Three sentences into Blaine's monologue, the subject of his grandfather's ram disappears forever. It would be one thing to simply follow a digression faithfully, but Mark Twain's wit uncovers genius in the details. We go from Bill Yates to Seth Green to Sarah Wilkerson to Sile Hawkins, who is really "Filkins" ("Si Hawkins" will resurface in *The Gilded Age*), to a Miss Jefferson, who lent her glass eye to old Miss Wagner, "that hadn't any, to receive company in," and so on down the line of absurdity. There is also a wooden leg in this procession of body parts reminiscent of "Aurelia's Unfortunate Young Man." And there is even a parting shot at the notion of divine authority in a woman who "married a missionary and died in grace—et up by the savages. They et *him,* too, poor feller—biled him." But not to worry: "Prov'dence don't fire no blank ca'tridges, boys. That there missionary's substance, unbeknowns to himself, actu'ly converted every last one of them heathens that took a chance at the barbecue."

The ways of Providence weren't so funny in Mark Twain's final years if we are to accept the persistent claim that they were deeply pessimistic. (They were, but he never lost the sense of himself as the humorous butt of the cosmic joke.) He later wrote parodies about heaven, according to Edgar Lee Masters in his castigating biography, when he should have been satirizing the material and political corruption of his own country. Born in 1868, Masters, now an almost forgotten poet save in college anthology selections from his 1915 *Spoon River Anthology,* comes across in his biography of Lincoln as a neo-Confederate who imagined that with the Civil War, Lincoln and the Republican Party had sold the ideals of Jefferson down the river. More influential critics have castigated Twain for his abandonment of essentialism for what became relativism in the twentieth century. When he first presented an early chapter of the deterministic *What Is Man?* to the Monday Evening Club of Hartford on February 19, 1883 (then entitled "What Is Happiness?"), it was met with scoffs and jeers.[5] It is very possible that the scholarly emphasis on his late-life pessimism even today would not be so strong if he had become a muckraker instead of an immoralist attacking Judeo-Christian ideology. In other words, the most effective way to undermine his brutal satires on conventional religious beliefs, published after his death, was to suggest that he was philosophically naive and even childish when it came to the push and shove of eternity. But the mere fact that Twain could have made so much fun of man's insignificance in the cosmos (for example, as a diseased microbe in the body of a drunk) confirms not only his credentials as a supreme satirist but his maturity and indeed courage in the face of nothingness.

Starting with chapter 63, he recycled some of the Sacramento *Union* letters from Hawaii, cutting out substantial sections from thirteen of twenty-five letters, but revising the wording only of the parts he reused. Here the subject of missionaries continues and is contrasted with the literally stark naked innocence of the natives. (When he encounters a bevy of nude native women bathing in the sea, he leaves out of the *Roughing It* version the statement that he not only ogled them but also "went and undressed and went in myself.")[6] Here also we find the clear implication that these white missionaries have come to the earthly paradise to infect it with the Big Lie. They show the island innocents "what rapture it is to work all day long for fifty cents to buy food for next day with, as compared with fishing for pastime and lolling in the shade through eternal summer. . . . How sad it is to think of the multitudes who have gone to their graves in this beautiful island and never knew there was a hell!"

In chapter 77 the narrator encounters on the island of Maui another of those mysterious strangers who appeared to Mark Twain (and *within* him) from time to time. This stranger is naturally a storyteller, indeed a teller of tall tales who repeatedly contradicts the narrator's sense of reality by pointing to what he claims to be an even more remarkable fact than the one the narrator has just mentioned. He will appear again and again in the fiction of Mark Twain and finally emerge as the odd but gifted printer's apprentice in "No. 44, The Mysterious Stranger," who, it turns out, is Satan's nephew. "Somehow," Twain tells us, "this man's presence made me uncomfortable." Ultimately, the mysterious stranger is shown to be the biggest liar of all, who when found one day "hanging to a beam of his own bedroom," has even lied in his own suicide note. ("No. 44," however, shows the incongruence of lies about life in telling the Truth about human life.) In real life, Twain had encountered in the town of Lahaina the eccentric Francis A. Oudinot, a Southern sympathizer hiding out from the Civil War. In *his* lie, he claimed to be a descendant of the famous marshal of Napoleon's army, Charles Nicolas Oudinot (1767–1847).[7] But he was probably just another "American claimant," a type of liar that Mark Twain would depict as the Duke and the King in his most famous book. He was about to discover their prototype in his next literary sojourn—in England and the land of titles.

24 A Book about the English

In the spring of 1872, following the success of *Roughing It,* Mark Twain considered himself not only a successful humorist but also a proven travel writer. His next sojourn would, he thought, take him to a book about the English. After spending the summer with his family at a seaside resort in Saybrook Point, Connecticut, he sailed by himself that August to England. Just before his departure, he told Orion about his self-pasting scrapbook, the only invention that would ever earn him any sizable sum of money, outside his inventions in fiction. By now Orion had lost his job at the American Publishing Company after alerting his brother to Bliss's financial shortcuts on the production of *Roughing It* and was trying to reinvent himself again. Whatever Orion touched turned to dust, while whatever his brother touched now turned to gold.

This Midas touch did not extend to his book about the English, however, which never materialized. But in the process, or the lack of it, he discovered that he was now the most popular American writer abroad. Such fame had its own problems. He was immediately embraced by the English and was invited everywhere by anybody of note. He thus found little time to work on his book—"too much sociability," as he told Livy. The other obstacle had to do with his intention to write a satire about English customs. The warm British hospitality, though, made him reluctant to mock their customs. He told Mrs. Fairbanks that his newfound English friends had taken him right into their inner sanctuary, it seemed. How could he make fun of them without violating their trust?[1] He would eventually write another kind of book about the English in

A Connecticut Yankee in King Arthur's Court (1889) that wouldn't be very flattering, but for now he was stopped in his tracks when it came to the English.

One has to wonder why, except for the need of another travel subject, he set out to write the satire in the first place. Did he harbor the American disapproval of social rank based on birth? His uproarious lampoons of royalty in *Huckleberry Finn* and frontal attack on English nobility in *A Connecticut Yankee* had to originate somewhere. There were the family tradition on his mother's Lampton side that they were heirs to the Earl of Durham and the belief on his father's side that the Clemenses went back to the English Clements, who were of noble blood, but Twain put no stock in it, as he told a distant relative, Jesse Leathers, in 1875. He would, however, try for such a title if he thought there was "a reasonable chance to win it."[2] As it turned out, he was treated so thoroughly like royalty that he was paralyzed to write about the British in any disrespectful manner.

Practically the only Englishman not to show him respect was the publisher John Camden Hotten. He had published the first English unexpurgated edition of Whitman's *Leaves of Grass* without paying the author any royalties. But Hotten, exploiting the absence of an international copyright law (not enacted until 1891), republished any American who sold, and that certainly included Mark Twain, whose books and uncollected sketches he had been reprinting since 1870, beginning with *The Innocents Abroad.*[3] Starting with *Roughing It,* Twain learned to publish his books separately in England, before the American editions (thereby securing both copyrights), but even this approach backfired when Canada, even though it was then formally part of the British Empire, pirated *Tom Sawyer* after it was published in England and months before it came out in the United States. As a result, cheap copies of the book flooded the U.S. market and undersold Twain's own edition. Twain would actually travel to England to be on British soil when *The Gilded Age* came out in 1873, but he didn't take that precaution in publishing *Tom Sawyer,* instead finding a representative in the American expatriate Moncure Conway, whom he met in England in 1872.

Perhaps if he had encountered more Hottens, Twain might have gone ahead with his book about the English. By November, however, he was telling his mother and sister that he had more or less given up on that subject. He had made some notes toward it, but those that survive do not suggest it would have been much of a success. Otherwise, he had had such a good time being wined and dined and making after-dinner speeches that he had literally fallen in love with "these English folks."[4] He hated to leave them, but departed on November 26, planning to return that spring with his wife and little Susy. In terms of literary output, he was somewhat at a standstill because, though he may not fully have realized it yet, he was passing out of his phase as a travel writer.

Although he had shelved the English book, he would not soon give up on the English. In fact he returned to England twice in the next two years, allowing only a day or two in the United States between his second and third crossing of the Atlantic. This suggests immense physical stamina on Twain's part, for shipboard travel was arduous and often dangerous. On his first return from England, his ship had weathered extremely stormy seas. He and Livy visited England and later Scotland and Ireland between May and November 1873. Only weeks later he was back in England for a lecture tour on Hawaii and his adventures in *Roughing It.* He was without his wife again, to her deep regret (she had insisted that he return from his first unaccompanied visit to England in 1872), and he would not sail home from Liverpool until January 1874. His daily companion for the next two months would be his old friend from California, Charles Warren Stoddard.

Stoddard was a homosexual visiting a country where sodomy was a criminal offense punishable by incarceration. A more famous writer and homosexual, Oscar Wilde, would suffer this penalty some two decades later. And like Wilde, Stoddard very much admired Whitman's "Calamus" poems, which celebrated "manly love," or what Whitman called "Adhesiveness," a term adapted from his study of phrenology. Apparently, few aside from gay readers believed that by the term "manly love" Whitman meant homosexual intimacy. Stoddard did, however, and he had repeatedly asked Whitman in 1870, after his own sexual liberation in Hawaii in the 1860s, to please comment on the "Calamus" poems. Stoddard, as he would suggest in his *South Sea Idylls* (1873), based on his sojourn in Hawaii, was not interested, in the words of an early twentieth-century critic of his book, in "customary brown maidens with firm breasts, lithe limbs, and generous impulses [something Twain had certainly noticed in his letters to the Sacramento *Union*], but the strong-backed youths, human porpoises who drive their canoes through the mists of the storm." "In the name of Calamus," he begged Whitman, "listen to me!" Whitman for his part finally answered, on receipt of "A South-Sea Idyll," an abbreviated version of the longer work that Bret Harte had published in the *Overland Monthly* in 1869. "I do not of course object to your emotional & adhesive nature," the poet told Stoddard, but he also warned him against "extravagant sentimentalism."[5]

Stoddard had come to London in October as an occasional foreign correspondent for the San Francisco *Chronicle.* Ambrose Bierce and Joaquin Miller, California writers of the Twain-Harte era, who were then living in England, had also encouraged him to come abroad because he could easily increase his income, they said, by selling magazine articles to the British. Yet Bierce, who evidently knew Stoddard more intimately than Miller, warned him to avoid any homosexual trysts. "You will, by the way, be under a microscope here," he told him. "Your lightest word and most careless action noted down, and commented on by men who cannot understand how a person of individuality in thought and conduct can be other than a very bad man. . . . Walk, therefore, circumspectly . . . avoid any appearance of eccentricity."[6]

Twain added fifteen dollars a week and the cost of lodging to Stoddard's income by making him his personal secretary during his lecture tour and their stay at the Langham Hotel in London. A few years later he told Howells, who had published Stoddard in the *Atlantic,* that he had hired him as a secretary to keep a scrapbook of the daily newspaper reports of the Tichborne Claimant trial going on at that time, but his true reason for hiring Stoddard was so that he would "sit up nights with me & dissipate."[7] As Twain later commented, he was simply looking for a drinking partner in Charlie, whose friendship with Twain ultimately prompted him to decline payment for his secretarial work. During the lectures in December, Stoddard accompanied Twain to the theater, sat in the empty royal box during the lecture, and accompanied him and his manager, George Dolby, back to the hotel for late-night drinking.

"How the hours flew by," Stoddard recalled years later, "marked by the bell clock of the little church over the way! . . . We sat by the sea-coal fire and smoked numberless peace-pipes, and told droll stories, and took solid comfort in our absolute seclusion." Since Dolby probably wasn't always present during their drinking sessions, we might wonder whether Stoddard, when intoxicated, didn't broach an intimacy with his friend, perhaps confessing or hinting at his sexual attraction to men. Although Twain may have suspected that Stoddard was a homosexual, he was probably tolerant, perhaps because he, too, may have had a personal history of unconventional sexual behavior, albeit heterosexual, in Nevada and Hawaii. He probably understood that his somewhat effeminate friend was different but that this difference did not make him morally corrupt. Despite his good times with Stoddard, he missed Livy dearly and because of it would cut short his lectures in Scotland and Ireland after Christmas. "Poor, sweet, pure-hearted, good-intentioned, impotent Stoddard," Twain called him in a letter to Howells a few years later when they were trying to get him a consulship through the influence of President Rutherford B. Hayes, Howells's cousin by marriage.[8] It is doubtful that Howells ever suspected Stoddard's homosexuality; otherwise, he probably wouldn't have given *South-Sea Idylls* such a favorable review.

Twain went home to America for the third time in two years, apparently empty-handed. Or at least that's what he may have thought at the time. But he did return for the publication of *The Gilded Age,* coauthored with Charles Dudley Warner (discussed in the following chapter). More important with regard to the long gestation of *Huckleberry Finn,* however, was the fact that he also returned with Stoddard's scrapbook filled with the newspapers' daily descriptions of the Tichborne Claimant trial. This trial had fascinated him at least partly because of his distant cousin Jesse Leathers' letters over the years urging him to finance an investigation into the Lampton family's claim to the earldom of Durham. The Tichborne case concerned the claim of an Australian butcher who insisted that he was Roger Tichborne, believed to have been lost at sea in 1854. When the claimant arrived in London in 1866 to press his case, the lost boy's mother accepted his claim. When she died in 1872, he lost an ejection suit against his alleged nephew, the reigning baronet, and was subsequently tried and convicted of perjury and served the next ten years in prison. To this day, it has never been determined whether his claim was valid or not.[9]

Twain made brief reference to the case in chapter 15 of *Following the Equator* (1897), but the preposterous idea of asserting a claim to royalty manifested itself first and most magnificently in the Duke of Bridgewater in *Huckleberry Finn.* Twain, as noted, attended one session of the Tichborne perjury trial and long afterwards remembered seeing and perhaps conversing with the supposed "Sir Roger." "He was in evening dress," Twain recalled, "and I thought him a rather fine and stately creature. . . . It was 'S'r Roger,' always 'S'r Roger,' on all hands; no one withheld the title, all turned it from the tongue with unction, and as if it tasted good."[10] Nobody said, as the King does in chapter 19 of *Huckleberry Finn,* "Looky here, Bilgewater." Twain's uncompleted book about the English would have more than one afterlife.

25 Colonel Sellers

The Gilded Age, a satirical novel about government corruption in postwar America, appeared at the end of 1873, while Twain was still in England. He had written it with Charles Dudley Warner in five or six months earlier that year. It was a subscription book issued by the American Publishing Company (and by the Routledges in England), but, despite Twain's name recognition, not to mention Warner's reputation as a genteel humorist, it did not sell nearly so well as either *Roughing It* or *The Innocents Abroad.* (These sales may have had something to do with the fact that *The Gilded Age* was possibly the very first American *novel* to be issued by subscription.) The project had apparently been undertaken almost whimsically on a dare from the authors' wives during a dinner party in Hartford, soon after Clemens returned from England in 1872.[1]

James Fenimore Cooper, not one of Twain's favorite fiction writers, as we shall see, wrote *Precaution* (1820) on a similar dare from his wife as to whether he could write a better novel than Jane Austen. It was his first novel, and it was a failure, both artistically and commercially. He succeeded the next year with *The Spy* (1821), a forgotten classic about the American Revolution. Today, a visitor to Cooperstown, New York, where Cooper grew up, will find that the author has also been largely forgotten by the locals, who reinvented Cooperstown in the twentieth century as the home of the Baseball Hall of Fame. Indeed, the tide may have first turned against our greatest historical novelist with Twain's 1895 essay (discussed in chapter 43) that became because of its hilarity one of his most anthologized works in the second half of the twentieth century.

Practically all that remains of Cooper in Cooperstown is a lonely statue where his house once stood around the corner from the now bustling Hall of Fame. Today's visitors seem never to notice the seated author of the Leatherstocking Tales.

Cooper has not been forgotten, of course, in the annals of American literary history, but Warner has, apart from his identification with Twain. If Twain's contributions to American literature had ended with *The Gilded Age,* he would still be remembered but only as a minor travel writer and humorist. He was yet to make a full discovery of his Hannibal past and the river, whose culmination is not found so much in *Tom Sawyer* as it is in "Old Times on the Mississippi" and *Huckleberry Finn.* Neither Cooper nor Twain achieved their greatness by answering those dares from their wives, because in both cases the undertaking was a distraction from their identity-themes. For Cooper it was the Revolution, the sea, and the frontier. For Twain it was Hannibal and the river, where he met all "the damned human race" that he would ever need to know in order to write as he did.

To some extent, Twain's half of *The Gilded Age* also came out of his past, mainly in the use of his father's worthless land in Tennessee and his mother's cousin, James Lampton, as Colonel Eschol Sellers (changed, after the real Eschol Sellers threatened to sue, to "Beriah Sellers" and in the subsequent play to "Mulberry Sellers"). Twain saw Lampton for the last time in a hotel room in St. Louis in 1885 while on a lecture tour with George Washington Cable. With Cable in the next room, Sam got his voluble cousin to hold forth. After Lampton's departure, the New Orleans writer, who had recorded some of the visitor's talk, stuck his head in the door and said, "That was Colonel Sellers."[2] Twain's part of *The Gilded Age* also included his first substantial literary use of steamboating and the Mississippi River. In chapter 3 he introduces Uncle Dan'l from his Florida days on Uncle John Quarles's farm. In the novel, he is one of the slaves owned by the Squire or "Si" Hawkins family who regularly tells scary stories to the children, just as the real Uncle Dan'l had done for young Sam and his cousins. The story in the novel that frightens the Hawkins children is about "de Almighty," which turns out to be a steamboat coming down the river in the black of night. In the following chapter, Twain even includes a fatal steamboat race, despite knowing (as he must have known) that such a race had likely been the root cause of the explosion of the *Pennsylvania* and the death of his younger brother in 1858.

When the poet Masters criticized Twain for writing religious satires instead of political ones, he partially misjudged *The Gilded Age,* which targeted not only Congress and the Grant scandals but also the temporary insanity plea. The corrupt Senator Dilworthy is modeled on Senator Samuel C. Pomeroy, whose indictment for bribery was the subject of newspaper conjecture at the time. The novel's treatment of the insanity plea forms the basis of Laura Hawkins's defense for killing the bigamist she had unknowingly married. Masters was closer to the truth when he called the novel "a surface examination of a diseased body politic." Allusions to the shady dealings of the Grant administration, for example, were left somewhat oblique, presumably since Twain had already met the president and would in time profit from publishing the Civil War general's memoirs. For the most part, the story's thrust as a muckraking novel took a back seat to its political humor (which has not survived its age), but it went far enough to arouse the condemnation of several newspapers involved with the tawdry governmental politics of the day, including the influential Chicago *Tribune.*[3]

Aesthetically, the plot of the novel is rather chaotic and today obscure. Twain wrote the first eleven chapters, which tell the story of a patriarch in Tennessee very much resembling his father, all the way down to his running a village post office. His son Washington is based upon the dreamy Orion. The children include two youngsters, picked up along the way as the family migrates to Missouri and a river reminiscent of the Salt River (in the novel there is a scheme to secure federal funds to dredge the newly named Columbia River). One of the children is Laura, who eventually kills her husband with impunity, tries to lecture about it, and dies of a heart attack. The family is initially answering the call of Colonel Sellers, who eventually gets involved with Senator Dilworthy in schemes not only to reroute rivers and railroads but also to rededicate the worthless Tennessee land as a site for a trade school for ex-slaves. Warner took over at chapter 12 with a plot that involves a more traditional love affair between Philip Sterling and Ruth Bolton; it is never satisfactorily integrated with Twain's story line. The rest of the novel was completed by each writer taking his turn in the development of this zigzag plot. Today, the novel is—after Twain's book about Joan of Arc and perhaps *The American Claimant* (1892)—his least read work. Mostly, its title has survived to designate a greedy era in American history.

The Gilded Age was attacked in the press for being a lackluster novel that was promoted and sold by subscription advertisements even before the critical verdict could be heard. Several important magazines such as *Scribner's* and *Harper's* declined to review the book, and even the faithful Howells simply relegated it without comment to the "Other Publications" list in the *Atlantic.* Twain tried to use his influence with Whitelaw Reid, Horace Greeley's successor at the helm of the New York *Tribune,* but Reid, who had earlier solicited Twain for articles for the *Tribune,* refused to allow Edward House to review the book, either out of an animosity for House or because House was a personal friend of Twain's, or both. "Ask House to tell you about Whitelaw Reid," Twain wrote his coauthor Warner in the spring of 1873 when the still-unpublished book was being heralded as a potential best seller. "He is a contemptible cur, & I want nothing more to do with him," and Twain didn't have much to do with Reid for almost thirty years. For his part, Warner would soon lose his faith in the quality of their joint work. "On second thought," he told the critic Thomas Wentworth Higginson only weeks after the book appeared, "it is not best to send you The Gilded Age. . . . I have already found out that it is not much of a novel."[4]

As we have already seen and shall see again, Mark Twain never permanently lost faith in anything he wrote, and Warner's frailty in such matters may have lost him thousands of dollars when the novel was turned into a successful play. It is clear that he and Twain early on realized the book's possibilities as a play, most likely because of its ready topicality. They took out a dramatic copyright on the novel's adaptation in the spring of 1873. But when Gilbert B. Densmore, an editor and drama critic of the *Golden Era,* dramatized the play for a San Francisco production, Twain immediately threatened suit and ultimately purchased Densmore's play for two hundred dollars and the promise of two hundred dollars more if he used the material in his own dramatization. Because the Densmore play was based exclusively on Twain's characters, Twain asked Warner to relinquish his dramatic rights. In his authorized biography, Paine made it a point to argue that Warner "very generously and promptly" conceded that the play version was the property of his coauthor. He added, however, "Various stories have been told of this matter, most of them untrue."[5]

What Paine left out of his less than impartial picture of Warner's stolid indifference to losing a significant amount of money he probably deserved was the answer to a letter Paine had received from Twichell about the matter. Paine may have hoped that Twain had at least offered his coauthor a nominal payment for relinquishing dramatic rights to their joint enterprise. For regardless of whether the play was based solely on Twain's contribution, Twain would never have written the hit that became *Colonel Sellers* without having first coauthored *The Gilded Age* with Warner. On June 1, 1911, Twichell told Paine that there had been "some unpleasantness between them," but whether it was about the royalties from the book or Twain's claim for exclusive rights to the play is not known. This suggestion about "unpleasantness" may be supported by John Hooker, Twain's Nook Farm landlord in Hartford, who told his brother Edward on January 8, 1875: "Clemens has made a real stroke with this drama—It is too bad Charles Warner was not with him in it."[6] Hooker's expression of pity for Warner's loss, along with the authorized biographer's defensive posture on the matter, suggests that there was nevertheless some uncomfortable feeling between the coauthors. Perhaps Warner and Hawley's earlier slight of Twain when he had become interested in buying into the *Courant* came into play. Whatever the case, Twain's insistence on cutting out Warner, without so much as a token share of the play revenue, while voluntarily paying Densmore for the use of his text, shows him to have been a victim himself of the very Gilded Age that he and Warner had criticized in their novel. This gold-rush mentality would culminate in Twain's greatest folly—his monomaniacal investments in the Paige Compositor. In the meantime, as Colonel Sellers would say (in the play, not the novel), "There's millions in it."

The man who made the Colonel famous and the play almost as popular as the dramatic versions of Washington Irving's *Rip Van Winkle* and Stowe's *Uncle Tom's Cabin* was John T. Raymond. Raymond had been in the Densmore production in San Francisco in the spring of 1874, and it can be said that his performance as Colonel Sellers was what sold the play. This fact did not entirely please Twain because he thought Raymond consistently failed to bring out the full humanity of the flesh-and-blood original, James Lampton, and had merely portrayed his delusional and thus humorous side. Besides being a little defensive about exploiting a relative loved by his mother, Twain may have simply resented the fact that Raymond was the key to the play's commercial success. He even belittled his performance in one curtain speech. Yet as one contemporary remembered, there was an unequal division of labor in the play's success:

> Sellers gleams faintly on the printed page,
> As drawn by Clemens in the "Gilded Age,"
> But dominates, in Raymond, all the stage.
> Long may we live to see before us stand
> That humorous figure with uplifted hand![7]

Raymond was already a popular actor, but this role made him nearly as famous (for a time, at least) as Joseph Jefferson became in his title role in *Rip Van Winkle.*

Colonel Sellers (touted as "Mark Twain's Drama" in the printed program) officially opened at the Park Theater in New York City on September 16, 1874. Twain claimed to have completely rewritten Densmore's dramatic adaptation "three separate & distinct times," ultimately using fewer than twenty of his lines, but "so much of his plot" that he doubled his payment to Densmore. This assertion is found in a response to a criticism of his dealings with Densmore that appeared in the New York *Sun* on November 2 and was reprinted, with a dismissive first paragraph, the following day in the Hartford *Evening Post.* Twain immediately drafted his response, but it was never mailed, possibly because he thought the *Evening Post*'s denial of the *Sun* account made his own denial unnecessary. The only public response which argued that Twain was the sole author of most of *Colonel Sellers* came from Raymond in the *Sun* of November 3, but then, the actor was already financially linked with the author, splitting the profits fifty-fifty.[8] Without Densmore's version, apparently lost, there is no way of knowing precisely how much Twain used of the other's work. The fact is, however, that Mark Twain was never again successful as a playwright in spite of many endeavors in that direction. But this play was an immediate success that ran consistently for 119 nights, closing on January 9, 1875. Because of its successful opening season (not counting the performances in San Francisco and Rochester in the spring and summer of 1874), it was often revived and played six-week seasons between 1876 and 1888, ending only (and significantly) with Raymond's death.[9]

Reading the play today and finding genuine humor in it is difficult. Without Raymond, it is like the novel, a melodrama with a few satiric asides. American drama, of course, did not find its spark until the twentieth century. Today even the dramatic versions of "Rip Van Winkle" and *Uncle Tom's Cabin,* though superior to *Colonel Sellers,* have mostly lost their appeal (especially the one based on Stowe's classic for its distortion of the character Uncle Tom). The character of Sellers is immediately introduced with an imbedded off-color joke about his chasing "after every 'Ignus Fatous' that comes along." The Great Illusionist responds with vaudevillian angst that that is "no way to talk to me, you ought to know better. I'm too old a man. . . . I'll swear I've never heard the woman's name before."[10] There is a faint hint in the play that the Colonel is actually Laura's father, suggesting the illicit sexual relations that form the basis of the plot of *Pudd'nhead Wilson,* but nothing ever comes of it. The only slave with a speaking part is Uncle Daniel, who is present for the steamboat race and collision. Nine years of Sellers's foolish speculation in everything from mules to a perpetual motion machine have passed by the opening of act II. The only constant that looms over the Washington Hawkins family is the Tennessee land, which is never sold.

Laura Hawkins (the character's name is that of Twain's childhood sweetheart) takes center stage with all her problems. Her adopted brother, Clay, is in love with her, but she falls for a Confederate soldier who, unbeknownst to her, is already married. Laura had been in search of a noble mission in the spirit of Florence Nightingale or Joan of Arc, but she is ultimately consumed by her own egotism. Senator Dilworthy, whose exact model Sam had met when he visited Washington, D.C., on his father-in-law's behalf in 1870 in a lobbying effort worthy of the Gilded Age, does not make a stage appearance, but his scheme to assist ex-slaves by getting the government to purchase the Tennessee land is fully aired, along with the senator's "love for the Negro alone [which] actuates him."[11] Twain merely plays with this subject of race in the play, but it will soon emerge as a subtheme in works beginning with "A True Story" and culminating in *Huckleberry Finn* and *Pudd'nhead Wilson.*

"That's what Governments are for," exclaims Sellers in act III with regard to the various schemes under way to enrich private citizens. "It's only within the last few years, that the science of government has been thoroughly understood. Our fore fathers never had statesmen like ours." Here Twain, having interned as Senator Stewart's secretary in Washington in late 1867, begins to unload the full force of his humor upon Congress as useless and corrupt. When Lafayette Hawkins ("Washington" in the play) praises Sellers by saying that he ought to be in Congress, Sellers protests, "What have I ever done to you to justify you in making a remark *like that?*" The play ends with Laura's shooting her bigamist husband and being tried and acquitted on a plea of temporary insanity. When asked how anybody knew she was insane at the time of the crime, Sellers, who was the first to come upon the murder, testifies: "She—said she was sorry she killed him." In other words, she was about as sorry as an undertaker at a funeral. "Let us endeavor," Twain said in one of his famous quotations, "to so live that when we come to die even the undertaker will be sorry."[12]

Twain is said to have made between fifty and seventy thousand dollars for his half of *Colonel Sellers* during its thirteen-year run. It paid the bills, but much more important work was already under way by the time the play had its New York debut.

26 Mississippi Memories

Even before Twain made so much money on the play, he was becoming rich from his books. By the end of 1874 the American Publishing Company had bound a total of almost 245,000 copies of *The Innocents Abroad, Roughing It,* and *The Gilded Age.*[1] By the time *Colonel Sellers* closed its first season in New York in January 1875, he was awash in memories of the South, which flooded his imagination and would form the basis for *Tom Sawyer, Life on the Mississippi,* and *Huckleberry Finn.* These works would bring him not only more money but permanent literary fame. His recollections of boyhood had possibly been stirred by the family plots he had devised for *The Gilded Age.* (He began *Tom Sawyer,* a much more extensive narrative about childhood, six months before joining forces with Warner on the political novel.) He was now a southerner living in the North, and yet the South kept inserting itself into his consciousness. This upheaval of memories began in 1872, and greatly intensified during his fourth summer at Quarry Farm when he heard about the "troubles" of Mary Ann Cord, a former slave and then his sister-in-law's cook in Elmira, and wrote about them for the November 1874 *Atlantic* in his newly built octagonal study in the woods a short walk from the house at Quarry Farm. The publication was his first appearance in the prestigious magazine.

"A True Story, Repeated Word for Word as I Heard It" was a frame story told in black vernacular by a slave mother who, having been sold away from her seven children, was reunited with one of them during the war. Writing it may have stimulated or refocused Twain's thinking about both blacks and slavery, subjects merely italicized in the public mind after the Emancipation Proclamation. It was also one of his earliest experiments with a black dialect. He published something very similar later the same month in the New York *Times,* a sketch entitled "Sociable Jimmy," which features a ten-year-old black whose medley of free associations at least vaguely recalls Twain's earlier use of the digression story, such as in "His Grandfather's Ram." Both "A True Story" and "Sociable Jimmy" feature black characters who brought back to life for Sam Clemens vivid memories of Uncle Daniel and the others on the Quarles farm in Florida, Missouri. These African American voices were an essential part of the fabric of Mark Twain's greatest art, which was now beginning to emerge.[2] Only a month before these publications, on October 24, his Mississippi River memories had surged on yet another front during a walk around the Hartford countryside with Joe Twichell. Sensing the sure success of "A True Story," Howells had been eager for more from Twain's pen, but it wasn't until Sam started reminiscing with Joe about his steamboating days that he realized he had more material for the *Atlantic.* "What a virgin subject to hurl into a magazine!" Twichell had exclaimed,[3] and so it was.

Mark Twain's seven articles on the subject were almost unprecedented. An anonymous article in *Harper's* in 1870 entitled "Down the Mississippi" devoted only a few sentences to the profession of piloting. Another piece in *Scribner's* may have been—along with the conversation with Twichell—part of the impetus for Twain. Edward S. King's contribution to a series entitled "The Great South" appeared in October 1874. King alluded to the "quaint, dry humor" of the pilots and their fondness for storytelling. He also mentioned Mark Twain specifically as one of those who had served an apprenticeship on the river. Having stumbled on the dramatic possibilities of *The Gilded Age* through Densmore's script, Twain may have reacted in a similar manner to King's article, thinking that somebody was stealing his thunder. He had indeed considered writing a book on the subject as early as 1866. In 1871 he told his wife while on the lecture circuit, "When I come to write the Mississippi book, *then* look out!"[4] Whatever the case, it was always Mark Twain's destiny to write about the Mississippi River.

One measure of the enthusiasm with which the "Old Times" pieces (adapted later as the material for chapters 4–17 in *Life on the Mississippi*) were received is how quickly and widely they were copied by the other journals and newspapers around the country. This pirating before American magazines began to copyright their materials also took the form of a small book by an unscrupulous Canadian publisher using Twain's title. (Belford Brothers would give Twain more of the same when *Tom Sawyer* appeared.) In asking Twain for the articles, which ran from January to August of 1875, Howells had hoped to boost the *Atlantic* circulation (perhaps to recover from the drop in the subscription rate after Stowe's disastrous article on Byron in 1869), but the magazine may have sold even fewer copies than before, because the Twain articles sent to newspapers were in many cases republished verbatim instead of merely serving to advertise the *Atlantic.* Such exploitation was simply the result of popularity; it had plagued him on the lecture circuit, too, when newspapers had often printed his lecture nearly verbatim before the audience in the next town could hear him deliver it.

Although the articles formally set out to describe the "science" of piloting (which they did for a reading audience that knew relatively little about the antebellum culture of the Mississippi River), the main draw for readers today is the nostalgia that Twain evokes in these pieces, for he was indeed living in that past again when he sat down to write. "When I was a boy," he began, "there was but one permanent ambition among my comrades in our village on the west bank of the Mississippi River. That was to be a steamboatman." He captured the point of view of the boy on the river in that era who would eventually morph into the hero of *Tom Sawyer* and culminate in the narrator of *Huckleberry Finn.* One by one, he wrote in the *Atlantic* series, all other boyhood ambitions disappeared before the possibility of life on the river. These village boys might hope that God would allow them someday to become pirates, but when this fantasy faded, "the ambition to be a steamboatman always remained."

The sense of the river's sanctuary lay in the fact that it was securely in the past. That evocation of escape is at its most profound when it embraces Huck and Jim adrift on the river under the stars, safe if only temporarily from the greed and bigotry of the land. Such scenes suggest America's comparative innocence before the Civil War. Afterward, with the expansion of the country's influence throughout the world, it was well on the road to the loss of agrarianism and the greed of capital.[5] Even *Pudd'nhead Wilson* (1894), which reflects Twain's later cynicism about America, is one of his most vivid and compelling works because it is set before the war, when the country was shaping the future artist's vision. And it must be remembered that Twain's audience was reading these works on this side of the Civil War. Contemporary readers, of course, might share the author's sense of personal nostalgia, having experienced their own youth during the same time period, but the bigger pull was its invocation of a better past, one in which they always finally did the right thing.

Twain was writing in the era of literary realism, the same period in which Howells's protagonists could still grapple successfully with right and wrong and not be ruled exclusively by hereditary and environmental forces. It is only in the later chapters written for *Life on the Mississippi* that this spell is broken, when the account includes a view of the river and its life *after* the war and the demise of the steamboat. In the *Atlantic* articles, on the other hand, we find the basis for Twain's other strong works. Here the Mississippi Valley of the 1840s comes alive for really the first time in his oeuvre. Hannibal returns as the fictional St. Petersburg, and the Mississippi River comes back, carrying all the glory and greed of its antebellum culture. Here we get an eye-level view of life from a teenager growing up in Hannibal. It would be practice for the point of view he later created in *Huckleberry Finn,* which mixes reality with illusion to show us the absurdity of the commonplace. The narrator resents, for example, the boy in town who is the first to become an apprentice engineer on a steamboat. This envied youth had, we are told, both money and hair oil. The narrator here is the same one who gave those lectures around the eastern states, except now the travel book takes us not to Europe, the Nevada territory, or Hawaii but back to the sanctity of boyhood. Indeed, during his second lecture tour in 1871–72, he began writing that lecture on the boy. But "An Appeal in Behalf of Extending the Suffrage to Boys" was perhaps too full of political sarcasm to succeed, and he scrapped it even before giving it. His aim had been to poke light fun, or "good-natured satire," at woman's suffrage, a movement that he later supported.[6]

Sam had naturally learned the river "like a book," but that was important only insofar as he managed to become an acceptable if no better than average river pilot. He had also learned the river well enough to set *Huckleberry Finn* along its winding stream. He learned to read like a book all the people who made up the river's carnival of life—not only the deadbeats who conned their way from St. Louis to New Orleans and back but also the ignorant folk in all those hamlets and ramshackle towns along the river. "Old Times on the Mississippi" was clearly a dress rehearsal for the adventures of Tom and Huck, or the bad boy who never came to grief and the good boy who did not prosper, in the sense that it crystallized the backdrop of their dramas.

It is somewhat ironic that Twain complains that learning the science of piloting undercut the romance of the Mississippi. "Now when I had mastered the language of this water and had come to know every trifling feature," he writes in what became chapter 9 of *Life on the Mississippi,* "all the grace, the beauty, the poetry had gone out of the majestic river!" If this loss were in any way real, it could only be in the later chapters of the book, which recount Twain's visit after the war and the death of the steamboat industry. For in reconstructing the life of the pilot before the war, he presents a picture of relative, if not absolute, freedom. Not only was the pilot paid as much as the vice president of the United States, but he outranked all the officers on the boat, including the captain, as long as the vessel was underway. Even the details of piloting in those days are romanticized, or at least exaggerated. Most pilots were risk takers (something Mark Twain was not, at least as a pilot), and many serious accidents occurred on that busy stream of commercial traffic. Yet it is the romance of it all that is transferred to the world of Tom Sawyer and Huck Finn. T. S. Eliot, another famous American writer who hailed from Missouri, called the Mississippi "a strong brown God" in his *Four Quartets.* The river was a living presence whose currents in Mark Twain's world carry readers back to childhood and innocence.

In "Old Times" Twain first recovered this world that became the setting of his other river novels, including *Pudd'nhead Wilson.* In what became chapter 11, he talks of the "small-fry craft" that steamboat captains dismissed as "an intolerable nuisance." One of these resembles

Huck and Jim's raft, run over in chapter 16 of *Huckleberry Finn.* He even anticipated the novel's two frauds or false claimants to royalty in the deckhand who was either "an earl or an alderman" (chapter 5 of *Life*). In what became chapter 12, there is the puppy-love bragging and posing we find in *Tom Sawyer.* When the "pretty girl of sixteen" visits the pilothouse with her aunt and uncle, both the youthful narrator and another cub pilot vie for her attention. This other cub pilot, like Huck on the raft in chapter 16, dives deep enough during a mishap to keep from being killed by the boat's paddle wheel.

Mark Twain, too, was diving deep into his memories of the Mississippi Valley before the war. As we shall see, *Adventures of Huckleberry Finn* bears the marks of a number of books he was working on simultaneously, with his usual fits and starts, not just the river books but also *A Tramp Abroad* and *The Prince and the Pauper.* Yet the river had the main hold on his imagination. When he expanded "Old Times" into *Life on the Mississippi,* he was defeated in his effort to recapture the magic of the earlier chapters in the *Atlantic.* In the chapters following the material from "Old Times," he turns his autobiographical tale of youthful aspirations and naiveté into an adult travel book. But the true traveling was to be found in the combination of the river with his past before the age of fifteen, the age at which, he once told the widow of Will Bowen, he would have been happy to have been drowned.[7]

At the time of the preparation of *Life* in 1882, the most important part of that memory was already well under way in the composition of *Huckleberry Finn.* That year he pulled the "raft passage" out of his novel and inserted it in *Life* "by way of illustrating keelboat talk and manners, and that now departed and hardly remembered raft life." It became chapter 3 with the title "Frescos from the Past," signaling the nostalgic nature of the boy's personal history. It is the episode (now officially restored to *Huckleberry Finn,* after the discovery in 1990 of the long-lost first half of the holograph of Twain's novel) in which Huck swims out to a barge full of inebriated raftsmen to discover whether he and Jim have already passed Cairo and thus missed their escape route from slavery up the Ohio River. Written in the tradition of the tall talk of the Old Southwest, this passage features two "prodigious braggarts," drunkards who exaggerate their ferocity until a much smaller raftsman calls their bluff. The raft scene introduces Huck for the first time in his own right and out from under the shadow of Tom Sawyer. It is told in Huck's voice, the same one that will tell the sequel to *Tom Sawyer,* which had been narrated in the third person. Here is Huck's actual debut in American literary history.

The raft scene probably just as well belongs in *Life on the Mississippi,* where it gives one of the more dramatic depictions of river culture, for in *Huckleberry Finn* the passage of more than five thousand words strikes some readers as a digression containing nothing essential to either plot or theme. And while its achievement in depicting the local color of that bygone era is at least equal to that of A. B. Longstreet (in *Georgia Scenes*) or Thomas Bangs Thorpe (in "The Big Bear of Arkansas"), it is also unoriginal in the sense that it follows too rigidly the formulaic structure of the vernacular tales that precede it. Twain warned his publisher to keep it out of the novel's prospectus (a volume of sample chapters that vendors of subscription books carried to potential buyers in the hinterlands), because he feared that including it there might cause the new book to be perceived as a "reprint" of *Life on the Mississippi.* Later, in the effort to slim down *Huckleberry Finn* to make it more of a physical match for *Tom Sawyer,* for which it was advertised as a sequel, the publisher urged that the raft scene be removed from the printer's copy even before typesetting began.[8]

The important point in all this is that the fully formed Huck Finn first surfaced in *Life on the Mississippi*—a story of a general past that gives us our initial glimpse of his personal history, which would become the subject of an American classic. The Huck of the raft scene was first created in the summer of 1876 during the first phase of the composition of *Huckleberry Finn.* Although at the outset he appears to the public as Tom Sawyer's sidekick in *Tom Sawyer,* the true Huck wasn't far behind. But this river rat with a conscience would have to go through several more modifications or transformations, in Twain's other works of this period that served as part of the foreground to *Huckleberry Finn,* before emerging in his own right.

27 The Riley Book

Considered as adult literature, *The Adventures of Tom Sawyer* is possibly the most overrated work in American literature. If Mark Twain had never written *Huckleberry Finn,* it would today be regarded as simply one of the era's great paeans to the American boy, in the tradition of Thomas Bailey Aldrich's forgotten classic (*The Story of a Bad Boy*) "about the pleasant reprobate" who "in spite of the natural outlawry of boyhood," as Howells put it, "was more or less part of a settled order of things." Instead, paired with the "sequel" that became an American classic, it has been either overexposed or overpraised in the public mind. *Tom Sawyer* was the novel that ultimately fulfilled the contract with the American Publishing Company for the diamond mine book that had sent the fated John Henry Riley to Africa before his untimely death.[1] Like "Jim Smiley and His Jumping Frog," it has a stranger—too well dressed on a weekday for St. Petersburg, as the omniscient narrator observes. But this youthful rival is soon dispatched by Tom and thus dismissed as nothing more than an extra in the plot, whereas the other outsmarts Jim Smiley and becomes the prototype for Twain's other, more mysterious strangers. *Tom Sawyer*'s title and chief features are even better known to the average reader than those of its so-called sequel. Its memorable fence whitewashing scene, for example, is as famous as the plight of the henpecked husband who takes a twenty-year nap in Washington Irving's "Rip Van Winkle." Neither story was entirely original with its author. *Tom Sawyer* combines the detective story with the boy's tale, while the idea of "Rip Van Winkle" was borrowed from a German folktale. At least Irving's story contains something resembling a literary theme—the idea that while things change, they also stay the same. When Rip wakes up, he is no longer a subject under George the Third but a citizen under George Washington. He merely exchanges a termagant wife for a termagant daughter. Twain's novel is also a dream—the author's reminiscence of childhood—but where is its theme, other than the sentimental one that childhood is a time of innocence and worthy of celebration? Its distinguished achievement clearly lies in the genre of children's literature, and it should not be judged by the standards of adult fiction.[2]

Yet it was also a major contribution to the local-color movement that had arisen after the Civil War opened Americans' eyes to geographical areas beyond what had been their hundred- or two-hundred-mile travel radius from home. As Walt Whitman wrote of his soldier brother George: "He has marched across eighteen states, traversing some of them across and back again in all directions. He has journeyed as a soldier since he first started from this city [Brooklyn], over twenty thousand miles; and has fought under Burnside, McClellan, McDowell, Meade, Pope, Hooker, Sherman and Grant."[3] Moreover, Americans during this postwar period, when the South was becoming increasingly resentful of the continued presence of federal troops, welcomed this walk down memory lane. For its part, the North was becoming weary of the Negro and his cause (gained in war and lost in peace, as Frederick Douglass sadly concluded in 1894) and so was now losing interest in its continued punishment of the South.[4] It, too, yearned for the simplicities of childhood.

One of the reasons for the misclassification of *Tom Sawyer* is that Mark Twain himself could not decide whether he was writing a children's book or one for adults. In his author's preface, he says: "Although my book is intended mainly for the entertainment of boys and girls, I hope it will not be shunned by men and women." Earlier, while finishing the book, he told his friend Howells, "It is *not* a boy's book, at all. It will only be read by adults. It is only written for adults." Yet in another letter to the editor, after Howells had worked over the manuscript for him, Twain stated that the book was "now professedly & confessedly a boy's and girl's book." He added significantly that this designation bothered him "some nights, but it never did until I had ceased to regard the volume as being for adults."[5] Clearly, he could not hold up his head high enough when under the impression that he was writing for children. Once it was admitted, the task was easier to live with. He simply hoped, as he confessed in this preface, that *The Adventures of Tom Sawyer* would not be "shunned" by adults.

The embryo for the novel, in the opinion of Bernard DeVoto and others, is a sketch labeled by Twain's literary executor as the "Boy's Manuscript," penned in late 1868 (not 1870, as guessed by Paine). As John Gerber observes, Twain wisely abandoned it because—probably like "An Appeal in Behalf of Extending the Suffrage to Boys"—it was too much of a burlesque to succeed.[6] Yet the idea of the boy stayed with him, fortunately until its culmination in *Huckleberry Finn,* where he would confront rather than extol what he had believed as a boy. In *Tom Sawyer,* where slavery is practically never mentioned, he had stayed within the boy's sanctuary of naiveté and innocence. Tom, the boy Sam had been in Hannibal, becomes in the "sequel" to his story the adult his creator became in Hannibal before the war, the one who voted against Lincoln in the 1860 election. Indeed, Tom is almost wholesomely good in his own book, but a hypocrite in Huck's, withholding the crucial information that Jim is already free. Twain states in the preface to *Tom Sawyer* that the adventures recorded in the novel were not only his own but those of his schoolmates as well. We know that his model for Huck Finn was Tom Blankenship, but in many ways the model wasn't this member of the Hannibal underclass but the "boy," or person, Twain hoped he had become by the time he wrote *Huckleberry Finn:* one who followed his conscience in a corrupt society. The other boy—Tom Sawyer—was in fact "drawn from life" in the sense that he was a stand-in for the consensus in this slaveholding village, a consensus that the young Sam Clemens had innocently subscribed to at the time.

Twain may have written as many as a hundred pages of manuscript for *Tom Sawyer* by the time he broke off to work on *The Gilded Age.* He didn't get back to the story until the spring and summer of 1874, and he finished the book the following spring and summer, all or most of the writing having been accomplished at Quarry Farm. After Howells read and critiqued the manuscript, he told Twain on November 21, "It's altogether the best boy's story I ever read," but he had made a number of corrections. After recovering from bronchitis during the Christmas season of 1875, Twain finally opened the package with Howells's editing and accepted almost everything without even reading through the manuscript. "There [never] was a man in the world so grateful to another as I was to you day before yesterday," he wrote his friend on January 18, "when I sat down (in still rather wretched health) to set myself to the dreary & hateful task of making final revision of Tom Sawyer, & discovered . . . that your pencil marks were scattered all along. . . . Instead of *reading* the MS, I simply hunted out the pencil marks & made the emendations which they suggested."[7]

Twain hated to revise anything, but *Tom Sawyer* may have been more irritating than other works. For one thing, he had not soared to the same romantic heights in the book as he had in the "Old Times" sketches. That kind of profound engagement wouldn't recur until *Huckleberry Finn.* Indeed, until the story in *Tom Sawyer* gets fully into its rhythm with the grave-robbing scene and the murder of Dr. Robinson in chapter 9 ("When you fairly swing off," Howells observed about the last two-thirds of the text), it is self-consciously if also cleverly narrated. Tom becomes almost a puppet in this patriarchal storyteller's hands. When the boy tricks one of his comrades into whitewashing the fence, he is a "retired artist." This young man, who is old enough to be sexually attracted (we would assume) to Becky, is also innocent enough to show off to the new girl in town by balancing a straw upon his nose. This exaggerated state of innocence may have been conceived when Twain was still considering taking him into adulthood in the story. In any case, the author seems to have been at odds with himself in organizing the tale. The plot at first wanders from episode to episode as if he were merely arranging vignettes from his past. Tom matures somewhat during the novel, but he experiences no epiphany or attack of conscience like that which besieges Huck. Regardless of Twain's indecision on the matter, the book was finally written for children. Unlike its "sequel," it was no bildungsroman, or novel of adolescence in which a young protagonist verges on the difference between childhood illusions and adult reality.

Twain's Tom would never have inspired the creation of Holden Caulfield in J. D. Salinger's *The Catcher in the Rye.* Huck, on the other hand, did influence Salinger and many other writers besides.

The American publication of *Tom Sawyer* was fraught with difficulties. Howells, as he promised, started "the sheep to jumping in the right places" by giving the book a glowing review in the *Atlantic* for May 1876, but it appeared six months before the book itself was published. Because of production delays at the American Publishing Company, the American edition of the book did not appear until December. In the meantime, to again prevent pirating in England and (he thought) in the colonies, Twain had arranged with Moncure Conway to have the British edition appear first. But this routine protective strategy backfired when Belford Brothers of Toronto, the unscrupulous firm that had pirated "Old Times," began in the summer of 1876 to publish cheap editions of *Tom Sawyer* by reprinting the English edition put out by Chatto and Windus. Belford Brothers claimed that Canadian law superseded British in this case. Since Clemens had not sent an agent to Canada or gone himself (as he would with *The Prince and the Pauper*) to obtain Canadian copyright for *Tom Sawyer,* it was not protected there.[8] Twain was naturally bitter and threatened to write only plays in the future, thinking he could reproduce the success of *Colonel Sellers.* "Belford has taken the profits all out of 'Tom Sawyer,'" he told Conway as the American edition finally came out. "We find our copyright law here to be nearly worthless, and if I can make a living out of plays, I shall never write another book."[9] But there would be no more dramatic successes like *Colonel Sellers.*

This was a rather devastating blow, which manifested itself throughout the 1870s with his going back and forth between at least three manuscripts. He had already collected what he considered the best of his short pieces under the heading of *Sketches New and Old* in 1875. He faced many distractions. He was now the father of two daughters with the birth of Clara in 1874. He was active in several Hartford societies, including the Monday Evening Club. He and Livy fell into a heavy schedule of entertaining at their grand Hartford house, often inviting the Howellses and the Aldriches as weekend guests. He was now in his early forties and in the prime of life. He was an accomplished author, whose greatest work lay just over the horizon. He touched on Huck's life in the "sequel" in the last chapter of *Tom Sawyer.* It was cut from that novel at Howells's suggestion, and possibly became the first chapter of *Huckleberry Finn.*[10] Here we meet Huck at the home of the Widow Douglas, and his tale starts out almost as innocuously, in terms of Twain's satire and irony, as *Tom Sawyer.*

When Twain changed the point of view of this chapter to the first person, however, he began to speak in a voice that would hardly suit the Victorian standards of New England. It was not simply the American vernacular that had replaced the English narrator's silver tongue, but the American point of view as well—which used language, words so full of Whitman's vocabulary that they would bleed, as Emerson once noted of *Leaves of Grass.* The trouble began in Boston and would suggest that Mark Twain was almost as much of an affront to the Boston Brahmins and their literary way of depicting the world as that upstart from Brooklyn who had once published without permission a letter of Emerson's praising *Leaves of Grass.* Twain, too, was seen as stepping out in the wrong direction. Already, the newspapers were picking up his audacious opinions. In the earliest recorded interview with the press, he told the Chicago *Evening Post* of December 21, 1871, that he was glad that the prince of Wales, who would become King Edward VII in 1901, was recovering from typhoid fever. "I'm glad the boy's going to get well," he told the reporter. "For he will probably make the worst king Great Britain has ever had." He developed a public brashness that the press loved—and exploited. He spoke of "politician scum" to the New York *Herald* during the Hayes-Tilden presidential race of 1876.[11] It was the beginning of the era of Mark Twain the Humorist, who whenever he visited New York or Boston would usually be interviewed by the press and whose political views were savored by journalists looking for material to sell newspapers. The public welcomed him. The literati were rather puzzled, but since he was now an *Atlantic Monthly* author, Howells generously suggested that he speak at the journal's seventieth-birthday dinner party for John Greenleaf Whittier.

28 Banned in Boston

The most memorable event for Mark Twain in 1877 should have been his second visit to Bermuda, this time in the welcome company of his "pastor," Joe Twichell. As we will recall, Twain had made a brief first visit there a decade earlier at the tail end of the *Quaker City* cruise. His second visit in May would set in motion a pattern of returning there numerous times throughout his life, particularly in his final years, for the island reminded him of his happy childhood in the Mississippi Valley as well as his time in the paradise he had found in Hawaii.[1] But for sheer biographical importance, this particular Bermuda interlude is easily overshadowed by the failure, both imagined and real, of his speech at the *Atlantic Monthly*'s seventieth-birthday dinner for John Greenleaf Whittier on December 17.

We remember it today as Twain's speech about three drunks purportedly named "Mr. Longfellow, Mr. Emerson & Mr. Oliver Wendell Holmes" who invade the cabin of a miner in the foothills of California. The dinner at the Brunswick Hotel in Boston involved fifty-eight distinguished male writers of the day. Women were invited only to the after-dinner speeches, which began at 10:15, when the doors were opened to a select public. The diners included not only this noble trinomial of literary saints—Henry Wadsworth Longfellow, Ralph Waldo Emerson, and Oliver Wendell Holmes—but also such now largely forgotten writers as Charles Dudley Warner and Thomas Wentworth Higginson, whose work was typical of what we would now call the age of Howells. Present as well, of course, was the ex-westerner Howells himself, by now—it was thought—thoroughly scrubbed of his Ohio backwoods odor. In a description the following day in the New York *Evening Post,* George Parsons Lathrop, Nathaniel Hawthorne's son-in-law, made the gathering sound like something out of James Russell Lowell's *A Fable for Critics* but without the friendly satire: "Here robust and cheerful, with an expression of richly courteous dignity, stands Longfellow, a white-haired Hyperion. There, Emerson, himself beyond seventy, but to all seeming wonderfully well and wearing that incurious but searching inquiry which in a company like [this] gives him the air of one who does not suspect his own fame." The article named the most prominent writers present, including Whittier himself, "quietly talking with a group of friends at one side of the room" in the east dining hall of the hotel.[2]

The dinner began sharply at 7:00 P.M. Its seven courses were washed down with Sauterne, sherry, Chablis, claret, and Burgundy—objected to the following day in a formal resolution by the local chapter of the Woman's Christian Temperance Union. Such lubrication must have placed more than a few of the auditors in an alcoholic haze that has perhaps forever compromised the accounts of how Twain was actually received that evening. According to Henry Nash Smith, who has written the fullest account of the evening and its aftermath: "Henry O. Houghton [publisher of the *Atlantic*] made a short address of welcome and introduced Whittier as guest of honor. Whittier excused himself from speaking and asked Longfellow to read a sonnet, 'Response,' composed by Whittier for the occasion. Houghton then introduced Howells as toastmaster, and Howells introduced Emerson, who . . . recited Whittier's 'Ichabod.'"[3] Howells himself made a short speech, Holmes read a new poem of his own, and Charles Eliot Norton responded with a toast to Lowell, who was absent as minister to Spain. Howells then read letters from those dignitaries unable to attend, after which he introduced Mark Twain. This wasn't actually Twain's first appearance as a speaker at an *Atlantic* dinner, and that may have been part of the problem. He had attended and spoken briefly at his first *Atlantic* dinner on December 15, 1874, following the publication of "A True Story" in the journal the previous month. Because of his perceived success as a charming humorist (that earlier time, he spoke somewhat impromptu on "The President of the United

States [Grant] and the Female Contributors" to the *Atlantic*), he was expected this time to give a performance in line with his recent *Atlantic* pieces, not just "A True Story," but the "Old Times" pieces of 1875.[4] His latest book after all was *Tom Sawyer,* a lighthearted tale ostensibly written for children. In other words, he was expected to offer safe comic relief to a program laden with high seriousness and deep sentiment.

To those fifty-eight writers, with Howells perhaps excluded because of his own lingering fear of being an outsider, Mark Twain may have represented potential anarchy. Smith concludes his lengthy analysis of the dinner with the suggestion that the speech "expressed a deep-seated conflict" on Twain's part regarding the literary Brahmins of New England. Another literary executor of the Twain estate and lifetime student of Mark Twain's, Bernard De Voto, even theorizes that *The Innocents Abroad* had possibly been a burlesque of Longfellow's travel books.[5]

Twain rehearsed the story of his shame over the speech in a chapter from his autobiography published in the *North American Review* in December 1907. He recalled being preceded at the podium by William Winter, drama critic for the New York *Tribune* and nemesis of Walt Whitman for "inappropriate" writings in *Leaves of Grass.* Initially, Winter had been one of the drinkers along with Howells who were friendly to Whitman during his days in 1860 at Pfaff's Broadway saloon in New York, but Winter had since defected and would soon denounce the poet whose book became the first to be "banned in Boston" in 1882. (Howells, too, would later keep his distance from Whitman, but as we shall see later on, Twain contemplated publicly supporting the "obscene" poet.) We don't know what Winter thought of Twain's characterization of the putative Emerson as "a seedy little bit of a chap," or for that matter his description of the pretended Holmes as "fat as a balloon" and the impostor Longfellow as having the physical build of "a prize-fighter," but to any reader out west when Twain was writing hoaxes for the *Enterprise,* the wholly inaccurate physical descriptions would have signaled the farcical nature of his talk that evening. (Holmes, for example, was hardly "fat as a balloon," but so short that he had to have special hooks in his front parlor so that he could reach them to hang his hat.) All Twain recorded was that the pleasure of the evening for everyone ended when Winter sat down and he stood up to deliver a memorized tale that turned the faces of his audience "to a sort of black frost."

Twain was followed by William Henry Bishop, a writer now completely forgotten in the annals of American literature. His first romance, entitled *Detmold,* was just beginning its serialization in the *Atlantic.* Twain remembered that the faces of his auditors that evening, as he finished his own performance, wore the "expression faces would have worn if I had been making these remarks about the Deity and the rest of the Trinity." Exactly such remarks about "the rest of the Trinity" had already been literally made long ago in Emerson's own "Divinity School Address," after which he had become persona non grata at Harvard for more than thirty years. Only in recent years had Emerson, one of Twain's alleged victims that evening, been hailed as a member of the (literary) godhead. Twain recalled or claimed that the shock of his address was so severe that his successor at the speaker's platform lost all composure and could not complete his address. Having "burst handsomely upon the world with a most acceptable novel," Twain noted in his autobiography, Bishop crumbled. "He was facing those awful deities . . . with a speech to utter. No doubt it was well packed away in his memory, no doubt it was fresh and usable, until I had been heard from."[6]

Bishop, coincidentally, was born in Hartford. During his eighty-one years he wrote many other books, taught Italian at Yale in the 1890s, and occupied two different consulships in Italy. Indeed, he had modeled his early work after that of his mentor Howells, who himself had also enjoyed a consulship in Italy and later sponsored Bishop for admission to the American Academy of Arts and Letters. Like many so-called realistic novels in the dawning age of Social Darwinism, however, Bishop's *Detmold* ran the risk of waxing sentimental. A cautionary tale about Americans trying to discover themselves in Verona, where they worship its ancestral history and lush landscapes, its marriage plot features Louis Detmold, an architect schooled in Ruskin who has followed his love Alice Starfield abroad in the hope of persuading her to reconsider his proposal of marriage. Alice herself is a typically proud Victorian heroine who is headstrong in ignorance of the fact that she actually loves Detmold.

Detmold, however, has a skeleton in his closet. Long ago his father committed a vague financial crime not unlike the one Silas Lapham, Howells's most famous protagonist, is tempted to commit to save his business. (Typically, in such Realistic genres, the hero may suffer personal misfortune, but the loss does not rob him of his dignity.) By now Detmold's father has fully atoned for his mistake, but the shame endures. When an Italian rival for Alice's hand reveals the ancient crime, it turns out that Alice, the adopted child of a wealthy American family, is actually the daughter of Detmold's father's partner in crime. The melodrama bristles with the ideology of American or Emersonian individualism. "The self-made man is our cornerstone," Detmold declares, and blames American women (not invited to the Whittier banquet, we recall) for perpetuating most of the American snobbishness and love for the undemocratic ways of Europe. Howells may also have been attracted to Bishop's rather patronizing defense of American humorists in the novel. They are, Detmold states, "something more" than humorists—like Artemus Ward and Howells's friend and guest that evening, Mark Twain—who "have a much better claim to statues than a great many who get them. . . . I go even further," Detmold exclaims. "I wish to see a bust of the Jumping Frog in Central Park."[7]

In fact, Bishop didn't lose his composure at the Whittier birthday dinner, as Twain remembered in his autobiography, but delivered his speech as planned. Furthermore, the rest of the speeches went forward as well. The *Post* the next day in its report of the dinner did not even mention Twain's speech, while the Boston *Globe* of the same date noted that it had "produced the most violent bursts of hilarity." The negative response emerged a couple of days later. Once the Boston *Transcript* pronounced the speech "in bad taste," similar newspaper verdicts followed. And for Twain this reaction was also probably fueled by Howells's statement to him in a letter on Christmas Day that "every one with whom I have talked about your speech regards it as a fatality." At Howells's suggestion, Twain sent letters of apology to Emerson, Holmes, and Longfellow, all of whom (with the possible exception of Emerson) quickly regarded the speech as generally harmless and even entertaining. Gradually, Twain forgave himself as "God's fool," and a few weeks later even told his friend Mary Fairbanks that it was one of the funniest things he had ever written. Later—almost twenty-nine years after the event, in 1906—his social secretary Isabel V. Lyon recorded in her diary that even though Twain took the blame for the Whittier speech in his autobiography, he was privately, in her words, "chuckling with delight over the speech. . . . 'Oh [he exclaimed], it will do to go into print before I die' and the couch [shook] with him and his laughter." He subsequently insisted on reading the Whittier speech to Lyon, word for word.[8]

Some today still insist that it *was* funny, and it is. Possibly, it is more entertaining today than the Jumping Frog story that first made him famous, particularly in the way that Twain sets New England's greatest verse against the arid landscape of the Sierra Nevada mines of California. Here, it should be remembered, Clemens himself had failed at silver mining in 1862 and at the time had yet to discover his calling as a writer. Now, as he said on this fateful evening in 1877, standing before the country's "biggest literary billows," he was "reminded of a thing which happened to me fifteen years ago, when I had just succeeded in stirring up a little Nevadian literary ocean-puddle myself." In the story, the three miners cheat at cards and threaten to brawl until their host falls asleep. He wakes just in time to spot the three miners leaving his cabin. Longfellow, who is making off with the host's only set of boots, is called out as "Evangeline." The fraud impersonating that century's leading poet then answers with the following lines from Longfellow's most famous poem, "A Psalm of Life":

Lives of great men all remind us
We can make our lives sublime;
And, departing, leave behind us
Footprints on the sands of time.

Twain was performing as he was expected to—having fun with some sacred verses. It was a traditional frame story with the exception that "The Miner's Story" within the frame is told by the "fourth littery man," Mark Twain, a younger version of the outside narrator. But while poets like Whitman were being parodied constantly for their experimental verse, writers like Longfellow, Holmes, and Emerson were then considered sacrosanct. Yet it wasn't the poets themselves who objected, but their admirers. Apparently, neither Longfellow nor Holmes took offense. Longfellow responded on January 6, 1878, to Twain's apology by saying he was "a little troubled, that you should be so much troubled about a matter of such slight importance." He added, "The newspapers have made all the mischief." And initially the newspapers had supported Longfellow and Holmes's favorable impression of Twain's speech. The day after it, the Boston *Globe* noted: "Mr. Longfellow laughed and shook, and Mr. Whittier seemed to enjoy it keenly."[9]

Only Emerson, the review said, appeared "a little puzzled about it." We know that by this point he was entering a phase of dementia, and this condition may have come into play here. But if fully alert, he too wouldn't have minded Twain's joke at his expense. The author of "The Comic" knew, as he wrote in that essay, that man was "the only joker in nature" because he alone possessed an appreciation of incongruity, which is at the heart of not only humor but the challenge of nature itself as an emblem of God or the Oversoul. In other words, we become grotesque and the object of humor, the transcendentalist decreed, when we fall out of harmony with nature. If any Emerson was offended, it was his daughter Ellen, one of the many admirers of these Schoolroom poets and New England Brahmins. For her there would be no statue of the Jumping Frog in Boston Common, or in Concord for that matter. In answering for her father, Ellen Emerson, who had become his secretary and constant companion at his lectures and other public events, responded (to Mrs. Clemens, incidentally) that the Emerson family was disappointed since "we have liked almost everything we have ever seen over Mark Twain's signature."[10] That is to say, they had appreciated him merely as a humorist. Twain, in spite of his real or simulated contrition about the speech, must have found Ellen Emerson's condescending letter as galling as Whitman, another vernacular writer associated with Emerson, would find her brother Edward's slight of him in *Emerson in Concord* (1889). Yet Twain had recently put away the manuscript of *Huckleberry Finn* after running out of gas, as he often put it, and he was having a hell of a time as a writer. He was so low at that point that he couldn't even have insisted that Concord take him for anything except a clown.

Whitman had been an object of scorn to the Emerson family ever since 1855 for twice publishing without permission the Concord philosopher's famous letter of greeting to the poet "at the beginning of a great career." First Whitman had it published in the New York *Tribune* of October 10. Then, as if this liberty were not sufficiently offensive, the poet copied (and answered) it in an appendix to his 1856 edition of *Leaves of Grass* and plastered its most prominent clause in gold letters on the spine of his book. Not only Emerson's family but also his many friends and acquaintances were outraged. Yet Emerson said nothing at the time. He even struck his "tasks," as he promised Whitman in the letter, and visited him in Brooklyn. Had Emerson been in possession of his full faculties in 1877, he no doubt would have responded as nobly as Longfellow and Holmes did. It wasn't the great writers but their New England audience that was so protective of the region's culture and so fearful of the barbarism of the West and New Yorker ideologies such as Whitman's. This group of writers, it is sad to say, included Howells, who maintained throughout his life that his friend had "trifled" with the personalities of the great on that bedeviled December evening.[11]

The question remains as to why Twain publicly subscribed to the view of his speech expressed in the *North American Review* as scandalous, while privately rejoicing in it. As noted, he had defended the speech to Mrs. Fairbanks shortly after the event. The answer may be that Twain did not want to openly disagree with his friend Howells's interpretation. Moreover, the rather pompous *North American Review,* which published his account of the Whittier dinner in 1907, probably wouldn't have published any other view. But Twain also knew when something was truly funny, and to protect himself in perpetuity, he included in that December article a copy of the 1877 speech with only slight and insignificant changes.[12] He knew that the best humor had to be irreverent, but also that that irreverence, as the basis of humor, could never be personal or spiteful. That made it merely local and quickly dated, like the drollery of so many other humorists of his era (and ours) who relied on current events for their material. (In poetry it would be the difference between a sentimental poem for a particular person and an elegy whose personal subject is never named so that the lament becomes universal.)

Twain hadn't in fact attacked the personalities of Emerson, Longfellow, and Holmes, nor would that have been humorous if he had; it was the story's incongruity that put their grand poetic lines in the mouths of three drunks. Twain discovered a great lesson in all this, one that he would apply in his greatest book: the impersonal was the gateway to the greatest humor. Twain's speech would have been in bad taste, as some of the newspapers later charged it was, if its humor had in fact depended on personalities and belittled actual people, but this tall tale merely deflated bloated sentiments, such as those in Longfellow's "A Psalm of Life." In *Huckleberry Finn,* the protagonist is most hilarious (deadly so) when, in observing human behavior, he naively juxtaposes hard reality with the sentimental or craven distortion of it. Of course, his creator had probably sensed the difference long before, even before Jim Smiley bet against the parson's fervent hope that his wife would recover from her life-threatening illness.

29 The Innocent Abroad Again

"I HAVE THE HONOR TO REPLY TO YOUR LETTER JUST RECEIVED," the automatic letter with his facsimile signature said, "THAT IT IS MY PURPOSE TO WRITE A CONTINUATION OF TOM SAWYER'S HISTORY, BUT I AM NOT ABLE AT THIS TIME TO DETERMINE WHEN I SHALL BEGIN THE WORK." Perhaps the form letter, datelined Hartford, 1877, with a blank for the month and day, was one of Twain's first attempts at cloning himself through the latest technology, a small way toward turning out more books; for *Tom Sawyer,* in spite of its difficult American birth, proved so popular that letters from readers demanding a sequel arrived "WITH SUFFICIENT FREQUENCY TO WARRANT THIS METHOD OF REPLYING."[1] The letter was a bit disingenuous in saying that such a sequel had not already been begun. Between July and September of 1876, while *Tom Sawyer* got ravished by the Belford Brothers and languished in proofs at the American Publishing Company (for reasons due both to Bliss's trying to sell too many books by subscription at the same time and Twain's temporary loss of interest in *Tom Sawyer* because of the nearly yearlong lag in production), he had completed 446 manuscript pages of *Huckleberry Finn,* specifically the first twelve and a half chapters plus what became chapters 15 through the middle of 18, where Huck meets Buck Grangerford. Until 1990, when the first half of Twain's manuscript was found in an attic in Hollywood, it was thought that the first of three (or possibly four) phases of Twain's writing of it ended with the steamboat crash in chapter 16. This was the part of the book Twain told

Howells he liked only "tolerably well" and that he might "pigeon-hole or burn the MS when it is done."[2]

Unfortunately for its continued progress, Twain found other fish to fry in the years intervening between phases one and two of his masterpiece, which did not recommence until the waning weeks of 1879. He wrote *A Tramp Abroad* and *The Prince and the Pauper.* He marketed his only successful nonliterary invention, Mark Twain's Patent Self-Pasting Scrap Book, through Dan Slote's firm beginning in 1877. The following year he published *Punch, Brothers, Punch! and Other Sketches,* mainly as "a 10-cent advertising-primer" to boost sales of his scrapbook.[3] He also wrote a series of essays on his second trip to Bermuda, published in the *Atlantic* between October 1877 and January 1878. His life contained so many distractions that he decided he had to hide from it in order to write. "Life has come to be a very serious matter with me," he told his mother on February 17, 1878, in one of his increasingly infrequent letters to Jane Clemens, still living in Fredonia. "I have a badgered, harassed feeling, a good part of my time. It comes mainly of business responsibilities and annoyances, and the persecution of kindly letters from well meaning strangers—to whom I must be rudely silent or else put in the biggest half of my time bothering over answers." All this added up to the admission that "I cannot write a book at home," and now "home" meant not only Hartford, from which he could previously escape to Elmira, but the United States itself. "I have about made up my mind," he told his mother, "to take my tribe and fly to some little corner of Europe and budge no more until I shall have completed one of the half dozen books that lie begun, up stairs."[4]

In fact, his brother Orion seemed to be doing at least as much writing, while also switching back and forth between journalism and the law and working on nonliterary inventions of his own. When he sent Sam a sample of his working novel that winter, his brother advised that instead of imitating Jules Verne's science fiction, he ought to parody his work. "I think the world has suffered so much from that French idiot," he added, "that they could enjoy seeing him burlesqued." But that work went nowhere. Sam privately complained to his mother a few days later: "Orion sends his hero down . . . into the interior of the earth, . . . [where] he meets & talks with a very gentlemanly gorilla. . . . Can you imagine a sane man deliberately proposing to retain these things & print them, while they already exist in another man's book?" His older brother, his former boss in Hannibal, Sam concluded, was "absolutely destitute of originality."[5]

Before sailing with his family, a servant, and Livy's childhood friend Clara Spaulding on the *Holsatia* on April 11, Twain traveled to Fredonia to say goodbye to his mother and sister Pamela as well as his niece Annie Moffett, now married to a civil engineer dabbling in real estate, Charles L. Webster. He also visited Buffalo and at least one of his old friends, David Gray, an editor on the Buffalo *Daily Courier.*[6] Twain was apparently delighted to discover that Bayard Taylor, a well-known travel writer and translator of Goethe's *Faust,* was embarking on the same ship, having been appointed U.S. minister to Germany by the Hayes administration. He attended a farewell banquet for Taylor on April 4 at Delmonico's and even made a very short speech. It was a typical gathering of the literary elite, or what we would call today the literary establishment, of Victorian America. Howells was present, of course, along with many of the *Atlantic* writers he had published.[7]

Taylor had earlier been selected by the Centennial Commission in Philadelphia to write a national hymn, while Walt Whitman sat across the Delaware River in working-class Camden and issued a privately printed "Centennial Edition" of *Leaves of Grass.* Perhaps brooding over his exclusion from the hundredth-anniversary festivities for the nation that he had hailed in 1855 as "essentially the greatest poem," Whitman had set off an Anglo-American debate in 1876 over the shabby treatment he felt he had received from the establishment. Describing himself in an anonymous article in the *West Jersey Press* of January 26, which was widely quoted in England, Whitman said that twenty years after the first edition of his book, he had been systematically ignored. Naming the *Atlantic* as among those literary magazines refusing to publish his poems, he added: "All the established American poets studiously ignore Whitman. The *omnium gatherums* of poetry, by Emerson [whose 1874 anthology *Parnassus* had failed to include a sample of Whitman's work], Bryant, Whittier, and by lesser authorities, professing to include everybody of any note, carefully leave him out."

Among these "lesser authorities" Whitman doubtless included Taylor, who had become what was then the equivalent of today's U.S. poet laureate, only after the centennial honor had been turned down in rapid succession by Longfellow, Lowell, Holmes, Whittier, and William Cullen Bryant. This lesser authority had also joined those critical of Whitman in the 1876 debate over the American treatment of *Leaves of Grass.* In a guest editorial in the New York *Tribune* of April 12, 1876, entitled "American vs. English Criticism," Taylor had said of the transatlantic defense of Whitman that the English brain had become bored with respectable American utterances: "They are so tired of hot-house peaches and grapes, that they find a strange delight in the pucker of unripe persimmon. They place the simulated savagery of Joaquin Miller beside the pure and serene muse of Longfellow. Poe is exalted to the rank of a leader and pathfinder." And Whitman, he said, they hail "in terms fitting to no one less than Homer and Moses combined."[8]

This was the writer Twain had celebrated at the farewell dinner at Delmonico's in April. (In the wake of his Whittier birthday dinner speech, he planned to refer in this one [but didn't] to "the dangerous weapon of speech.")[9] Taylor was also the one with whom he so looked forward to crossing the Atlantic—a smoking partner in a day when most men smoked cigars, but also a smoker with a heart condition that would help to end his life before the close of 1878. One wonders what they talked about during those two stormy weeks at sea. For in denouncing two years earlier the English preference for the unripe utterances of vernacular writers, Taylor had also taken aim at the postwar popularity of American humorists and, in particular, at Twain's first great model in the genre, the "almost vanished" Artemus Ward. In 1876, at least, Taylor still thought George Horatio Derby, or "John Phoenix," superior to Samuel Langhorne Clemens, or "Mark Twain." Yet he was relieved that the recent "raptures [the English] bestow upon Mark Twain have [at least] not damaged the pure ideal of Humor which Lowell has given us." Mark Twain was going abroad for more reasons than he realized.

Bayard Taylor had not been in attendance at the Whittier speech, but he had likely heard all the stories about it by the time the two men crossed the Atlantic together. As the *Holsatia* prepared to sail, the press recorded the movements of the new minister and the new star on the literary horizon. "The new Minister," the New York *Times* of April 12 reported, "was smoking another of those large cigars . . . when a peculiar-looking caravan drove down the pier. It might once have been a coach, but it had been transformed into a sort of pyramid on wheels. . . . The lifting of a few dozen trunks from the top of the pyramid disclosed the Gilsey House coach, shining with gilt. It has brought to the steamer Mr. and Mrs. Samuel L. Clemens, a lady friend of Mrs. Clemens, several children, and a nurse." "Having checked off his family into the saloon," the report continued, "he came out upon the deck to shake hands with the new Minister." It went on to overhear their conversation, in which both men spoke words for public consumption, with Taylor as the straight man to Twain's comic. On board the two talked more seriously, with Twain admiring Taylor's formal learning and strong memory for reciting poetry. But by the turn of the twentieth century he would observe in his autobiography that although Taylor "had written voluminously in verse," practically "all his poetry is forgotten."[10] At that juncture in history, Whitman's had been largely forgotten, too, and Twain worried about the longevity of his own posthumous fame.

Critics and biographers have speculated that Twain was lying low by going abroad after the Whittier speech, but like so many great writers, he never lost faith in his talent—or, for that matter, in the speech he had given on that December evening in 1877. As noted, his letters of apology to the three supposedly offended auditors were sent mainly to console Livy and especially to protect his friend Howells, whom he feared had been the one truly hurt by the affair. Rather, Twain was going abroad to finish, as he had told his mother, at least one of a "half dozen books" he had begun. The editors at the Mark Twain Project at the University of California at Berkeley speculate that these unfinished works may have included drafts of "Captain Stormfield's Visit to Heaven" (a work that would require many more years of simmering); *The Prince and the Pauper*; a play entitled "Simon Wheeler, Detective" (a failure that he later tried to turn into a novel); "The Autobiography of a Damned Fool" (featuring his bungling brother Orion, whose antics almost got him into one of the stories that fill in the narrative plank of *A Tramp Abroad*); a burlesque diary of Methuselah; and of course, *Huckleberry Finn*.[11] Yet once they reached Hamburg on April 25 and Twain was able to spend the next fifteen months traveling around Europe, his fancy turned to yet another book, indeed another travel book, that would become *A Tramp Abroad* in 1880. (Then, "tramp" often indicated a walk or trip, not just a homeless person.) Travel books would always be Mark Twain's refuge from the responsibilities of the novelist, whose work required a firmer structure. Yet *A Tramp Abroad,* as the editors of the Penguin edition of the book note, also returns to the narrative plank of earlier books such as *Roughing It* by interspersing humorous sketches with autobiographical and historical matters.[12]

After the *Holsatia* reached the port of Hamburg, the veteran travel writer began immediately filling up notebooks that would provide the grist for his next book. He noted how clean the northern city and indeed all of Germany looked. There were no beggars, or "tramps," in the country, and their absence here was contrasted with their numbers in neighboring countries, especially France and its section of the Alps. He had little patience for the idle poor at this stage in his life; panhandlers would come right up to the front door of his mansion in Hartford. The Clemens party visited different German cities, including Frankfurt, before settling into the grand Schloss Hotel in Heidelberg, overlooking the Rhine Valley and the rapidly flowing Neckar River. They stayed in Heidelberg from May 4 until July 23, when they traveled to Baden-Baden, on the edge of the Black Forest, to await the arrival of Joe Twichell. He was coming over at Twain's expense for the month of August.

They were all straining to learn and speak German, which Twain would famously satirize in an appendix to *A Tramp Abroad* ("The Awful German Language"). One journal entry directly anticipates a portion of what got into print. "Some of the words," he wrote in his journal while still in Heidelberg, "are so long that they have a perspective . . . like the receding lines of a railroad track." Students dueling at the University of Heidelberg also caught his attention. "One knows a college bred man," he noted, "by his scars."[13] *A Tramp Abroad* is an uneven medley that reflects the occasionally different points of view of this writer in exile, some of which are deadly serious and others of which are utterly hilarious. His somber descriptions of the student warriors who coolly smoke cigarettes and sip wine before doing battle bespeak his undisguised horror at the violence. Like Huck following the slaughter of Buck Grangerford and other warriors of the Tennessee and Kentucky backwoods, this narrator sums up the student injuries as a "fearful spectacle . . . better left undescribed." Still, the former Buffalo journalist who had ridiculed the French for their quick surrender during the Franco-Prussian War then undercuts this serious meditation on the calm brutality of German dueling with a chapter titled "The Great French Duel." Since French duels are performed in the open air, the narrator says dryly, "the combatants are nearly sure to catch cold."[14]

Twichell arrived in Baden-Baden on August 1. He was deeply touched by his friend's invitation and thrilled at the expectation of their almost exclusive time together. "To walk with you, and talk with you, and sleep with you, and say my prayers with you, and see things with you, for weeks together," he had written on June 8, "why, it's my dream of luxury."[15] For the next month, they made excursions together through the Swiss Alps, sojourns punctuated by regroupings with the rest of the Clemens party at various cities and spas. Much of Twain's travels with Twichell, who became "Harris" in the travel narrative, formed the backbone of his book. While waiting for him in Baden-Baden, Twain, who had what sounds like the gout, took advantage of the medicinal baths. This detail didn't get into *A Tramp Abroad,* but it sets the stage for Huck's up-a-stump encounter with the harelip at the Wilks residence in *Huckleberry Finn.* In fact, the encounter with the American lady in chapter 25 of *A Tramp* had doubtless suggested the entire scene. The narrator's pretending to remember the woman from "back home" when he doesn't remember her at all is as hilarious as Huck's trying to support his own pretense of being an Englishman in chapter 26 of *Huckleberry Finn.* It is also reminiscent of his earlier battle of wits with Judith Loftus, the backwoods river wife who sees through Huck's masquerade as a girl.

This particular scene in *A Tramp* is a parody of the American tourist and his glaring ignorance of all things foreign. In a bet with Harris the narrator pretends to confuse a young American woman with somebody else as a way of striking up a conversation with her and ends up in "the tightest place I ever was in." The intended victim of the ploy is immediately convinced that they are the oldest of acquaintances and proceeds to allude to a series of mutual friends. It culminates with the mention of old Darley, who would attempt to enter the house during the winter. "I was rather afraid to proceed," the narrator writes. "Evidently Darley was not a man,—he must be some other kind of animal,—possibly a dog, maybe an elephant."[16] Like Huck with Joanna Wilks, the narrator gets into a "sweat"—until he discovers that Darley is a black slave. On another occasion, the narrator meets a bore about to enter Harvard who repeats himself endlessly, reminding us of Twain's earlier skits using mindless repetition. This story also smacks of Twain's slights to the Boston intelligentsia, following the Whittier speech.

On August 9, Sam and Joe took a boat trip down the Neckar, which Twain turns into a rafting trip in chapter 14. "The motion of the raft," the future chronicler of that most famous boy on the river writes, "is the needful motion; it is gentle, and gliding, and smooth, and noiseless; it calms down all feverish activities, it soothes to sleep all nervous hurry and impatience; under its restful influence all the troubles and vexations and sorrows that harass the mind vanish away, and existence becomes a dream, a charm, a deep and tranquil ecstasy." "It's lovely to live on a raft," Huck tells us in chapter 19 of his "autobiography." He and the runaway slave Jim "had the sky, up there, all speckled with stars, and we used to lay on our backs and look up at them."[17] Like childhood itself to Twain's mind, the raft on the river is a sanctuary from the cruelties and paradoxes of life ashore, though this spell is soon broken by the appearance of the two frauds being chased out of a river town they have been caught bilking.

A Tramp Abroad consists of forty-nine relatively brief chapters that cover Twain's time in Germany, Switzerland, France, and Italy. The unspoken running joke is that their tramps through the Alps (in which they, for example, climb Mount Blanc by telescope) are largely devoid of any real hiking, because they take the train or some other conveyance at the earliest opportunity. The narrative plank creaks more than once during this exercise in absurdity, but it is saved by its humor, more or less. This is assuredly true with Twain's now celebrated story imbedded in chapters 2 and 3, "Jim Baker's Blue-Jay Yarn." The bird becomes frustrated at trying to fill up a hole with acorns, only to discover that it is a bottomless pit, in reality an empty miner's cabin with a hole in the roof. The plot itself isn't funny or in any way the point, but the characterization of an animal with human qualities is. "Animals talk to each other," we are told. "And as for command of language—why *you* never see a blue-jay get stuck for a word. . . . They just boil out of him!" Twain employs incongruity in suggesting, for instance, that jays never use bad grammar, "don't belong to no church," and haven't "any more principle than a Congressman . . . a jay can out-swear any gentleman in the mines. You think a cat can swear. Well, a cat can; but you give a blue-jay a subject that calls for his reserve powers, and where is your cat?"[18] Twain was falling back on the humor of the Old West, where he had in fact first heard this story from one of the Gillis boys. That humor would shine much more consistently through his magnum opus, but first he had to find his way back home.

30 Down and Out in Paris and London

It can be safely said that by March 1879 Mark Twain had come to hate the French and, by that summer, was reassessing his high estimate of the British. It may have been the weather, for the winter of 1879 was one of the most severe in France and indeed Europe. Yet his moodiness toward the French should have been uplifted somewhat by his Parisian surroundings. The Clemens party lived in the luxurious Normandy Hotel, on the corner of rue de l'Échelle and rue St. Honoré, in the very center of the City of Light, on its elegant Right Bank in the first arrondissement. The hotel was adjacent to the Palais Royal and what is today the city's old opera house, which was brand new in 1878. The area was then—as it is now—one of the most expensive and delightful places to stay in Paris. Just north of the rue de Rivoli and within walking distance of the Tuileries and the Louvre, the Clemenses' hotel was virtually across the street from the famous Théâtre Français. As Livy told her nephew, the hotel was a "much more expensive place than we intended to stop in, but we could not suit ourselves better."[1]

It is difficult to say just what set off this irritation engulfing his most recent impressions of both France and England. It may have been partly the letdown after Joe Twichell went back home in September 1878. He wrote "Old Joe," whose companionship he valued second only to that of his wife: "It is actually all over! I was so low-spirited at the station yesterday & this morning when I woke, I couldn't seem to accept the dismal truth that you were really gone, & the pleasant tramping & talking at an end."[2] Or it may have been the sudden death of Bayard Taylor in

Germany that December. Twain had written him a letter from Munich, where the family had resided for three months before coming to Paris on February 28, only a week before the new American ambassador's death, wishing him a speedy recovery from a recent illness. Taylor, while he favored the New England writers of Emerson's generation, had, two years earlier, accepted Mark Twain as "distinctly American in our literature" because his art was "*truly,* vigorously, and picturesquely embodied." And because—unlike Whitman's—it could be read aloud during the family hour, or "under the evening lamp," as it was known in the nineteenth century.[3]

Curiously, Taylor's Victorian attitude toward literature was no more moralistic than Twain's hostility toward the French. In that same (anonymous) editorial in the *Tribune* of 1876, Taylor had criticized Whitman's *Leaves of Grass* as a vulgar revival of "the old Greek reverence for the human body and delight in all its functions." Similarly, in notes for a chapter about French morality (ultimately excluded from *A Tramp Abroad*), Twain exploded in a burst of puritanical denunciation. Mixed in with his complaints about the French weather ("this eternal winter") were castigating remarks about the French culture of sex. "Frenchman speaking admiringly of a little girl," he wrote, "'What! seven years old & still virtuous?'" (His first daughter, Susy, had just turned seven.) Even the company of the great Russian novelist Ivan Turgenev and other now famous writers didn't distract him from his Francophobia. "'Tis a wise Frenchman that knows his own father," he wrote in his journal on May 12. He noted that married women had lovers and that "every man in France over 16 years of age & under 116, has at least 1 wife to whom he has never been married."[4]

Here was Mark Twain—who as a carefree bachelor had very likely explored the darker precincts of New Orleans, Virginia City, San Francisco, and Honolulu—attacking the French for doing, as the joke would have it, what they knew best. Married for almost a decade in 1879, and as faithful as he had once predicted to his sister-in-law that he would be, after admitting that while still single he had slept with chambermaids, he now found not only Frenchmen but the entire nation of France "wholly savage" and in dire need of American and English missionaries.

"Scratch an F," he raged, "& you find a gorilla." America, on the other hand, wrote the coauthor of *The Gilded Age* and the marital adventures of Laura Hawkins, "is the most civilized of all nations. Pure-minded women are the rule, in every rank of life of the *native-born.* The men are clean-minded, too, beyond the world's average."[5]

Mark Twain was clean minded, too. At least that was his reputation, to all, that is, but his former cronies in the West and those select readers of the privately circulated *1601,* an off-color parody of European aristocratic manners in which Queen Elizabeth and other members of her court politely discuss such crude matters as flatulence, sexual intercourse, and masturbation. In the age of Victoria (when the double standard in matters of sex was supposedly for the protection of "women and children"), the satire was perhaps a natural runoff from his study of sixteenth-century British history, begun before his latest trip abroad and undertaken for the composition of *The Prince and the Pauper.* That novel, featuring the brutality of English life three hundred years earlier but which Twain suspected came right up to the present, may have triggered his shift in attitude toward the British, even before he imploded on the French. Indeed, he claimed in his Paris journal that up to the previous century, British civilization had been no better than that of the Zulus or the Shoshone Indians.[6]

Mark Twain would never write a book about the French that contained the indictment suggested in his private journal attacks; his French book would have to wait until the 1890s and then focus on French virtue in the character of Joan of Arc. Of course, he had already tried once to write one about the English. Now he was about to try again—or to continue—picking up the incomplete manuscript of *The Prince and the Pauper* once he returned to the United States, even as he finished *A Tramp Abroad.* Both books were penultimate to completing *Huckleberry Finn,* but *The Prince and the Pauper* contains the initial elements of not only his masterpiece but also *Pudd'nhead Wilson,* as well as *A Connecticut Yankee in King Arthur's Court.* It is rather telling that the only book of Mark Twain's to be almost unanimously classified as a children's book should contain the major seeds of his most ambitious work. But then, *Huckleberry Finn* began as a boy's book. *The Prince and the Pauper* lives today mainly as a drama for children, which is also rather curious considering that Mark Twain could never write a successful play (it wasn't he who would successfully dramatize *The Prince and the Pauper.*) Furthermore, it was supposed to be his attempt to write "serious" or upscale Victorian fiction on a par with Howells and the others of his era. It was not a frivolous gesture when he prefaced *Huckleberry Finn* with the caveat that anyone looking for the usual ingredients of high literature—a moral or even plot—would be prosecuted, banished, or shot. For *The Prince and the Pauper* is one of the most moralistic and carefully plotted books that Mark Twain ever wrote. Here he worked extra hard to write "literature." In *Huckleberry Finn* he was—he initially thought—simply writing a sequel to *Tom Sawyer.* And indeed when he finished his masterpiece, he hardly realized what he had accomplished.

The Prince and the Pauper features yet another Tom, the impoverished Tom Canty, along with Edward VI, look-alikes who inadvertently exchange roles.. That allows Twain to show in contrasting depictions both the poverty of the masses in sixteenth-century England and the astonishment of a young prince who is exposed to it for the first time and eventually resolves to strive for reforms in his kingdom, much in the way that Huck will ultimately resolve to "go to hell" for Jim. Twain took his epigraph for the novel from Shakespeare's *The Merchant of Venice,* about the "quality of mercy" lacking in English life. The idea of switched boys anticipates the theme of switched babies in *Pudd'nhead Wilson,* where the difference between them is not only economic but also racial. Tom as "king" even rejects his mother, foreshadowing Chambers's essential rejection of *his* mother. This Tom is also like Tom Sawyer in that "the little Prince of Poverty" loves stories of chivalry and romance, thereby making it easier for him to adapt to the routines of royalty once he has been switched into the court of Henry VIII. The prince's sister, Lady Jane, in her questioning of the "mock prince," anticipates the harelip Joanna Wilks, who interrogates Huck.

Once the real prince is exposed to the miseries and dangers of his kingdom, he meets up with Miles Hendon, another wandering claimant deprived of his true rightful identity. Like Huck and Jim, Edward and Miles go on an epic journey that exposes the different levels and kinds of social injustice and human folly. There is even a scene in chapter 13 in which Hendon, like Huck in the scene with Judith Loftus, demonstrates his male ignorance of the women's art of sewing, or how to thread a needle. When Henry VIII dies, Canty, still as the false prince, asks a question similar to the "Is he dead?" query at the sight of an ancient mummy in *The Innocents Abroad:* "Will he keep?" Twain looks backward as well as forward, then, as he moves inexorably toward his magnum opus. When the king is forced to beg for his "poor afflicted brother," he forecasts Huck on the raft with the slave catchers pleading for his sick father. But again Twain pulls in details and incidents from everywhere. In chapter 18, Edward Tudor wakes up thinking he is lying next to a corpse, "newly dead and still warm." It turns out to be a living calf, but as Twain earlier recalled, coincidentally in chapter 18 of *The Innocents Abroad,* the body he woke up to as a boy in his father's Hannibal JP office was both human and dead. And like Huck and Jim on being reunited after the Grangerford episode, the prince and Hendon jog "lazily along" in chapter 25, "talking over the adventures they had met since their separation." Finally, the switching of the two boys in *The Prince and the Pauper* resembles the identity exchange between Huck and Tom at Aunt Sally's. Like Tom Canty's exchanging his rags for royalty, Huck Finn the river rat becomes "respectable" as Tom Sawyer.

All of this was no doubt percolating in Mark Twain's subconscious as he grumbled about the French and began to change his mind about the English. In fact, he had already written "The Great Revolution in Pitcairn," a sketch anticipating his anti-imperialistic and anti-British theme in his second "book about the English," *A Connecticut Yankee.* In "The Great Revolution" a "mysterious stranger" tries unsuccessfully to reshape an island culture of ninety people, who before his arrival enjoyed nearly idyllic conditions. The sketch was initially intended for *A Tramp Abroad,* but ended up in the March 1879 issue of the *Atlantic Monthly.* While visiting Great Britain, he met as he had in Paris other writers and artists of note. There was a dinner with Henry James, whom Livy liked very much, and James Whistler, whom she didn't. They visited the grave of Shakespeare at Stratford-on-Avon, and Twain met the "great Darwin" on another side trip, this time to the Lake Country. He said little about the meeting at the time in his journal, but three years later upon the death of Charles Darwin, he recalled the two had been embarrassed at being introduced to each other as great men. He also recalled that Charles Eliot Norton told him Darwin said he "always read himself to sleep with my books."[7] There is no evidence that Twain read himself to sleep with *Origin of Species* (1859), but he had perused *Descent of Man* (1871) and later joked that Adam now stood to be exchanged for a monkey and forgotten.[8] Earlier, of course, in *The Innocents Abroad,* his narrator weeps at the grave of Adam as though he were a close relative.

After fifteen months abroad, the Clemens party sailed for home on the *Gallia* out of Liverpool on August 23, 1879. They had stayed away too long, and this may have been a factor in the shift in Twain's mood toward France and England, if not Germany and the other places they had visited on the continent. When their ship reached New York harbor on September 2, a New York *Sun* reporter said that Twain looked older and grayer than when he had gone abroad, while a *Times* correspondent described "the nearest surviving kin of the jumping frog" as ageless in that his hair was "no whiter than when he last sailed for Europe." The *Times* did note, however, that he came back with even more luggage than he had left with—a total now of twelve trunks and twenty-two freight packages. It took six hours for him to get everything through customs. He was the last passenger to leave the ship, partly because one of his trunks was temporarily lost. Twain told Dan Slote, "I was lucky to get through at all, because the ship was loaded mainly with my freight." Much of it was intended for the Hartford house, enough new things to prompt an expensive redecorating by Louis Comfort Tiffany. But for now the Clemenses were headed for their summer home in Elmira, which they would occupy through October before returning to Hartford. By the end of the year he had given the speech for Grant in Chicago (see chapter 8) and another *Atlantic* birthday speech in Boston, this time for Oliver Wendell Holmes, at a breakfast in honor of the author of *The Autocrat of the Breakfast Table.* Given the staleness of the humor of that book today, perhaps even then to Twain, much of whose humor still lives, he did well and did not "embarrass himself" as many thought he had done two years earlier at the Whittier dinner. In fact, he no doubt endeared himself to Holmes and others in the audience by publicly confessing that he had unconsciously stolen the epigraph to *The Innocents Abroad* from Holmes's *Songs in So Many Keys* ("To My Most Patient Reader and Most Charitable Critic, My Aged Mother . . ."). He spoke of his earlier apology to Holmes and the response (from "the first great man who ever wrote me a letter").[9] This time, after so many months abroad, the "fit" with American literary royalty felt a little less alien.

Yet Twain was entering deep and treacherous waters as the decade of the 1880s opened before him. He would accomplish his greatest invention with *Adventures of Huckleberry Finn,* but there would also be other inventions that would eventually threaten him with financial ruin. The artist who allegedly hated art would ultimately become the businessman who hated business.

PART III The Artist and the Businessman

31 Associations New and Old

A Tramp Abroad would be Mark Twain's last book with the American Publishing Company for years to come. It had been a difficult work to finish, what with all the cuts and revisions. Yet, probably because of its advance publicity by way of early reviews and published excerpts, the book, released in March 1880, sold well—in its first year more than sixty thousand copies in the United States. Elisha Bliss died the following fall. Twain had been less and less satisfied with the man who had sold so many of his books by subscription. Paradoxically, it was the success of *A Tramp Abroad* that brought about the rupture in his eleven-year streak with the Hartford publisher. He broke with Bliss when he realized that the de facto "half profit," or fifty-fifty split between author and publisher that Bliss had agreed to since *Roughing It* (amounting to 7.5 percent of the list price), was a lie. When for the first time the term "half profit" actually appeared in the contract for *A Tramp,* Twain found that he made significantly more money than he had on all the previous books.[1]

He had also been courted for some time by James R. Osgood, who had come up through the ranks at Ticknor and Fields of Boston. By the late 1870s, Osgood had bought out the original owners and eventually joined forces with Henry Houghton. But that arrangement had soon foundered, and by 1881 he was in effect starting over as James R. Osgood and Company without Houghton's old list of established authors.[2] Now dispossessed of Emerson as well as the Schoolroom poets of Boston, Osgood needed to expand his range of authors—indeed, extend it to the widening class of readers that improved transportation and the rapid postwar advancement of print technology had created by bringing down the price of the average book. His new acquisition of authors who wrote in the vernacular and appealed to this broader readership included not only the humorist Mark Twain but also the controversial poet Walt Whitman.

Not that the first major book Osgood published—or copublished—with Twain was written in the vernacular. *The Prince and the Pauper* was nonetheless published as a subscription book. This method of book sales, which probably inspired the Sears Roebuck catalog as a way to reach potential customers beyond the urban bookshops, turned out not to be Osgood's strong suit, but the general arrangement between the publisher and Twain evidently worked out well enough for their association to carry over to *Life on the Mississippi*. In effect, with Osgood, Twain reversed the unfair ratio between publisher and author that he had resented in his dealings with Bliss, agreeing to pay Osgood exactly the 7.5 percent royalty Bliss had paid him on *Roughing It*. Moreover, Twain, after Bliss, still needed somebody to manage his literary affairs. In fact, the need was even more acute because his business interests had begun to expand beyond simple nonliterary inventions of his own.

He now owned the majority interest in a patent for Kaolatype, a new and still untested engraving process he had purchased from Dan Slote, whose company retained the rest of the stock. Slote, Woodman, and Company was supposed to market the product, but when that investment failed to live up to its promise even after Twain contributed additional funds, Twain got Charles L. Webster, his niece's husband in Fredonia, to investigate. Webster reported in the spring of 1881 that Slote, in siphoning off so much of Twain's money, was either "a knave or a fool." Webster's conclusion, along with suspicions that Slote and his company had also cheated Twain on the profits from his self-pasting scrapbook, ended their close friendship of fifteen years, which had started on the *Quaker City* cruise. When Slote died suddenly a year later, Twain told Mary Fairbanks: "If Dan had died thirteen months earlier, I should have been at the funeral, and squandered many tears; but as it is, I did not go and saved my tears." His "mother" Fairbanks, who had also known Slote on the same cruise, tried to remind her "son" that at least before his ex-friend found himself in a financial corner he *had* offered "a notable friendship—made so by your book it is true, but consistently sustained by after years of mutual service and sympathy."[3] But iron had already entered Sam's soul.

One would think that after such a disappointing foray into business, Clemens might stick to writing, even in the heyday of American inventors. But Mark Twain's arrangement with Osgood led him to become not only his own publisher but also by the mid-1880s a heavy investor in yet another invention in the rapidly expanding printing and publishing field. He had already met, in 1880, a machinist and inventor named James W. Paige. Only a few years earlier, another self-taught engineer, Thomas Edison, now hailed as the "Wizard of Menlo Park," had invented the phonograph and the first commercially practical incandescent lightbulb. As an investor and part owner of the Farnham Type-Setting Company, which rented space in the Colt Firearms Factory in Hartford, Paige—no doubt encouraged by Edison's example—worked away at perfecting his automatic compositor, or typesetter.

That year Sam Clemens had also welcomed into the world his third daughter, Jean, born in Elmira on July 26, another event that proved ominous in his life. Indeed, 1880 would be a major turning point. It ushered in both prosperity and eventually also the pessimism now attributed to him during the last years of his life.

The Prince and the Pauper was published to favorable reviews in the United States and not-so-favorable ones in Britain, where some critics resented Twain's emphasis on the brutality of the English throne in the sixteenth century and snidely suggested he restrict himself to American humor. He now turned to the Mississippi River to complete a book prompted by the success of his "Old Times on the Mississippi" articles in the *Atlantic* in 1875. He intended to revisit St. Louis and the Mississippi in preparation for it. He asked his friend Howells to accompany him, but Howells was too busy, so he made the journey instead with Osgood and a stenographer from Hartford named Roswell Phelps. But before their trip that April, Twain became interested in another matter at the James R. Osgood Company.

Osgood had taken a chance and published the sixth edition of *Leaves of*

Grass in the fall of 1881, becoming Whitman's only commercial publisher since the war. Whitman, now practically worshipped in some quarters as the "Good Gray Poet," had given one of his popular lectures, "The Death of Abraham Lincoln," in Boston that fall, and this appearance led to his signing on with Osgood, who had previously known Whitman in the 1860s as a fellow drinker at Pfaff's. In turning over his latest manuscript, what became the final and definitive edition of *Leaves of Grass,* the poet had cautioned his old acquaintance: "Fair warning on one point—the old pieces, the *sexuality* ones, about which the original row was started & kept up so long, are all retained, & must go in the same as ever." The bard was referring to the recurring attacks on his book since its initial publication in 1855. He now considered *Leaves of Grass* his life's work, a "cathedral" in which the early sexual poems were no longer at the center of its altar but still held their rightful place in the overall structure. But that's not the way Boston district attorney Oliver Stevens saw the matter. On March 1, 1882, he informed Osgood, just as he was preparing to journey down the Mississippi River with Twain, that Whitman's book violated "the provisions of the Public Statutes respecting obscene literature" and ordered its withdrawal from sale immediately.[4] *Leaves of Grass* thus became the first book to be "banned in Boston," setting off a blizzard of letters to the editor in both the New York and Boston papers.

Mark Twain wrote one of those letters to the Boston *Evening Post.* "The Walt Whitman Controversy" was left unfinished and, perhaps like *1601,* never really intended for publication. His argument in support of *Leaves of Grass* pointed to the hypocrisy of allowing all kinds of pornography from antiquity to stay in print (and on the bookshelves of respected homes) while living authors like Whitman were censored and even prosecuted criminally for far less offensive material. Such "classic" writers as Rabelais, Boccaccio, Cervantes, Chaucer, and Shakespeare were in every gentleman's library, but not the "new bad books" such as "Swinburne's and Oscar Wilde's poems, & Walt Whitman's 'Leaves of Grass.'" "Are they handy for the average young man or Miss to get at? Perhaps not. Are those others? Yes, many of them."

At this point, the humorist fully unmasked himself: "Now I think I can show, by a few extracts, that in matters of coarseness, obscenity,

& power to excite salacious passions, Walt Whitman's book is refined & colorless & impotent, contrasted with that other & more widely read batch of literature." "In 'Leaves of Grass,'" he went on, "the following passage has horrified Mr. Oliver Stevens by its coarseness." Among the lines that the district attorney had singled out as obscene, Twain must have been thinking of the following two, given the scatological Rabelais passage he contrasts them with: "I keep as delicate around the bowels as around the head and heart, / Copulation is no more rank to me than death is." What followed instead in his letter were two lines of ellipses and a bracketed statement supposedly from the *Evening Post* editor saying, "We are obliged to omit it.—ED. Post." "How pale and delicate it is," Twain continued, perhaps echoing Whitman's use of "delicate," "when you put it alongside this passage from Rabelais." Throughout, he makes it clear which passages from these classical works he is citing, and his next example, from *The Life of Gargantua and Pantagruel,* is also ostensibly censored by the *Post* editor, but it is ranker than anything found in Whitman. The letter goes from example to example drawn from a variety of classics, introducing salacious passages, but always pretending to have the prim editor bleep them out, to conclude that there is not "an educated young fellow of nineteen, in the United States," who has not read them.

"After that," Twain continues, evoking and eliding a scene in the *Heptameron of Margaret, Queen of Navarre* in which a girl is ravished in front of her mother, "Whitman is delicate enough, isn't he?" He concludes with "The Venial Sin" in Balzac's *Droll Stories.* In a final parodic spin on the mores of the day, Twain writes that he has mislaid his English copy of it and so quotes from the French translation, certainly a more appropriate conduit in light of his recent, if private, trashing of that culture. Translated to English, it would have read: "The hermit undressed himself immediately, and the small angel did so as quickly. When each was naked, Rustique dropped to his knees, and put the poor innocent in the same position. There with hands joined, he cast his eyes on———." He concludes this mock letter to the editor by saying that he would not complain if the editor censored his quotations from the classics: "Yes, you know that indecent literature is indecent literature; & that the effects produced by it are exactly the same, whether the writing was done yesterday or a thousand centuries ago; & that these effects are the same, whether the writer's intent was evil or innocent." This fascinating tribute by one major writer of the nineteenth century to another breaks off with the phrase "Whitman's noble work," obviously the beginning of another paragraph. This hanging fragment may be evidence of Mark Twain's acknowledgment of a literary equal, but, like all those other honest but risky statements about art and morality left behind in unpublished nineteenth-century manuscripts, it would be lost to Twain's world and only published posthumously in ours.[5]

The following month, Twain paid final homage to the man who had greeted Whitman "at the beginning of a great career" back in 1855. Emerson was fading rapidly in the spring of 1882. He had already been failing mentally by the time of the 1877 Whittier dinner. Twain, Whitman, and Emerson, coincidentally, had all been "banned in Boston," more or less, at junctures during their careers. Emerson had become persona non grata at Harvard for a generation following his "Divinity School Address" there in 1838; Twain had been denounced by proper Bostonians after the Whittier debacle; Whitman's sixth edition of *Leaves of Grass* had been censored there. Boston, the literary cradle of America's rebellion against what Emerson called "the courtly muses of Europe," was losing its place in the transcendentalist hunt for the ultimate "end" or purpose of nature (even Whitman's raw nature) as an emblem of God, as Emerson had put it in *Nature.* It favored the past over the present in literature. Even humor, as the late Bayard Taylor had perceived it, still found its literary apex in James Russell Lowell instead of Samuel Langhorne Clemens, alias Mark Twain.

In early April, Twain went out to Concord with Howells, who he was still hoping would accompany him on his trip down the Mississippi. There is an indirect reference to this visit in his 1882 notebook, one that puzzled Twain scholars for many years. He wrote, "Emerson & Artemus Ward"—strange bedfellows until we discover in a later notebook entry of late 1906 or early 1907 that it is a reference to Emerson's befuddlement during one or more of his lectures as he became increasingly plagued with aphasia. Apparently, Twain heard a story about it on the day of his visit to Concord from Emerson's son Edward, whom he had known since 1872 when the two were passengers on the *Batavia* sailing home from Liverpool. The two had been brought together as familiar acquaintances after having witnessed a harrowing spectacle at sea in which their ship's captain rescued of a number of people from a sinking vessel despite a raging storm. In the later notebook he wrote of an incident in which Emerson lost "his scraps & his place" during a late lecture and was allegedly confused by some members of the audience with the literary comedian who had launched Mark Twain's career.[6] Emerson died on April 27, a day before Twain returned to New Orleans for the first time in twenty years.

32 Return to the River and the Lecture Circuit

On April 17, 1882, Mark Twain attended a dinner at the Union League Club in New York City. The next morning, in the company of Osgood and Phelps, he took a train for St. Louis. By April 28 they were in New Orleans, having journeyed down the Mississippi first on the *Gold Dust* and then on the *Charles Morgan.* During the trip south, Twain tried to go under a pseudonym so that his fame wouldn't hamper his ability to draw out the pilots, but he was recognized almost immediately. One of the sailors in the pilothouse quipped to Sam that he had heard a shaggy visitor "use your voice. He is sometimes called Mark Twain." At Cairo, the *Gold Dust* nearly ran over a raft. Twain recorded in his diary that he felt "an old-time hunger to be at the wheel and cut [the raft] in two," but the incident no doubt reminded him of what he had already written about Jim and Huck's raft almost getting sliced in half by a steamboat in chapter 16 of the novel he had left half finished in Hartford. The trip also strengthened his sense of the landscape when he returned to finish *Huckleberry Finn.* Going down the river, he noted the changes in its course and other details that would make their way into the later chapters of *Life on the Mississippi.*[1]

While on the *Charles Morgan,* which he had boarded in Vicksburg, he overheard and recorded the conversation of two black laundresses. One of the ex-slaves got nostalgic for the old days as they passed a beautiful plantation near Baton Rouge. The other strongly disagreed, saying "it was mighty rough times on the niggers." "That's so," admitted the first. "I come mighty near being sold down here once; & if I had been

I wouldn't been here now; been the last of me." The other said that she had actually been sold down the river as far as Mississippi, and that if she had gone "furder down," she too wouldn't be there today to remember it. "Occasionally," Twain concluded, "the big laundress would drop into song & sang all sorts of strange plantation melodies which nobody but one of her race would ever be able to learn."[2] In returning to the South and the Mississippi River, it appears, Twain was also revisiting the questions of race and slavery—indeed, perhaps confronting these issues directly for the first time since writing "A True Story" in 1874.

His old mentor Horace Bixby was in New Orleans to greet him. By this time, the fifty-five-year-old pilot was commander of the Anchor Line steamer *City of Baton Rouge.*[3] Before leaving Hartford, Twain had also made arrangements to meet both George Washington Cable, who still resided in New Orleans, and Joel Chandler Harris, who was coming there from Atlanta, where he wrote for the *Constitution.* Twain had met Cable in Hartford in 1881, when the author of *Old Creole Days* (1879) and *The Grandissimes* (1880) vacationed in New England. Before that, Cable had written for the New Orleans *Picayune.* He had also been a Confederate cavalryman in the Civil War, but he was well on his way to becoming a champion for the civil rights of freed slaves. His books were popular in the North and initially so in the South (except with Creoles), but his political opinions were ultimately denounced in his homeland. In 1884 he would reluctantly decide to relocate to Massachusetts. Harris, on the other hand, was warmly regarded in the South for his *Uncle Remus* tales. Twain, too, admired the way he captured the black dialect. As Eric Sundquist notes, Harris's tales of Brer Rabbit and Brer Fox "do not entirely whitewash the Old South but maintain a taut balance between minstrel humor and a subversive critique of slavery and racism." They encoded, another critic points out, slave themes of the trickster figure.[4] Mark Twain would ultimately go beyond both these writers in treating the whole matter of black slavery and the troubled white conscience.

Along with Osgood and Phelps, Twain stayed at New Orleans's commodious St. Charles Hotel, with its barrooms, restaurants, and Grand Salon—a circular hall with white walls and red carpets, endless mirrors and crystal chandeliers. Cable came right over from his home on

Eighth Street, in what is known today as the Garden District, to take the visitors for a daylong tour of the city. Twain kept referring to Cable personally as "Life on the Mississippi," and later in his book of the same name he called the author of *The Grandissimes* "the South's finest literary genius," in whom it had "found a masterly delineator of its interior life and its history." On their first afternoon together, the party lunched on delicious pompano in the West End on Lake Pontchartrain. Cable took them to a mule race held to raise money for the Southern Art Union. The next day, Saturday, they were guests at Cable's home. And on the following, Harris arrived from Atlanta. On Monday the trio of authors read from their works in Cable's study. That is, Twain and Cable read from their works. "Uncle Remus was there," Twain told Livy, "but was too bashful to read; so the children of the neighborhood flocked in to look at him (& were grievously disappointed to find he was white & young) & I read Remus' stories & my own stuff to them, & Cable read from the Grandissimes & sketches."[5] The day was topped off with a dinner at the home of Cable's friend James B. Guthrie, a lawyer and local Shakespearean. The evening was filled with music, song, and story until after midnight. Cable sang some of the dialect songs that he would use during his tour with Sam in 1884–85.[6]

Twain spent a total of nine days in New Orleans, the city he had haunted as a young pilot and the last place he had seen his brother Henry before his death on the *Pennsylvania* in 1858. At sunset on Saturday, May 6, Twain and his traveling companions boarded the *City of Baton Rouge,* captained by his old teacher Bixby. When it reached St. Louis six days later, Osgood temporarily left their river sojourn to attend to business in Chicago. Two days later, May 17, Twain boarded the *Gem City* and found himself back home in Hannibal. It was a sad homecoming in one sense, and this may be why he recorded none of the particulars of his visit in his letters home about the town that had molded him. "The romance of boating is gone, now," he confided to his journal. "In Hannibal the steamboatman is no longer a god. The youth don't talk river slang any more. Their pride is apparently railways." He also found the South there "sophomoric"—the speech "flowery & gushy." For some reason, perhaps because of the return to his poor beginnings there, he counted up his current investments. They included more than twenty concerns and totaled $68,950.[7] The Paige typesetter accounted for $5,000 of the total.

In visiting the river and in particular Hannibal, he probably realized for the first time how fully his past had vanished. The "Old Times" pieces had come from that vanished past. As a result they are much more romantic and engaging than the later chapters in his Mississippi memories, which are weighted down with postwar realism. Railroad tracks ran rudely along the river in front of Hannibal now, and the village shuddered slightly as trains rumbled by almost every hour or so. The era of the steamboat was almost dead. He had come back to the river not only to turn his *Atlantic* pieces into a book but also to stimulate memories that had been initially stirred up by writing about the region in both the "Old Times" pieces and *Tom Sawyer.* Possibly some of the pessimism that invades *Huckleberry Finn* resulted from that eye-opening return. At New Madrid, on the party's way north ultimately to Minnesota, he made an entry in his journal about the infamous Darnell-Watson feud, which had already become the basis of the Grangerford-Shepherdson feud in chapter 19 of *Huckleberry Finn.*[8] He noted the way two of the young Darnells were shot in the back. In the novel, Buck Grangerford and his cousin are similarly gunned down. He even recorded how the two feuding families attended the same church services together. He left Hannibal on the *Minneapolis* after a three-day visit.

Before concluding his tour up the river at St. Paul on May 21 and going home by train two days later, he visited a number of upper-river towns, including Keokuk, where he had lived in 1857. The next day, his boat stopped in Muscatine, Iowa, another family landmark since Orion had edited the Muscatine *Journal* there between 1853 and 1855 and had printed nine of his younger brother's earliest travel letters from New York and Philadelphia. He was returning to write a book, *Life on the Mississippi,* that more than likely he really did not want to write. Like *A Tramp Abroad,* it would be another tedious exercise of pushing a travel book beyond its natural life in order to satisfy the bulk expected by buyers of subscription books. Back in Hartford, he asked his publisher Osgood to "set a cheap expert to work to collect local histories of

Mississippi towns & a lot of other books relating to the river for me." By the next year, when *Life on the Mississippi* was issued, he was referring to it as "this wretched God-damned book."[9]

In the spring of 1882 Osgood published *The Stolen White Elephant, Etc.,* which features a story originally written in 1878, another of the pieces omitted from *A Tramp Abroad,* and recycled pieces from *Punch, Brothers, Punch!* "The Stolen White Elephant" was a rather tedious burlesque of a notorious body-snatching case in New York City that Twain had written while in Munich. It was another way to keep his name before the public, and in this case attention to the book was enhanced by P. T. Barnum's importing from England an elephant to whom he gave the same name that Twain had used for the pachyderm in his story—"Jumbo." That summer or fall, Twain invented a complicated history board game (not produced until 1891) that never made him any money.[10] He was, however, revisiting the *Huckleberry Finn* manuscript that he had put away in 1876 after completing some fifteen chapters. Since 1880 he had written four more chapters, the ones that introduce the river frauds known as the Duke and the King and carry the story through Sherburn's killing of Boggs (chapter 21). He had also written the "Notice," which would help make up the preliminaries to his greatest work:

> Persons attempting to find a Motive in this narrative will be prosecuted; persons attempting to find a Moral in it will be banished; persons attempting to find a Plot in it will be shot.
>
> By Order of the Author
> Per G. G., Chief of Ordnance

This farcical announcement perfectly reflected his mood during the writing of the other books and stories he managed to produce as he rummaged through his imagination for the true story of Huck and Jim. It was applied to the book in almost a note of exhaustion over the sheer impossibility of finding true humanity or higher meaning in a Darwinian universe. Speculation has it that "G. G." stands for "General Grant," whose praises he had recently sung in Chicago in 1879. Grant was a soldier whose earliest of "superstitions," as he wrote in the memoir Twain would publish in the same year as *Huckleberry Finn,* "had always been . . . not to turn back, or stop until the thing intended was accomplished."[11] It was an unrealistic credo that worked only in war, not in the deeper complexities of life. Huck might "go to hell" for Jim, but he could never get him to heaven.

About as close to the saints that Twain ever got was spending the winter of 1884–85 lecturing and entertaining with George Washington Cable, a devout Christian who never traveled on Sundays. On their lecture tour they were publicized as "twins of genius." Cable, whose literary imagination came right out of the French Quarter of New Orleans and its surrounding plantations and hamlets, was as soaked in the South as Mark Twain. Essentially, both men had been members of or sympathizers with the Confederate army. By the time of their pairing, each had become a "Yankee." Both now felt keenly a certain irony in their alienation from their southern roots. In a photograph taken at the outset of their lecture tour, the two men stand together in a casual pose that exudes absolute confidence in themselves as writers and performers. Twain stands with his coat open and his right hand in his hip pocket. A watch chain trails off across his vest to his left side. Cable, almost a head shorter than Clemens, is seen leaning slightly into his friend. He is dressed in a long coat fully buttoned with his left hand in his hip pocket. He is bearded, with a moustache trailing down to his collarbone. His neatly combed black hair contrasts with Twain's ruffled, slightly graying look. There is a slight smile on Cable's face, but it seems to come from his eyes. Twain, beardless with full moustache, looks as though he has a great deal on his mind.

Their lecture manager was Major James B. Pond, a colorful entrepreneur who in 1875 had purchased Redpath's Lyceum Bureau in Boston and afterward opened a lecture bureau of his own in New York City. It is not absolutely clear just why Mark Twain returned to the lecture platform. It may have been mainly for the money, for he was feeding a number of investments that now included increasingly frequent cash infusions to the Paige typesetter. Moreover, he generally wasn't very fortunate with other investments. In January 1883, for example, he bought more than two hundred shares in a railroad company in Oregon at seventy-five dollars a share. Six months later he sold his two hundred shares—plus another hundred purchased later for four thousand dollars—for a pitiful twelve dollars a share, or a loss of more than fifteen thousand dollars.[12]

Twain and Cable's joint program, which opened in New Haven on November 5, 1884, consisted of readings in which (as it was advertised) "the pathos of one will alternate with the humor of the other."[13] At first it was hoped that the tour would include not only Cable but also Howells, Aldrich, and even the shy Harris, but it eventually came down to these two writers, performing at the height of their careers, Clemens approaching his apex while Cable had already crested. Clemens's primary selections naturally consisted of memorized readings from his forthcoming *Huckleberry Finn,* which would officially be published in February 1885 at the close of the lecture tour. His material also included excerpts from *A Tramp Abroad;* his coauthored (with Howells) failure of a play, *Colonel Sellers as a Scientist* (advertised in at least one program as "Colonel Sellers in a new role"); and older items such as the Jumping Frog story, the Blue-Jay yarn, and occasionally "A True Story."[14] This work would have been in general harmony with the anti-slavery subtheme of *Huckleberry Finn* since he included in his performance the scene in which Huck decides to "go to hell" and help Jim escape from slavery. Significantly, he presented nothing from his recently published *Life on the Mississippi,* which had not sold well.

Cable read from his works, including *Dr. Sevier,* a novel that had been serialized in the *Century* for the past year and published by Osgood that September. It was set in New Orleans between 1856 and the end of the war. As Arlin Turner, Cable's ablest biographer, observes, this novel departed from the pattern of Cable's earlier and more picturesque works by focusing on contemporary problems in the South such as the need for prison reform, better sanitation, and poverty relief for ex-slaves and poor whites. It was not primarily a Creole story; nor did it touch more than lightly on the problem of the civil rights of freedmen, which would soon become Cable's main political focus. Yet it did contain a passage that enraged the South and effectively kept the Cable-Twain team from ever thinking of taking their lecture tour below the Mason-Dixon line: the admission by one of his characters that the cause of the North in the war had been right. The controversy that ensued came from the *Century* serialization of the book. That October, the magazine printed a letter from a Southerner saying that while Cable had the right to say what he did, the sentiment was not shared by most of his compatriots. In the November issue, however, Cable, who had considered for many years the consequences of speaking out against his homeland, threw more oil on the fire. He said that regardless of whether the war had been fought over either the right to secede or slavery, the first would have clearly allowed the continued existence of the second and the ultimate ruination of Southern life.[15]

This publicity got the tour off to a rough start, but it soon became insignificant because they spoke only to northern audiences. And while Cable was reflecting the political turn his fiction was taking, Twain was gradually departing from his role as a humorist ("a position entirely his own," one of the announcements said) as he drew the essence of his performances from his literary masterpiece. *Huckleberry Finn,* what Justin Kaplan has rightly called "a fresh-water" *Moby-Dick,* was not publicly recognized as a masterpiece until Andrew Lang's essay "The Art of Mark Twain," published in the *Illustrated London News* of February 14, 1891 (coincidentally, in the year of Melville's death and years after *Moby-Dick* itself had already been forgotten for more than a generation).[16] Yet the moral seriousness of *Dr. Sevier* and *Huckleberry Finn* is, historically speaking, more evident in the new direction in which each work would take its author in a general assault on the human (and social) condition.

Overall, though, their lecture programs were short on moral seriousness; they were primarily entertainment that depended in large part on the interaction of these two public personalities, both accomplished veterans of the platform. Together they made more than a hundred appearances in eighty cities, beginning in New England and Canada, moving west to Pittsburgh and through the Midwest, and revisiting several more cities in Canada before concluding in New York. They used no formal introducers. Usually, Cable would appear on stage and announce, "I'm not Mark Twain," before singing a couple of slave and Creole songs and doing his first reading. Twain would subsequently amble out on stage, looking as if he didn't know where he was or what he was expected to do. He would then proceed as he had in the old days, only now giving "readings" instead of pretending to lecture. Sometimes the two would come onstage together with Twain in the lead and Cable, noticeably shorter, following like a son behind his father. According to one report, Twain would turn and say, "Lays sun gen'l'men, I intorduce to you, Mr. Caaa-ble."[17]

They both had an easy sense of humor that came through not only in their performances but also in newspaper interviews they did together in most towns and cities just prior to or following their performance. These in themselves were a form of ongoing advertising for their readings. On one occasion, when a reporter in St. Louis lamented the poor quality of their images in woodcuts in the magazines, Twain answered that he thought that Cable's picture flattered him, while his own depiction did not begin to do him justice.[18] He did grumble privately to his wife from time to time because Cable neither drank nor smoked and attended church services at least twice a week. He also thought at times that Cable took up more than his half of their two-hour program, but these strains did not extinguish their friendship or mutual respect. More than once he told Livy that Cable was a great man. In a letter of February 3, 1885, from Chicago, he expressed his admiration for Cable's championship of the freed slaves: "He is a *great* man; & I believe that if he continues his fight for the negro (& he will,) his greatness will come to be recognized." Since it was Twain who made the lecture arrangements with Pond, he realized, after paying Pond and Cable, around $17,000 for the entire tour. Cable earned a salary of $450 a week and expenses, whether he lectured or not, as well as an additional $60 when more than two matinees were held a week.[19] In all, Cable probably made more than $7,000.

33 Mark Twain and the Phunny Phellows

One of the reasons Mark Twain grumbled during the tour with Cable is that it effectively returned him to his role as a literary comedian and underscored his fame as a "phunny phellow." He had just written an American masterpiece, but here he was doing theatrical high jinks on stage with a southern novelist and a local colorist. (Although he did not at first quite realize its full literary and historical power, Twain did ultimately consider *Huckleberry Finn* his best work more often than not.) His performances consisted of readings from his more humorous pieces over the years, but they also included the passage in which Huck decides to "go to hell" for a runaway slave. The novel's publication coincided with the end of his tour with Cable in February 1885. It may have seemed to him that he was somehow reverting to the status of an Artemus Ward. We remember his second lecture tour in the winter of 1871–72, when he scrambled around for a topic, beginning with "Reminiscences of Some un-Commonplace Characters I Have Chanced to Meet" but quickly turning it into "Artemus Ward, Humorist." After that failed to entertain his audience, he resorted to selections from *Roughing It* and finished out the lecture season triumphantly (see chapter 21). Yet even at that time, he was succeeding mainly as a phunny phellow, the author of a work that, when published in 1872, was considered by most reviewers as a "funny book of the journalistic sort." "You will remember, maybe, how I felt about 'Roughing It,'" he wrote his Buffalo friend David Gray in 1880, "that it would be considered pretty poor stuff, & that therefore I had better not let the press get a chance at it."[1]

During the postwar period and into the early twentieth century, the humor of the Old Southwest on which Mark Twain was raised divided into two complementary streams—one a shallow rough-and-tumble brook, the other a deeper and more sedate stream, but both leading to the great sea change in American literature, Realism. The first consisted of the phunny phellows who manipulated language with misspellings and malapropisms to satirize political events of the day (several wrote imaginary interviews with Lincoln, and one even remembered the assassination with little regret). It was mainly newspaper humor later collected into books sold by subscription presses of the same kind that would issue most of Mark Twain's books. Like Clemens himself, many of these literary comedians began as tramp printers before the war. Their work was first made popular in the newspapers through exchanges of material with other papers and ultimately through syndication.

Twain's contemporaries in this line shared the same literary godfather: Artemus Ward, whose real name was Charles Farrar Browne. Browne employed a cordon sanitaire required of all humorists because the "better people," as Walter Blair writes, in both North and South did not as a rule go for native humor.[2] Such better people included Sam Clemens's own wife and children. By the 1890s Mark Twain had emerged as the best of a group of forty or fifty such writers. Perhaps the Oxford honorary degree in 1907 finally freed him from the pack, or allowed him to believe he had established himself as more than a humorist. It is therefore not surprising that he overvalued the honor by subsequently wearing his scarlet gown on inappropriate occasions, such as his second daughter's wedding.

Curiously, Artemus Ward was, like Twain, also lionized in England before his death in 1867. And because of his success many other humorists flourished in the United States right along with Mark Twain in the postwar years. Most assumed fictional names to tell their stories on the lecturer's stage, in the newspapers, and through collections of their materials in books. There was David Ross Locke, whose "Petroleum Vesuvius Nasby" reminds us of Sam Clemens's hyperinflated very first nom de guerre: "W. Epaminondas Adrastus Perkins." Other representative funny men were Charles Henry Smith ("Bill Arp"), Henry Wheeler

Shaw ("Josh Billings"), Edgar W. Nye ("Bill Nye"), James M. Bailey ("The Danbury *News* Man"), and Melville D. Landon ("Eli Perkins"). As time went on, a few dropped the mask and wrote under their own names, including Finley Peter Dunne, Eugene Field, and Walt Whitman's friend and disciple John Townsend Trowbridge.

The other stream of development led to the rise of the local colorists. Indeed, it was their movement that accounts at least in part for the deepening of Mark Twain's fiction in which the extravagance and exaggeration of the humorists (e.g., in either *The Innocents Abroad* or *Roughing It*) take on the regional and local identity of place (e.g., "Old Times on the Mississippi," *The Adventures of Tom Sawyer,* and *Adventures of Huckleberry Finn*). After the war, readers were curious about different regions and their cultures, having themselves traveled about the country as soldiers, or having relatives and friends who had. Moreover, many were nostalgic for the seemingly pastoral America before the war—even in the Old South, then defeated and struggling under its devastation, both during and after Reconstruction. The demand for a new American regional literature was met by a number of monthly magazines founded in the decades leading up to or immediately following the war—*Harper's Monthly, Putnam's Monthly, Atlantic Monthly, Scribner's Monthly,* and others.

Two writers who were famous before the war—indeed whose writings even helped precipitate it—evolved into local colorists after the war was over. John Greenleaf Whittier, whose anti-slavery poems had fueled the abolitionist movement, published in 1866 "a winter idyll" called *Snow-Bound* that evoked the harsh New England winters he had witnessed as a child. Harriet Beecher Stowe, author of *Uncle Tom's Cabin* and Mark Twain's neighbor in Nook Farm, reminisced about growing up in Massachusetts and Connecticut in a series of books culminating in *Old Town Folks* in 1869.[3] A third successful writer, Bret Harte, whose career sprang almost solely from his publication of "The Luck of Roaring Camp" when it appeared in the *Overland Monthly* in 1868, looked back a couple of decades as he depicted life in the California mines following the Gold Rush of 1849. Similarly, Joel Chandler Harris took his readers back to the slave quarters before the war. Cable, of course, sketched out the lives of the Creoles of Louisiana, and somewhat later, Edward Eggleston wrote about the Hoosiers in Indiana. In a real sense, most of them were defining their regions the way the writers of Down East and the Old Southwest had, but now the pictures were about more than mere eccentricities or oddities of character and language. Exaggeration was replaced by Realism, of which this local color movement was the beginning. It set the stage not only for the nuanced descriptions of life in the works of William Dean Howells and Henry James but also the vernacular narratives of Mark Twain.

Twain must have felt the pull of both currents as he struggled with his public image. He knew well what he owed to the humorist tradition. Without it, he would never have become Mark Twain. Yet he sensed that if he remained a humorist only, or was merely remembered as one, he might be forgotten with the other phunny phellows. He had long realized his difference from the most prominent of them, starting at least as early as his lecture on Artemus Ward. What he himself said, he told Livy back then, "fetched" his audience, while what he quoted from Ward did not. Twain's humor at its best was not topical; rather, it was full of pathos and profoundly engaged in the horrible or hilarious joke of the human condition. He was in fact saved from the fate of the humorist by the local color movement, which introduced him to literary realism. Yet there would likely never have been either a Mark Twain or the American literary realism movement without the irreverence of the phunny phellows. This fact is nowhere better illustrated than in the very story that helped launch Twain's national career as a humorist, "Jim Smiley and His Jumping Frog." Its irreverence evokes the very heart of comedy, when the compulsive gambler Jim Smiley bets that the clergyman's wife will die. It ultimately takes a stranger—a mysterious stranger in the larger context of the human condition—to bring down such a fanatically selfish human being, a gambler with a vicious streak that Twain ultimately attributed to the entire human race.

A century after his death, we can see Mark Twain more clearly not only in relation to the humor and realist movements but also in the context of literary naturalism, or determinism. As he wrote book after book, always thinking that he was simply making a living, his era was steadily giving way to the malaise of the end of the century. The American West as the land of freedom and second chances had dissolved into myth by the time of the White City at the Chicago World's Fair of 1893, the same year when Frederick Jackson Turner announced that the frontier had closed. "The translation of land into capital," in the words of historian Alan Trachtenberg, "of what once seemed 'free' into private wealth," undercut the agrarian dream and set Americans upon the uncharted waters of the twentieth century.[4] It was in this fin de siècle tradition that Twain's humor took on its seriousness. For even though so many of his novels are set in the antebellum past, he was in fact reflecting the problems of postwar America. Beginning with *The Gilded Age,* which directly addresses the rampant materialism of many Americans after the war, the greed in his characters grows stronger and stronger until it becomes literally funny. He takes this human folly to Europe in *A Tramp Abroad* and extends it to our English forebears in *The Prince and the Pauper.* As we shall see, Mark Twain's vision from here on out becomes darker and darker until it culminates in "No. 44, The Mysterious Stranger," an account of a journey so deep into the heart of darkness that Mark Twain chose not to publish it.

34 Webster and Paige

During the 1880s two quite different individuals emerged in the life of Mark Twain, and their involvement with him would have dire consequences. It was the decade in which he triumphed with *Adventures of Huckleberry Finn* and failed (critically, at least) with *A Connecticut Yankee in King Arthur's Court.* Indeed, his literary highs and lows during this period are almost perfectly reflected in his fortunes and misfortunes as a businessman and an investor. First, there was Charles Luther Webster, who had married Annie Moffett, Sam's niece by his sister Pamela, in 1875. He hailed from Dunkirk, New York, thirty miles from Fredonia, where Annie had moved with her mother at the age of eighteen. In the census for 1870, Webster is listed as the son of a retired farmer and his wife, and as a draftsman (he later became a self-taught civil engineer). Then there was James W. Paige, a man made for this American era of rampant advances in technology that turned the U.S. Patent Office in Washington, D.C., into one of the government's busiest agencies. He was a machinist and inventor who lived in Rochester, New York, in the 1870s and moved to Hartford in 1877 at the invitation of the Farnham Type-Setting Company, which had agreed to sponsor the development of his typesetting machine.

Webster, according to his mother-in-law, Pamela Moffett, had a "very nervous temperament" and eventually suffered from a debilitating case of neuralgia. When he was nine years old, he accidentally killed a young girl with a gun.[1] He died before the age of forty, in 1891, leaving behind a widow and three children. The inventor Paige designed, built, and tinkered endlessly with what Twain ultimately considered his infernal machine, the Paige Compositor. He also fancied himself as something of a playboy. In 1892, having enjoyed Twain's lavish financial support for years, Paige was sued by a stage actress for breach of promise for the grand sum of $950,000. The newspapers that carried the story reported his net worth at between $2 and $3 million. His accuser never collected a dime, and Paige, whose personal wealth—like his invention—was mostly a chimera, died a pauper in Chicago in 1917, precise age unknown.[2] Twain immortalized both men in his letters and autobiography. "I have never hated any creature with a hundred thousandth fraction of the hatred which I bear that human louse, Webster," he told Orion. He said of Paige in his autobiography that if he had the inventor "in a steel trap I would shut out all human succor and watch that trap till he died."[3]

After his marriage to Annie, Webster went into business selling real estate in Fredonia. He also got involved with the Fredonia Watch Company, which turned out to be a fraud. Webster discovered the truth about the company, but not before he personally sold his Uncle Sam some four thousand dollars' worth of shares. Together they frightened the company into returning most of the money, and Twain then put his nephew in charge of the Kaolatype stock being managed by Slote, Woodman, and Company. Gradually, he became Twain's full-time business manager, and then junior partner in 1884 with the creation of Charles L. Webster & Company. Twain initially set up this publishing house to issue *Huckleberry Finn,* thinking he could do a much better job himself than what Osgood had done to sell *Life on the Mississippi* by subscription. (Osgood, as noted earlier, simply had no experience in the field of subscription publishing, as opposed to the traditional way of selling books through his publisher-owned bookshop.) Following the great commercial success of *Huckleberry Finn,* the firm published Grant's *Memoirs,* another triumph but also the last big strike before a series of eighty-six more books with mediocre to poor sales that were published between 1885 and 1894. (See appendix B.) Failures included the life of Pope Leo XIII in 1887, as well as a number of Civil War memoirs whose sales potential had been overestimated after the Grant volumes, which had earned the general's widow almost $400,000 in royalties and Twain personally almost $100,000.

One of the severest drains on Charles L. Webster & Company was the publication (within three years) of an eleven-volume anthology titled the *Library of American Literature,* coedited by the poet-businessman Edmund Clarence Stedman and Ellen Mackay Hutchinson in 1891. The capital outlay was enormous because these subscription volumes had to be produced, sold, and delivered as a set before they brought in any income whatever. When the Panic of 1893 washed over the country, Webster & Company was unable to borrow enough money to sustain the overextended enterprise. Interestingly, this ambitious selection of texts was quite democratic, including not only Whitman but also his most enthusiastic supporter and a minor poet and fiction writer in his own right, William Douglas O'Connor, author of the panegyric on Whitman entitled "The Good Gray Poet" (1866).[4] It did not include, however, Sara Parton, better known as "Fanny Fern," a popular feminist writer and a devotee of Whitman's.

Aside from complaints to his sister and brother, Twain saved most of his vitriol concerning Webster for an autobiographical dictation of 1906. By that time, his authorized biographer, Albert Bigelow Paine, was on hand to hear the rancorous remarks, but he never included the material in either his 1912 biography or his 1923 edition of the autobiography. In fact, he dismissed Clemens's account as "the result of misunderstanding and disagreement," saying that "Webster was probably vainglorious and irritating, but in all the letters and records there is nothing to show that he was not working for the best interests of the firm, or that he ever was unfair in his mistakes. In fact, he was very industrious—and literally worked himself to death."[5] When Twain's true feelings about his niece's husband became public in Bernard De Voto's *Mark Twain in Eruption* in 1940, Webster's son Samuel published *Mark Twain, Business Man* in 1946, a defense of his father's actions with regard to the firm and its failure.

The truth is that neither Twain nor Webster was very astute at business, or at least at accounting (resulting in a bookkeeper theft of twenty-five thousand dollars discovered in 1887). After the coups of *Huckleberry Finn* and the Grant memoirs, the company acquired a reputation as one of the most prestigious presses in the country, and it should have succeeded. Simply put, it was poorly run, guided by little or no effective marketing plan. As publishers, Twain and Webster chose one loser after another, even though Webster did manage on several occasions to talk Twain out of making contracts for obvious failures. One of them was the proposed continuation of Grant's life from where it leaves off in the *Memoirs,* to be written by one of the general's sons (a biography never published).[6]

Another problem between them was that Twain the artist didn't want to be bothered with business matters, yet he often complained that he wasn't kept adequately informed about company profits and expenditures. He also couldn't understand the firm's financial statements, and—given their bookkeeper's embezzlement—apparently Webster couldn't either. Twain also used his nephew-in-law as a personal factotum, asking him to purchase this or that item for his "Aunt Livy" or sending him up to Hartford to check on renovations and repairs to their house while the family spent the summer at Quarry Farm. On one occasion, he even expected Webster to travel all the way from New York City to Elmira just to discuss a particular problem the company was then experiencing. Webster was at a particular disadvantage in dealing with Twain because his senior partner was also his wealthy uncle. Yet he would occasionally flare out at his "Uncle Sam" when asked do his personal bidding, such as handling his unprofitable inventions and patents, including an impractical bed clamp designed to keep children from kicking off their bed covers (duly tested on the Webster children). Twain's attitude toward Webster was doubtless tainted from the beginning. Shortly after Webster made his move to New York in the spring of 1881, his mother-in-law told her son Sam Moffett that she "always believed that C[harley]'s moral nature was weak and undeveloped."[7] Such idle speculation would have made the family rounds to Pamela's younger brother, who all along thought he was doing his niece a favor by hiring Webster in the first place.

The conflict that developed between them arose because, while Twain had finished his masterpiece by 1885, he still had less and less time for writing because of the demands of other "business." During the first half of the 1880s, everything looked positive. Yet the distractions of the second half of the decade went beyond simple business problems with

Charles L. Webster & Company. All along, the smooth-talking Paige was increasing his death grip on Twain's imagination (and his money). Twain had first met the mechanic-turned-inventor in the Colt Fire Arms Manufactory in Hartford, where he was working away not only on his typesetter but on another invention for improving the telegraph. Justin Kaplan has described the whole ordeal and is best at capturing Twain's utter fascination with the financial possibilities of the technology. Twain was persuaded by Dwight Buell, a Hartford jeweler, to see the prototype and to meet Paige. "Until he saw it in action," writes Kaplan, the former printer "had not believed such a machine could exist. Soon after he saw it and fell under the spell of its inventor, . . . he began to believe that it was about the only machine of its kind that did exist."[8] There were others undergoing perfection, however, including the Merganthaler Linotype, which would ultimately sweep the field of competition, but Twain's state of denial along with his unbounded faith in James W. Paige kept him a prisoner to a tragic illusion.

Twain's notebooks are full of fantasies about how much money the typesetter would earn, exact calculations as to how many newspapers would either buy or lease it and how much they would be forced to pay. He was obsessed with the machine, which usually functioned well enough with light workloads, but never performed reliably enough to meet the relentless demands of a daily newspaper. It was as if all those notions of getting rich—dreams that first danced through his head when he was a young teenager in Hannibal and everybody was either leaving or traveling through town on their way to the Gold Rush of 1849—had suddenly rematerialized. He spent much of his time trying to interest other investors, but, as the machine failed test after test and Paige repeatedly tore down his machine of eighteen thousand parts to make corrections and improvements, Twain was left as virtually its sole financial backer. Over the decade, he may have invested as much as $200,000 on the project. Estimates vary and go as high as $300,000—roughly $6 million in today's dollars. While his publishing company was still making money, Clemens apparently used part of that profit, or at least his personal share, to fund the machine. He even resorted to spending part of his wife's inheritance. By 1887 Livy's share in J. Langdon & Company had dwindled to less than $55,000, and that was its value before Twain began siphoning part of it away to sustain Paige's folly.[9]

He soon began to lose money in the publishing company, too. And all the while there were frequent requests for loans, major sums, often from near strangers. Calvin Higbie, his old mining partner from the Aurora days, to whom he had dedicated *Roughing It* ("When we two were millionaires for ten days"), asked him for a $20,000 loan. One of General Grant's sons, Jesse, persuaded Twain to pay $5,000 for a trip he made to London to look into a railroad investment that came to nothing. Evidently the Grant family thought it had found a magic fountain in Webster & Company and even challenged its bookkeeping on the *Memoirs*—this despite the fact that Grant's widow had received from the company the biggest royalty check in history up to that time. Jesse also wanted to become a partner in Webster & Company before he would allow it to publish Grant's letters to his wife (another Grant book the firm did not issue). To Twain's credit, he regularly contributed to worthy causes, such as sending two black students through an all-black college in Pennsylvania and financially helping another African American to finish Yale Law School. He generously supported a promising sculptor, Karl Gerhardt. He even gave Walt Whitman money on more than one occasion. In 1887 he contributed fifty dollars to funds Whitman's disciples were raising to provide him with a summer cottage, money that ultimately helped build the aging poet's mausoleum.[10] Yet Twain was also digging his own grave, financially. In addition to everything else, he was paying Paige an annual salary of $7,000. He was perpetually fuming over Paige's endless delays, only to be charmed again and again into continuing his support every time he confronted the inventor, who simply could not be hurried.

As business went down, costs went up. Webster moved the firm to larger offices, having earlier hired a stenographer, Fred A. Hall, to take dictation from General Grant for the *Memoirs.* Hall soon became a junior partner in the firm and finally replaced Webster when he fell ill in 1888. Hall had also filled in for Webster during his two trips abroad, once in August 1885 to secure foreign rights for the Grant *Memoirs* and again in June 1886 for an audience with the pope, who in return for publishing his biography made the Protestant Webster a papal knight. That was the most Webster & Company got for publishing a book the partners cynically thought all American Catholics would want to buy if not read. Hall himself was a manipulative sort who did not hesitate to deceive authors when he thought it necessary. One of the firm's books was entitled *The Legends and Myths of Hawaii,* purportedly written by the current king of the islands. When its ghostwriter, Twain's former associate at the Virginia City *Enterprise,* Rollin M. Daggett, grew impatient in 1888 because another book was placed ahead of it in the publishing schedule, Hall suggested that they could "have a die made and bind up a few volumes. . . . We can easily dispose of these, send three or four of them to [Daggett], and that will keep him quiet."[11] Nor was Hall shy when Twain, later that year, conspired with him to force Webster into permanent retirement so that they could stop his salary, which had continued after his initial departure.

Webster did retire permanently in the fall of 1888 with a final compensation of around twelve thousand dollars (really a free loan from Twain, not the company, which was already in the red and beginning to borrow from the Mount Morris Bank in New York). In retirement Webster was periodically seen on the streets of Fredonia in his papal regalia, and it was known that he liked to be addressed as "Sir Charles Webster." Privately, Twain spoke of him as "not a man but a hog," thinking erroneously that Webster had pilfered small sums while still running the firm. Yet he paid out the pension because of his regard for his niece.[12] Webster enjoyed only three years of retirement before dying in 1891, probably of pancreatic cancer. Twain, who refused to write to Pamela directly while she resided in Webster's home, did not attend his funeral. Nor did Livy. Six years later he told his sister: "I am not able to think of [Webster] without cursing him & cursing the day I opposed your better judgment of the lousy scoundrel & thief & sided with Annie in her desire to marry him. The thought of that treacherous cur can wake me out of my sleep."[13] By this time Webster & Company had long since declared bankruptcy.

By then Twain had washed his hands of Paige, too. In February 1891 he finally untangled himself from the "machine" and, in an agreement three years later, freed himself of any lingering financial responsibility for it. When told that Paige had signed on the dotted line, the weary writer, then about to travel the world to repay his publishing firm's debts, replied: "I am glad Paige has signed. I wish it was his death-warrant." Earlier, when every potential investor including his brother-in-law had failed to commit, Clemens had assumed almost complete financial responsibility for the machine and had to be formally released from that obligation.[14] Before this final and complete break with Paige, he had held out hope that one day the inventor would stop his incessant dismantling and reassembling of the five-thousand-pound machine and announce its definite completion. Its success would still have brought Twain—or his heirs, it seemed more probable—millions. In 1891, sounding like Colonel Sellers, he wrote Orion (whose own version of the typesetter had been the Tennessee Land): "It is worth billions; & when the pig-headed lunatic, its inventor, dies, it will instantly be capitalized & make the Clemens children rich."[15] Serious or not, he was echoing the refrain of their father, John Marshall Clemens, as well as his literary incarnation in *The Gilded Age*. In chapter 1, Squire Hawkins tells his wife as the impoverished family is about to answer Colonel Sellers's call for them to move to Missouri: "I have taken up Seventy-five Thousand Acres of Land in this county—think what an enormous fortune it will be some day! Why, Nancy, enormous don't express it—the word's too tame!"

35 A Romance of the White Conscience

Twain's edginess in getting *Adventures of Huckleberry Finn* ready for publication in 1884 shows in some of the prefatory material he inserted at the last moment—as if to delay that final plunge into this "sequel" to *Tom Sawyer.* For this book would take him deep into the American experience of slavery, a topic first stirred in "A True Story" but hardly touched on in his first two novelistic uses of the matters of Hannibal and the Mississippi. Slavery as an institution had effectively died with the Emancipation Proclamation of 1863, but its impact on the country and this writer surely had not. That is one of the reasons why this particular "boy's book" is so compelling, not only to Twain's readers in the nineteenth century but to readers ever since: it evokes the human ideal of doing right in the face of inconvenience and indeed ruin. Huck does what Silas Lapham does in Twain's best friend's novel *The Rise of Silas Lapham,* published the same year. In a moment of crisis, he refuses to act in his own behalf when it will injure another. Silas, of course, is consciously doing right by refusing to take advantage of naïve investors in order to save his company from bankruptcy. Huck, on the other hand, makes a similarly risky sacrifice but thinks he is doing wrong. Therein lies the difference between Howells the realist and Twain the emerging naturalist in the mid-1880s. For Twain, Huck's "sound heart" is not ruled by any common standard of morality but is simply that way through another Darwinian accident.

Apparently somebody at Charles L. Webster & Company (or the photoengraver the company used) didn't care for either Jim the sympathetic slave or Twain's implicit determinism, because the engraving for the illustration at the end of chapter 32, depicting Huck's being greeted by Aunt Sally and Uncle Silas, was sabotaged to show the sway-backed Uncle Silas with an erect penis protruding through his trousers, the caption now conveying a double entendre: "Who do you reckon it is?" The defaced illustration made it into the prospectus (sample pages of the book to be used by the subscription book salesmen) and into the signature of the first printing of thirty thousand copies.[1] This act of subversion, whose perpetrator was never discovered, naturally outraged Clemens, who was forced to delay publication beyond the 1884 Christmas season in order to recall every copy of that page in the prospectus and the book and to replace them with the original undamaged engraving (only one or two survived to tell the tale).

The plot of the novel is probably as generally familiar as the fence whitewashing scene in *Tom Sawyer,* certainly more recognizable to most readers today than the plot of the first Hannibal book. It picks up with Huck living at the home of the Widow Douglas on the hill overlooking St. Petersburg. He is kidnapped by his father, who wants Huck's share of the money that he and Tom found in the earlier novel. Huck escapes to Jackson's Island, where he finds the slave Jim, owned by Miss Watson, sister of the Widow Douglas. Jim "runs off" to avoid being sold down the river. Their subsequent river journey takes them through different levels of southern society that are described in almost anthropological detail—from a backwoods wife to family feuds and river con artists. During his retreat from the world with Jim, as they travel on a raft downriver at night under the stars, Huck decides to risk being known as a hated abolitionist and to help Jim escape from slavery. Jim is ultimately sold by the Duke and the King—two frauds who take over the raft—and ends up a prisoner on Aunt Sally's farm in Arkansas, where he is being readied for return to his owner. Twain, as he later wrote, literally moved the farm of his Uncle John Quarles and Aunt Patsy downriver to Arkansas to become the farmhouse residence of Tom's Aunt Sally and Uncle Silas. Huck is obliged to pose as Tom and agrees to help Tom, posing as Sid, free Jim. Huck is both surprised at and disgusted by Tom for agreeing to "steal" a slave, but as we ultimately learn, Tom knows that Jim is already free and is simply seizing the opportunity to use him as a pawn in his exotic escape plans. All is discovered by the adults, and Jim ends up officially free. Huck resolves to "light out for the Territory," where his creator had gone to escape the war in 1861, rather than remain in a society in which Jim will never be truly liberated. The issue of Jim's real ultimate fate, of course, is not addressed in a novel that required a happy ending.

The first edition, oddly, had two frontispieces, perhaps the result of the author's last-minute decisions. From the start, there was the first of E.W. Kemble's sketches throughout the book, this one showing Huck standing before a fallen dead tree holding a rifle in his left hand and a shot rabbit aloft in his right. The second was a photograph of a bust of the author's profile, done by Karl Gerhardt, a Hartford artist Twain had supported during his study in Paris for many years. In order to help Gerhardt get the neck right, Twain had a photograph taken of himself stripped to the waist (see the frontispiece to this biography). In the Gerhardt bust, Twain essentially exchanges the usual accoutrements of an author for the gaze of a Roman general whose orders may not be disobeyed.[2] In a way, the trade-off is similar to Whitman's achievement in the frontispiece to the first edition of *Leaves of Grass,* where he exchanged the author's black coat and tie for the uniform of the workingman who wrote poems about such nontraditional subjects as jobs and sex. But Twain was more inhibited in his visual plunge into the vernacular, mainly because he, as well as his family, didn't want to be confused with the underclass Huck. Traditionally, the outside narrator in southwestern humor took pains to distinguish himself from his inside or vernacular storyteller. Hence, it was prudent to juxtapose this backwoods figure in *Huckleberry Finn* with a classical bust of somebody suggesting Twain's difference from his first-person narrator.

Almost twenty years later, when Twain's nephew, the journalist Samuel E. Moffett, was writing a biographical piece about Mark Twain that would be published in 1903, he submitted a draft to the family for its approval. In a recently discovered letter, Clara wrote on behalf of her mother (then quite ill) asking her cousin to clear up any lingering notion of similarities between author and narrator. "There has been so much said in the papers lately of my father's being himself the original of Huckleberry

Finn," she wrote, "that my mother has worried at the thought that many might really believe him to be one of the poor whites of the South." She then asked for some small changes (marking the place where they ought to appear), explaining "that his family was of good origin in reduced circumstances, & again on the second turned-down page mention that his parents on both sides had been slave holders." (Moffett complied, but on the issue of slave ownership he softened that fact by substituting "forefathers" for "parents.")[3] Twain himself had always pointed to Tom Blankenship, the son of one of Hannibal's town drunks, as the model for Huck, but in light of Livy and Clara's nervous request and indeed the family's general preference for such works as *The Prince and the Pauper* and even his life of Joan of Arc, published in the 1890s, we might wonder if indeed he wasn't basing this character, certainly in terms of Huck's humorous distinctions between illusion and reality, partly on himself.

Regardless of that possibility, Clara's request gives us a new context for Sam Clemens's return to the South in *Huckleberry Finn.* Whitman might dream in the grass about democracy for all, but it would have to be dreaming, nevertheless. His narrator might take in a fugitive slave as the speaker does in section 10 of "Song of Myself," but the flesh-and-blood writer behind the narrator maintained that, even though he was against slavery, it had to be upheld until Congress officially banned it. Whitman even lost the friendship of one of his closest literary allies over the issue. After the war, Sam Clemens wrote the same kind of romance about antebellum America, this one featuring a white boy and a runaway slave making their journey down the middle of America. Progressive on the issue of race in his own time, if not in ours, Twain consequently allows Huck to come up to later standards only when adrift from a society in which certain human beings are treated like livestock. In spite of his time on the raft, during which he becomes personally close to Jim, Huck remains to the end a victim of his environment, impulsively telling Aunt Sally once he's ashore that nobody but a "nigger" (i.e., a slave and a nonhuman) was killed in a reported steamboat explosion.

Yet Clara and her mother were wrong on one significant count. The narrator of *Huckleberry Finn* is none other than Mark Twain on the lecturer's platform, nonchalantly lounging about the stage the way Huck lounges through life, trying to distinguish illusion from reality. Huck can't, for example, see the advantages of Miss Watson's heaven over the obvious pleasures of hell. "Then she told me all about the bad place," we learn in the opening chapter, "and I said I wished I was there. . . . *She* was going to live so as to go to the good place, . . . so I made up my mind I wouldn't try for it." Later, in a 1901 speech, Twain spoke of a dying man who couldn't make up his mind as to which place to go—"both have their advantages, 'heaven for climate, hell for company!'" In short, almost at the same time Clara asked her cousin to help squelch the idea that Huck Finn and Mark Twain were one and the same, Twain was publicly reinforcing that identification. This book, his greatest achievement, did in fact come largely from real life, and by conscious design. "If you attempt to create & build a wholly imaginary incident, adventure or situation," he wrote in 1887, "you will go astray. . . . But if you found on a *fact* in your personal experience, it is an acorn, a root, & every created adornment that grows up out of it & spreads its foliage & blossoms to the sun will seem realities, not inventions."[4]

While Twain was writing his book, he read and jotted marginalia in William Still's encyclopedic *The Underground Rail Road,* which is a compilation of black narratives of experiences on the Underground Railroad. Known as the "Father of the Underground Railroad," Still, whose parents were emancipated slaves, published his book in 1873. The stories he gathered, in which fleeing blacks were constantly in danger of being betrayed (as Frederick Douglass, Jervis Langdon's friend, had been in his first attempt to flee his Maryland masters), are full of suspense. Certain signals were used to assure the next passengers on the Underground Railroad that the way was safe. On the flyleaf of his copy, Twain wrote about a slave in Richmond, the mother of a three-year-old daughter. Her brother, an escaped slave living in Elmira in 1844, "cut two duplicate hearts out of pink paper, & wrote on one, 'When you see this again, you will know.'" The escaping mother and her child "saw & recognized the duplicate heart," Twain wrote, and subsequently succeeded in reaching her brother in Elmira.[5]

One of the most overlooked aspects of *Huckleberry Finn* is the danger that threatens Jim throughout their travels. If Twain had forgotten the deadly perils of the runaway slave in the South, Still's book must have reminded him of the facts. Jim's danger seldom shows up during the main part of the novel, when Huck and Jim travel at night or when their purpose of getting Jim to freedom is upstaged by the various episodes along the river in which Jim cannot be a central player. But it looms large at the beginning of the novel and it is underscored at the end when Tom is shot while pretending to be an abolitionist. Even though Jim sacrifices his own freedom to care for the wounded Tom, the farmers who corner Jim are ready to hang him. They don't, merely because he is somebody else's property, not because of any recognition of Jim's humanity. To them Jim is never—as Huck says about Jim—"white inside." In fact, in their utter contempt for any slave, they "cussed Jim considerable," Huck tells us in his noncommittal voice, "and give him a cuff or two, side the head." (To "cuff" a slave, who was often addressed as "Cuffy," was to hit him or her with the back or cuff of the hand.) Finally, Huck tells us, when the whole story of Jim's sacrifice is told by the doctor who treats Tom, "they all agreed that Jim had acted very well, and was deserving to have some notice took of it, and a reward. So every one of them promised, right out and hearty, that they wouldn't cuss him no more."

These and other events like them in the late chapters are why it is important to finish the novel and not stop when the river adventures are over, the point beyond which Hemingway said "the rest is just cheating." The story not only has to end somewhere, but those final chapters—after Tom's annoying insistence on the details of how Jim's escape should properly be carried out—round out the story and bring it to a realistic close. Aesthetically, if anything ought to be skipped in reading *Huckleberry Finn,* it is the raft scene left out of the original edition because it had been included in chapter 3 of *Life on the Mississippi* as a way for Twain to satisfy readers hounding him for a sequel to *Tom Sawyer.* While it is a fine example of humor of the Old Southwest, a tradition that Twain culminates, it is otherwise something of a digression from the plot of *Huckleberry Finn.*

As critics of the novel over the past century have noted, its plot is episodic in its forty-three short chapters (not counting the outsized raft scene). It begins in Hannibal, or St. Petersburg; in these opening chapters, Twain was, as noted, writing his "sequel" to *Tom Sawyer,* in which Huck is named on the title page as "Tom Sawyer's Comrade." Tom is in control of things until chapter 4, when Huck steps into his own story by discovering his father's footprint in the snow, identified by a cross in the left heel to ward off the devil. The ominous footprint tells Huck that his father, the town drunk, is lurking nearby. When Pap appears in the next chapter, Huck's story can be said to have begun in earnest. He leaves Tom Sawyer's world of romance and its harmless consequences—indeed, Clemens's childhood memory of Hannibal—for the ugly reality of river life in the Mississippi Valley that Sam Clemens had absorbed as a river pilot before the Civil War.

As the story unfolds, it is not only Jim who becomes a fugitive but Huck as well—not just from his father, who had imprisoned him in a deserted cabin on the Illinois side of the Mississippi, but now also from society itself because he is in the company of a fugitive slave. Additionally, as a member of the underclass—the very society of poor whites that Clara and her mother wanted to make sure was not confused with their own family roots—Huck fears that he will be accused of lesser crimes than abolitionism, such as helping the Duke and the King cheat the Wilks girls. On his journey with Jim, Huck is also constantly trying to find out who he is. When he gets to Aunt Sally and Uncle Silas's farm, he discovers that he has to pretend to be Tom Sawyer instead of Huckleberry Finn. Indeed, he *becomes* Tom in the shenanigans orchestrated by the real Tom, who is passing under the pseudonym of his brother Sid. But this is simply the culmination of a series of false identities beginning with Huck's disguise as Sarah Mary Williams in the river cabin of Mrs. Judith Loftus, the backwoods wife who detects his male identity and, being too clever by half, dismisses him as a runaway apprentice. He is then thought to be dead before he comes back to life as George Jackson at the Grangerfords. Next, he is the valet to the bogus English relatives of the Wilks family.

Mark Twain himself was operating under a false identity—certainly as far as his Victorian-minded family was concerned. They preferred his pseudo-Virginia identity wrapped up in the trinomials of John Marshall Clemens and Samuel Langhorne Clemens, the first given in honor of a lawyer who eventually became chief justice of the Supreme Court, and the second the surname of a vaguely remembered friend of his father's.[6] Neither name had any prior family connections. But then names are often meaningless in the American universe of new beginnings. Twain's fascination with royal titles, indeed his ironic and satirical use of them, comes right out of the American grain. His use of the Duke and the King in the novel was of a piece with the opening shot of his frontal attack on British nobility in *A Connecticut Yankee in King Arthur's Court*. In that novel, as we shall see, the source of the vitriol that flowed from his journals as he wrote the book is now British instead of French. And what had merely buffeted the British sensibilities in *The Prince and the Pauper* turns lethal in *A Connecticut Yankee*. Matthew Arnold, who criticized Grant's grammar in his *Memoirs* in 1887, helped bring the acid to the surface in Twain's reconsideration of the British and their condescending view of American culture (and corresponding dismissal of its humor). In the spring of 1888 Twain planned but never executed a formal response to Arnold's widely read attack on American culture.[7]

Readers have often wondered why Jim can't simply cross the Mississippi River to the free state of Illinois. Twain knew along with his original audience that fugitive slaves were not "free" or safe in border states, that slave catchers would illegally apprehend them and bring them back into slave territory. Anyway, Jim's momentum is caught up with Huck's on Jackson's Island. He has a raft, and a raft goes in only the direction the river flows; hence, they ironically flee south in search of freedom. Going up the Ohio River by steamboat from Cairo wouldn't have been any safer. Moreover, Twain's steamboat piloting experience didn't include the Ohio River; the part of the Mississippi with all its bends and other impediments that was seared in his memory lay between St. Louis and New Orleans. Clearly, Twain, when he began imagining Huck's journey, didn't know any more than his main character did just where the river would take them—only that it had to be south.

He had picked up ideas for the book while visiting the river in 1882. All those river shacks, feuds, and frauds that made up its life got absorbed into this panorama of southern life before the war. And there were frauds off the river, as well, who contributed to the characters in the novel. The King, for instance, was modeled in part after Charles C. Duncan, the skipper of the *Quaker City* who had so infuriated Twain not only during *The Innocents Abroad* cruise but also in the late seventies. Then there had been several exchanges between the two in newspapers. Mainly, Duncan raised the author's ire when he remembered publicly in lectures the day when Twain and Edward House had come from Pfaff's in a slightly intoxicated state so Twain could apply for a berth on the *Quaker City* cruise.

Jim himself is modeled on blacks Twain knew personally, not only Uncle Daniel from the Quarles farm but also his Hartford butler, George Griffin. As a southerner, Twain was more familiar with black people than were most whites in the North, but he also viewed them from the viewpoint of a benign southerner, judging them to be a gentle but ignorant people whose activities and antics charmed as well as amused. Jim is the perfect butt of Tom's romantic elaborations. His willingness to endure them irritates many readers today. And indeed it may be unrealistic, but this was the way many whites in the country were trying to remember blacks during and after Reconstruction, when *Huckleberry Finn* was being written and published. Whites were more and more afraid of what would become of future generations of blacks who had not grown up as slaves, and it is not unreasonable to assume that Twain sensed some of these feelings. The fear, of course, led to the country's shameful period of black lynchings between 1880 and 1920. In 1901 he talked with Frank Bliss, Elisha's son who succeeded his father at the American Publishing Company, about the possibility of a book to be called the *History of Lynching in America.* "Yesterday," he told him, "I wrote an acid article on the subject ('The United States of Lyncherdom') for the North American Review." Neither the book nor the article was ever published in Twain's lifetime because, as the *North American Review* editors warned him, it would cost him his southern readership. Yet it tempted him for a time. "The lynching-book still haunts me," he told Bliss. Twain had earlier—in the Buffalo *Express* of August 26, 1869—complained of lynching, but he did so in an unsigned editorial.[8]

Naturally, *Adventures of Huckleberry Finn* is hardly perfect in terms of its depiction of race relations according to the post–civil rights movement standards of our own time. (As one critic has recently observed, Huck may simply recognize "that he likes Jim better than he does Miss Watson.")[9] The novel fares much better in its ironic, certainly subtle indictment of slavery. It was the book for its time in America's racial history as much as Stowe's masterpiece was for its era. While *Uncle Tom's Cabin* appeared before the war and at the beginning of the rise of abolitionism in the North, we ought not to forget that *Huckleberry Finn* appeared at the height of American racism and black oppression at the end of Reconstruction, when the Ku Klux Klan was formed in the South and the thousands of black lynchings soon began. Its ultimate achievement is to show just how hypocritical whites, including kindhearted ones like Huck, can be when it comes to blacks. Indeed, Twain demonstrates how black racism in the United States ran even deeper than the institution of slavery itself. Mark Twain ultimately reveals the reader—not only in America's antebellum period but today—to be in most cases prepared to go to the extremes Huck does in attaining Jim's freedom *only* when slavery is no longer either a fact or even a temptation. In other words, the white reader gets a free ride in the sense that he or she can come down on the side of justice without running the risk of breaking the law—because the law, if not the consequence, of slavery had disappeared by the time of the publication of *Huckleberry Finn* in 1885.

Even to Huck most of the time, Jim is largely a burden that he all too easily forgets about during their periods of separation. The indifference that so many whites felt toward blacks becomes clearer in *Pudd'nhead Wilson,* but it is obvious enough in *Huckleberry Finn.* And its dramatic demonstration there is what makes the book such a scathing indictment of slavery—if not altogether the racism then engrained in the white mind. Slavery, as noted, is more roundly condemned—more directly attacked—in Stowe's great novel, but there the owners of slaves, or at least some of them, are pitied for their plight. Moreover, slavery itself, before Eliza's need to flee the household, has almost the benign appearance of John Pendleton Kennedy's *Swallow Barn; or A Sojourn in the Old Dominion* (1832), a series of Irvingesque sketches intended to paint slavery and southern life in general as a warmhearted institution in which blacks like Uncle Tom are truly the bosses of their own domains. Harriet

Beecher Stowe, who aside from a brief period in Kentucky had never visited the South, mainly mastered the arguments against slavery. Mark Twain knew the South firsthand. He also understood human nature—on both sides of the Mason-Dixon line—with regard to race relations in America in the wake of slavery.

We find none of Stowe's noble depictions of slaves in *Huckleberry Finn,* only superstitious slaves whose presence outside of their usefulness is hardly noticed by whites. Even Huck, in spite of his brief transformation on the river, reverts to referring to slaves as things. "When I start in to steal a nigger, or a watermelon, or a Sunday-school book," he tells Tom in chapter 36 as they begin the antics to free Jim, "I ain't no ways particular how it's done so it's done." The story can be read as a novel of adolescence in which the protagonist wakes up as a potential criminal in a corrupt society. With this book, Mark Twain himself woke up. He would never again believe in the possibility of an innocent or carefree Huck Finn. External forces, to be sure, were drawing him out of his Howellsian cocoon of realism with its romantic way of viewing a Darwinian world. His incredibly complex financial state was beginning to turn into the nightmare it would become by the end of the decade.

Something else snapped within. Mark Twain finally submitted to the tragedy behind all the jokes he had been making about what he would ultimately term "the Creator's pet" in *Letters from the Earth,* his final work and a scathing satire on the human condition written in the year prior to his death. When it was finally published with Clara's consent in 1962, coinciding with the agreement between the writer's surviving daughter and the University of California Press for a limited edition of his papers, a project that continues today, it not only reinvigorated interest in Mark Twain but re-alerted his reading public to his serious side.[10] Yet it was not in 1909 but in the years during which he wrote his masterpiece that he realized that there was no more territory to "light out" for—merely the "damned human race" of cosmic microbes. Mark Twain tried several times to get Huck back to the boyland where he might make the right choice, but all his sequels to that world failed because the escape out west or into space or back into antebellum Hannibal had already been closed off.

36 Publishing Grant

"It had never been my intention," Mark Twain recalled in his 1906 autobiographical dictation, "to publish any body's books but my own." He was referring to the publication of Grant's *Memoirs* and his own *Huckleberry Finn* by Webster & Company, formed after his break with Osgood & Company in 1884. James Osgood had failed miserably, in Twain's opinion, in his subscription sale of *Life on the Mississippi,* and he didn't want to go back to the American Publishing Company with his sequel to *Tom Sawyer* because that "company had been robbing me for years and building theological factories out of the proceeds."[1] But on the evening of November 19, 1884, following his joint appearance with Cable at Chickering Hall in New York City, he decided that he wanted his publishing company to get the contract for Grant's memoirs. He claimed he had heard strangers coming out of the hall mention Grant's intention to publish them through the Century Company, but in fact he had actually learned of the plan from the editor of *Century* magazine, Richard Watson Gilder, who had commissioned four of Grant's Civil War essays for his journal.

Twain's mood the day of his visit to the Grant residence at 3 East 66th Street on the east side of the newly constructed Central Park may have been a bit sour. As would happen more than once during his 1884–85 tour with the sentimental Cable, his performance had, in the press, been unfavorably compared to Cable's. According to the *New York Times* of November 19, "Mr. Cable was humorous, pathetic, weird, grotesque, tender, and melodramatic by turns, while Mr. Clemens confined his efforts to the ridicule of such ridiculous matters as aged colored gentlemen, the German language, and himself." It might as well have been Grant instead of Cable who upstaged him, for he had been mildly obsessed with the general ever since his own rather embarrassingly brief military service in 1861, the near-encounter with Grant in Missouri he would soon exaggerate in his own Civil War essay, "The Private History of a Campaign That Failed." U.S—"Unconditional Surrender"—Grant had always loomed in Twain's conscience as a rebuke to his boyish behavior as a Marion Ranger. Now he could perhaps assuage his guilt and win over the conquering general, who was nearly broke because of his fated partnership with Ferdinand Ward, the "young Napoleon of finance" who had fled the country to avoid prosecution for schemes in which he pledged the same security for several different bank loans. Grant was also battling cancer at the base of his tongue. Had he not procrastinated when he first felt the awful pain in his throat, he might have survived. Even in those relatively dark ages of medical science, it was an ailment that had been successfully treated with surgery. Yet by the time his overly delicate and euphemistic physicians reluctantly used the word "cancer," it was too late. The growth had invaded the surrounding cells that lined the soft palate.

Now the cigar-smoking Twain sat before the ailing Grant and one of his sons, Fred (a former soldier who would die of the same disease in 1912 at the same age), and belittled the *Century* offer in no uncertain terms. Twain was probably as blindly confident about the success of Grant's memoirs as he had been about so many earlier business deals that had lost him thousands of dollars. Indeed, here sat two men who were remarkably similar: both had grown up poor with the burning desire to become rich. Mark Twain had succeeded by his writing, not his investments thus far, but neither had anything in the investment portfolio of Ulysses S Grant ever come to full bloom. Denied the Republican nomination for a run at a third term as president in 1876, he had since failed to make (and keep) enough money to become financially independent. This shortcoming contrasted sharply with the success of his well-heeled and highly placed friends, many of whom had doubtless benefited through their relationship with the conquering general of the

War Between the States and two-term president of those reunited states. Even his home on East 66th Street had been purchased with funds collected by those prominent friends. "Any number of them," as biographer William S. McFeely observes, "could have taken Grant into their firms, but none of them did." Now after the failure of his heavy investment in the Mexican Southern Railroad and the financial loss as well as taint of the scandal from his "silent" partnership in the failed Grant & Ward firm (that would be Buck Grant, another son, christened Ulysses S, Jr., and Ferdinand Ward), the senior Grant was nearly destitute, the object of pity, and—worst of all—possibly implicated in some of Ward's financial trickery. An editorial in the New York *World* asked in its headline, "Is Grant Guilty?" The nation at large merely felt sorry for its hero and wanted him left alone.[2]

Twain never doubted the general's impeccable character and towering greatness, not only as a public figure but also as a writer. He had urged Grant to write his memoirs long before the Century Company commissioned the essays that led to its offer of a book contract. Since his triumphant "fetching" of the silent and stony-faced Civil War icon in 1879 in Chicago (see chapter 8), Twain had come during their subsequent meetings to appreciate Grant as "a fluent and able talker—with a large sense of humor, and a most rare gift of compacting meaty things into phrases of stunning felicity."[3] He was confident that the commanding general's memoirs would outsell many times over those of William Tecumseh Sherman, published nine years earlier. Notably, his prescience in this case was rooted in his intuition and experience with language, not with investing. And Grant, as it turned out, more than fulfilled Twain's expectations—even proved to be a much better writer than his intended ghostwriter and former member of his military staff, Adam Badeau, already the author of a three-volume history of Grant's military career (1882) and another on Grant's life since the war. While Grant was writing his book, it was often asserted in the press that Badeau was doing it for him, a claim Webster & Company strongly, and correctly, denied.

A few days after his visit with Grant in the fall of 1884, Twain described the experience to his daughter Susy. General Lew Wallace, author of the popular *Ben Hur* (1880), was present. He, too, was contributing to the

Century magazine's series on the Civil War. "Mrs. Grant got up & stood between Gen Wallace & me," Twain bragged to the teenager, who was then beginning a biography of her father. Mrs. Grant then said, "'There, there's many a woman in this land that would like to be in my place & be able to tell her children that she had stood once elbow to elbow between two such great authors as Mark Twain & General Wallace.'" "We all laughed," Twain continued and, more to the point, told Susy that he took the compliment as an opportunity to encourage Grant to finish his memoir. "Don't look so cowed, General," he teased him. "You have written a book, too, & when it is published you can hold up your head & let on to be a person of consequence yourself."[4]

No doubt, Twain "fetched" the general as he had in Chicago, but he now dared him to place his literary mind on the printed page. Following the success of his *Century* articles at a mere five hundred dollars apiece ("easily worth ten thousand dollars apiece," Twain guessed after the first one had "lifted the *Century*'s subscription list from a hundred thousand to two hundred and twenty thousand"), the Century Company had offered Grant a standard contract of a 10 percent royalty on their list price. It based its terms on Sherman's success with his memoirs, which sold between 200,000 and 300,000 copies. "Strike out the ten percent from the Century offer," Twain suggested to Grant, "and put twenty per cent in its place. Better still, put seventy-five percent of the net returns in its place." Grant demurred, saying that no company would pay him that much, no matter how great his military reputation. Twain told him that there wasn't a reputable publisher in America who would not be more than glad to pay the terms he named. That included, he coyly suggested, the American Publishing Company, which along with several other presses eventually did offer much more than the Century Company's initial bid.[5] We should keep in mind that this was the Gilded Age, the term originating in part with Twain and Warner to describe a time when moguls like Carnegie and Rockefeller were amassing huge fortunes. Why not writers as well? The ongoing success of *Huckleberry Finn* underscored the possibility.

At a second meeting at Grant's house, Twain dropped all pretense of being neutral and made his own offer for the memoirs. Sensing the deep popular appeal of Grant's book, he knew that a well-run subscription house could sell many more copies and pay much more per copy than a trade press could, by hawking the prospectus in the hinterlands where so many military veterans (and potential readers) resided. He suspected that the American Publishing Company would jump at the deal on the very terms he proposed to Grant, but his mention of his former publisher was clearly a ploy to plant the *idea* of subscription publishing in Grant's mind even as he was about to sign with the Century Company. Once this alternative was broached, Clemens knew that he would be in the running with his own subscription house. It would take some time before the general decided, first to reject the Century Company's initial offer, then to turn down all other offers to the exclusion of the one from Charles L. Webster & Company. Its namesake, Twain's hardworking "nephew-in-law," would follow up on the offer, making calls on Grant while Twain continued the lecture tour with Cable.[6] Grant signed their contract in late February 1885 and spent the rest of his life—literally—completing his memoirs, published in two volumes, the first of which appeared at the end of 1885, nearly six months after his death. Volume 2 was issued in the winter of 1886.

Webster & Company had acquired a sure thing because Grant's writing of his memoirs was well under way by February. Yet as Twain was leaving the Grant residence soon after the signing of the contract, Fred Grant "stunned" him by confiding that his father's physicians had been holding back on the general's true medical condition. "In fact they considered him to be under a sentence of death and that he would not likely to live more than a fortnight or three weeks longer."[7] He had completed about half of the second volume, or 900 of the eventual total of 1,232 printed pages in both volumes. Yet he also had to revise both volumes and check his facts against other military accounts—all of this under the threat of a premature demise, one the general surely sensed as his throat tightened and he was forced to carry on all communications with penciled notes.

News of the general's failing health began to fill the nation's newspapers that spring and summer. The spurned Century Company, which had commissioned and publicly advertised his four Civil War articles, had yet to receive the last one. That commitment was ultimately finessed by dividing the third twenty-thousand-word essay on the Battle of Vicksburg into two articles, thus satisfying the contract.[8]

There were other rather painful distractions. As Webster & Company celebrated the advance subscription sales of the *Personal Memoirs of U.S. Grant* (allegedly at one hundred thousand sets by the end of May and swiftly climbing), press reports began to grumble about Twain's having taken unfair advantage of the Century Company in securing the Grant contract with inside information through his association with the *Century* editors, Richard and Joseph Gilder. Jeanette Gilder, whose literary vision was as progressive as that of her brothers (she had commissioned a series of "out-door sketches" from Walt Whitman for the *Critic* in 1881), furnished a fairer account to the Boston *Herald*. This encouraged Twain on July 6 to ask the newspaper for a special favor: that it show him, before printing, any malicious claims similar to what had already appeared in the New York *Advertiser*. "I will correct them, & at the same time will leave untouched all statements about me which are *true*, howsoever damaging they may be."[9]

Still, the rumors of Twain's alleged exploitation persisted and even expanded into a tale in which the wealthy humorist had taken direct advantage of the dying and impoverished general. As the end approached, Twain could do nothing but bite his tongue and keep silent (and later commit his defense to his autobiography). He told the sculptor Karl Gerhardt, who had won the commission from the Grant family to do the general's death mask, that he wanted to contribute to the fund to cover the artist's work. He would give five hundred dollars, but his name, he told Gerhardt, "need not to go on the subscription list and so furnish the shabbier half of the world a chance to say General Grant's publisher is craftily trying to advertise himself." "I'm like Brer Rabbit," he told his old friend Ned House only days before the general's death, "I 'ain't sayin' noth'n.' . . . Everybody thinks I sneaked in & got the book by underhand processes: whereas I merely sneaked in & told the General *what terms to require of the Century people*."[10]

Grant was fading fast, but he was as intractable and resistant in the face of death as he had been in the face of war. In fact, what evidently kept him going was the work on the memoirs. "The last time I saw Gen. Grant alive," Twain recalled a decade later, "was a few days before his death. He knew that his end was very near. He was sitting in his chair, fully dressed; his book was finished, and he was putting one or two finishing touches to it with his pencil—the last work he was ever to do."[11] Reduced in circumstances and humiliated by the Ward scandal, he had written not only to save his wife and family from financial ruin but to relive the days of his absolute glory as a soldier and military leader. He wrote with the same spontaneity and clarity that had dictated his military plans and orders during the war. Now the world would soon know that this natural warrior was also a gifted writer. In the preface to the *Personal Memoirs,* Grant euphemistically called his literary labor "a pleasant pastime." But he also revealed that he wrote the second half of volume 2 after "I had reason to suppose I was in a critical condition of health." This preface was dated July 1, and Grant died on July 23, 1885. Its coolness and reserved tone barely obscured the pent-up passion of the so-called "Silent Man," or "the Sphynx," as Twain called him in 1895.[12]

The obtaining of Grant's memoirs may have been, as Twain said, an afterthought, but its success unfortunately led Webster & Company to believe, especially after the similar success of *Huckleberry Finn,* that anything it touched would turn to gold. Both *Huckleberry Finn* and Grant's *Memoirs* were books that circumvented the troubling aspects of the contemporary post-Reconstruction era in American history and returned to a time when the issues were more clear-cut: Twain's novel cast back to the antebellum era of slavery, avoiding the confusing terrain of post-slavery race relations in the United States, and Grant's memoirs invoked the Civil War itself, reinscribing Grant as a war hero and diverting attention from his subsequent political failures. The American reading public clearly was seeking that kind of retreat, and this enthusiasm led Webster & Company to publish at least three more military memoirs, which didn't sell that robustly, especially the posthumous recollections of General Philip Sheridan in 1888. All this was leading down the road to ruin, but neither Twain nor his partner, Charles L. Webster, at this point had any doubts about the company's success. Among the better sellers were books by Mark Twain himself—reissues of *The Prince and the Pauper* in

1885 and 1887;[13] *The Stolen White Elephant and Other Stories* in 1888; *A Connecticut Yankee in King Arthur's Court* in 1889; a pamphlet entitled *Facts for Mark Twain's Memory Builder* (part of Twain's financially unsuccessful board game), a reprint of *Life on the Mississippi,* and a cheap edition of *Huckleberry Finn* in 1892;[14] *The American Claimant, Merry Tales* (containing "The Private History of a Campaign That Failed"), and a cheap reprint of *The Prince and the Pauper,* also in 1892; *The £1,000,000 Bank-note and Other New Stories* in 1893; and—just before the declaration of bankruptcy—*Tom Sawyer Abroad* in 1894. Charles L. Webster & Company did not survive long enough to publish *The Tragedy of Pudd'nhead Wilson* (1894), which would take Twain back to the American Publishing Company.

37 Brooding in King Arthur's Court

A Connecticut Yankee in King Arthur's Court represents the first and last time Mark Twain published in a literary work the kind of satiric diatribe that would typify the tenor of his posthumous publications. The English reaction to it was unsmiling disapproval. As the reviewer for the *Pall Mall Gazette* said, Mark Twain might as well have burlesqued the Sermon on the Mount. His trifling with Sir Thomas Malory's *Morte Darthur,* the very first prose masterpiece in English following the Middle Ages and a national romance embodying the core ideals of British and Western civilization, was simply more than most English readers could take. This marvelous romance had set the pattern for such English classics as Edmund Spenser's *The Fairie Queene* and, more recently, had inspired poet laureate Alfred, Lord Tennyson's *The Idylls of the King.* The story—or stories, as twentieth-century scholars have discovered—of *Morte Darthur* sees the idea of manhood, as evoked by King Arthur's Round Table, as part of the knighthood of Christianity. The *Pall Mall Gazette* added that Twain's ridicule of the Quest for the Holy Grail (the chalice of the Last Supper) was simply a vulgar American attack on the central symbol "of the individual effort to arrive at perfection in personal life, to attain high, unselfish, irreproachable conduct."[1]

Twain's purpose had been less to mock Malory than to ridicule the shortcomings of English monarchy and aristocracy, both medieval and modern. Nor were those his only satiric targets, which also included the Roman Catholic Church and the American robber barons of his own Victorian age. But the attack on aristocratic privilege, cruelty, and incompetence was the most blatant, made doubly so by Daniel Carter Beard's pro-labor illustrations for the text. In some of his drawings, Beard (with Twain's approval) used quite recognizable faces as models—Tennyson as Merlin, Jay Gould as a slave driver, Queen Victoria as a hog, and the prince of Wales (later Edward VII) as a "chucklehead." With jokes like that, it's a minor miracle Twain had any English friends left at all

Behind all three of his themes lay his gathering anger about both the flagging sales of Webster & Company and the repeated disappointments in the development of the Paige Compositor. The voice we hear in the talk of the Yankee narrator as he complains about the backwardness of Camelot is the same one we hear in the impatiently worded letters Twain wrote to Webster and in his complaints about Paige's latest dismantling of his invention. In both *Huckleberry Finn* and *A Connecticut Yankee,* the narrator exposes human and social inequities. The anger in the first book, however, is conveyed ironically through a naive but clever teenager, while its expression in the second is from none other than Mark Twain himself, speaking also in the first person. The unsentimental, irreverent, and straight-talking Yankee undercuts whatever deep ironic purpose Twain had in mind when he decided to write his own version of Camelot. For, as James M. Cox observes, "instead of converting the indignation which stands behind satire into ironic observation, apparent indifference, and mock innocence which constitute it, Twain paraded his indignation in front of the world to be criticized."[2] Missing now was the stealthlike irreverence found in the works between *The Innocents Abroad* and *Huckleberry Finn.*

Briefly, the story of *A Connecticut Yankee* concerns Hank Morgan, a nineteenth-century mechanic and foreman for the Colt Fire Arms Manufactory in Hartford (where the Paige typesetter was being infinitely perfected). In a fight with one of his workers, Hank is knocked unconscious. He wakes up in sixth-century England and is almost executed as a captive of an adventuring knight, but saves himself through knowledge of a solar eclipse about to take place, using it to convince King Arthur and his court that he has magical powers superior to Merlin's. During the next ten years he seeks to improve the country by covertly introducing nineteenth-century technology, at first hoping simply to make a profit but later intent on reforming the morals of Camelot and undercutting its class system by introducing democracy. In the end, he is both frustrated by the failure of reform to have any lasting effect on human beings and, more directly, thwarted by the Catholic Church, which controls the ideology that keeps the system in place. The tale concludes by having Hank electrocute thousands of knights, leaving him trapped in Merlin's cave behind a mountain of corpses. Merlin, who has been upstaged by Hank's more scientific magic, gets his revenge, before being accidentally electrocuted himself, when he condemns Hank to a death worse than that of the knights: a living one in which he will sleep for the next thirteen centuries until he wakes up again in the present, yearning for his life in the sixth century, during which he had married and fathered a child. The tale's irreverent treatment of Malory's classic in the effort to satirize English nobility added to the British resentment Twain had originally stimulated with his earlier "book about the English," *The Prince and the Pauper.*

Interestingly, Twain was personally delighted with *Morte Darthur.* He had been familiar with its great legends as early as 1880, when he purchased a children's edition for the family library. He was reintroduced to the work in 1884 when Cable bought him a copy of the standard Globe edition in Rochester during a stop there on their lecture tour. Reveling in its tales of chivalry and adventure, he and Cable spoke its archaic dialect in jest to each other. During their stop in Indianapolis in the winter of 1885, he wrote his daughter Susy: "When I get home, you must take my Morte Arthur & read it. It is the quaintest and sweetest of all books." He quoted from memory a passage on the death of Launcelot, comparing its eloquence to that of Lincoln's Gettysburg Address. When a year later Mary Fairbanks evidently expressed shock that he would satirize this classic, he protested that his story was simply a contrast with life today. "Of course," he continued, "I shall leave unsmirched & unbelittled the great & beautiful *characters* drawn by the master hand of old Malory." At the time of this letter, he had written only three chapters of his book; they made good fun of Malory's romance without attacking the ideal of chivalry itself. But when he took up the book again in the summer of 1887, his stance toward his subject took a dramatic turn.[3]

"It is enough to make a body ashamed of his race," Hank exclaims in chapter 8, on the sham of aristocracy, "to think of the sort of froth that has always occupied its thrones without shadow of right or reason, and the seventh-rate people that have always figured as its aristocracies." The writing of *A Connecticut Yankee* became on-the-job training for the later anti-imperialist and debunker of Christian myth.

As noted in chapter 35, Matthew Arnold's criticism of American culture had irritated Clemens and had whipped up his anti-British sentiment in a flourish matched only by his denigration of the French in his journals a decade earlier. "Yours is the civilization of slave-making ants," he wrote in the summer of 1888, much in the way that Hank Morgan belittles aristocratic claims. "A monarchy is perpetuated piracy. In its escutcheon should always be quartered the skull & cross-bones." He got a good deal of his Anglophobic propaganda from George Standring's *People's History of the English Aristocracy* (1887), a book he even thought of reissuing through Webster & Company as a companion volume to *A Connecticut Yankee.* Standring's thesis was that England's only hope lay in its shifting away from a monarchy to a republic, and that efforts in that direction had been undercut in 1886, a year before the celebration of Queen Victoria's golden jubilee. At home Twain had also become interested in the U.S. labor movement.[4]

The diatribe that ultimately controlled the tone of *A Connecticut Yankee* was not simply vituperative; it was also frequently filled with pathos. In his moving descriptions of profound human suffering endured by the common man at the hands of the nobility, Twain stripped away Camelot's romantic veneer. In chapter 18, "In the Queen's Dungeons," Twain paints a vivid picture of the suffering that Morgan le Fay, King Arthur's wicked sister, causes without the slightest hesitation or pang of conscience. Calling her a Vesuvius, he writes: "As a favor, she might consent to warm a flock of sparrows for you, but then she might take that very opportunity to turn herself loose and bury a city." Of a husband and wife separated and jailed indefinitely because the bride had refused *le droit du Seigneur,* the custom that entitled her lord and master to first connubial rights, he describes the couple "as kerneled like toads in the same rock; they had passed nine pitch dark years within fifty feet of each other, yet neither knew whether the other one was alive or not. All the first years, their only question had been . . . 'Is he alive?' 'Is she alive?' But they had never got an answer; and at last that question was not asked any more—or any other."

This "humorist" could depict human suffering powerfully, but he could also be cleverly funny. When he wasn't lashing out at the nobility directly, Twain satirized it with the same wit that ran through his early work and that by now had made him famous. In an episode typical of *Morte Darthur,* Hank Morgan, by now known in Camelot as "Sir Boss," sets off in chapter 11 with the demoiselle Alisande la Carteloise, or "Sandy," to liberate forty-five "young and beautiful" princesses who have languished in "cruel captivity for twenty-six years." (As Hank notes in chapter 19, time has no impact on either the youth or the prowess of the inhabitants of Arthur's kingdom. In Malory's tale, for example, Launcelot and his illegitimate son, Galahad, are physical equals. Morgan le Fay in *A Connecticut Yankee* is described as "fresh and young as a Vassar pullet.") The quest, pursued over several chapters, is almost forgotten by Hank, but when they do arrive at the "ogre's castle" in chapter 20, it turns out to be "nothing but a pig-sty." It is not a pig-sty, however, in the ideologically trained eye of Sandy, who sees what one would expect to find in Camelot—captive princesses, not pigs. "When I saw her fling herself upon those hogs, with tears of joy running down her cheeks, and strain them to her heart, and kiss them," Hank concludes, "I was ashamed of her, ashamed of the human race."

Twain's assault is on the ideology that is the foundation of class differences. Behind the sham of nobility, he found the Catholic Church. Much of his invective toward the Church found its ballast in William Lecky's *History of European Morals* (1874), a book that Twain had first read, heavily marking his personal copy, in the mid-1870s, not long after his first visit to England. "Though Clemens' concept of the Church as villain was probably not inspired by Lecky alone," writes Howard Baetzhold, "in *A Connecticut Yankee* he drew most of the ammunition for his assaults from the historian's well-stocked arsenal."[5] Indeed, one of the factors, if not literary weaknesses, of this novel is that it was, unlike *Huckleberry Finn,* almost exclusively driven by political theory.

Standring and Lecky, it appears, were involuntary ghostwriters of a Mark Twain classic.

In *History of European Morals,* Lecky argued demonstrably that between the fall of Rome and the Renaissance the Catholic Church had consecrated the idea of secular rank among the nobility as a way to retain its own influence through such superstitions as the divine right of kings. In effect, the freemen that Hank comes to want to release from their social bonds were brainwashed into believing in the sanctity of their own slavery or menial social condition, the way the Protestant church in the United States, as reflected in *Huckleberry Finn,* had convinced the narrator who woke up in the antebellum days of Sam Clemens's youth that slavery was moral and upheld by the Bible.

Twain had been arguing with Lecky ever since the writing of Huck's tale. While he used his anti-Catholic material in *A Connecticut Yankee* in both books, he disagreed with Lecky the intuitionist, who held that man was endowed with a moral sense that could overcome circumstance. Commenting in chapter 18 on Morgan le Fay's casual cruelty as a sovereign right, Hank declares that "training is everything. . . . We have no thoughts of our own, no opinions of our own." Granting that our being might hold a thimbleful of individuality, he insists that everything else is "contributed by, and inherited from, a procession of ancestors that stretches back a billion years to the Adam-clam or grasshopper or monkey from whom our race has been so tediously and ostentatiously and unprofitably developed." Twain allowed, however, for "that one microscopic atom in me that is truly *me.*" It would have been nice to think it was that part of Huck that decided to "go to hell" in order to save Jim, but by the time Mark Twain sat down to write his next book about slavery (*Pudd'nhead Wilson*), he had probably decided that Huck's story was merely a romance, indeed, as much of a dream as Hank's sojourn in Camelot.

Much of the plot of *A Connecticut Yankee* after the liberation of the hog/princesses reads rather tediously today, but it would have been interesting to most readers in 1889, partly because of Hank's arguments about protection and free trade. In "Sixth Century Political Economy" (chapter 33), in which artisans do not understand inflation and are thus deceived by "high wages," Twain mirrors the conflict between capital and labor in the American 1880s. It was during this decade that the membership of the Knights of Labor approached seven hundred thousand. Ever since the Civil War the American economy had grown voraciously, but workers' wages—with the decline of the artisan worker after the war—had not kept up with the success of the various business trusts and monopolies. Begun almost twenty years earlier as a secret organization in order to protect itself from retaliation from the companies it opposed, the Knights of Labor had recently won a number of strikes for the eight-hour working day, culminating in its victory in the Union Pacific strike of 1884. Its support of workers included women and blacks, though not Asians. Women, previously limited to the arduous occupation of sewing, flooded the new labor pools created by such inventions as the typewriter and the telephone switchboard. Switchboard operators were known as "hello girls." In *A Connecticut Yankee,* Hank's child with Sandy—supposedly one of the new generation in Camelot not to be held back by the old superstitions of social rank—is called "Hello Central."

The influence of the Knights began to wane around 1886, as Twain began his novel. The union fell into disagreements with competing labor groups. In one of his political cartoons in *Harper's Weekly* during 1886, which must have attracted Twain's attention, Thomas Nast—whose houseguest Twain had been in 1884—depicts the Knights' opposition to the skilled craft unions in a scene in which two knights joust as capital looks on approvingly, much in the way King Arthur and Queen Gwynevere in *Morte Darthur* look upon tournaments in which knights kill or maim each other for fame and honor. The Knights of Labor also lost its allure with the public and the press by becoming involved in a number of May Day strikes that failed. The Haymarket Riot of May 4, 1886, in Chicago essentially finished off the organization when it was unfairly blamed for the bloodshed. Chicago at the time counted eighty thousand Knights but an even greater number of immigrants committed to socialist doctrines. Eight of these alleged anarchists were rounded up and quickly sentenced to death in a legal lynching that infuriated Howells but seems not to have upset Twain.[6]

Yet this former printer was cautiously committed to labor movements that were relatively free of the taint of socialists and communists. On March 22, 1886, he read his article entitled "The New Dynasty" to the Monday Evening Club. His interest in labor may have been sparked in part by his involvement in the campaign for an international copyright agreement. In January he had testified before the Senate Committee on Patents about the issue. One of those also arguing before the committee, a printer and member of the Knights of Labor, claimed (falsely) that his union counted between four and five million members in order to buttress his demand that all foreign books sold in the United States be printed there. Condemning power as normally leading to oppression, Twain found an exception in the Knights because they supposedly banded together for the welfare of *all* workers, not just bricklayers or stenographers. By virtue of the strength of his union's membership, this mere artisan had more clout, he told the Monday Evening Club audience, than James Russell Lowell had when *he* appeared before the same Senate committee in support of the international copyright law, because the labor leader spoke, as Twain rather awkwardly stated it (perhaps revealing his own lingering skepticism about the masses), as "the nation in person speaking; and its servants, *real*—not masters *called* servants by canting trick of speech—listening."[7]

Twain must have found himself in the same paradox that Hank Morgan does—indeed, *A Connecticut Yankee* can be seen as a reflection of Twain's social and economic dilemma in the 1880s. Here was a rich entrepreneur, the owner of a publishing company and an investor (at the rate of $5,000 a month) in the development of the Paige Compositor, arguing for union labor before the elite members of the Monday Evening Club in Hartford, the citadel of insurance brokers and investment bankers, the very kind of unproductive laborers to whom the Knights of Labor refused membership, along with gamblers and liquor producers. Hank, the dispossessed heir of Huck, is forced to kill off part of the society he has generally been trying to improve. Ultimately, Twain produced a dystopia in an era of utopian novels encouraged by the advances of technology (for example, the immensely popular *Looking Backward,* by Edward Bellamy, published a year before Twain's novel). Bellamy's protagonist is turned out of the very kind of Eden that had housed the white romance of *Huckleberry Finn.* Hank's reality is that the human race is condemned to acting out endlessly the same mistakes that Huck naively thought could be avoided. As a result, there is no happy ending in *A Connecticut Yankee,* no lighting out for (or return to) Camelot and Malory's fantastic sense of time.

38 Progress and Poverty

Mark Twain continued to hammer away at British nobility in his next novel, published in 1892. He had begun *The American Claimant* in the mid-1880s as an unsuccessful drama cowritten with Howells; it had been adapted from the play version of *The Gilded Age* and was ultimately entitled "Colonel Sellers as a Scientist." Matthew Arnold's attack on the irreverence of American newspapers is ridiculed in the story by contrasting them with the British press, which is seen as nothing more than a propaganda tool for the glories "of the petted and privileged few, at cost of the blood and sweat and poverty of the unconsidered masses."[1] (Ironically, in this era of the robber baron, American newspapers were doing the same favors for big business.) Twain did not actually compose *The American Claimant* until the spring of 1891, but the British grievances festered in his mind long after the completion of *A Connecticut Yankee,* especially when English reviewers assailed that book upon its appearance in 1889. He would eventually reconcile himself with the British, when his concerns about unearned privilege broadened into disenchantment with the excesses of political power on both sides of the Atlantic.

"When I finished Carlyle's French Revolution in 1871," he told Howells in August 1887, "I was a Girondin; every time I have read it since, I have read it differently—being influenced & changed, little by little, by life & environment, . . . & now I lay the book down once more, & recognize that I am a Sansculotte!—And not a pale, characterless Sansculotte, but a Marat." It was in that same summer that his theme in *A Connecticut Yankee* turned anti-imperialist. When in chapter 13 Hank comes upon freemen laboring without pay on their bishop's road, their subjugation reminds him of "reading about France and the French, before the ever-memorable and blessed Revolution, which swept a thousand years of such villainy away in one swift tidal wave of blood." Hank subsequently concludes that there were two "'Reigns of Terror' . . . the one wrought murder in hot passion, the other in heartless cold blood; the one lasted mere months, the other had lasted a thousand years." He added in his letter to Howells that his changed reading of Carlyle had come from within because "Carlyle teaches no such gospel."[2] Twain had traveled a long way from his days in Hawaii in the 1860s, when he first came upon a feudal system, though one already on the wane. Although he instinctively disapproved of Hawaiian royalty, he was at the time more interested in American missionaries who, while they clothed and civilized the indigenous population, also taught them about another "royal" paradise called heaven and how difficult it was to get there.

In the 1890s, when Charles L. Webster & Company was also on the wane, it issued reprints of five of Henry George's economic and social screeds, including his controversial *Progress and Poverty,* first published in 1879. George had argued for a "Single Tax" on unused land owned by the rich as a remedy for the country's social and economic ills. At the same time Twain was entertaining radical ideas and publishing radical books, he was also happy in the knowledge that his Paige typesetter wouldn't have to join a printer's union. When in 1887 his own brother, now permanently unemployed and on a regular monthly stipend from Sam, tried to assist a journalist working on an article about his famous brother, his younger brother flatly refused him permission to make public any aspect of his very guarded private life, saying: "I have never yet allowed an interviewer or biographer-sketcher to get out of me any circumstance of my history which I thought might be worth putting some day into my *auto*biography."[3] He was apparently still laboring under the illusion that everything he touched would turn to gold.

Orion was one of the American "roughs" who had never received a college education. Twain valued this kind of American over the dyspeptic college graduate who never got his hands dirty. Though Orion would prove the exception to Twain's notion of a "divine average" of American labor, the older brother had the same aspiration for getting rich as an inventor that Sam, another non–college graduate, harbored. James W. Paige, the inventor in whom Twain still placed all his confidence, also had no university training. In a February 1887 talk before the Monday Evening Club on "Machine Culture," one applauded by Howells when he read the text, Twain reminded his audience that most of the inventions of the nineteenth century had not been the work of "college-bred men." "What great births you have witnessed!" he told Walt Whitman, another school dropout and skeptic of higher education, on his seventieth birthday. "The steam press, the steamship, the steel ship, the railroad, the perfected cotton-gin, the telegraph, the telephone, the phonograph, the photogravure, the electrotype, the gaslight, the electric light, the sewing machine."[4] Twain believed, as he has his advocate of labor (who "got his education in a printing office") say in chapter 10 of *The American Claimant*, that the nineteenth century was "the only century worth living in since time itself was invented." It was the era, at least during the last part of the century, when monarchies began to weaken and the common man started to rise.

Twain had grown up in the era of the American lyceum movement, in which many in the working class could overcome a lack of formal education by studying a subject and delivering a lecture on it to their peers. Teaching a subject, they joyfully discovered, was the most effective way of mastering it. Such lyceum gatherings served as the country's first "adult education." Here one could raise himself up by dint of arduous study after a hard day's work in the factory or shop. By Twain's adulthood after the war, those who had succeeded without college were beginning to mix with college-bred men. After hearing the printer in his remarks outclass those of the Harvard-educated James Russell Lowell before the Senate Committee on Patents in 1886, Twain thought that the time for the self-educated working man had arrived. Yet as the decade progressed and his Connecticut Yankee failed to erase the ideology of class from Camelot, Twain ultimately lost faith in this "divine average." Twain's egalitarianism—at least with regard to the working class—never got beyond the theoretical.[5]

The American Claimant was originally serialized in the New York *Sun* between January 3 and March 27, 1892, marking the first time Clemens had ever serialized a complete work. Its twenty-five brief chapters were subsequently published by Webster & Company with illustrations by Dan Beard, now his favorite illustrator. The novel, usually dismissed as a farce, has rarely been reprinted except as part of uniform editions. It ought to be featured in its own edition, because it is full of Mark Twain's wit (in one scene a sham painter is said to have "libeled the sea"), and it most immediately anticipates *Pudd'nhead Wilson* with regard to lost identities. *The American Claimant* also works out Twain's modified criticism of aristocracies. It is in part the story of Colonel Mulberry Sellers, who becomes the "American claimant" to the House of Rossmore in England upon the death of Simon Lathers (adapted from the name of Twain's mother's cousin Jesse Leathers, who had urged Clemens to finance an inquiry into the Lampton genealogy leading back to the earl of Durham). Twain makes the Colonel, now fifteen years older, almost as poor as he had depicted him in *The Gilded Age,* and Washington Hawkins remains loosely based on the hapless Orion.

Unlike previous claimants in the fiction of Mark Twain, this one is not lying. As the true earl of Rossmore tells his son the Viscount Berkeley back in England, the authentic earl had come to America several generations earlier and "disappeared somewhere in the wilds of Virginia, got married, and began to breed savages for the Claimant market." His disappearance allowed his younger brother to quietly assume his title back home. The current heir Berkeley, however, bristles with anti-royal propaganda and decides to go to America to surrender his title to the Sellers family. Once there, however, he is declared dead in a hotel fire and takes the opportunity to shake off his aristocratic identity. The reality of having neither friends nor money in a new country soon becomes clear: he finds himself penniless and without any means of support. When, out of desperation, he asserts his noble rank at a typically austere and noisy boardinghouse in Washington, D.C., he is promptly ridiculed. Like the prince in *The Prince and the Pauper,* he finds himself out in the cold; there is even a comrade named Barrow who facetiously accepts his claims the way Miles Hendon does the claims of the prince in *The Prince and the Pauper.* Taking the name of Tracy, Berkeley subsequently becomes an artist of cheap chromos and falls in love with Sally Sellers, the Colonel's daughter. Although once a believer in the family quest, she has thrown off all her father's pretensions to royalty and, in a humorous twist, now fears that Tracy loves her only because he believes in *her* social rank. Upon hearing of his son's impending engagement to an American woman, Berkeley's father comes to America to reestablish his son's identity. He hopes to break up the love match with the family of the American claimants, but he is immediately charmed by his future daughter-in-law, and thus the aristocratic family from both sides of the Atlantic is brought together again through the marriage of Berkeley to Sally.

In the book's farcical subplot the Colonel and Hawkins originally think that Berkeley is a rematerialized spirit from the hotel fire and fear that Sally has fallen in love with a ghost. At one point, Hawkins tries to discourage her infatuation by persuading her that her lover is a criminal by the name of S.M. Snodgrass, the son of a mad scientist who named all his children after dread diseases. "S.M," we soon learn, stands for spinal meningitis—ironically, a disease that would five years later visit Sam Clemens's family and change it forever. For now, he was changing politically, having lost completely the romantic fancy of *Huckleberry Finn* and still recovering from Hank's failed experiment with the human race in *A Connecticut Yankee.* In chapter 22 of *The American Claimant,* Berkeley says good-bye to his youthful objections to nobility. He is ready to return home to England and resume "his position and be content with it and thankful for it for the future, leaving further experiment, of a missionary sort, to other younger people needing the chastening and quelling persuasions of experience, the only logic sure to convince a diseased imagination and restore it to health." Berkeley clearly spoke at this juncture for Mark Twain, who was now content, as we have noted, to be a theoretical socialist and a practical capitalist.

In June 1888 Twain could not attend the commencement at Yale University to receive an honorary master of arts, but he did use the occasion to speak up for his own "labor union," the fraternity of humorists. He was particularly gratified at this time to receive the degree, he wrote the school's president, because the "late Matthew Arnold [had] sharply rebuked the guild of American 'funny men' in his latest literary delivery."[6] Twain's sense of the divide between college-bred individuals and non–college graduates extended into the realm of literature. He was a blue-collar writer, a humorist, who had written an American classic but barely knew it. "I am the only literary animal of my particular sub-species," he told a friend, "who has ever been given a degree by any College in any age of the world, as far as I know."[7]

He told Orion, who still lived in Keokuk with his wife, Mollie, and his mother, now suffering dementia in the final years of her long life, that he probably should have made the effort to go to New Haven. But life then seemed overwhelming. With his mother failing, Sam planned a visit to Keokuk in the spring of 1888, but it was canceled because of another family illness, terminal as it turned out, that of Theodore Crane, the husband of Livy's adopted sister, Sue. Sam's mother-in-law was also approaching the end of a long life, though she was clearheaded to the last—with an evolving sense of humor that eventually erased her initial sense of shock at her son-in-law from the West. "Mother dear," he told her the day after his fifty-third birthday: "Thank you ever so much for my end of that check; I shall buy something nice & warm with it—whisky, or something like that."[8]

The following year he reached another hallmark when his long friendship with Edward House came to an end through an apparent misunderstanding over who had his authorization to dramatize *The Prince and the Pauper.* Its production in the winter of 1889–90, adapted for the stage by Abby Sage Richardson and produced by Daniel Frohman, who had instigated Richardson's agreement with Twain, led House to file an injunction, claiming that Twain had promised *him* the right to dramatize the play. Ironically, the only "play" from the works of Mark Twain to survive him (aside from the recent production of *Is He Dead?* discussed in chapter 47) was *The Prince and the Pauper,* though not this particular version, which he hated.[9] He pretended to remain undisturbed by the ugly publicity over House's claims, which were rehearsed in the *New York Times.* Clearly favoring House in reporting on the litigation, the *Times* contrasted Twain's personal wealth with House's relative penury. It reported on February 26 that House claimed Twain had not only asked him to dramatize the play but also reasserted their agreement the previous December, offering him between one-half and two-thirds of the proceeds from the production. Twain later explained that he had tried his "level best" to persuade House to dramatize the play, but that House didn't think it would be profitable. Years before, House had gone to Japan as a music and drama critic for the *Tribune* and had become an English professor at the University of Tokyo. There he had adopted a young divorcée named Koto, ostensibly to become her foster parent and protector. He brought her to the United States in the mid-1880s and made himself an unwelcome guest in the homes of Twain and his Hartford neighbors. By this time, he was crippled with gout, but financially sustained by a generous pension from the Japanese government as well as royalties from his librettos for comic operas. House returned to Japan in 1892, where he lived as an invalid cared for by Koto until his death in 1901. Twain ultimately blamed him for his 1873 falling out with *Tribune* editor Whitelaw Reid, who had refused to allow House to review *The Gilded Age.*[10]

Although the suit against Twain was ultimately dismissed, the House affair left its scars because of all the attention the press had given the proceedings. The Fourth Estate had emphasized the plaintiff's disabled state. Readers may well have been reminded of the claims a few years back that Twain had exploited his friendship with the late General Grant. And it was only one of a dozen or more distractions he faced at the close of the decade. "The machine is finished," he told his wife on New Year's Eve 1888, but the saga of the Paige typesetter in fact was far from over. He didn't even have time for a young writer named Hamlin Garland, who would publish his classic of prairie realism, *Main-Travelled Roads,* in 1891. An evolving naturalist himself, Twain clung to the realist tradition at least in his literary friendships. "I am heels over head in work and cannot possibly spare time for giving the subject you speak of the proper thought," he told Garland in the winter of 1889. At home his wife became afflicted with a series of minor health problems as well as the first signs of a weak heart that marked the beginning of her downward spiral of more than a decade. That spring she contracted conjunctivitis, or "pink eye," which, before the availability of antibiotics, lasted well into the summer.[11] Twain himself suffered from severe bouts of rheumatism. The Clemens family was by then back to its seasonal retreat outside Elmira, but Crane's looming death, occurring on July 3, dispelled any sense of relief from the daily grind of life. His passing would mark the end of all but one of their summers at Elmira.

Susy entered Bryn Mawr College outside Philadelphia in the fall of 1890. Sam's firstborn daughter, she was probably his favorite, especially since she showed early signs of authorship in beginning her father's biography. During the summer before her entry into college, he praised a sample of her writing, saying, "I knew you could write, if you would take the pains." In looks, unlike her sisters, she favored her father, especially in the mysterious and distant appearance of their eyes. Like her sisters, she was an attractive young woman, ethereally Victorian in her bearing but also brightly modern. Susy remained at Bryn Mawr only one academic year, and at least one biographer has speculated that her parents removed her from the school because of a lesbian relationship she had developed with another student, Louise Brownell. The letters Susy wrote her from Europe are intensely affectionate, though also typical of nineteenth-century terms of endearment between young female adults. Signing herself "Olivia," she told Louise a few months after leaving college, "My darling I do love you so and I feel so separated from you." We will probably never know the true reason for her early departure from Bryn Mawr, but Karen Lystra has speculated that it was to help out the family financially.[12]

Evidently, Susy enjoyed the academic work at the school, an institution for which she had to take an extra exam to gain admission since she had originally intended on going to Smith. But she didn't like the dormitory food or, if her mother is to be believed, the permissible late hours. In a letter to a friend apparently considering Bryn Mawr for her daughter, Olivia Clemens wrote at the beginning of 1891 that Susy suffered from homesickness as well as a lack of sleep in rooms in which the other girls "sit up too late." Twain was "homesick," too, for Susy and sought out excuses to visit her at college. A classmate, Evangeline Walker Andrews, described Twain's eldest daughter as emotional and high-strung.[13]

During one of his visits to Bryn Mawr, he put on a performance for the students and perversely included a ghost story called "The Golden Arm" after his daughter had begged him not to tell it. She had first heard him read the story in public at Vassar when she was thirteen and objected to its startling close, which made the audience jump as "one man." Susy may also have been embarrassed because the story had to be told in black vernacular. As soon as he began to recite it, as her classmate recalled, "Olivia [Susy] quietly fled up the aisle, I following." She went into an open classroom and "flung herself down and with her head on a desk wept aloud! . . . There was nothing to do or to say, no comfort that I could give her. . . . The applause was thunderous and people began to pour out of the Chapel. Finally, Mr. Clemens appeared and seeing Olivia in the classroom, he rushed in, and in a moment he had her in his arms trying to comfort her." When she protested the telling of the story and asked him why he persisted, he responded that he couldn't think of another story to tell, only of her voice saying not to tell the story.[14] Twain's emotional ties with his first daughter remain something of a mystery—even in this age of armchair psychoanalysis.

Clara, two years younger than Susy, was apparently the most stable of the Clemens girls. She was not interested in going to college, because her talents were already focused on music. She had begun taking lessons twice a week from a student of Liszt in New York City. The youngest child, Jean had a major interest in the care of animals, especially horses; she seemed perfectly normal until she reached the age of ten in 1890. That year her parents noticed a "sudden and unaccountable change" in her personality. It was the first sign of epilepsy, a disease not medically diagnosed until 1896 and one not fully understood in Jean's lifetime.[15]

With the arrival of the new decade, Twain pretty much found himself with his hands both full and empty. The "machine" was eternally not ready for investors' inspection. His play was an artistic embarrassment and its controversial origin a public relations nightmare. His wife began to suffer more serious health problems, and both his mother and his mother-in-law died in 1890. Livy lost her treasured mother, and Sam his "first and closest friend." The family thought of going abroad. With the typesetter and the publishing firm draining his income as well as Livy's inheritance, Twain decided to close up the Hartford house and reside for six months or more in Europe, where it was cheaper for them to live. By now his dreams of eventual typesetter wealth had begun to flicker.

39 Europe on Only Dollars a Day

Twain went abroad with his family in June 1891 to save money, because with his dwindling income he could no longer afford the high cost of maintaining the Hartford house. Yet he ended up taking nothing less than the grand tour of the best Swiss, French, and German hotels, spas, and operas—paying couriers, waiters, porters, private teachers for his daughters, and other agents, according to the ritual of the now wealthy Americans (his "tribe" as he called them in a series of travel letters reminiscent of *A Tramp Abroad*) traveling abroad in Europe. Passengers on the *Quaker City* back in 1867 had been charged twelve hundred dollars apiece and were advised to carry an extra five hundred in gold. Now it was 1891. Twain, of course, was paying only for one-way tickets to Europe, not the luxury rates of the *Quaker City,* but the comparison gives us some idea of what he was spending; indeed, getting to Europe was probably the largest part of the whole expense. The United States had returned to the gold standard thirteen years earlier. As a result, its currency exchanges with western Europe remained stable throughout the time the Clemens family lived abroad. Yet the exchange rate, which was one dollar to five French or Swiss francs in the 1890s, wasn't the reason Europe was cheap for Mark Twain.

Europe was *not* cheap for the average American, who in the nineteenth century rarely went abroad anyway, but only for rich Americans who could afford to purchase nontradable goods and services, those that couldn't be sold in the United States, such as spas with medicinal waters and tickets to Wagnerian operas in Bayreuth, just outside Nuremberg.

The cost of staying for weeks in a luxurious European hotel was significantly less than maintaining the Hartford house. Moreover, considering the heavy flow of European immigrants to the United States in the 1890s, it is not surprising that the people who performed all the menial tasks for guests of the hotels the Clemens family frequented worked for considerably less than their American counterparts. It is no wonder that Aix-le-Bains was the first place Sam and Livy went, leaving their three daughters, the recently widowed Sue Crane, and their Hartford maid, Katy Leary, in Geneva. In the 1890s Swiss and nearby French spas were a particularly good deal for the wealthy American.

After an initial three days in Paris, they arrived in Geneva on June 18, and by the 29th were immersed in the medicinal baths at Aix-le-Bains. They remained there almost to the end of July. "What I came here for . . . ," he wrote in the New York *Sun*, in the first of six widely syndicated letters that paid him a thousand dollars each, "was the baths." He spoke of his right arm, disabled with rheumatism. "There are a great many curative baths on the continent, and some are good for one disease but bad for another." Such medical quackery—or myth—proffered every kind of bath: for the nose, the ears, the throat. The typical course of medicinal treatments consisted of fifteen showers and five tub baths in gothic bathhouses made of white marble masonry, all at around ten dollars per course with occasional tips of ten cents. "Two half-naked men seated me on a pine stool," he wrote, "and kept a couple of warm-water jets as thick as one's wrist playing upon me while they kneaded me, stroked me, twisted me, and applied all the other details of the scientific massage to me for seven or eight minutes."

Staying in Bavaria during the first two weeks of August to attend a series of Wagnerian operas, Twain reported in his second letter to the *Sun* that he was both pleased and overwhelmed by the operatic performances and the scene in general. "If your seat is near the center of a row," he wrote of this "Wagner temple," "and you enter late you must work your way along a rank of about twenty-five ladies and gentlemen to get it." The opening performance he and his family witnessed was *Parsifal*, whose first act (of three) lasted two hours, something he enjoyed, he wrote, "in spite of the singing." *Parsifal* is loosely based on the epic poem about an Arthurian knight of the same name, and such a drama no doubt perversely appealed to the recent author of *A Connecticut Yankee*. The next day, Clemens was outside the opera house as the second intermission for *Tannhäuser* was coming to an end, when the beautiful daughter-in-law of the German emperor appeared on the balcony, stopping the returning audience "dead in its tracks." The princess quickly hid herself. Twain observed that she had a kind face and was "without airs; she is known to be full of common human sympathies." Yet in the anti-royal voice of Hank Morgan he added, "This kind is the most harmful of all, for wherever they go they reconcile people to monarchy and set back the clock of progress."[1]

In late September, leaving his family in Lausanne, he embarked alone on a ten-day boat trip that began on Lake Bourget. He went by canal to the Rhone River, which took him ultimately down to Arles, where he took a train back to Lausanne. While still on the boat trip, he wrote to Livy of "the early dawn on the water—nothing can be finer, as I know by old Mississippi experience." He witnessed "the most superb sunrise! the most marvelous sunrise! & I saw it *all*—from the very faintest suspicion of the coming dawn all the way through to the final explosion of glory."[2] The Clemenses spent the winter in Berlin, and by the beginning of 1892 Sam was figuring they would remain in Europe for two or three more years. In March he and Livy went to Menton, France, another spa town on the sea just north of Monte Carlo. They traveled in Italy in April and May and settled in Bad Nauheim, Germany, the following month.

In June he made the first of almost a dozen trips across the Atlantic while the family remained in Europe. He had left home to save money, but he could see from Europe that he was also losing it through his publishing company, especially from the financial strain put on it by the *Library of American Literature* volumes. So he traveled back to America to deal with that situation, and he also wanted to check on the typesetter, in which he still owned significant stock, although he decided not to meet with Paige, who had relocated his operation to Chicago. Clemens did go to Chicago, briefly, and wrote Orion from his hotel that the family was "in the clouds" because the physicians in Bad Nauheim had informed them, somewhat paradoxically, that Livy did not have heart disease, "only weakness of the heart-muscles." That alone, he told his brother, "was worth going to Europe to find out."[3] Not only Livy but Jean and especially Susy as well would suffer medical problems during their stay in Europe. Subject to "many savage moods," as her sister Clara would later remember, Susy could not eat or sleep regularly and lost weight, while taking singing lessons that would ultimately send her to another health spa to rest her strained voice.[4]

Twain rejoined his family in Bad Nauheim, and it was in this town just north of Frankfurt that he conceived and first began work on *The Tragedy of Pudd'nhead Wilson.* From there on August 7 in a letter updating his brother-in-law on Livy's health, he spoke of opposing her wish to spend the winter in Florence. After finally losing that argument and agreeing to find a villa there, he told Charlie Langdon, using an image from *Pudd'nhead Wilson,* that he was humbled, like his fictional creation Chambers, "& have gone up in the gallery with the niggers."[5] He also began "Tom Sawyer Abroad," a novelette that even his family thought a product of an imagination straining to succeed at any cost. "My family (tough people to please)," he told Fred Hall, who was now running Webster & Company and also acting as Twain's literary agent, "like it first-rate, but they say it is for boys and girls. They won't allow it to go into a grown-folks' magazine." But he had a number of irons in the fire, including the planned dramatization of *The American Claimant* with the celebrated producer Augustin Daly. He continued to make progress on *Pudd'nhead Wilson,* thinking he was writing a story called "Those Extraordinary Twins," which, for a time, he was. He called it "the howling farce," which he had laid aside "to ferment while I wrote 'Tom Sawyer Abroad.'" By now he could sense that the story about the twins was something new with him: "It is clear out of the common order—it is a fresh idea—I don't think it resembles anything in literature."[6]

In September 1892 the Clemens tribe moved to the villa Twain had rented in Florence for around three hundred dollars a month. Yet the journey there took longer than expected. They had to stop over in Lucerne for ten days because of Livy's illness. They had stayed in Bad Nauheim "a little too long," he told Susan Crane, who had by then returned to the United States. They feared erysipelas, but one wonders whether Mrs. Clemens wasn't a typically unhealthy middle-aged woman in the nineteenth century who was in need of exercise and a better diet. Her doctors in Lucerne didn't think she was seriously ill.[7] Once in Florence her health seemed to return, and Twain very much enjoyed the isolation of the Villa Viviani, located in the village of Settignano, three miles outside of Florence.

"We have been in the house several days," he told Sue Crane on September 30, "& certainly it is a beautiful place,—particularly at this moment, when the skies are a deep leaden color, the domes of Florence dim in the drizzling rain, & occasional perpendicular coils of lightning quivering intensely in the black sky about Galileo's Tower." Those conspicuous towers and domes down in the city, he thought, looked the same as in the time of Boccaccio or Dante. Yet the Italian language was an obstacle, but one that Jean, now twelve, was quickly overcoming. The house, built only two centuries before (not at all old in the Old World), had a gigantic hall that dwarfed everything in it, including Clara's piano. But it made "an eloquent theatre" in which the Clemens girls performed operas and plays. Clara was anxious to move—and did soon move—to Berlin by herself to continue her music lessons, but could not just yet because of a recent outbreak of cholera in that city. ("She watches the [cholera] reports anxiously," Susy told Louise Brownell, "and *hates* to be lingering away from that indispensable Mr. Moritz Moszkowski!" her piano teacher. Later, she would marry a musician, though not this one, today known for his encore piano pieces at the end of concerts; he would die in poverty in Paris in 1925.) So the family was all together for a time, huddling around the mother hen who was ordered by a new doctor to "be in bed by 10 at the latest, & take her breakfast in bed & lie there an hour afterward. . . . She is to drink sparingly . . . & keep an account of it for the doctor to cipher on. She is to eat nothing, & very little of that." "She will prosper, now," Twain told his sister-in-law, almost prayerfully. All they lacked, he concluded, was a cat. And they soon found one of those, too.[8]

"Some day," the distracted author told Hall, "I hope to get to work on the Extraordinary Twins again, but I can't guess how much of a book it will make." On November 10, he thanked Chatto and Windus for a book on the new science of fingerprinting he had asked them to send ("I shall devour it"), signing his letter with two thumbprints. But as usual, he was working on more than one book at once and had earlier asked his English publishers to send him an encyclopedia article on Joan of Arc. This subject would for a time be dearest to his heart, at least partly because he identified the young martyr with his daughter Susy. By the beginning of December, he had sold "Tom Sawyer Abroad" to Mary Elizabeth Mapes, longtime editor of *St. Nicholas Magazine,* where it would be butchered by her editors as it was serialized in 1893–94. He had needed the money somewhat desperately and hadn't asked many questions about its possible censorship, especially since it took him only three weeks to write and netted four thousand dollars. And by the end of 1892 Twain had made the shift from the "Extraordinary Twins" to "Pudd'nhead." "I begin, to-day," he told Hall, "to entirely re-cast and re-write the first two-thirds—new plan, with two minor characters made very prominent, one major character dropped out, and the Twins subordinated to a minor but not insignificant place." He added: "*The* minor character will now become the chiefest, and I will name the story after him—*'Pudd'nhead Wilson.'*"[9]

This was the first of two major turning points in the composition of *Pudd'nhead Wilson* because Twain's reading of Francis Galton's *Finger Prints* (1892) gave him a fresh and scientific way of tying the plot together. A year after *Pudd'nhead*'s triumphant book publication in 1894 ("the best work you've ever done," one admirer told him, "except the Prince & the Pauper"), he had already forgotten the source's name but not the book itself, "which interested me too much & which I used with so much freedom. . . . Mr. Chatto sent it to me when I was writing *Pudd'nhead Wilson;* & that accident changed the whole plot & plan of my book."[10] Actually, it took more than the fingerprinting book to solve Twain's plot problems. The manuscript, which he ultimately reduced to around fifty-eight thousand words, still contained more than eighty thousand words. It probably retained too much of the original farce of "The Extraordinary Twins." For although he sent Hall a "finished" manuscript, or typescript, in February 1893, he later retrieved it to continue work on it that spring when he returned to America. The second turning point would occur that summer when he was in the throes of his first real panic over his financial condition since going abroad.[11]

"Get me out of business!" he pleaded with Hall on June 2, fearing that the Mount Morris Bank would foreclose any day on its thirty-thousand-dollar loan. Yet almost two months later, on July 30, he declared, "*This* time 'Pudd'nhead Wilson' is a success!" Indeed, the work had diverted him from his misery over finances. "I am almost sorry it is finished," he told Hall six weeks later when he was ready to ship back the scissors-and-paste typescript. "It was good entertainment to work at it, and kept my mind away from things." It was during this revision that he separated the conjoined twins. His wife may have objected to his writing facetiously about the physically handicapped. (One wonders how he got the harelip past her in *Huckleberry Finn*.) Twain had most recently gotten the idea of using "Siamese twins" after seeing an exhibit of the Tocci brothers, Giovanni and Giacomo. He had long been fascinated with such "twinship" ever since seeing the team of Chang and Eng in Barnum's circus. In 1869 he had written "The Personal Habits of the Siamese Twins," in which he speculated on the dilemma of two different personalities, one a drinker and the other a teetotaler, in the same body.[12]

As was the case with so many of Mark Twain's plots, this one evolved out of aesthetic doodling in which Siamese twins were finally separated and Wilson found a way to shed his title of "pudd'nhead" long after he had admitted that he would have killed his half of a barking dog. Yet Sam Clemens would continue to try to shake off, or at least diminish, the humorist's side of *his* literary reputation. He was soon hoping his book on Joan of Arc would help, but ironically *Pudd'nhead* had not only reinforced his reputation as a humorist but also planted the seeds of his ultimate reputation as one of the world's great humanists. As late as 1934 J. Henry Harper, however, one of the founders of Harper's, which would publish Twain's complete works along with such important secondary works as Paine's 1912 biography and Clara's *My Father, Mark Twain* (1931), included *Joan of Arc* as one of the works that shot the humorist out from under the humanist. *Huckleberry Finn* was included in Harper's list of the best, but not *Pudd'nhead Wilson*. It would soon be forgotten until the South of so many Dawson's Landings woke up to the Civil Rights Movement in the middle of the twentieth century.[13]

40 A Dream Sold Down the River

The Tragedy of Pudd'nhead Wilson has given modern critics extensive grounds for consternation and disagreement (even the use of the word "tragedy" in the title is challenged on both textual and thematic grounds). In the wake of the civil rights movement and affirmative action, its plot is inevitably troubling to today's reader. It is clearly informed by Twain's own state of conflicted feelings about blacks and race in the 1890s, a point of view that was absorbed into his pessimism about the so-called "damned human race." In its final evolution out of a farce later labeled a "comedy" in the American Publishing Company's book publication of the novel in 1894, it is the story not of Pudd'nhead Wilson but of the slave Roxana, or Roxy, and her son Valet de Chambre, known as Chambers—whom she switches with the master's son, born Thomas à Becket Driscoll, causing each to be called by the other's name for most of the novel. "To all intents and purposes," Twain writes in chapter 2 of his book, "Roxy was as white as anybody, but the one-sixteenth of her which was black out-voted the other fifteen parts and made her a negro"—and a slave. Her son, conceived with a white man, was accordingly thirty-one thirty-seconds white—and a "nigger." This term—what is today referred to in most college classrooms and throughout the media as the "N-word"—was then synonymous with "slave." Either word signified an unchangeable state of inferiority that underscored and encapsulated the tragedy of race relations, one that in Twain's view was nearly as bad for whites as it was for blacks. Both are the helpless products of "training," a concept he had broached in

A Connecticut Yankee. Yet Roxy and her son are doubly bound by this deterministic law, for they are "black" by birth and shaped by an environment controlled by whites.

Twain may have been initially inspired to write his tale about the bogus distinctions of the color line as early as 1890, when Louisiana passed a law requiring separate accommodations for blacks and whites on railroads. Homer Plessy, who was one-eighth black, challenged the law in court and lost. He appealed all the way to the U.S. Supreme Court, which issued its notorious "separate but equal" ruling in 1896.[1] In this era, because of his mixed race, Plessy was designated as an "octoroon" in the idiosyncratic terminology of hypodescent, a classification system then practiced in Latin America and in the southern United States, particularly in Louisiana. A mixed-race person with predominantly "white" ancestry was called, depending on how many black grandparents he or she had, a quadroon, octoroon, quintroon, or hexadecaroon. Mark Twain did not invoke that terminology for Roxy, or anyone else, but as a quintroon, she would be assigned by "fiction of law and custom" to the race of her one black ancestor—that is, her socially inferior one. The decade of the 1890s was a time in which whites, increasingly anxious about the behavior of blacks brought up outside the institution of slavery, often turned to racial violence. Between 1889 and 1923 nearly twenty-five hundred "blacks," no matter how many parts white or black they may have been, were lynched. At the turn of the century, as previously noted, Twain himself thought to publish an article, even a book, documenting and denouncing the shameful practice.

Instead, it was Theodore Dreiser, another writer of the American vernacular, who spoke out in "Nigger Jeff" (originally named, interestingly, "Nigger Jim"), his finest short story, published in 1901, the year in which Twain wrote "The United States of Lyncherdom." As a newspaper reporter in 1893, Dreiser had witnessed a lynching outside St. Louis and never forgotten it. Earlier, his best friend, Arthur Henry, had published *Nicholas Blood, Candidate* (1890), a story that anticipated the genre of novels sympathizing with the activities of the Ku Klux Klan, the most popular of which would be Thomas Dixon's *The Clansman* in 1905. In Henry's story, a physically imposing black man alarms the city of Memphis when he runs unsuccessfully for mayor. Henry, progressive on most political questions of his day, was probably taking commercial advantage of the Negrophobia in America with a racist novel that he later tried to forget, perhaps was even ashamed of, since he never told Dreiser of its existence. "Does anybody doubt that America has among her possibilities a Reign of Terror?" Henry asked rhetorically in his epigraph. "We have 8,000,000 children of the night among us, and, like the shadows of a dark and stormy night, they spread swiftly. . . . Let us look at them."[2]

Such was the racial climate in the United States when Twain took one of his last looks back at the town that had once hosted the relatively harmless boyhood adventures of Tom Sawyer. When *Pudd'nhead Wilson* first appeared as a serial in *Century* between December 1893 and June 1894, the word "tragedy" did not appear in the title. The story was taken generally by the white audience of that day as a humorous parable about the ways not only of southern blacks and whites in the antebellum era (the action of the novel begins in 1830) but also, by implication, of blacks in the 1890s, who were generally considered harmless but also potentially dangerous to a society that had once enslaved their antecedents. "Tragedy" was added to the title only when the American Publishing Company issued it. Frank Bliss paid extra to include the revised text of "The Extraordinary Twins," which was called a "comedy" to set it off from the "tragedy" of *Pudd'nhead Wilson.* To include it, Twain apparently had to remove whatever Livy found offensive, though at that point, given his impending financial disaster, she may have compromised her principles. The novel was copyrighted in her name to protect his royalties in case of bankruptcy. When this strategy was first broached, he told Hall, his literary agent and still head of the struggling Webster & Company: "What I am mainly hoping for, is to save my royalties . . . for if they go I am a beggar."[3]

Yet *Pudd'nhead Wilson* is indeed a tragedy in the sense that the fragile possibility of racial equality is destroyed by the "fiction of law and custom."[4] In *Huckleberry Finn,* Twain had tricked the typical (white) post-Emancipation reader into freely cheering for the successful escape of a fugitive slave, whom he otherwise would have cared little about. Neither the reading audience of the 1880s nor its successors in the twentieth century any longer had an emotional investment in "the nigger Jim" as property. Hence, they were enabled, after the fact, to do the "right thing." In *Pudd'nhead Wilson* Twain also turns the tables by making the victims of American racism almost entirely white. It was only in the illustrations for the 1899 "deluxe" edition of the novel, when America's Negrophobia reached its zenith, that Roxy was absurdly depicted as having black skin. The 1894 illustrations were faithful to Twain's descriptions of a woman (with brown hair) only one-sixteenth black. Roxy is Twain's most feminine literary character and one of his few memorable women after Aunt Rachel in "A True Story." In that 1874 story, there is no question of the color of Aunt Rachel's skin; she is clearly a *black* victim of white injustice.

Roxy is doubly a victim because she is mostly white, though not white enough. The "one-drop" theory about black or Indian blood would continue well into the twentieth century (in fact, it still operates in some legal ways, such as tribal decisions about who is or is not a genuine member, and in several extralegal ways, having only disappeared legally in 1967), and it helped to reintroduce Twain's classic to the reading public in the 1960s, when the word "miscegenation" was still a pejorative. In the interim, the novel was nearly forgotten or dismissed as a farce, not only about foreigners who happened to be twins (even conjoined ones in "The Extraordinary Twins") but also about blacks ignorant enough to name a son after a bathroom attendant ("Valet de Chambre"). "It's de nigger in you" is the refrain heard from the lips of not only Roxy but Twain as well, who explores the curse of American inferiority based on race. "Why were niggers *and* whites made?" Tom asks himself once he has been told that he is a black and potentially a slave. Twain is sympathetic and even empathetic toward his black characters, just as he was toward blacks he knew both as a boy and as an adult. He describes Roxy as "the heir of two centuries of unatoned insult and outrage" and the peals of black laughter as available only to angels "and the bruised and broken black slave." At the same time, however, he is paternalistic and even condescending, evincing the prejudice of a reformed southerner, or "Yankee" who generally thought that all the slave ever needed was emancipation.[5]

Briefly, the story is putatively about another Yankee, David Wilson, who makes the mistake of facetiously calling for the death of his half of an invisible barking dog and is thus branded a "pudd'nhead" by the clueless and smug little town of Dawson's Landing, another stand-in for Hannibal. In revisiting Hannibal in his fiction this time, Twain sold it down the river to below St. Louis, where the slave's burden was harsher. As the result of Wilson's "blunder," this Orion-like protagonist is prevented from succeeding as a lawyer and spends the next twenty or so years as a surveyor.

He also takes up as a hobby the new science of fingerprinting, and in the course of this activity over the years collects the prints of everyone in Dawson's Landing. This includes those of Thomas à Beckett Driscoll and Valet de Chambre, born on the same day. The first is the wholly white child of Percy Driscoll and his wife, while the second is the slightly black offspring of Roxy and one of the leading white residents of the town, Colonel Cecil Burleigh Essex, who soon dies. Both children are placed in the care of the Driscolls' slave Roxy, who, after the birth of Valet de Chambre, "was up and around the same day," while Mrs. Percy Driscoll dies within a week of giving birth. One day before his own untimely death, Percy Driscoll explodes over the petty thievery of his household slaves and threatens to sell the guilty ones down the river. Fearful that her own son will suffer such a fate someday, Roxanna, as already noted, switches her baby son with the master's fully white child. The result is that her son grows up "white" and is known as "Tom," while the real heir grows up as "black" and a slave, and is known as "Chambers." Both become the ward and property, respectively, of Percy's brother, Judge York Driscoll, another leading citizen of the town who lives by the Code Duello of a Virginia gentleman. Roxy, who was freed on the death of her master, Percy Driscoll, remains in the Driscoll household to rear both children.

Reminiscent of the title character in "The Story of the Bad Little Boy," the nominal "Tom," we learn in chapter 4, was, following the switch, "a bad baby, from the very beginning of his usurpation." It would have been easy in the 1890s to read this plot as the parable of the freed slave who squanders his freedom, causing mayhem in the white community—much in the way Nicholas Blood does in Arthur Henry's racist potboiler. Yet the false Tom, it becomes clear in Twain's narrative, does not fail because he is "black" but because of the master-slave culture that brings him to condemn if not despise all blacks, including his own mother, Roxy. The false heir grows up and goes to Yale for two years, long enough to learn to tipple and gamble. Twain was perhaps subconsciously extending a possible slight to Yale, which had in 1888 awarded the "humorist" an honorary masters degree. It also reflects the consensus among artists of that era who lacked university training that such academic privilege made fops of the American breed. "Tom's eastern polish," we read in chapter 5, "was not popular among the young people [of Dawson's Landing]. They could have endured it, perhaps, if Tom had stopped there; but he wore gloves, and that they couldn't stand, and wouldn't; so he was mainly without society."

"Tom's" gambling indebtedness eventually drives him to become a thief who loots the houses of Dawson's Landing. Roxy, who, after Tom and Chambers reach adulthood, goes "chambermaiding" on the Mississippi, returns to ask "Tom" for financial support. When he contemptuously refuses her, she pulls out her hidden ace and informs him that he is not "white" but in fact her son, and she can prove it. In fact, she can't, but he is successfully bluffed and allows her to share the profits of his thefts. She becomes an accomplice in crime merely out of economic desperation; otherwise, Roxy believes wholly in the proud heritage of her white blood.

Indeed, in switching her baby to avoid his being sold down the river, she is fortified by the example of whites. "'Tain't no sin—*white* folks has done it," she exclaims in chapter 3, recalling fragments of the biblical tale of King Solomon. She emulates whites by celebrating the false heritage of the F.F.V., the same way that Twain's own father had. Even though she tells her son that slaves "ain't *got* no fambly name," she goes on to tell him in chapter 9: "You ain't got no 'casion to be shame' o yo' father, *I* kin tell you. He was de highest quality in dis whole town—Ole Virginny stock, Fust Famblies, he was." It wasn't only the Old World of Europe, where Twain was writing this novel, that reminded him of the pomposity of fancy names and titles. He had expressed his ridicule for aristocratic airs in *A Connecticut Yankee* and before that in his parody of the Duke and King's claims of nobility in *Huck Finn.* Yet in *The American Claimant* and *Pudd'nhead Wilson* he shows how these claims tempt even the democratically minded American, who was otherwise brought up to disapprove of unearned privilege and the pomp that accompanied it.

The town's reception of the Twins, especially in the farce, is Twain's burlesque of the American fascination with nobility. The Twins are the issue of old Florentine families. The fact that they are also physically joined may underscore Twain's ridicule of unearned social rank. In what Twain called in 1894 "The Suppressed Farce," the Twins become the houseguests of Aunt Patsy Cooper and her daughter Rowena. Mother and daughter agree that the names of Luigi and Angelo Capello are "perfectly beautiful! Not like Jones and Robinson and those horrible names." When the "double-headed human creature with four arms, one body, and a single pair of legs" arrives, the town is overwhelmed with pride.[6] Eventually "Tom," jealous of the attention the visitors are receiving, insults the Twins and is kicked by one of them. In the court case that follows, it is impossible to determine *which* twin committed the assault, and the case is dismissed.

Here we have the nexus between the two stories that allowed Twain to perform his literary Caesarean and complete *Pudd'nhead Wilson.* It is clear in this story that the kicking is done by Luigi, who is subsequently forced into a duel with Judge Driscoll, after "Tom" attempts to substitute legal retribution for the Code Duello. As a result, the judge disinherits him (not for the first time) and, to save his family honor, challenges Luigi to a duel that is inconclusive. Driscoll is just as proud of his "first fambly" status as Roxy is of her (secret) connection to it. When he discovers after the unsuccessful duel that Luigi had killed a man (however justly), he refuses to duel with someone who is not a "gentleman" and plans to shoot him in the back. But before he can act, the judge is killed by "Tom," who is ultimately apprehended and convicted of murder. Instead of being hanged, however, he reverts to slave status and is sold down the river.

At the time Twain was writing his book, he was increasingly worried about his financial future and bracing himself for the probable bankruptcy of his publishing company. These fears washed over into his story. When Percy Driscoll dies, his estate has gone into bankruptcy and is able to pay only sixty cents on the dollar of its debts. (Twain initially planned in his company's bankruptcy to pay only fifty cents on the dollar before Livy insisted on full payment.) Now with the addition of a slave who has not been included as property in the original bankruptcy proceedings, the creditors return. Technically, the guilt for the murder, as the governor determines when he pardons "Tom" and allows the creditors to sell him down the river, lies not with the murderer but with the "erroneous inventory." "Everybody saw," Twain concludes his novel, "that there was reason in this. . . . If 'Tom' were white and free it would be unquestionably right to punish him . . . but to shut up a valuable slave for life—that was quite another matter."

Mark Twain ends his story by returning to his title character. By winning the Twins' case, Pudd'nhead Wilson reinvents himself and becomes the mayor of Dawson's Landing. Yet the true protagonist of the story, Roxy, who also had been sold down the river temporarily by her own son, is left out in the cold. David Wilson's "long fight against hard luck and prejudice was ended," but Roxy's battle against a much more virulent and insidious prejudice is allowed to continue. Twain abandons his heroine the way Nathaniel Hawthorne had abandoned Hester Prynne in *The Scarlet Letter,* after allowing that the sin of adultery with Arthur Dimmesdale had "had a consecration of its own." Twain had begun his story the way Hawthorne had—intending to celebrate his heroine. At the outset he describes Roxana as a white woman whose one-sixteenth of black blood "did not show. She was of majestic form and stature, her attitudes were imposing and statuesque, and her gestures and movements distinguished by a noble and stately grace. Her complexion was very fair, with the rosy glow of vigorous health in the cheeks, her face was full of character and expression, her eyes were brown and liquid." If Hawthorne, in the forest reunion of Hester and Arthur, wrote the most erotic scene in nineteenth-century American literature, Twain is a close second in this most sexual description. While he stresses his heroine's nobility and stateliness, we still get a clear impression of Roxy's potential sensuality.[7]

Yet everything for Roxy goes downhill from this ecstatic picture in chapter 2. Even before the description, her black dialect threatens to bring her down to size. Her strong sense of survival, certainly as noble as that of any white person in the novel she might emulate, is treated condescendingly. "Was she bad?" the narrator asks. "Was she worse than the general run of her race? No." Twain blames her behavior on the "unfair show" of their environment. Yet even her son "Tom" fails, and he—unlike Huck's Jim—is white on the "outside." Roxy's "whiteness" doesn't save her, either. It can't, of course, in the world out of which comes *Plessy vs. Ferguson*. The only "black" it can't enslave is the "white" one called Chambers; training does that. ("The poor fellow could not endure the terrors of the white man's parlor, and felt at home and at peace nowhere but in the kitchen.")[8] Just as Hawthorne couldn't let his heroine go unpunished in antebellum America (Dreiser did do that fifty years later in *Sister Carrie*, with the result that his own publisher condemned the book), Twain couldn't leave Roxy be. At the close of *Pudd'nhead Wilson* she is a scorned woman. He could no more save her than he could dare to publish "The United States of Lyncherdom" in 1901. His novel would have been condemned—if not for its sympathy for blacks, then certainly for its unrealistic conclusion in the emerging Jim Crow society of the South—and the influence of that policy in the North, where his novel had far more readers.

41 Family Matters

On January 18, 1893, from Florence, Clemens wrote his old friend Mary Fairbanks, whose husband had recently gone through the bankruptcy he increasingly feared for himself, that he had ground out "mighty stacks of manuscript in these 3½ months, & some day I mean to publish some of it." These stacks probably included "Tom Sawyer Abroad" and "The £1,000,000 Bank-note," but the book he was working on at the moment was neither of these. "That is private," he told her, "& not for print, it's written for love & not for lucre, & to entertain the family with, around the lamp by the fire." The work he sought to cloak in mystery and would publish anonymously was *Personal Recollections of Joan of Arc* (1896), which he intended as a companion piece to *The Prince and the Pauper* and which Howells imagined would be as popular as *Ben Hur* (1880). The use of the word "personal" in the title was a double entendre since Susy, almost twenty-one, was something of a martyr herself, having been taken away from her friends at Bryn Mawr. She experienced "sudden sieges of complete homesickness," she admitted to her former Bryn Mawr classmate Louise Brownell. Telling Mrs. Fairbanks that Clara was thriving in Berlin at the Willard School for American young women, Twain added, "I'm afraid Susy isn't, for she is with us away out here on the hills overlooking Florence." Though only two or three actual miles from the Tuscan jewel on the Arno, where Dante was first dazzled by his Beatrice, it seemed like "forty in fact, as I realize when I have to drive down there twice a month." Susy usually accompanied him to Florence, and their slow return, an uphill journey, usually concluded after dark.[1]

Over the previous twenty-one months, Susy had discovered that her darling Louise was conventionally religious, something Mark Twain's eldest daughter was not, and that Louise had mixed her religious idealism with Victorian notions of romance. (They both adored Elizabeth Barrett Browning's *Aurora Leigh.*) Susy also learned that her friend had acquired other emotionally close girlfriends; this provoked slight fits of jealousy. When Louise finally revealed her attraction for a Bryn Mawr classmate named Elizabeth, Susy fired back that she had understood "that side of you from the first, the *very* first. What *has* surprised me is that having it you could feel any love for, or drawing toward me, . . . I have wondered all along if you have seen me as I am." Then she went on to make what was tantamount to an admission of lesbianism. "Your love for Elizabeth is largely based upon spiritual reverence. . . . I love you first and last because—*I love you,* and the honoring and reverencing are quite secondary and subordinate; so much so that if I neither revered nor honored you, I should still love you."

"Indeed," she further revealed, "I have loved once, *twice* where I did not even *respect.* You see darling, here is where we differ vitally." By this time, Susy felt that she had waited long enough for letters that finally satisfied her completely. "The point of all this discourse," she told Louise, who would marry, bear four children, and earn a Ph.D. in Greek and English from Bryn Mawr in 1897, "is that I am confirmed in my fear that perhaps it would not be safe for me to tell you as much about myself as I should like to. How do I know you mightn't break off our relations on the spot?" She closed by suggesting that Louise was "rather *implacable inflexible puritanic.*" Their correspondence continued for another year or more but with an acknowledged difference. "What you say," Susy told Louise in her next letter, "is true to a certain extent about my leaning more on my love for you than on yours for me."[2]

If the idea of his daughter's homoerotic tendencies ever occurred to him, Sam probably left no record of it. Three days after writing Mrs. Fairbanks, he was consumed by eighteen-year-old Clara's affliction with Daisy Millerism. Ever since Henry James's *Daisy Miller* (1878) had been the reading rage for those wealthy enough to go abroad, these Americans had been especially self-conscious about their European image.

And Mark Twain, who had made so much fun of European manners in *The Innocents Abroad,* now sounded more like Winterbourne's aunt in James's novella, who finds the Miller family's social intimacy with their courier appalling. "From the outspoken frankness with which you tell about excluding yourself with forty officers," he told Clara, "one is compelled to believe that you did not know any better. . . . The average intelligent American girl who had never crossed the ocean would know better than to do that in America. It would be an offence against propriety there—then what name shall it be called by when done in Berlin?" Speaking for her mother as well, he concluded, "An American girl in Europe cannot offend in the least degree . . . and not get herself talked about."

Within the year, he would extend this dissertation on the moral purity of Victorian women to his "In Defense of Harriet Shelley," published in the *North American Review* in 1894 and collected in *How to Tell a Story and Other Essays* in 1897. It was an attack on Edward Dowden's 1886 life of Shelley, which had blamed Harriet Shelley, the poet's first wife, who committed suicide in 1816, for his infidelities. About the same time that Sam Clemens was writing his defense of Harriet, all the time respecting the genius of Shelley as a poet, Susy Clemens was reading Dowden's biography. While sympathetic toward Harriet's ordeal with Shelley, who left her—with two children—for Mary Wollstonecraft Godwin in 1814, Susy couldn't help telling Louise: "Shelley I am sure wasn't quite sane but he *is* adorable!" Clearly, Susy was losing her desire to return to puritanical America and was becoming acclimatized to the ethereal life of Florence and upper-crust Europe in general. Her father may have sensed this development in his daughter, whom he always sought to protect from the world. As with Joan of Arc, Susy was doubtless in his mind when he wrote his witty defense of Harriet Shelley. One of his reasons for devoting so much time and effort to the twenty-thousand-word essay was that he feared that the biographer's "version is accepted in the girls' colleges of America"—colleges like Bryn Mawr, presumably.[3]

For Twain, the isolation from that or any society at the Villa Viviani otherwise set his imagination free, for it was about this time that he began to write the kind of philosophical fiction that culminated in works like "Which Was the Dream?" and, later, "3,000 Years among the Microbes." On Susy's twenty-first birthday, he told his other "Susy," his sister-in-law Susan Crane: "I dreamed I was born, & grew up, & was a pilot on the Mississippi, & a miner & journalist in Nevada, & a pilgrim on the Quaker City, & had a wife & children & went to live in a Villa in Florence—& this dream goes on & on & *on,* & sometimes seems so real that I almost believe it *is* real."[4] It was almost as if he had died and gone to heaven, or at least some extraterrestrial place, after writing *Pudd'nhead Wilson.* His moorings were somehow loosed after that last fictional return to the river. David Wilson, the latest version of the mysterious stranger who had moved in and out of his fiction ever since "Jim Smiley and His Jumping Frog," had solved a crime using science, a subject Twain would become more intensely interested in, especially evolutionary biology. Fingerprints proved that we could never truly change. By the end of the decade, Wilson would rematerialize in "The Man That Corrupted Hadleyburg."

Twain sailed for America on the *Kaiser Wilhelm II* on March 22, 1893, his second trip back home since going abroad in the spring of 1891. He got caught up with his old friend Howells, who "was really the same Howells that we used to know," he told Livy. At the home of Mary Mapes Dodge, he had dinner with Rudyard Kipling and his wife, who were then living in Vermont. Twain first met the author of *The Light That Failed* in 1889 when Kipling sought him out for an interview in Elmira. The future anti-imperialist had no problem with the imperialistically minded fiction of this up-and-coming literary star. Indeed, *Huckleberry Finn* may have influenced Kipling's *Kim* (1901), a novel Twain read every year, so he wrote in 1906, for the "deep and subtle and fascinating charm of India [that] pervades no other book as it pervades *Kim.*"[5]

On his trip he managed to get to Chicago again, this time in the company of Hall, to learn what progress Paige had made in the production of the first fifty typesetting machines and to try (in vain) to modify their financial arrangement. Paige had a knack for always embedding deep in any contract something that worked to his advantage. Only a day or two after his arrival, Twain came down with a severe case of bronchitis that kept him in bed for the next two weeks. Not only did he fail to see

Paige, but he also missed the World's Fair of 1893. The White City, as it was called, was located in Jackson Park on Lake Michigan. It spawned both Chicago's renaissance in art and architecture and the nation's first serial killer, who used the Columbian Exposition to attract and snare his twenty-seven or more young female victims.[6]

Back in New York City by April 26, Twain took to his bed again. "I've a mind to stay right here," he told Orion, meaning until he was scheduled to sail back to Europe May 6. He told his sister Pamela that he had been "very close to pneumonia for a week in Chicago" and that he had suffered it for thirty-five days a year earlier in Berlin. Though he feared he had damaged his right lung, he continued to smoke his pipe and cigars. Twain returned to Europe with a profound sense that because of his illness, he had accomplished nothing. He was struggling to protect his family from impending poverty but feeling helpless to stop its steady march toward them. The family was already leaning on Livy's letter of credit. "We are at a heavy expense, now," he told Hall. "We are skimming along like paupers, and a day can embarrass us." He fretted over "the Mount Morris volcano," an increasingly impatient New Jersey bank that was Webster & Company's biggest creditor.[7]

In June the Clemenses broke up housekeeping in Florence. Susy went to Paris with a chaperone to study singing under the well-known vocal teacher Blanche Marchesi. The rest of the family moved to Munich briefly, Clara joining them upon her graduation from the Willard School. From Munich in July, the family visited the baths at Krankenheil-Tolz in Bavaria, mainly for Livy's sake, since she wasn't feeling that well when they departed from their Italian villa. The following month they were back in Munich and headed for other baths in Franzenbad—this time for Susy. Her voice teacher had sent her home, finding her physically unfit for the rigor of singing lessons and in need of rest and strengthening. Marchesi recommended the cure at Franzenbad. "Here in Franzenbad," Susy told Louise in September, "there seems to be more room than usual for that faithful friend of mine, the ennui." Unlike Clara, who was up to that time steadfast in her desire to become a pianist, Susy was more reserved or hesitant about her artistic aspirations. "Oh how I hate the tastelessness of things!" she told her Bryn Mawr love. "And how I would rather *live* in this life and let the half dead condition wait till later!" Life in this case meant Louise. "Oh my beloved I cannot tell you how precious you are to me," Susy wrote. "I wish that when I see you I could just slip into your room and take you in my arms."[8]

In October the family would establish its winter quarters in Paris, presumably so that Susy could resume her voice lessons there. Clara was finished with any lessons or schooling for a while and decided to return to the United States. She and her father sailed on the *Spree* on August 29, 1893. Upon their arrival in New York, Clara accompanied him on a trip to Hartford and then went to stay with her Aunt Sue in Elmira. Twain spent the winter season in New York City, staying initially at the Lotos Club "for economy's sake." But he soon moved in with his old friend and family physician Dr. Clarence C. Rice on 19th Street. Soon thereafter, he established longer-term quarters at the Players, in another "cheap room." He was back in America, his third visit since leaving it in 1891, to face a looming double crisis, and fortunately for him, he came upon a dark angel, perhaps ultimately suggesting in the deep reaches of his literary imagination the satanic figure of "The Mysterious Stranger" texts. His name was Henry Huttleston Rogers, known to many as the Mephistopheles of high finance.[9]

42 A Friend at Standard Oil

Henry Rogers was a couple of years younger than Twain, whose writings he had admired for years. Twain's depictions of small-town life, especially in *The Adventures of Tom Sawyer,* reminded Rogers of his own humble beginnings, from which he had risen to become John D. Rockefeller's leading financier and vice president at the Standard Oil Company. Worth today's equivalent of thirty-nine billion dollars, Rogers could have modeled for Dreiser's Frank Cowperwood in *The Financier* (1912). He was ruthless but human, financially cold-blooded yet artistically sensitive. That combination blended well with the strengths and weaknesses of Mark Twain, the artist and businessman, who was now desperately in trouble. Rogers understood the writer's reckless nature when it came to making money, especially his madness about the Paige typesetter, in which even Rogers had obligingly invested.

Twain's return to the United States in the fall of 1893 marked the first of two New York phases in which he hobnobbed with the rich and famous, regularly attending grand dinners and yachting with America's version of European nobility, robber barons such as Rockefeller and Andrew Carnegie. Twain was famous, and it was in the interests of Rogers and Rockefeller to associate themselves with his popular image in order to balance the monstrous one that Ida Tarbell would soon be constructing in her 1902 series of articles that led to *The History of the Standard Oil Company* (1904). That book was the harbinger of the kind of muckraking that would be published in the first decade of the twentieth century and would open the way for well-researched fictional attacks not only by Dreiser but also by Upton Sinclair, David Graham Phillips, and other writers, now forgotten. Mark Twain has been accused of both joining the plutocracy that these younger writers opposed and helping to improve the public image of Standard Oil in the press. Some of the biggest threats to American industry in the last part of the nineteenth century and the beginning of the twentieth were the trusts that Theodore Roosevelt is today remembered for destroying (possibly one of the sources of Twain's later antagonism for that president). Rogers was a director of thirteen of these trusts and, along with Rockefeller associates John D. Archbold and William Rockefeller, controlled the many companies that made up the monopolistic Standard Oil Company. "We are not in business for our health," Rogers proudly admitted to a government commission investigating his organization, "but are out for the dollars."[1]

This was the man who told Twain when they first truly met in October 1893 (they had briefly been introduced two years earlier on a yacht) to *"stop walking the floor"* over his financial troubles. "You may have to go to walking again, but don't begin till I tell you my scheme has failed." Twain was almost childlike in his relief. "I have got the best & wisest man in the whole Standard Oil group—a multi-millionaire—a good deal interested in looking into the typesetter," he told his wife. He had also told Rogers about a near-miss debacle at Webster & Company. Only a month earlier, the company had almost gone under but had been saved for the time being. "The billows of hell have been rolling over me," he told his wife. "It looked for days as if we must go under, for lack of $8,000 to meet notes coming due to-morrow, Monday. I raced up to Hartford & back again. At Hartford I wrote Sue [his sister-in-law Susan Crane, some of whose money was also invested in the machine] telling her I had no shame, for the boat was sinking—send me $5,000 if she possibly could." But Sue didn't have the money, and neither did the banks on Wall Street in the first wave of the Panic of 1893. Already, millions were out of work across the country. Moreover, his Hartford acquaintances of many years didn't seem sympathetic enough either. On his return from Hartford, he went to bed physically and emotionally exhausted. It was at this point that Rogers fully intervened not only with shrewd financial advice but also with money of his own.[2]

To give the company breathing room, Rogers arranged for his son-in-law, William Evarts Benjamin, to purchase the burdensome *Library of American Literature.* Then he turned to Paige and the typesetter and eventually whittled down the agreements between the Chicago and Hartford interests to a manageable level for all concerned. "A singularly clear-headed man is Mr. Rogers," Twain told his wife on December 4. "This appears at every meeting." If nothing came of Rogers' managerial wizardry, he thought, only Paige would be to blame. Rogers pursued the inventor like a rat in a cage. "Paige will never sign [the proposed amended contract] unless hunger compels him," Twain continued. And hunger—or desperation—did bring him around. Indeed, Rogers' persistent pursuit of the wily inventor began the steady slide to his ultimate demise in 1917 in that potter's field in Chicago.[3] His decline and utter disappearance are emblematized in the fact that not a singe photograph of him has ever been found.

Rogers was not only Twain's financial savior; he was his frequent companion in society and the sporting playgrounds around New York. It was even remarked that the two men resembled one another. Twain's letter to his wife of January 4, 1894, throws a sidelight on history now forgotten. Rogers had purchased tickets to watch the "Coffee Cooler"—a Harlem native who became the "Colored Middleweight Champion of the World" that evening—"dress off another prize fighter in great style." Twain used the term "prize fighter," but he actually witnessed one of the early "glove contests" in America, what we know today as boxing, with six-ounce gloves and a stated number of rounds of fixed length. This was different from actual prizefighting, which was illegal and which permitted bare knuckles and endless rounds stopped only by a fighter's being knocked down. John L. Sullivan, the first American recognized as a heavyweight champion of boxing, had participated in the last bare-knuckle championship against Jake Kilrain in 1889 in Mississippi, where the fight lasted seventy-five rounds. "A round consists of only 3 minutes," he told Livy, describing these glove contests with set rounds as opposed to interludes between knockdowns. "Then the men retire to their corners & sit down & lean their heads back against a post & gasp & pant like fishes. . . . Only one minute is allowed for this; then time is called & they jump up & go fighting again. It is absorbingly interesting."[4]

Later that month, Twain went to an exhibition bout involving Gentleman Jim Corbett at Madison Square Garden. Corbett had become the heavyweight champion in Florida three days earlier, defeating Charlie Mitchell. Twain met the champion in his dressing room after the fight, later telling Livy that the architect Stanford White, one of the occupants of the ringside box Rogers had rented, escorted him there. (At a later time, the publisher J. Henry Harper claimed to have introduced Twain to the champion.) Corbett himself did not remember it. Since Twain's report was written right after the alleged meeting, however, the following interchange with the champ may be reliable. "You have whipped Mitchell, & maybe you will whip [Peter "Black Prince"] Jackson in June—but you are not done, then," the five-foot, eight-and-a-half-inch, 150-pound writer teased the six-foot, one-inch, 200-pound boxer, fantasizing over a bout between America's best writer and America's best boxer. "He answered so gravely," Sam told Livy, "that one might easily have thought him to be in earnest—'No—I am not going to meet you in the ring. It is not fair or right to require it. You might chance to knock me out, by no merit of your own, . . . & then my reputation would be gone & you would have a double one.'"[5]

Following the boxing, Twain danced until four in the morning to a Hungarian band at the Players Club. "I had danced all those people down," he told his wife, "& was not tired. I was in bed at 5, & asleep in ten minutes. Up at 9." That afternoon he walked three miles to Rogers' house and returned at 5:30. This wiry chain-smoker of nearly sixty manifested remarkable stamina. On another evening in the subfreezing January weather, he told Livy, "I did errands in Boston till 11 a.m.; reached N.Y. [by train] at 5:30 pm; left my satchel at the station & walked 17 blocks in the snowstorm to Mr. Rogers.'" Following dinner, the two men played billiards until 10:30, "talking typesetter now and then," after which Twain walked back in the storm to the station to retrieve his satchel and take a cab back to the Players. Rogers more than once observed that his friend never seemed to show physical fatigue.[6] It may have been that he was simply walking on air in his anticipation that

Rogers would eventually release him from his financial worry. Actually, during this American visit, he suffered frequently from bronchitis and a nagging cough, which Dr. Rice tried to relieve with various remedies.

Apparently Twain had not told his Hartford friends, or anybody outside the family, that "Hell-hound Rogers" was now his principal financial adviser and even silent partner. Hence, when George Warner, his former Hartford neighbor and brother of Twain's coauthor of *The Gilded Age,* approached Webster & Company with a manuscript by a friend that arraigned the Standard Oil Company individual by individual (very likely Henry Demarest Lloyd's influential *Wealth against the Commonwealth,* published by Harper & Brothers in 1894), Twain declined the opportunity, not with any defense of the Standard Oil Company and his friend Rogers but with the excuse that his publishing company was not accepting any new manuscripts. Indeed, since the firm was teetering on the edge of bankruptcy, that may well have been true. But he told Livy that what he truly wanted to tell Warner, what he "*wanted* to say [was]—'The only man *I* care for in the world; the only man I would give a *damn* for; the only man who is lavishing his sweat and blood to save me & mine from starvation & shame, is a Standard Oil fiend.'" "'If you know me,'" he continued, "'you know whether I want the book or not.' But I didn't say that. I said I didn't want *any* book; I wanted to get out of the publishing business & out of *all* business."[7]

Ethically speaking, Twain had made a similar compromise when his father-in-law had been attacked in the press back in 1869 for driving up the price of coal with his monopoly of interests; the Buffalo *Express,* which Jervis Langdon had helped Twain purchase, fell curiously silent while criticism continued in other regional newspapers. Yet even his brother Orion, who had thrown away a political career in Nevada for the principle of teetotalism, changed his tune about the trusts when he heard what Rogers was doing for his younger brother and—by extension—himself. "I have been abusing the Standard Oil Company," Orion readily confessed. "I did not know it was run by angels."[8]

Another perhaps more indirect beneficiary of Rogers' generosity, Samuel E. Moffett, Twain's nephew, would offer the same point of view in his *Cosmopolitan* article about Rogers for the magazine's "Captains of

Industry" series in 1902. Having been a journalist for the Hearst newspapers, and now managing editor of *Cosmopolitan*, Moffett went on to become an editorial writer for the New York *World* and then for *Collier's Weekly* before his life was tragically cut short in 1908, the victim of a stroke while bathing in the ocean off the New Jersey shore. His Uncle Sam had monitored his career since its beginning, and there is little doubt that he influenced Moffett's favorable piece about Rogers in 1902. By that time the Tarbell articles had thoroughly tarnished the name of Rockefeller and many of those connected with him. "Some men who have won great success are indifferent to public opinion," Moffett wrote. "Mr. Rogers, keen, cool, and at times grimly hard as he is, is sensitive on that side. He knows that Standard Oil methods are not popular." Clearly measuring everyone, especially Standard Oil critics, by their financial portfolio, Moffett wrote, "You may be a person of utter financial insignificance, making less in a year than he can make in an hour, but . . . he will devote two hours of argument in an attempt to convince you that the recording angel would be wasting time in inspecting the books of the Standard Oil Company." "The notion that the Standard Oil monopoly rests in any degree upon railroad discrimination"—favoritism in shipping charges, a central accusation against Rockefeller—"is a pure delusion," Moffett concluded before going on to describe Rogers' generous contributions to the New England town of his youth.[9]

"Inclined to keep piety and business separate," as Moffett put it, Rogers was loyal to his friends and favorites, not only to Mark Twain but also to the seaside town of Fairhaven, directly across the harbor from the famed whaling port of New Bedford, prominent in Herman Melville's *Moby-Dick*. He and his wife were at the time of his budding friendship with Twain in the process of giving Fairhaven a new courthouse and post office. For the opening ceremony on February 22, 1894, Rogers asked his friend whether he would accompany the family and make a few remarks. "He was as shy & diffident about it as if he were asking me to commit suicide," Sam told Livy about ten days before the Fairhaven visit. "But said Mrs. Rogers was afraid it was asking too much of me & was sure she could never get up the courage to do it." "Think of that!" he closed. "Why, if they should ask me to swim the Atlantic

I would at least try."[10] Today, the Rogers fortune has declined, mainly because of the Great Depression of the 1930s, but Fairhaven has become a summer tourist attraction that commemorates on its website "the magnificent European-style public buildings built between 1885 and 1906 by Standard Oil Company millionaire Henry Huttleston Rogers, a native of the town." Perhaps typical of Rogers' sense of philanthropy, the surviving gothic edifices stand more as a monument to Henry Rogers than anything else. Andrew Carnegie, a financier equally as ruthless, left the nation hundreds of libraries, including one in Pittsburgh that helped Theodore Dreiser become a writer.

Mark Twain may have been guilty of joining the American plutocracy in the final years of his life and of becoming its clown and defender, but in 1894 he was desperate to protect his family from the encroachments and embarrassments of poverty. He worried constantly about them—about Livy, who was increasingly ill; about Susy, who was endangered by what we would today call anorexia; by Jean's more and more obvious epilepsy. Only Clara, who had returned to Europe in November, seems to have been unmarked by the harshness of life then. Twain wasn't about to compromise their safety. His final years, without most of them, after the productive decade of the 1880s through the composition of *Pudd'nhead Wilson,* suggest that his immediate family had been the heart and the soul of the man and the writer.

By the end of February 1894, it was becoming clear that, while the typesetter still held promise, Webster & Company was in deep trouble in spite of its sale of the *Library of American Literature.* Rogers was advising Twain to sell everything to the Century Company "on the best terms I can get," but the publishing house was interested only in acquiring the Twain titles from the Webster list, not the others. Webster & Company's sales were depressed, and—incredibly—Twain was starting to blame the Grant *Memoirs*—"that terrible book! which made money for everybody concerned but me." (His argument in the main was that the success of the book, subsequently "insanely managed" by Hall—yet another scapegoat—had led him into debt.) "It owes me a hundred & ten thousand dollars," he ranted to his sister Pamela. "It owes Livy about sixty thousand, & it owes banks and printers eighty-three thousand." His only consolation was the success of *Pudd'nhead Wilson,* still being serialized in *Century.* When assured repeatedly that it was his best work since *The Prince and the Pauper,* he said to Livy privately, "I could have said, 'No, *sir*—it don't even *begin* with Joan of Arc.'"[11] *Adventures of Huckleberry Finn* wasn't even on the radar screen.

Twain returned to his family in Paris in mid-March 1894, after a six-month absence, satisfied that this trip had accomplished more than the last. Yet he had to rush back to the States the very next month, marking his fourth crossing since 1891, because of the imminent bankruptcy of Webster & Company. It finally occurred on April 18, four days before he arrived. Twain and Hall were hoping that its creditors would allow them to resume business in order to pay their debts, but the Mount Morris Bank refused. Indeed, the only real sympathy came from "a stranger out in New York State" who sent Twain a dollar and planned to organize a dollar relief fund for his favorite writer (shaming and exasperating Livy). Webster & Company owed the bank alone almost thirty thousand dollars. As partial payment for what the firm owed Mrs. Clemens as the principal creditor, Rogers arranged to have all copyrights to her husband's books transferred to her name. At one point the bank hoped to cash in on the coming success of *Pudd'nhead Wilson,* but Twain parried that he would have to ask the "author." "It was confoundedly difficult at first for me to be always saying 'Mrs. Clemens's books,' 'Mrs. Clemens's copyrights,' 'Mrs. Clemens's type-setter stock,' & so on but . . . I got the hang of it presently," he told his wife, who was now beginning to get a bit accustomed to the ordeal. "I was even able to say with gravity, 'My wife has two unfinished books, but I am not able to say when they will be completed or where she will elect to publish them when they are done.'"[12]

Twain sailed for Europe again on May 9 to a summer of relative rest and relief, leaving Hall to take the blame for the Mount Morris debt (even though Twain would have to repay it because Hall had secured that particular loan in 1892 behind his back).[13] It would not be until October that the other shoe would drop.

43 Broken Twigs and Found Canoes

"I'm writing a review of Fenimore Cooper's Deerslayer," he told Livy on May 16, 1894, on his way back to England, "the most idiotic book I ever saw." It is not entirely clear why Twain decided to target the work of James Fenimore Cooper, one of his literary forefathers, but "Fenimore Cooper's Literary Offenses" became the most anthologized of all his writings. His comment to Livy that March about his expectations for *Joan of Arc,* after he had received so much praise for *Pudd'nhead Wilson,* suggests he was worried about being known, or remembered, simply as a humorist. The essay appeared in the *North American Review* in 1895, and it hilariously made the point that Cooper was a slovenly writer, even as it gave a lift to Twain's credentials as a serious literary craftsman. "In one place in *Deerslayer* [1841], and in the restricted space of two-thirds of a page," the former printer announced in his essay, "Cooper has scored 114 offenses against literary art out of a possible 115." Some of what Twain wrote may have been edited out of the published version in the interest of space, or perhaps even as a covert slight for ridiculing one of America's most cherished writers at the end of the nineteenth century. He told Richard Watson Gilder three years later: "The North American Review didn't want it; they were afraid of it. I had to *make* them take it, at the revolver's muzzle."[1]

While living at the Players on Gramercy Park in New York City earlier in 1894, he had been keeping company with a number of established critics and journalists, some of whom thought highly of Cooper. One of these was Brander Matthews, at the time a professor of English at Columbia

University. "We must be a little wary," Twain said in his essay, "when Brander Matthews tells us that Cooper's books 'reveal an extraordinary fullness of invention.' As a rule, I am quite willing to accept Brander Matthews's literary judgments and applaud his lucid and graceful phrasing of them; but that particular statement needs to be taken with a few tons of salt." Just before Christmas 1893, Twain had given an impromptu speech at a dinner honoring Matthews. He was grateful for his "platform training," he told his wife, because he had not had time to memorize the speech he had written out about this friend and critic, someone who had praised *Huckleberry Finn* when it was first published. He observed that other speakers (he had agreed to be last) had spoken well of the guest of honor, but, he said, they had overlooked "the most notable achievement of his career—namely, that he has reconciled us to the sound of his somber & awful name—namely—Bran-der Math-thews!"

Twain enlarged on that odd but simple point, saying that "his lurid & desolating name—BRAN-der MATH-thews! B-r-r-ran-der *Math*-thews! Makes you think of an imprisoned god of the Underworld muttering imprecations & maledictions. . . . The first time you hear it," he continued, "you shrivel up & shudder; & you say to yourself that a person has no business using that kind of language when children are present. . . . And on the other hand when the veteran profane swearer finds all his ammunition damp & ineffectual from long exposure, how fresh & welcome is the dynamite in that name—B-r-r-RANder M-m-ATHthews! You can curse a man's head off with that name if you know how & where to put the emphasis." It was an enormous success, and no one suspected, he told Livy, that it had been merely his "bold delivery that made it seem a good speech."[2]

Twain's *North American Review* essay began with three epigraphs from eminent scholars and writers—one then dead, the British mystery novelist Wilkie Collins, who had stamped Cooper "the greatest artist in the domain of romantic fiction yet produced by America." Brander Matthews was quoted as saying that Cooper's woodsman Natty Bumppo was "one of the very greatest characters in fiction." The third was Thomas R. Lounsbury of Yale, who had written on Cooper in the "American Men of Letters" series in 1882, edited by Charles Dudley Warner. Twain's epigraph quoted Lounsbury declaring that *The Pathfinder* and *The Deerslayer* were the best of Cooper's novels "as artistic creations." This praise for the very kind of vernacular fiction that Twain was even then trying to get beyond with *Joan of Arc* may have been irksome to the writer who wasn't yet counting on *Huckleberry Finn* to give him the reputation he enjoys today. "It seems to me that it was far from right," he said of these august experts, "to deliver opinions on Cooper's literature without having read some of it."

Cooper's reputation had already suffered over the years because of lawsuits he had launched against newspapers that he thought had libeled him. He had also aroused the ire of his countrymen for criticizing the rude manners of Americans he had noticed after living, like Twain, abroad for a number of years. Moreover, as Cooper's most recent biographer notes, his works had suffered somewhat from hasty book production resulting in sloppy copyediting and faulty proofreading.[3] Yet none of these facts overrides the truth about Cooper's redundancy as a storyteller. Twain had accused Cooper, among other things, of writing awkward and superfluous sentences. But his most serious charge was that Cooper's fiction was unrealistic, or, one might say, "romantic" in Twain's age of Howellsian realism. Today it might be likened to chastising a Turner Classic for lacking realism and subtlety, but the target of Twain's satire also included Cooper's didacticism in the Leatherstocking novels. Even in *The Deerslayer,* which contains more forest adventure than *The Pioneers* (1823) or *The Prairie* (1827), we find the embedded political theory that distracts from the narrative, even while it makes Cooper our most important historical novelist in the tradition of Sir Walter Scott. The argument that underlies the extended adventures of Natty Bumppo (another name for "Deerslayer" in the series) is that European civilization with its laws and traditions has come to the wilderness, and, in spite of all of Nature's goodness, law must inexorably dominate the wilderness.

Yet in these novels the wilderness is ultimately respected. Cooper may have been our first environmentalist writer. Unlike his fellow New Yorker Walt Whitman, who in "Song of the Redwood Tree" celebrated the death of the giant Sequoias as part of the western progress of democracy, Cooper tempered his faith in the westward movement of civilization with a respect for nature's virginal beauty. Natty Bumppo in *The Pioneers,* for example, is convicted of shooting a deer out of season, even though he has a greater respect for nature than most and has also recently, through his wilderness skills, saved the life of the daughter of the very judge who sentences him. Although Cooper, unlike William Gilmore Simms, his southern counterpart, did not know Indians firsthand, he did extensive historical research. But to Twain, who grew up on another frontier only a few hundred miles from hostile Indians and who did not much like them, the picture that Cooper drew—whether friendly or hostile—was irresponsibly romantic and, in a word, false.

Cooper's characters are clearly more emblematic than realistic, for he was often using them to make a political argument in his novels. *The Deerslayer* opens with a long discussion between Hurry Harry and the young protagonist, still uninitiated in actual combat with the red man, as to what constitutes honorable behavior in time of war. Twain also chose the weakest titles in the Leatherstocking saga to attack, for while *The Deerslayer* and *The Pathfinder* were cast in the earliest period of the overall chronology, they were written last, in the 1840s, when Cooper, in need of money, was persuaded to add them to the other three novels already in the series. No detail, it seems to the modern reader, was too small or unworthy of discussion in *The Deerslayer* and *The Pathfinder.* Cooper was pretty much defenseless in the face of Twain's minor tour de force, whose hilarious wit to this day continues to have a bad effect on his reputation. Yet the theme of these stories—the clash between nature and civilization, the individual and the state—was very similar to what Twain himself pursued in his magnum opus. Cooper's Daniel Boone–like hero—whom Twain in his essays mockingly calls "Deerslayer-Hawkeye-Long-Rifle-Leatherstocking-Pathfinder-Bumppo"—is surely one of the literary ancestors of Huckleberry Finn. Both possess an inborn sense of moral justice in society and yet prefer the innocence and purity of that natural utopia beyond civilization—the wilderness forest in Cooper's case and the river in Twain's. Both seek its isolation. Both have sidekicks who are racial minorities in the societies from which they seek to escape. For Cooper's hero the sidekick is Chingachgook (pronounced "Chicago" in Twain's essay on Cooper) and for Twain it is "the nigger Jim" (miscalled "Nigger Jim" in too many commentaries of the last century, the misnomer actually tracing back to the publicity for the Twain-Cable tour).

But in terms of realistic plot and detail, Twain was almost as fanciful as Cooper in the sense that both the Leatherstocking Tales and *Adventures of Huckleberry Finn* are romances in which many of the crucial details require the reader's willingness to suspend disbelief, if not outright credulity. In saying that Cooper's series ought to have been called the "Broken Twig Series," Twain joked that Cooper "prized his broken twig above all the rest of his effects, and worked it the hardest. It is a restful chapter in any book of his when somebody doesn't step on a dry twig and alarm all the reds and whites for two hundred yards around." Yet how many times does Huck or someone else in Twain's Mississippi Valley novels magically come upon a canoe or a raft when he needs one? By Twain's standards, we might call his river fiction "The Found Canoe Series." Indeed, the very idea that an adolescent redneck brought up to believe that slavery was biblically ordained would ever go against the rules and become a hated abolitionist is, in and of itself, helplessly romantic. This is not to say that the gritty scene in which Huck decides to "go to hell" for helping Jim escape does not rise on its own terms to realism.

Attacking or satirizing a writer of a previous generation was scarcely unprecedented, of course. Swift had assailed Dryden in "A Tale of a Tub" and "The Battle of the Books." Byron had ridiculed Southey on several occasions. Wordsworth had criticized Pope. And Shelley had found fault with Wordsworth in "Peter Bell The Third" for abandoning the principles of the French Revolution and becoming conservative in his old age as poet laureate. Twain would have read about this last authorial assault in Dowden's biography of Shelley. Twain's approval of the French Revolution, as evidenced in *A Connecticut Yankee* and in his correspondence, would have landed him on Shelley's side in the pseudonymous "Peter Bell," in which the preface declares that Peter (i.e., Wordsworth) "changes colors like a chameleon and his coat like a snake."[4]

On the American side of the Atlantic, Twain's old friend and now enemy Bret Harte had once parodied Whittier, something Twain himself had come close to doing in his Whittier birthday dinner speech of 1877. In 1871 Osgood and Company had published a volume of Harte's poems that contained "Mrs. Judge Jenkins," billed as "the only genuine sequel" to Whittier's "Maud Muller," a sentimental poem about the restrictions on marriage between members of different social classes. Whittier's theme was actually about the lost dreams of youth, but his plot line set him up for easy ridicule, especially of his conclusion that "For of all sad words of tongue or pen, / the saddest are these: 'It might have been!'" Whittier's poem told of a judge who becomes infatuated with an illiterate milkmaid, Maud Muller, but comes to his senses and marries "a wife of richest dower, / Who lived for fashion, as he for power." In Harte's clever rejoinder, the judge comes back down the lane to Maud instead of getting on with those of his class "whose verbs and nouns do more agree." After sketching the judge's subsequent life with Maud's family, in which her father borrows money, her brother gets intoxicated, and his twin children look too much "like the men who raked the hay," Harte concludes:

> If, of all words of tongue and pen,
> The saddest are, "It might have been,"
>
> More sad are these we daily see:
> "It is, but hadn't ought to be."

Whittier had been known for his anti-slavery poems before the war, when Sam Clemens still mistrusted such northern ideas. So he may well have subconsciously agreed with Harte, even though he consciously despised him, the way he doubtless agreed with Shelley about Wordsworth.

Cooper's "offense," other than writing for his own contemporary audience instead of Twain's, was that the American Scott had been championed by the academic, literary arbiters of the day, such as Professor Lounsbury (who later edited Whittier). From the mid-1880s onward, efforts to create an American academy of distinguished writers of all kinds led various American journals to poll their readers on who should belong. *The Critic* in 1884 asked its readers to send in "a list of the names of the forty American authors of the sterner sex whom they deem most worthy of a place in a possible American Academy." In the early balloting the top places went to the writers of the previous generation, usually northern, such as Holmes, Lowell, and Whittier (but curiously not Cooper). Howells (fifth) and Bret Harte (eighth), no doubt to Twain's displeasure, ranked considerably higher up than he did at fourteenth. As such polls proliferated, Twain—the humorist—was usually not even among the top ten. Thomas Bailey Aldrich (seventh), George Washington Cable (twelfth), and Henry James (thirteenth) likewise outranked Twain. The other vernacular writer who is today ranked as a major American artist, Walt Whitman, came in twentieth out of a field of forty.[5]

Twain had made yet another round-trip crossing of the Atlantic, between July and August, when he joined his family, now located at Étretat, a spa on the coast of Normandy. He had placed *Joan* with Harper's, though it was first to be serialized in *Harper's Monthly* (anonymously so that readers wouldn't expect humor), but he was still working on Cooper. "I have been sitting here all day," he told his wife from New York shortly before he sailed back to Europe, "grinding away at those old Cooper articles. I was far from satisfied with them; but now I have cut them down to a single article . . . & I think I am quite well satisfied with it; well enough, in fact, to offer it for publication."[6]

Cooper could now fend for himself while Twain turned his attention to Joan of Arc, who was at this point becoming another of his literary personages—indeed, a kind of historical/fictional daughter whose courage nearly obsessed him. Yet his *real* daughter Susy, the one whose blood connections and emotional neediness had given him an almost tactile connection with the Maid of Orléans, was at the same time in utter distress. After waiting three years for her first reunion with Louise Brownell, who that summer came to Oxford to pursue postgraduate studies, Susy was dreadfully disappointed, even beside herself, after Louise evidently made it clear that she did not want to continue their relationship on the same emotional terms. Livy had given Susy permission to travel to England despite her fragile emotional state, but Louise chose not to repay the visit by coming to France. "I don't know how to write you," Susy told her lost friend. "There seems to be nothing to say, *nothing* in all the world."

Evidently Louise was about to return to America without seeing Susy again. "I would not, *could* not dream this would happen and that I should lose you now *now* at the moment of having you again, after all these years of waiting. *It is impossible. I cannot believe it. It cannot be true.*" "Why didn't you, why couldn't you come to Étretat?" Susy pleaded. "Oh I have *lost* you and can do nothing." In September her father tried to console his friend Howells on the death of his father. "Sympathy is for the living," he told him, "& sincerely you have mine."[7] He closed with his usual refrain about the dead being better off than the living. Although he couldn't know it, he was soon to suffer his own death in the family, for, in her brooding condition and fragile physical state, Susy had less than two years to live.

44 Back Home and Overland

In the fall of 1894 the Clemens family sublet a house from a friend in Paris on the Right Bank for $250 a month—in what is today the seventh arrondissement. Clemens later described the place at 169 rue de l'Université as "large, rambling, quaint, charmingly furnished and decorated, built upon no particular plan, delightfully uncertain and full of surprises." It reminded Livy of their Hartford house, which she now longed to reoccupy after more than three years of living abroad. On their way from the Normandy coast, however, they had to stop a week in Rouen because Susy, perhaps in a delicate state over her frustration with Louise, came down with a serious case of bronchitis. Rouen was also the place of St. Joan's trial and execution in 1431. In the same letter to Rogers in which he reported that Susy's fever had risen to 104 degrees, he spoke of the ancient city as having little of note remaining about his Joan. "Even the spot where she was burned is not as definitely located as one would expect it to be," he wrote, adding, "But there is a new statue of her—and the worthiest one that has been made yet."[1] He would now get back to his book.

Yet he was distracted again that December when the Paige Compositor went down for the last time. It had failed a crucial test at the Chicago *Times-Herald.* As Rogers later told Albert Bigelow Paine, it was too much like a human being and not enough like a machine. There was nothing left but to break the calamitous news to Twain in Paris. "I *seemed* to be entirely expecting your letter," he told Rogers, "and also prepared and resigned; but Lord, it shows how little we know ourselves and how easily we can deceive ourselves. It hit me like a thunderclap."[2] The long night of hoping was over, and Twain now knew that he would not get any help from the typesetter in repaying his company's debts. There was some financial compensation when the Mergenthaler people bought up the rights to Paige's invention for $20,000, but Twain no doubt got very little of that. The irrepressible Paige was last seen applying for a patent on a pneumatic tube.

Instead of returning to the Hartford house, Clemens and his family would have to rent it. "I have got to pay the creditors of CL Webster & Co a heavy sum before the year closes," he told Frank Whitmore, the Hartford businessman who had been handling Twain's affairs in Hartford while he had been abroad. "I want *repairs* on the house reduced at once to $15 a month, even if the roof fall in. . . . We've *got* to rent that house, or sell it or burn it." He wisely crossed out the last clause, but he was feeling desperate. Empty, it cost $200 a month to maintain, not counting taxes and insurance. One of the very few expenses he couldn't cut was Orion's stipend. "My brother will have to have his $50 a month again [it had been briefly cut in half]—that can't be helped. He has nothing else to live on." He even asked Whitmore to take a 50 percent cut in pay, now that there was no typesetter interest in Hartford to worry about. He calculated that he could live on $13,000 a year if he remained in Paris or moved to Vienna. Four thousand of that, he told Rogers, came out of the "rags" of Livy's estate. He was still realizing $1,500 a year from the American Publishing Company royalties, and Chatto and Windus provided another $2,000. That meant he would have to earn another $5,000 or $6,000 just to "keep the tribe alive."[3] Where would the money for the Webster debts come from?

Twain returned to the States again for a month in March 1895 to arrange for the Harpers' publication of *Personal Recollections of Joan of Arc* (which began its anonymous serialization the next month) and to discuss a plan for a uniform edition of his works—every writer's dream in the nineteenth century (such editions of Emerson and the Schoolroom poets were already available). It was an emotion-filled trip for him, for he was finally letting go of his Joan and also making preparations for plans to ease himself out of personal debt that now amounted to around $100,000. Since digging himself out entailed the rent of the Hartford house, he went there to inspect it. Katy Leary had supervised the undraping of the furniture and its general preparation for leasing.

When he got off the train at Hartford, he told Livy, he didn't even want to go near the house. "But as soon as I entered, . . . I was seized with a furious desire to have us all in this house again & right away, & never go outside the grounds any more forever—certainly never again to Europe." It almost took his breath away, he continued. "Katy had every rug & picture and ornament & chair exactly where they had always belonged, the place was bewitchingly bright & splendid & homelike & natural, & it seemed as if I had burst awake out of a hellish dream, & had never been away, & that you would come drifting down out of those dainty upper regions with the little children tagging after you." The painful truth was still not clear to him: they could never go home again to Hartford.

The house was in every way a monument to the woman he loved. "You did it all," he told her, "& it speaks of you & praises you eloquently & unceasingly."[4] Although he thought that with *Pudd'nhead Wilson* he had abandoned the practice of dedications in his books, he decided nonetheless to dedicate *Joan of Arc* to Livy, "tendered on our wedding anniversary [in 1896] in grateful recognition of her twenty-five years of valued service as my literary adviser and editor / 1870–1895." It was the last novel he would publish during his lifetime. He thought at times it was his best, but posterity has not agreed. Twain followed the life of this saint (canonized in 1920) as accurately as he knew how, given the fact that he had been reared within an anti-Catholic ideology.

What he conceived as a labor of love turned out to be one of infatuation, for he had temporarily found somebody outside of his immediate family who had no equal and "no blemish," as he made clear at the close of the essay he appended to his French chronicle. Otherwise, the chronicle of Joan in Twain's hands is lacking in nuance and genuine drama, apart from the actual history of his subject during France's war with England. Only on the brutality and senselessness of war did the future author of "The War Prayer" appear to hesitate. After a battle in which everyone pays homage to this military leader who had the directness of Grant, Joan, in Twain's version, is seen to weep for the mothers of the slain enemies. Later on in the story, Joan is asked whether God is on the side of the French and hates the English. Her answer evades the question by suggesting that God had allowed the English to dominate the French during the Hundred Years' War in order to chastise France for its sins. Mark Twain's unconditional love for Joan comes through most dramatically when he describes the torture of her existence during her trial and execution.

It seems as if Twain was otherwise afraid to tamper much with the facts of this future saint, whose existence he had supposedly first learned about as a boy in Hannibal, when a leaf from a book describing Joan's mistreatment in Rouen supposedly, by his later account, flew in front of him.[5] Moreover, the entire exercise must have struck him as almost sacrosanct, for this book, though publicly dedicated to Livy, was secretly inspired by his own daughter's suffering—her continued unhappiness and depression, which she barely concealed behind the blank countenance we see in her pictures taken about this time.

By the time he was back in Paris in April, Twain had decided that he would embark on an international lecture tour in order to pay off his debts. His friend Sir Henry Stanley, whom he had known since 1867 and who had since made a great success as a public lecturer, encouraged and advised him. He hated lecturing and had sworn after the Cable tour that he would never do it again. He did not enjoy, as he would tell his nephew Sam Moffett in a newspaper interview that summer, "the hard travel and broken rest inseparable from lecturing," and he certainly would not have embarked on such a scheme at this late turn in his life if he could have avoided it. "I could have supported myself comfortably by writing," he said, "but writing is too slow for the demands that I have to meet; therefore I have begun to lecture my way around the world."[6]

When Sam Clemens finally returned to the United States with his family in May 1895, he had crossed the Atlantic fifteen times in the previous four years—on average, nearly once every four months. Yet in spite of his age and current health problems (he suffered from both gout and a severe case of carbuncles that kept him bedridden for forty days in June and July), he came home only to immediately leave it again for a lecture tour that would take him even farther away from home than before. The family spent almost all its time in Elmira before the tour kicked off in Cleveland on July 15. Before that, he was forced to get up from a sickbed to make an appearance in court in New York City when one of his creditors, a printing concern that had made a great deal of money from Webster & Company, heard that he was back in the United States. Twain blamed his own lawyers for allowing him to be so humiliated, but the scare put him in constant fear that his lecture receipts would be seized. Rogers eventually calmed these financial waters sufficiently so that Twain could concentrate on developing lectures, or readings, for his tour.

There were actually two tours, the domestic and the international. Before sailing for Australia to begin his international circuit, arranged through Robert S. Smythe of that country, he decided to lecture his way across North America. As the thermometer was already hitting triple digits that summer, he followed a northern route across the Great Lakes and into Minnesota and Montana on his way to the state of Washington and finally into British Columbia, where he would deliver his final overland lectures in Vancouver and Victoria. These lectures were arranged through Major James B. Pond, who had handled the Cable tour ten years earlier. For his services, Pond received a quarter of the lecture receipts. Twain also hoped to give a series of lectures in San Francisco, which he hadn't visited for twenty-seven years, but he was disappointed to learn that the city would be largely empty of potential audiences in August, and so he did not go there. Pond's wife went along. Twain was accompanied by his wife and daughter Clara. The other two daughters did not want to go, Susy claiming that she preferred to continue her singing lessons and Jean not wanting to miss enrolling in her mother's alma mater, Elmira College. The girls—even though Susy was now legally an adult at twenty-three, she was regarded as a dependent just like Jean, who was almost fifteen—stayed with their Aunt Sue in Elmira, planning to rejoin their parents and sister in London one year later at the end of the tour. Whatever their reasons, Twain could not have afforded at this point to pay travel expenses around the world for his entire family. He had initially decided to take only Livy, because he thought the sea voyage would be good for her health. Clara, who actually did want to go on the tour, was included on the excuse that Livy would not be taking a maid.[7]

The Cleveland lecture was a disaster. Seated behind him on stage at the Stillman Music Hall were five hundred unsupervised boys. "I got *started* magnificently," he told Rogers, "but inside of half an hour the scuffling boys had the audience's maddened attention . . . so I skipped a third of my program and quit." To make matters worse, he was preceded by "a concert of amateurs" whose family and friends "kept encoring them." Never again, he told Rogers: "There ain't going to be any more concerts at *my* lectures." Pond thought the lecturer looked "badly fatigued," and indeed he was barely out of his sickbed.[8] He had at least twenty more performances to look forward to before he sailed from Victoria in August. His course zigzagged along the Canadian border, going as far north as Winnipeg and as far south as Portland, Oregon. From Ohio they crossed Lake Erie to the Detroit River, which took them out on Lake St. Clair and up the St. Clair River to Lake Huron. From here they went from Michigan on Lake Superior to Duluth, Minnesota, where Twain went directly from the ship to the lecture hall on July 22. Immediately after the lecture, he and Pond boarded a train for Minneapolis to give another lecture. By the beginning of August, the party crossed the Rockies by a train that took nearly the entire day to climb eight thousand feet.

Heavy forest fires were blanketing the nearby hills in Washington and British Columbia. Twain, now largely freed from his carbuncles, came down with a cold by the time the party reached Vancouver on August 15, which made his voice hoarse and difficult to hear. Pond, in his diary, expressed continual amazement that he smoked so much. By this point, Livy, whose home cures seemed to give her husband some relief, was dreading the long voyage. And this was when they thought that the first leg would be to Hawaii on the way to Australia; but a cholera outbreak in Honolulu forced them to go directly on to Sydney, which they reached a month later.

Shortly before he sailed on the *Warimoo* out of Victoria, Clemens made a public declaration that would resonate around the country and throughout the world. He told the San Francisco *Examiner,* whose reporter was his nephew Sam Moffett and who had joined the overland traveling party in Seattle, that he would pay his debts in full in the next four or five years. He compared himself to Sir Walter Scott, whose romantic philosophy he detested, but who had also gone bankrupt and then repaid his debts. Twain dismissed the rumor that he was running away from his creditors by undertaking the world tour. Saying that his brain could not be mortgaged for debt, he nonetheless insisted that he wasn't a businessman, and that "honor is a harder master than the law. It cannot compromise for less than a hundred cents on the dollar."[9] Even though his partner Hall (never mentioned in the interview or anywhere else) owed one-third of the debt, he would pay that as well because Hall couldn't.

Pond, whose *Eccentricities of Genius* (1900) shows that he adored Twain,[10] took Kodak snapshots throughout the overland lecture tour. One of the last pictures shows Twain aboard the *Warimoo* with Clara and Livy on August 23 as the ship prepared for departure. Twain is standing by the rail smoking a long-stemmed pipe. He is wearing a nautical cap under which his pile of woolly hair, grayish white, is clearly visible. In front of the trio on the rail of the ship is mounted a notice in large bold letters reminiscent of the one that had launched *Adventures of Huckleberry Finn* hardly more than a decade earlier. "NOTICE," it read, "ALL STOWAWAYS WILL BE PROSECUTED AT HONOLULU AND RETURNED TO THIS PORT. BY ORDER." It might as well have said, "BY ORDER OF THE AUTHOR." For Mark Twain, now almost sixty, was starting over for the last time and taking no more chances.

45 Lost in the British Empire

It is generally accepted in Mark Twain scholarship, and among ordinary readers as well, that the death of Sam's eldest daughter in 1896 broke his spirit and turned him into a pessimist. What tends to be overlooked is that his work and his personality always had deep-seated elements of pessimism. Indeed, these elements exist in all serious thinkers. Even the optimistic Emerson, who also lost a favorite child shortly before he revealed the seeds of his darker thoughts in the essay "Experience," had indicated the same doubt about a benevolent universe in an earlier work entitled "Circles." In some cases, personal loss of this magnitude seems merely to trigger the full utterance of what has been there all along. "A man," Twain told a journalist when he arrived in Australia, "could never be a humorist until he could feel the springs of pathos."[1]

There was, however, a distinct change in Twain in the mid-1890s. Certainly, Susy's death was partly the cause, but among other things it is likely that the physical strain of the world tour was another, even though Clemens felt invigorated both during and immediately afterward. At its outset, he complained more than once to reporters that he was forced to undertake this long and arduous lecture tour at the age of almost sixty in order to pay another man's debts.[2] He was referring to Hall, of course, but this was a vast oversimplification of the financial situation. He was also in mediocre health, not nearly so vigorous as he had been during his stay in New York City just a year before, in 1894. More carbuncles plagued him during the yearlong tour, suggesting a deficiency in his diet. He was continually in danger of catching colds that sometimes led to bronchitis. Indeed, even the health of his immediate family members was rocky, compromised no doubt by their frequent changes of locale and the passive smoke from the many cigars and pipes Twain smoked every day. ("Mark Twain is an inveterate smoker," a reporter for the *Courier* in Ballarat, Australia, observed, "and when he relinquishes his cigar it is to transfer his attention to a pipe.") By the time the world tour concluded in July 1896 and the family had embarked on the *Norman* for Southampton, England, he had given at least one hundred readings in fifty-three cities. This itinerary took him not only to Australia (twice), but also to New Zealand, Ceylon (Sri Lanka), India, Mauritius, and South Africa.[3]

Because of a cholera outbreak in Honolulu, the closest Twain got to the islands he had roamed as a young man almost thirty years earlier was a glimpse of Diamond Head on Oahu. With the loss of his Hawaiian engagement, along with the one in San Francisco, he was already behind schedule in his scheme to pay off his debt. As it turned out a year later, his lecturing netted him only between $20,000 and $25,000, leaving him with a balance of $50,000 still owed to creditors. The *Warimoo* crossed the Equator on September 5 and arrived in Sydney on September 16. Here he spent nine days and lectured four times, billed as "Mark Twain at Home." He was described in the press upon his arrival as "spare and undersized." Still recovering from his last bout of bronchitis, he tried to limit himself to one cigar a day, to be enjoyed at bedtime. "But desire persecuted me every day and all day long," he later observed in *Following the Equator*; "so, within the week I found myself hunting for larger cigars" in order to better endure the limit of one a day. Within a month, this cigar had grown to a length of "four feet," the humorist suggested; he soon returned to the "liberty" of smoking ten regular ones each day.[4]

His advertised lecture billing allowed him to select just about anything from his oeuvre, and he often reached all the way back to material from his first *Jumping Frog* collection in 1867, such as "Aurelia's Unfortunate Young Man," the story about the accident-prone suitor who kept losing body parts. Another was "His Grandfather's Ram," a platform favorite that originally appeared as chapter 53 of *Roughing It* in 1872. The English-speaking world throughout the British colonies was familiar with his works, especially *The Innocents Abroad, Tom Sawyer,* and *Huckleberry Finn.* Audiences were therefore excited to "read" the author in person, and they also respected Twain as more than a funny man, finding sorrow in his stories as well as humor. One New Zealand correspondent later reported in "A Talk with the Famous Humorist" that his conversation "was not replete with 'funnyisms,'" that he was in fact "a brilliant conversationalist, who talks in polished and incisive English," in spite of the twang in his voice, something also noted by several other reporters during the tour. Twain's reading of Huck's decision not to turn Jim over to the slave catchers ("Small-pox & a Lie to Save Jim") particularly touched them, even though these British subjects lived in colonies where the indigenous peoples were an oppressed majority. In Natal, South Africa, where there were ten blacks to every white, Twain later recorded, "natives must not be out after curfew-bell without a pass."[5]

The future vice president of the American Anti-imperialist Society mulled over the situation in which more and more primitive and semi-primitive peoples from undeveloped parts of the world were being absorbed as new "countries" by European powers, especially Great Britain. He wasn't sorry, he wrote in *Following the Equator,* that "all the savage lands in the world are going to be brought under subjection to the Christian governments of Europe." "The dreary and dragging ages of bloodshed and disorder and oppression," he naively predicted, "will give place to peace and order and the reign of law." Yet he was uneasy when in Bombay he saw a servant struck in the same way his father had cuffed the family's slave Lewis back in Hannibal, "for trifling little blunders and awkwardnesses." Generally, he tried to smooth over the prickly problem of human aggression on the world stage by reasoning that "no tribe, howsoever insignificant, and no nation, howsoever mighty, occupies a foot of land that was not [initially] stolen."[6] This of course had been the point of condemning landed aristocracy in *A Connecticut Yankee*—that the victorious thugs of one generation became the kings and queens of the next. Now, however, he was abroad on British soil and in anxious need of lecture receipts, so he silenced his criticisms even as he stored up impressions that he would later use to condemn what he saw on this trip across the British Empire.

He finished his initial tour of Australia by the end of October, when he went first to Hobart in Tasmania and then to New Zealand to spend the next six weeks giving lectures. "We are having a darling time in Australasia—all three of us," he told his nephew Sam Moffett. "We don't seem to be in a foreign land, we seem to be at home." He was starting to enjoy lecturing again. Twain spoke of the labor problems in the United States and of the "negro problem, for which he frankly professed himself unable to see a solution," according to at least one interviewer. He was less optimistic about his own country's problems, it appears, than he was about those of the British Empire. This may have been because he was wary of engaging in the kind of facile analysis that European travel writers had often produced after visiting the United States.[7]

The Clemens trio spent Christmas in Melbourne and New Year's Day in Adelaide, where they embarked on the *Oceana* for the long voyage to Sri Lanka. By January 18 they were in Bombay. Twain's three "At Homes" in the city attracted large audiences. In Delhi an Englishman who had built a mosque for his harem and an English church for himself underscored the oil-and-water mix of the English and Indian cultures. "That kind of a man," Twain wrote in *Following the Equator,* "will arrive, somewhere." When they finally reached South Africa in early May 1896, Livy and Clara remained in Durban while Sam toured various towns. He told Rogers, to whom he had been sending lecture receipts to be applied to his debt, that he actually regretted seeing his tour come to an end: "I would like to bum around these interesting countries another year and talk." In early July he was reunited with his wife and daughter in Port Elizabeth. From there he congratulated Rogers on his recent marriage (his first wife had died not long after the dedication of the Fairhaven courthouse in 1894). He thought to cable his congratulations, but hesitated for fear that his telegram might arrive "in the midst of mourning for some bereavement." (The same message in a letter wasn't as likely to signal urgency and risk being opened and read during "mourning for some bereavement.") This empathic anxiety, however, proved ominous. "About the time this [letter] reaches you," he told Rogers, "we shall be cabling Susy and Jean to come over to England."[8]

He was especially anxious to see Susy because that winter she had suffered another bout of bronchitis. Her meningitis that summer may have been the indirect or delayed result of her cold, for the disease sometimes occurs when bacteria from an upper respiratory infection enter the bloodstream and infect the meninges. Thinking her poor health mainly psychosomatic, her father urged her to engage in mental healing. He was "perfectly certain," he told her, that such things as colds and carbuncles came "from a diseased mind, and that your mental science could drive them away." He closed with the phrase "From him who loves you." That spring he had to console Frank Whitmore on the death of his son.[9]

There is a pall that hangs over the book he wrote about this round-the-world lecture tour. *Following the Equator* is a pensive, even brooding work in which every significant human activity, except for the author's recollections, is clearly in the past and done for. It signals the end of the literary life in which he had usually balanced hope against futility. The fact that this travelogue was conceived mainly as a venture to continue to pay down his debt and written so quickly (without Twain's usual interruptions) is no doubt part of the reason for its seeming numbness. In spite of Twain's invigoration at the end of the tour, his record of it finds him in a state of psychological collapse. Two years after its publication, he told Howells: "I wrote my last travel-book in hell; but I let on, the best I could, that it was an excursion through heaven. Some day I will read it, & if its lying cheerfulness fools me, then I shall believe it fooled the reader. How I did loathe that journey around the world!"[10]

He concluded his book by describing the much-needed rest the family trio got on the voyage to England. "I seemed," he wrote, "to have been lecturing a thousand years, though it was only a twelvemonth." Yet he expressed pride in having made such a long trip, even if he didn't recall having enjoyed delivering most of the lectures. "It seemed a fine and large thing to have accomplished—the circumnavigation of this great globe in that little time," he wrote. Then the writer who came in and went out (though not quite) with Halley's Comet also commented on a report that "another great body of light had flamed up in the remoteness of space which was traveling at a gait which would enable it to do all that I had done in *a minute and a half*." "Human pride is not worth while," he wrote in the last sentence of *Following the Equator*: "there is always something lying in wait to take the wind out of it."[11]

The anxious parents sent that cable to retrieve Susy and Jean as soon as they arrived in Southampton at the beginning of August. Nervous about their long-awaited family reunion, Livy wanted to make sure she, Clara, and her husband were safely on land themselves before beckoning their two daughters across the sea. But not long after signaling the girls to join them, Twain reported in a letter to Pond on August 10: "Susy & Jean are not on their way hither, we do not yet know why." Not yet worried or alarmed, they took up quarters in the Highfield House in Guildford about an hour outside of London while they looked for a quiet house in the country where Twain could write his book. When the news finally came that Susy was ill, her condition was described as serious but not life threatening. "To-day," he told a friend in London, "we are troubled a little by news that our eldest daughter is ill in America. We cannot all get away immediately, but Mrs. Clemens & Clara will sail to-morrow & I shall follow 3 days later if the cablegrams do not improve meantime." On August 18, the day Susy died in Hartford, Twain received a cable that said his daughter was improving. He decided to postpone his trip in the hope that Livy would find Susy well enough along the road to recovery to bring her back to England in another month or so.[12]

This brief respite was shattered when he learned later that day that his daughter had died—"released" as her aunt and uncle said in their cable. Much as he had feared when writing to congratulate Rogers on his remarriage, tragedy had intervened between the sending and the receipt of his good tidings. Livy and Clara were still aboard the SS *Paris* on their way to America and not aware of what awaited them there. Twain began the first of what became a long series of letters to his wife in which he agonized over their loss. "Oh, my heart-broken darling," he wrote her on August 19, "no, not heart-broken yet, for you still do not know—but what tidings are in store for you! What a bitter world, what a shameful world it is." He cabled Dr. Rice to be on hand when their ship reached New York and to have all other friends and family kept out of sight, "for if you saw them on the dock," he told his wife in yet another letter that she would read after she learned of her daughter's death, "you would *know;* and you would swoon before Rice could get to you to help you."[13]

Dr. Rice joined the ship at quarantine, but would be too late to carry out this humane plan, for the terrible news had reached Clara and Livy the day before the ship docked. "On my way to the saloon for letters," Clara remembered, "I was told the captain wished to speak to me. . . . He handed me a newspaper with great headlines: 'MARK TWAIN'S ELDEST DAUGHTER DIES OF SPINAL MENINGITIS.' There was much more, but I could not see the letters. The world stood still. All sounds, all movements ceased. Susy was dead. How could I tell Mother? I went to her stateroom. Nothing was said. A deadly pallor spread over her face and then came a bursting cry, 'I don't believe it!' And we never did believe it."[14]

46 Mark Twain's Daughter

Olivia Susan Clemens died in the house in which she grew up. "Susy died at *home,*" Twain reminded Twichell, who had been on hand in Hartford when the end came. "She had that privilege." That winter when Susy caught her cold, she also became restless and nervous, perhaps tired of the isolation of Quarry Farm in Elmira. She had been "commanded" by her singing teachers in Europe "to live on a hill, . . . valleys being forbidden—and gather vigor of body" so that she could "go back to Paris and prepare for the stage (opera)." Her voice, they told her, "was competent for the part of Elsa and Elizabeth in Lohengrin and Tannhäuser." She went to Hartford to see old friends, staying at the Nook Farm home of Charles Dudley Warner and practicing her singing. By the summer, Katy Leary had traveled there to be ready to collect Susy and Jean, who had come separately to Hartford, for their voyage to England and the long-awaited family reunion.[1]

Twain had been having trouble with the first tenant of his Hartford house, so it evidently lay empty but fully furnished for at least part of that summer. Although Susy was staying at the Warners', she practiced her singing in the family home. When she became ill, the doctor advised Katy to move her into the Farmington Avenue mansion, and that is where Mark Twain's eldest daughter spent her final days. The doctor first diagnosed her illness as not very serious, then pronounced it meningitis, in the middle of what Paine describes as "that hot, terrible August of 1896." Dazed and confused, Susy roamed the Farmington Avenue house, dwelling on its familiar surroundings. At one point, Twain recorded in his journal, "she found a dress of her mother's hanging in a closet and thought it was her mother's effigy or specter, and so thought she was dead, and kissed it and broke down and cried." During her wanderings, she repeated, "It is because I am Mark Twain's daughter." "In the burning heat of those final days in Hartford," Twain recorded in Paine's edition of the notebooks, "she would walk to the window or lie on the couch in her fever and delirium, and when the cars went by would say: 'Up go the trolley cars for Mark Twain's daughter. Down go the trolley cars for Mark Twain's daughter.' This was no more than a day or two before the end." In her hallucinations, she imagined that she was the companion of a famous Parisian opera singer, a woman who, when she died sixty years earlier, had not been much older than Susy herself.[2]

Susy was twenty-four at the time of her death. The question remains as to what or who she might have become, whether she would have survived the burden of being "Mark Twain's daughter." "It kills me to think of the books that Susy would have written, and that I shall never read now," Twain told Rogers in the wake of his terrible loss. "This family has lost its prodigy." Ever since her early teens, when she began the biography of her famous father, it was clear that she was the most promising of the three girls. In a stream of letters to his wife, he rehearsed the misery of their loss. Noting that he possessed "no letter that Susy wrote me," he told Livy that he had "never wholly ceased to hope that some day Susy would take up my biography again. That is, I kept up a vague hope that she might take to making occasional notes and that my death would bring back the lost interest in the matter & that she would then write the book."[3] (Such a book would have to wait until 1931, when his only surviving daughter, Clara, published *My Father, Mark Twain.*)

Following the cue of her mother, Susy was said to have preferred the more serious Mark Twain to the humorist, but if so, she also maintained an appreciation for works like *Huckleberry Finn* and *Pudd'nhead Wilson.* While living in Florence and reading the romantic poets, she formed an acquaintance with the daughter of John Addington Symonds, the Victorian writer who bluntly asked Walt Whitman whether his "Calamus" poems about male friendship weren't tinged with the theme of homosexuality (Whitman dodged the question by claiming paternity of six illegitimate children). Among this Oxford star and closeted gay man's books was a biography of Shelley, whom Susy had found naughty but "adorable." Symonds's most distinguished work was the seven-volume *Renaissance in Italy* (1875–86), a study with which Susy might well have been acquainted. In Florence she was also an admirer and acquaintance of Vernon Lee, the writer of supernatural tales who was in turn a disciple of Pater and the cause of art for art's sake. Susy was delighted to have met Oscar Wilde, the aesthetic movement's most famous literary product, in 1891 while her family was vacationing in Ouchy, Switzerland. She described for her Bryn Mawr friend his "soft brown [suit] with a pale pink flowered vest, a blue necktie and some strange picturesque white flower in his button hole."[4] If Bryn Mawr awakened her intellectually, Florence, where other artists influenced by the symbolism and imagery of the Pre-Raphaelites abounded, nurtured her initial development into an aesthete for whom homoerotic or free love was, at least, an option.

That young woman, of course, was not the Susy whom Mark Twain was trying to remember in his letters, journals, and autobiography. Nor was she the genteel daughter of a proper Victorian mother who supposedly preferred the highbrow writings of Samuel Langhorne Clemens to those of Mark Twain, an image of Susy first put in place by Paine with the strong encouragement of Clara Clemens Gabrilowitsch. In the wake of Susy's death, her father "read her private writings" (including the letters of Louise Brownell, which her parents very likely burned, since they have not been found) and must have been dismayed by the secret change she had undergone while living abroad in Florence and Paris. "Bryn Mawr began it," her father told himself. "It was there that her health was undermined."[5] Yet there is no evidence that it was her health that changed at Bryn Mawr; it was her point of view, her concept of herself as no longer Mark Twain's daughter or "Susy," but Olivia Susan Clemens. Ill as she was in her final days in the Hartford mansion, there is something deeply suggestive in her delirious refrain about the trolley cars' obedience to "Mark Twain's daughter." Twain sensed something had changed as soon as she left for Bryn Mawr and so found any excuse to visit her there. He loved her as a daughter, but he didn't want to lose her to anyone else or anything else. That is why he kept hoping she would regain her interest in finishing his biography, even if he had to die to get her to do it. And this is why in 1906 he published in the *North American Review,* within selections from his autobiography, excerpts of what she *had* written.

Susy's biography of her father was more than nineteen thousand words—an extensive narrative for someone only thirteen years old. It breaks off in midstream, but what there is of it is a clearly focused chronicle. She was a precocious girl who, if we can believe her father, pondered the mysteries of the human condition as if she were an adult. As a child, he recalled, she was impressed and perplexed by the cyclical nature of existence. As a child of eight, she decided to stop praying. When asked why by her mother, she replied that the Indians had prayed to more than one god, "but now we know they were wrong. By and by it can turn out that we are wrong. So now I only pray that there may be a God and a heaven—or something better." Later on she wanted to know about the law of proportions; that is to say, how we discriminate between something deemed tragic and the sad but merely trivial things in life.[6] While Twain may well have been projecting his own theory of tragedy onto his memories of his daughter (the law of proportions comes up in "The Mysterious Stranger" manuscripts), it seems impossible that he was creating such recollections out of whole cloth. The fact alone that her parents sent her to a genuine college at a time when the women's rights movement was growing is itself significant. Even in the nineteenth century, Bryn Mawr wasn't simply a finishing school.

Twain blamed himself for his daughter's death as he had for the deaths of his brother and his only son. If he had not so foolishly gotten himself into business and then into such debt, the family would never have been forced to wander abroad for so many years; he wouldn't have had to undertake the lecture tour around the world; and they wouldn't have separated themselves from their daughter for a year before her death. Livy at least saw Susy in her coffin when she lay in state in the Langdon house before being buried in Elmira. Twain had to imagine it, which he did most vividly. "I seem to see her in her coffin," he told his wife. "I do not know in which room. In the library, I hope; for there she and Ben [Clara] & I mostly played when we were children together & happy."[7]

He also blamed God for the "ghastly tragedy" of Susy's early death. "How cruel it was; how exactly & precisely it was planned; & how remorselessly every detail of the dispensation was carried out," he told Howells, whose own daughter Winifred had died tragically in 1889. "Susy stood on the platform in Elmira at half past ten on the 14th of July, 1895, in the glare of the electric lights, waving her good-byes as our train moved westward on the long trip. . . . One year, one month, & one week later, Livy & Clara had completed the circuit of the globe, arriving at Elmira at the same hour in the evening, by the same train & *in the same car*—& Susy was there to meet them—lying white & fair in her coffin in the house she was born in."[8] This anger was part of the normal grieving process, of course, but the humorist in Twain could not help feeling battered by the incongruity of the tragedy. Another mysterious stranger, death, had come to town unexpectedly and turned the tables. Twain's pessimism, certainly enhanced by his worshipped daughter's death, simply acknowledged the cosmic scheme within and for which humor existed in the first place. Humor was finally all we had. Even Emerson had seen it in "The Comic." When anyone gets out of harmony with nature—that is, expects a world without death, even in the wildest reaches of his imagination—he inevitably becomes the object of humor and then of pity.

Livy returned to England with two daughters instead of three at the end of August. By the 11th of September the family had moved from Guildford to London—at 23 Tedworth Square, Chelsea, for $1,350 a year—"not to live in public there, but to hide from men for a time & let the wounds heal," he told Whitmore, who was again trying to rent the Hartford house for the Clemenses. He would write *Following the Equator* in the silence of Susy's permanent disappearance. He would not lecture anywhere in the coming year. He had expected to lecture in Britain that fall and perhaps in the United States in the spring, he told Orion and Mollie, "but the unspeakable bereavement . . . has necessarily quenched all desire to continue on the platform."[9] To keep safely hidden from the public eye during their yearlong bereavement, they gave out only the address of his British publisher, Chatto and Windus, except to close friends and family.

It was in the fall of 1894 that fourteen-year-old Helen Keller came into Twain's life. Now sixteen, this already celebrated deaf and blind woman was hoping to attend Radcliffe College and in need of money for that purpose. Prompted by the wife of Laurence E. Hutton, then at *Harper's Monthly,* Twain urged Rogers to help with Keller's support. (Rogers paid for all of Keller's time at Radcliffe.) Perhaps Clemens was moved in part by the fresh memory of his own daughter, also a college student, who had gone blind shortly before her death. "We have lost her, & our life is bitter," he told his wife on November 27, 1896, her fifty-first birthday: "We may find her again—let us not despair of it." In the meantime he began not to blame himself alone for the loss of Susy, but also Charley Webster, now more than five years moldering in his grave. Sam had not written his sister Pamela as often as he wrote Orion, he explained, for the letters he did write he often tore up before sending. "I was not able to keep Webster out of them, the primal cause of Susy's death & my ruin." Webster, he now insisted of the individual he had once so trusted with his business interests, had "no likeable qualities," unlike his successor Hall. He was "all dog." As time went on, he was even willing to expand the blame for Susy's death to the Warners and other neighbors in Hartford at the time.[10]

As he worked away on *Following the Equator* in the winter of 1897, his grief got heavier. "You have seen our whole voyage," he told Twichell. "You have seen us go to sea, a cloud of sail, & the flag at the peak; & you see us now, chartless, adrift—derelicts; battered, water-logged, our sails a ruck of rags, our pride gone. For it *is* gone." He hadn't fully realized that Susy was such an integral part of the rest of them. "I did not know," he told his old friend and confidant, "that she could go away, & take our lives with her, yet leave our dull bodies behind. And I did not know what she was."[11] In fact, he didn't know what she had become. At least until she got to Bryn Mawr, she was always "Susy," her diminutive nickname reinforcing the image of his darling teenage biographer and prenubile philosopher. There is no record whatever of either of her parents entertaining the prospect of her marriage, even though she was twenty-four—almost exactly the same age at which her mother married. And this was in a Victorian era in which the first and last question asked of any unmarried woman—the matter recently dramatized in Henry James's *Portrait of a Lady*—was, Whom would she marry? Instead, Twain kept rehearsing the parent-child scenario, never forgetting that his daughter's last word was "Mamma."

With the loss of the first daughter, the parents were keeping firm watch on the second (and the third, Jean, whose epilepsy would soon become still more apparent). When Clara took a fall at a London gymnasium in June, they canceled an engagement with James R. Clemens, a distant relative (father of Cyril Clemens, tireless promoter and amateur scholar of Mark Twain in the twentieth century who before long turned out to be a pest). When Clara decided to continue her piano training under the famed Theodor Leschetizky in Vienna, the whole family moved there with her that autumn, following a vacation in Switzerland. Sam and Livy were determined never again to separate themselves from either one of their remaining daughters. With Susy gone, the feeling was that anything could happen at any time. Telling his old friend Frank Fuller of his plans, Clemens announced that he had recently finished his new book—"and just in time, too, for by reports I am now dead. Posthumous works always sell better than others." When James Ross Clemens had recently been ill, the jumpy press leaped to the conclusion that Mark Twain was dying, a mistake he made famous by calling the report of his death an exaggeration. He claimed that he wasn't even trying to be funny, but it turned out to be one of his most enduring quips. The American public hadn't forgotten his financial dilemma. And a campaign to collect money to help him pay off the debt had begun at the New York *Herald*, but before it got off the ground, Livy made Sam insist that it be stopped and all money returned to the contributors. He was tempted not to stop it, for he was still feeling the fatigue of his debt, especially after going nearly all around the world to extinguish it, only to learn that lecture receipts were only enough to pay off a third.[12]

The success of *Following the Equator* (it sold thirty thousand copies within three months of its publication), along with wise investments made for the Clemenses by Henry Rogers, vanquished almost all of the debt by the winter of 1898.[13] But remarkably, Rogers also had to expend some effort to keep Twain from getting *back* into debt, for the speculator in Sam Clemens was still tempted by risky investments. By then, the family was ensconced at the lush Metropole Hotel in Vienna with its balls and dinners. It would be almost another two years before they returned to America, but Twain's final phase as a writer was already taking shape. The pain of Susy's death would never go away, but it was a fainter memory by the time they finally returned home without her.

PART IV The Mysterious Stranger

47 City of Dreams

In some ways, fin de siècle Vienna became the Clemens family's sanctuary from the lingering horrors of Susy's death. For one thing, Twain knew the Germanic culture better than most Americans and so, as America's most famous living writer, fit easily and even comfortably into the social fabric of the city. Having lived for extended periods in Heidelberg, Bad Nauheim, Munich, Berlin, and Weggis, Switzerland, he could understand and speak some German, though still with considerable discomfort. This center of the Austro-Hungarian Empire offered many distractions from the family's grief, although Twain in his letters and journals often wrote about it. To ward off the depression that accompanied it, he threw himself into his work, starting any number of literary projects, including the first two versions of "The Mysterious Stranger" and the small masterpiece that came almost directly out of the city's sometimes violent politics, "The Man That Corrupted Hadleyburg." After a few months in the Hapsburg capital, he told his friend Howells that he couldn't possibly survive "without work now. I bury myself in it up to the ears." It was mainly, he added, to shake off "the deadness which invaded me when Susy died."[1] No stoic when it came to the death of a loved one, he seldom kept these feelings to himself.

In a fine study, Carl Dolmetsch has painted in the background and most of the details for this important period.[2] The Clemenses had come to Vienna so that Clara might study piano with the famous Leschetizky. As Clara remembered it more than thirty years later, the family did not fully immerse themselves in the diversions of Vienna until Herr

Leschetizky committed himself to allowing Clara to become one of his pupils. She and her father went to the master's home at Karl Ludwig Strasse 42, where Clara made a plea in German and played the piano (she was more fluent at both than her father). "Poor Father," she recalled, "had to listen to a long speech addressed by Leschetitzky to him explaining what I needed in the way of technical preparation before he could accept me as a pupil for lessons with him," mainly lessons from one of Leschetizky's more senior pupils—his normal method of conducting his large classes of ten students or more. Clara saw her father's face "droop more and more as this German cataclysm fell upon him," until the other master in the room finally asked "for just one bit of information—were we to remain in Vienna?"[3] With that question answered in the affirmative, the last phase of Mark Twain's literary career began.

Clara never rose to the level of concert pianist, but she clearly had musical talent and at her best could skillfully play Chopin nocturnes, distinctly above the amateur level. She and Susy had been playing the piano since they were six or seven years old, when their Hartford neighbor and wife of Charles Dudley Warner first gave them lessons. After growing up on concerts and musicales in Hartford, it was almost natural for Clara to want to come to the musical capital of the world (even though that reputation for Vienna was coming to an end) to study with a master who had taught such famous artists as Paderewski and Schnabel. Another pupil, not nearly so famous but a musical prodigy to be sure, was Ossip Gabrilowitsch, Clara's future husband, known at the height of his career as "the poet of the piano." He later conducted the Detroit Symphony for eighteen years until his death from cancer in 1936. Clara met him formally at a dinner party her parents gave in order to bring together Charley Langdon, who was visiting with his family from Elmira, and Theodor Leschetizky, who was central to the social life of Vienna.[4]

The Clemenses were ensconced in the Hotel Metropole in the center of Vienna. They had initially tried for a furnished house, but the hotel, in its desire to advertise itself as the home-away-from-home of the famous Mark Twain, made him a very generous offer. For around $440 a month, they lived in an upper-floor suite that contained a parlor, a music room, a study, and four bedrooms. Normally such accommodations would have cost almost twice as much. The only drawback, as Twain told Rogers, was the bathroom, which was "50 yards distant, and as I was often tired and they didn't allow bicycles in the halls, I didn't take any baths that year. I was never so healthy and warm in my life." His joking aside, this may be the first indication of Twain's fascination at the end of the century with alternative medicine and health foods such as Plasmon, whose stock (to Rogers' chagrin) he soon began to buy. The apartment was otherwise well suited to his needs. Clara recalled how much her father wrote in it that first winter, "sometimes in bed and often pacing the floor. He walked rapidly back and forth from end to end of our long *salon* with his hands behind his back and his lips moving for half an hour at a time, and then sat down to a table and wrote."[5]

One of the first things he may have penned was "Conversations with Satan." It could have been his initial attempt at "The Mysterious Stranger" stories, one of several false starts since he had first thought of the idea two years previously in New Zealand. Earlier that year he had wondered in his journal why the world was not full of books "that scoff at the pitiful world, and the useless universe and violent, contemptible human race" and had concluded that writing such a book would amount to authorial suicide. He had a family to support, a responsibility that he felt all the more keenly in the wake of his financial problems. In the next few years he would publish a great deal of what he confessed were "potboilers." Since he couldn't afford to alienate his readers, he would write the other kinds of books—the kinds he sensed the world needed but would not accept—for his amusement only.

In "Conversations with Satan," looking down from his hotel room he spots "the figure of a slender and shapely gentleman in black coming leisurely across the empty square" in front of the hotel. The time was somewhat "past midnight," and Twain was standing before the window of his "work-room high aloft on the third floor of the hotel, and was looking down upon . . . the great vacant stone-paved square of Morzin Platz with its sleeping file of cab-horses and drivers counterfeiting the stillness and solemnity of death." "It was being whispered around," he wrote, "that Satan was in Vienna incognito." The prince of evil was dressed like an "Anglican Bishop."[6] After a brief but intriguing beginning, however, this narrative disintegrates into a boring discussion about German stoves and cigars. Twain next shifted the scene to Hannibal, but only briefly before cannibalizing what is now labeled as the "St. Petersburg Fragment" and using it as part of the first extant draft of "The Chronicle of Young Satan." Here the scene is the Austrian village of Eseldorf, and the Mysterious Stranger is Satan's nephew, who, Twain noted elsewhere, begs his uncle for more Christians to gobble up. "The Chronicle of Young Satan" is the second longest (at some sixty thousand words) of the three major versions of the story of the mysterious stranger, including the one called "No. 44, The Mysterious Stranger." This last, which is also known as the "Print Shop" version, is the longest at 523 manuscript pages. When Paine prepared a version in 1916 for Harper's, which retailed it as a children's tale, he silently bowdlerized, cut, and rewrote parts of "The Chronicle of Young Satan," grafting on to it the final chapter of "No. 44."

Vienna was working its way into Twain's literary imagination. The lure of the Viennese theater encouraged him to collaborate with the Austrian playwright Siegmund Schlesinger. Apparently, none of their collaborations was successful, and no fragments of their joint authorship survive. The experience did, however, briefly reawaken Twain's lifelong desire to become a successful dramatist. By early February 1898 he had completed a farce entitled *Is He Dead?* Based on his short story, "Is He Living or Dead?" which had appeared in *Cosmopolitan* for September 1893, it concerns the painter Jean-François Millet, who fakes his own death in order increase the value of his paintings. By August 1898 Twain was convinced that the play was best consigned to the fire. "I started in to convince myself that I could write a play or couldn't," he told Rogers. "I'm convinced. Nothing can disturb that conviction." Like *Colonel Sellers,* this play needed the skills of a better dramatist. In the case of *Is He Dead?* its production had to wait more than a century—for David Ives's embellishment, upon which the play opened on Broadway in 2007 and ran for four months.[7]

The family's social schedule was filled with dinners and recitals. Livy, probably for health reasons, limited her socializing, though she did host regular receptions in their quarters at the Metropole. Clara accompanied her father to the other events while Jean stayed home with her mother and Katy Leary, the Irish maid who had been with them for so many years in Hartford. By then Jean was indisposed, having already suffered six epileptic attacks. Her parents, as they confessed to the first Viennese neurologist they consulted, were afraid to tell her the real cause of her difficulty, saying instead that the attacks were merely ordinary fainting spells.[8] Besides going to social events, Twain also took an interest in the city's political situation, which was never dull.

As he noted in "Stirring Times in Austria," a longish essay he published in *Harper's* in March 1898, the Austro-Hungarian nation was a "patchwork quilt" of at least nineteen smaller nations or peoples who spoke different languages and held their so-called brothers of the empire at a distance and often in contempt. Twain was prompted to write his essay after witnessing a near riot in the Reichsrath on November 26, 1897. Noting that the legislators came from all walks of life and social levels—"princes, counts, barons, priests, peasants, mechanics, laborers, lawyers, judges, physicians," and so on—he concluded with this shocker: "They are religious men, they are earnest, sincere, devoted, and they hate the Jews."[9] As a result of this public comment and possibly others, Mark Twain was often mistaken for a Jew in Vienna, an identification that was exacerbated by his essay in *Harper's* for September 1898 entitled "Concerning the Jews." It was around the time of the Dreyfus Affair in Paris, about which Twain unsuccessfully proposed to write a book (even drafting its first chapter), and the anti-Semitism in Vienna was more virulent than anywhere else in Europe.

Forty years down the road, Vienna became the Austrian center for Hitler's Gestapo, which was in fact headquartered at the Hotel Metropole (blown up by a U.S. bomb in 1945). Vienna, indirectly at least, became the birthplace of the "Final Solution," in which six million European Jews perished, for it was while Hitler was working as a laborer in Vienna that the "danger of Judaism" had abruptly dawned on him. In the words of his architect and chief of armaments, "Many of the workers with whom he was thrown together had been intensely anti-Semitic." In fact, one of Hitler's principal mentors later on was Dr. Karl Lueger, who as mayor of Vienna during Twain's stay in the city engaged in anti-Semitic propaganda.[10]

Twain's defense of the Jewish people contained certain prejudices readily noticed today. Yes, he wrote, the Jew was smarter than everyone else (the central basis for hostility toward him, Twain added, not the Crucifixion), always took care of his own in need, and never required state welfare, but, because he had been systematically shut out of most professions, became the most professional at making money ("They all worship money," wrote the man who had once envisioned himself one of the richest in the world with the success of the Paige typesetter). Moreover, Twain continued, the Jew did not fully participate in the improvements of society ("When the Revolution set him free in France it was an act of grace—the grace of other people; he does not appear in it as a helper") but tended instead to be a parasite on it. Twain never used the word "parasite" in "Concerning the Jews," but this prejudicial commonplace of its day among Gentiles was implied when he wrote that few had participated in the military defense of the countries they inhabited. He was quickly challenged on this point and readily conceded it in a later postscript. In his essay he voiced some of the predictable canards against Jews. For the most part, however, such statements were overlooked because of the otherwise positive spin Twain put on the subject. These types of defenses were difficult to produce without incurring criticism. When Theodore Dreiser echoed some of the same sentiments in *his* defense of Jews during the 1930s, when anti-Semitism was turning deadly in Germany, he was roundly excoriated in the American press. (Ironically, his books had been banned in Germany because its censors thought "Dreiser" a Jewish name.)[11]

It becomes clear in Twain's essay that, to this Gentile, the Jewish people were an alien force. They were a force that he admired but did not altogether trust—the way the residents of a small Missouri town are wary of strangers—for example, David Wilson in *Pudd'nhead Wilson.* While saying that the Jew "seems to be very comfortably situated" in Viennese society, Twain wrote, he is nevertheless "substantially a foreigner wherever he may be, and even the angels dislike a foreigner." He was using the word "foreigner," he said, "in the German sense—stranger. Nearly all of us have an antipathy to a stranger, even of our own nationality."[12] Just as the Jew was a stranger in whatever country he called home, the

Mysterious Stranger was alien among humankind—with souls to be harvested on the grandest scale. Neither the Jew nor the Stranger was condemned by Twain; in fact, both were applauded for bringing more good into the world than the supposed do-gooders or reformers.

He had no prejudices against the Jew, he declared in the opening of "Concerning the Jews": "I can stand any society. All that I care to know is that a man is a human being—that is enough for me; he can't be any worse. I have no special regard for Satan [either]; but I can at least claim that I have no prejudice against him." And indeed he hadn't, ever since—as noted earlier—he had sat at his mother's knee as a boy and heard her ask, "Who prays for Satan—the one sinner that needed it most?" Ten years later, in one of his many statements that have become marketed as "Mark Twain Quotes," he told Henry W. Ruoff, another stranger, who was compiling a list of those who had most influenced the world, "Thunder is good, thunder is impressive; but it is the lightning that does the work." Ruoff had left off of his list Christ and Satan, who were the thunder and lightning of the Twain quote. In other words, Christ saved only one Christian in a hundred. Satan intimidated the other ninety-nine into heaven: "Satan's influence was worth very nearly a hundred times as much to the business as was the influence of all the rest of the Holy Family put together."[13]

By the time Twain began writing "Concerning the Jews," he had already launched "The Chronicle of Young Satan." His work and his social life were interrupted by Orion's death in Keokuk on December 11, 1897. The surviving brother added a one-time bonus of fifty dollars to the fifty he had been sending Orion and Mollie for years, even through his worst financial times. "Clara and I had started into society," he told Rogers, "and were dining and lunching and going to operas, and were getting at times cheerful once more; . . . but we are all once more under a cloud, through the death of my brother, and have resumed our former seclusion."[14] This period of confinement no doubt allowed him not only to make good progress on "Young Satan" but also begin "The Man That Corrupted Hadleyburg," about a town where there is yet another stranger.

48 Winter Fantasies

"Yes, sir, there *is* a Devil," Twain told one of his "closest friends"; "but you must not speak disrespectfully of him, for he is an uncle of mine."[1] "The Chronicle of Young Satan" is a dreamlike sequence of events. Little Satan tells the boys to call him Philip Traum, the surname being German for "dream." It seems almost intentional that the narrative, like most dreams, remains a fragment, for Twain was writing a number of them in Vienna and even just before. They were lazy recollections of his childhood in Hannibal, which had now become invested with the supernatural. In July 1897 he wrote out what amounts to an annotated list of the people, events, and social customs he remembered from Hannibal, calling the manuscript "Villagers of 1840–[5]3." Never intended for publication, it was a feat of remarkable memory and a way of collecting and organizing material for further fiction. A month later he wrote, or *began,* "Hellfire Hotchkiss," a story about a tomboy who performs a nearly miraculous rescue of a schoolmate who resembles Orion in his awkwardness. These works bled into the "St. Petersburg Fragment" and "The Chronicle of Young Satan." Twain was thrashing about, telling Frank Bliss of the American Publishing Company that he would be surprised to finish another book "within the next three years." To Rogers he announced, on November 10, 1897, the beginning of a new book (probably "The Chronicle of Young Satan"), but he added that of all the work "which I have begun since last August I have finished *not one single thing.*"[2] "The Chronicle," which he put down for an extended period at least once, breaks off suddenly.

A year earlier he had very likely been reading William James's *Principles of Psychology*—either the 1890 first edition or, more probably, the considerably shortened *Psychology: Briefer Course* (1892). He clearly did not read William James until 1896, for in 1894 he had told his wife that, while he had been visiting the Howellses in New York City, Eleanor Howells had "convinced" him that James was "right" about "hypnotism & mind-cure," the latter a remedy he then hoped would aid his daughter Susy. He ordered his own copy of James's "psychological book" while in London in 1896.[3] He may have met Sigmund Freud in the winter of 1898, whose *Interpretation of Dreams* was published in Europe a year later (though postdated 1900). When Twain gave his first public lecture in Vienna, on February 9, 1898, Freud was in the audience to hear "our old friend Mark Twain in person," as he told a colleague. Twain, doing bits and pieces from his world tour material, that night included "The First Melon I Ever Stole." Years later Freud alluded to the telling of this story in *Civilization and Its Discontents* (1930), recalling that, as Twain began the tale, he stopped and feigned doubt as to whether it *was* the first watermelon he had ever stolen.[4] It is plausible that Freud, on the brink of world fame, had a similarly direct impact on Twain, who consulted eminent physicians in Vienna about Jean and certainly could have encountered Freud in the process.

In the spring of 1897 Twain had begun writing "Which Was the Dream?" It employed his own recent life story to suggest that reality and the dream world are arbitrary and indistinguishable. The following year he started "The Great Dark," another family romance gone sour. He framed the idea in a notebook entry: "Last night [I] dreamed of a whaling cruise in a drop of water. Not by microscope, but *actually.* This would mean a reduction of the participants to a minuteness which would make them nearly invisible to God & he wouldn't be interested in them any longer."[5] Not only did this focus on tragedy in miniature anticipate "3,000 Years among the Microbes," but it also reflected the sentiments of Little Satan in his "Chronicle." While doing magic tricks for the boys Theodor Fischer (the narrator) and Seppi Wohlmeyer, Philip Traum creates clay workmen who construct a castle. When they act like humans and quarrel amongst themselves, their creator casually reaches out and crushes them, to the shock of the two boys. Subsequently, the workers cry over "the crushed and shapeless bodies" as Little Satan ignores them. "Often you would think he was talking about flies," the narrator observes.[6]

Echoing the thesis of *What Is Man?* (also begun, or recommenced, in the winter of 1898), Satan's nephew insists that man deserves everything that happens to him. This is because he is at bottom utterly selfish—and guilty because of his Moral Sense, or knowledge of right and wrong. All other animal life, characterized here by the "brute," inflicts pain innocently because it possesses no distinction between right and wrong, Little Satan tells the boys. But man with his Moral Sense does know the difference and thus inflicts "pain for the pleasure of inflicting it." With the Moral Sense, we are told, man can choose, and "in nine cases out of ten he prefers the wrong."[7] This idea, however, clashes head-on with the insistence that man lives in a deterministic world in which every move, however slight, is already planned out by God. The quandary we are left with is whether or not man is guilty in a world in which he ultimately *cannot* choose.

That same winter, in the midst of all his dreamscapes and philosophical pondering, Twain produced the one small masterpiece to emerge out of his twenty months in Vienna—"The Man That Corrupted Hadleyburg." In a town like St. Petersburg or Dawson's Landing, Hadleyburg's nineteen leading citizens wake up to the fact that they are primarily motivated by greed. Two real-life events helped to crystallize this tale for him. The first was the parliamentary riot in the Reichsrath, where—as Twain noted in "Stirring Times"—roughly nineteen different states were represented.[8] This raucous event was merely transferred to the Hadleyburg town hall. The second was the death of Orion. Edward and Mary Richards, the principal characters in the Hadleyburg story, remind us of that ever impoverished couple in Keokuk, Orion and Mollie Clemens. The stranger in the story is simply on furlough from the realm of "The Mysterious Stranger," here a vengeful adult. He is probably imagined as European, perhaps even that "slender and shapely gentleman in black" described in "Conversations with Satan," for he calls himself a foreigner "grateful to America" and he says he will soon go "back to my own country."

The mood of the story is decidedly Austrian in the formal way the characters react to one another. The town hall is draped in "festoons of flags." Its seating capacity is five hundred or more, not exactly the typical forum for a small American town like Hadleyburg. One night the stranger, who has led a dissolute life, drops off a sack of fake gold coins at the Richards household, saying that it should be given to the unknown person who helped him in a time of need when he passed through the town a year or two earlier. Since he does not know the name of this Good Samaritan, that person must identify himself by revealing what he said to the stranger when he helped him with a twenty-dollar loan ("You are far from being a bad man; go, and reform"). These words are contained in an envelope inside the sack. The stranger asks the Richardses to entrust it to the Reverend Burgess. Soon word of this visitation to a town that cherishes its reputation for honesty gets published in the local paper, and all the pre-chosen "Nineteeners" (as they are called) show up at a packed town hall, each with an envelope containing the words alleged to have been said to the stranger. In the interim the stranger has sent a second letter containing the winning phrase not only to Richards but secretly to the other eighteen leading citizens as well. One by one, at a meeting as disruptive as the one Twain witnessed in Vienna, Burgess opens the envelopes of the first eighteen to reveal the same statement and the obvious fraud.

Richards and his wife tremble in anticipation of having their envelope opened last, but Burgess mercifully stops at eighteen and later tells them that he was doing so to return a favor. Years before, Burgess had been accused of an unidentified offense, and Richards warned him just before his fellow citizens were about to ride him out of town on a rail. Actually, Richards had information to clear Burgess of the supposed crime, but he never came forward to save the clergyman's reputation. (Burgess eventually returned to the town but never recovered his congregation.) Richards has another skeleton in his closet. When the money first appeared, it was assumed that the Good Samaritan who aided the stranger was Barclay Goodson, by then deceased. A stand-in for Twain in his late cynicism, Goodson had lost a love match and remained a bachelor: "By and by [he] became a soured one and a frank despiser of the human species." All during his time in Vienna and afterward, Twain, who had lost a very special loved one in 1896, had ranted in letters to Howells and others about the worthlessness of the human race.

But, with Richards as a "friend," Goodson needed no enemies. When the object of Goodson's love died, Richards spread a rumor that the woman "carried a spoonful of negro blood in her veins." As a result of his guilty conscience, at least with regard to Burgess, Richards and his wife fear that the clergyman has somehow laid a trap for them, and both eventually pine away into their graves. No one ever is able to utter the full words of the stranger, who finally reveals that the entire affair has been a scheme to ruin the town's undeserved reputation for honesty. Appropriately, when the full statement that Goodson was alleged to have made to the stranger is revealed, we find that it advised him to reform or "you will die and go to hell or Hadleyburg—TRY AND MAKE IT THE FORMER."

Harper's Monthly paid Twain two thousand dollars for the story, which first appeared in its December 1899 issue. When he informed Rogers, who was now making more and more money for him through investments, he added that he was slightly puzzled that the magazine took the story, because "it had a sort of profane touch in the tail of it."[9] He was referring to the logo at the end of the story that quoted and distorted a line from the Lord's Prayer ("Lead us not into temptation"), but he also may have been hinting that, in publishing this story, he had in effect published the first and only version of "The Mysterious Stranger" that would see print during his lifetime, as it turned out. Hadleyburg's "foreigner" performs no magic, but he does maintain the mysterious stranger's same low opinion of the human race.

After a summer in Kaltenleutgeben, a dozen miles outside Vienna, the Clemens family rented quarters in a newer and more luxurious hotel for the following year. The Krantz, he told Rogers that summer, was "a kind of splendid Waldorf" and offered a parlor, dining room, a study, and four bedrooms at around $560 a month.[10] That fall he took another run at the story he was trying to tell in "The Mysterious Stranger." This time he shifted the action back to Hannibal and changed the point of view to the omniscient third person, producing another fragment of sixteen thousand words. In this version, he returned to Hannibal's "Schoolhouse

Hill," where his schoolmates lost their footing on the ice and "went skimming down the hill." In this version, Satan's nephew, renamed 44, appears at the school one day to perform miracles and learn things in mere seconds. More and more, it appears, Twain was becoming confined to the time of his youth, which had in previous retrospective writings seemed relatively carefree. Now, though, it was also susceptible to evil in the world. The six chapters are far inferior to either "The Chronicle of Young Satan" or "No. 44, The Mysterious Stranger," as Twain recycled incidents from the first fragment, mixed them with items from other works such as "Hellfire Hotchkiss," and even included a cameo appearance by his dead brother Orion, who "changed his principles with the moon, his politics with the weather, and his religion with his shirt."[11] (Even in death, it appears, Orion continued as the loving target of his brother's sense of humor.)

"You are the greatest man of your sort that ever lived," Howells had told his friend as Twain settled into Vienna to write these *serious* stories seething with anger toward God, "and there is no use saying anything else."[12] On the face of it, Howells's qualification ("of your sort") suggests the condescension that most Victorian era writers used when they praised humorists. The same attitude appears to color slightly his memoir *My Mark Twain* (1912). Yet humor was Twain's most important tool in becoming one of the greatest writers of American literature. "Against the assault of Laughter," Little Satan tells the boys in "Chronicle," "nothing can stand."[13] Mark Twain was at the top of his form when he used humor to expose hypocrisy and pretense. There is, for example, hardly any more moving condemnation of slavery than that found in *Adventures of Huckleberry Finn,* where its author is a magician who contrasts illusion and reality to reveal the stark truth about humanity. And there is no more original condemnation of the taboo on miscegenation than that found in *Pudd'nhead Wilson,* where practically all the principal characters are "white" but legally black. In "The Man That Corrupted Hadleyburg," nobody except Goodson and Jack Halliday is anything but ludicrous in his mendacity, and these two exceptions have developed into brooding pessimists. The only defense against becoming a cynic in Twain's world, it appears, is self-delusion and egoism.

Another project that occupied him while in Vienna was an edition of his collected works, growing to twenty-three volumes by 1903, issued by the American Publishing Company under the direction of Frank Bliss. Twain told Howells, "He is going to make a very handsome edition out of that Uniform, *very;* and moreover, he is working away with an energy which reminds me of his sainted father, who is now in hell." Frank Bliss wouldn't let go of the company's hold on Twain's earlier books. He and Harper's—before its bankruptcy (and immediate reorganization) at the end of the century—had been going back and forth on how they could jointly publish Mark Twain's works. In the end Harper's simply bought out and absorbed the American Publishing Company and its Twain list. Concluding that an author could not "successfully" introduce his own collected works, Twain suggested Howells for the job. Howells declined when Bliss would not meet his price, and Brander Matthews (BRAND-er MATT-hews!) wrote the introduction. Twain provided a short "Author's Preface," in which he staged a mock protest against touting his own works. "I cannot say without immodesty that the books have merit," he wrote. "I cannot say without immodesty that a 'Uniform Edition' will turn the nation toward high ideals & elevated thought; I cannot say without immodesty that a 'Uniform Edition' will eradicate crime, though I think it will."[14]

By the time they were well into their second year as residents of Vienna, everybody in the family but Clara thought it was time to return to the United States for good. Two barriers stood in their way. First, they wanted to live, for a time at least, in New York City before reopening the Hartford house, but Twain was afraid that they couldn't afford it. He even toyed with the possibility of dwelling in nearby Princeton, New Jersey, where his friend Laurence E. Hutton resided. Second, they were waiting for Clara to finish her piano lessons. When she abruptly abandoned them that winter, they thought even more about going home—before Clara as quickly took up singing lessons under a different teacher in Vienna. Thinking that her fingers were too short "to cover the technicalities" of the piano, she was now following the path of her dead sister, and her parents could only silently submit. By now the "dread" of leaving his "children in difficult circumstances" had subsided, but he didn't want to do anything else to interfere with their future—much in the way Little Satan suggested that the minutest change in a human being's preset life pattern could possibly mean a more severe "swindle of life."[15]

A third barrier to their overdue homecoming became more and more apparent. Jean's epilepsy was getting worse—the attacks more frequent. Nothing had helped her. None of the doctors she saw in Vienna could recommend anything more than frequent doses of potassium bromide, used as a sedative in the nineteenth century. Finally, he turned to Jonas Henrik Kellgren, whose course of "medical gymnastics" (today it would be called chiropractic) was available in both London and Sanna, Sweden, where the family went via London in August 1899. Obviously, the spinal manipulations didn't help ease or cure Jean's epilepsy, but for a time Twain convinced himself they were working. In fact, he took the course himself and raved about the sanitarium in Sanna to several close friends and even to William James, whom he urged to take the course. By the turn of the century, James had been diagnosed with a heart murmur. He didn't, however, go to Sanna for the Kellgren manipulations. The Clemens family resided in that small northern village until October and then returned to London, where Jean continued the Swedish Cure. The family clung to the hope that Kellgren's method would finally work. Their American homecoming, they feared, couldn't become a reality until it did.[16]

49 Weary Sojourners

Three months later—at century's end—they began to get impatient with Kellgren. "Livy is discouraged—& properly—about Jean's case," Sam told Sue Crane. Although his daughter's general health had clearly improved, "Livy considers that the treatment has done nothing with the disease. These people *have* cured this disease," he insisted. "We know this, or we should not meddle with it any longer; but we can't find out when Jean's cure is to begin, nor how many months or years it will take, for these idiots keep no record of their cases, & don't know any more about the phases & stages & other vital details of them than a cow might." Yet two weeks later Twain told Rogers that he thought Kellgren's course could have saved Susy from spinal meningitis. Jean's parents were lost in the maze of nineteenth-century medicine. Only forty years earlier, during the American Civil War, its hospitals had killed more soldiers than they saved. Jean's epilepsy, the Clemenses suspected, may have begun seven years earlier with a head injury she suffered as a girl.[1]

"I am tired to death of this everlasting exile," he told Rogers in the same letter. By this time, England was at war with the Boers in South Africa. He found London, then the largest city in the world, depressing "in these days of fog & rain & influenza & war." Privately, he told Howells, it was "a sordid & criminal war," and yet his head was with England, while his heart was with the Boer farmers, who had already taken charge of native South Africans on their part of the continent. Echoing the sentiment expressed in *Following the Equator,* he still subscribed to the idea that primitive peoples would be better off in colonies run by the major powers. But this heavy use of military force against the Boers revolted him and gave him second thoughts about the Spanish-American War, which had begun in 1898. After the initial American liberation of Cuba from Spain devolved into an invasion of the Philippines (the U.S. Navy needed coaling stations around the world), he told Joe Twichell at the end of January 1900: "Apparently we are not proposing to set the Filipinos free and give their islands to them; and apparently we are not proposing to hang the priests and confiscate their property. If these things are so, the war out there has no interest for me."[2] The groundwork was being laid for his anti-imperialistic writings, then just around the corner.

Reading about the British slaughter of Boer farmers and the American mistreatment of rebellious Filipinos, he soon changed his mind about the wisdom of so-called civilized powers overseeing "primitive" societies. In the summer of 1900 he wrote a letter to the London *Times* denouncing the political mischief of missionaries in China. Chinese peasants had risen up in the Boxer Rebellion (1899–1901) against foreign occupiers, slaughtering missionaries among others. "I do not know why we respect missionaries," he wrote in this letter to the editor that he wanted published anonymously ("Don't give me away, whether you print it or not," he told its editor, C. F. Moberly Bell). "Perhaps it is because they have not intruded here from Turkey or China or Polynesia to break our hearts by sapping away our children's faith & winning them to the worship of alien gods. . . . When a French nun in Hong Kong proposed to send to France for money wherewith to establish an asylum for fatherless little foundlings, . . . the Chinese authorities said, 'How kind of you to think of us—are you out of foundlings at home?'" He decided not to send the letter, but its perspective would flavor his most famous anti-imperialist essay, "To the Person Sitting in Darkness," published in the February 1901 *North American Review.* (The "person sitting in darkness" was a term taken from the Book of Matthew and used by missionaries when referring to "savage" or "uncivilized" peoples in the colonized lands. In an era of the railroad trust, the beef trust, the milk trust, and so on, he called these colonizing powers "The Blessings-of-Civilization Trust.")[3]

Mark Twain's fame was now such that it sometimes seemed to others that he would not object to any amplification of it. Several people had annoyed him by proposing to write his biography or publish letters from him they had received or found. These petitioners included Pond, Orion, Will M. Clemens, and even his nephew Sam Moffett (who subsequently published more than one biographical article on his famous uncle). Generally, Clemens said no in thunder. As early as 1887, Orion had asked permission to talk to a reporter about Sam's boyhood, even submitting a list of possible topics: "your philosophical dissatisfaction with your lack of a tail; your sleep-walking and entrance into Mrs. Ament's room; your year's schooling; your quitting at 11; your work in my office; your first writing for the paper (Jim Wolfe, the wash-pan and the broom); your going to Philadelphia at 17 . . . your swimming the river and back; ma's complaint that you broke up her scoldings by making her laugh; Pa's death." Sam replied: "I have never yet allowed an interviewer or biographer-sketcher to get out of me any circumstance of history which I thought might be worth putting some day into my *autobiography*." He added, "I hate all public mention of my private history, anyway. It is none of the public's business."[4]

Orion desisted, but not Will Clemens, who was unrelated to them ("I wonder what this bastard's real name is," Twain said to Moffett in the summer of 1900). Clemens had already published *Mark Twain: His Life and Work* in 1892 without either permission or approval from its subject. Now he proposed three more books—"The Mark Twain Story Book," "The Homes of Mark Twain," and an updated biographical sketch. "I am sorry to object," Twain wrote, hardly containing his anger. "But really I must. . . . A man's history is his own property until the grave extinguishes his ownership in it." Will Clemens, however, was not to be deterred. Saying that he observed the caveat against using any "of your copyrighted work," he insisted that Twain's speeches were fair game, "and there is no law against writing truthful facts concerning a man's life." Will Clemens promised to shelve the project for the time being, saying, "I've waited now forty years for other things—and I can add you to the collection now in storage."[5]

No doubt such assaults upon his privacy were part of what prompted

Twain to choose his authorized biographer, Albert Bigelow Paine, in 1906. Ever since Twain's day, writers and others in the limelight have abhorred the idea of having their lives laid out like a corpse to be probed and analyzed. Thirty years before his death in 1910, he might have been granted the sanctuary of a biography in the "American Men of Letters" series, but Twain was now in the twentieth century. Before it was over, one biographer would even suggest latent pedophilia. Privately, Twain told Sam Moffett that Will Clemens was a "singular tapeworm who seems to feed solely upon other people's intestines & who seems barren of any other food-supply. . . . He thinks it very harsh that after he has slaved all his life gathering sewage from my drain, I should drop ruthlessly down upon him & say 'Drop that!'" Through Rogers he instructed Colonel George Harvey, manager at Harper's after it emerged from bankruptcy that year, to watch out for any advertisements of Will Clemens's threatened books. As in the past, Mark Twain was ready to sue. Ever since he had become famous in the 1870s, there had always been somebody who wanted a piece of him.[6]

The family's winter in London was a cold one that seemed to last forever, well into the spring. They had tentatively planned to return to the sanitarium in Sanna for the summer, but changed their minds. No one but "Papa" had enjoyed the experience there. As Jean's health went up and down, they also set and canceled dates for their departure for America. He told one correspondent in June that Jean had recently "drifted into one of her bad times."[7] Because her illness confined her to the privacy of family life and kept her almost childlike, we don't know very much about this young lady who tried to keep up with her sisters but eventually focused on raising and grooming horses. Jean (a family nickname for Jane) had been named after her paternal grandmother, Jane Lampton Clemens, who had also been a skilled horseback rider in her youth.

That summer they moved once again, this time into a country house on Dollis Hill on the margins of London. "The house is on high ground in the midst of several acres of grasses & forest trees," he told Twichell, "& is wholly shut out from the world & noise."[8] It was here on the eve of his homecoming that he found again the serenity he had enjoyed in their rented villa outside Florence. That time had been productive, but now he was without Susy and Clara, who was preoccupied with her singing career. Livy continued to have her own medical ups and downs, and Jean apparently continued slowly to lose the battle against that mysterious malady called epilepsy. They recruited Sam Moffett to investigate several osteopaths in New York so that they might return to the United States before Kellgren was finished with her.

It may have been Jean's illness that drew Twain's interest back to Christian Science in general and prompted his objections to Mary Baker Eddy in particular. Susy's illness had first focused him on the movement because he put some trust in the "mind cure" that he'd heard about through Howells and his wife. The first of several essays, which would eventually be collected into a book, was "Christian Science and the Book of Mrs. Eddy." It appeared in the October 1899 issue of *Cosmopolitan*. He wasn't critical of Christian Science per se, which sought to replace medicines and surgery with exercise and massage. He did object, however, to its becoming another religion, or trust, as he put it—"the Standard Oil of the future." Borrowing from his early farce, "Aurelia's Unfortunate Young Man," the *Cosmopolitan* essay talked about a man who had fallen off a cliff and sustained an "incoherent series of compound fractures," causing him to resemble "a hat-rack." Taken to a Christian Science healer, he was told that his injuries were not real—that matter "has no existence; nothing exists but the mind."[9] Overall, the essay is droll but also somewhat tedious; it didn't bode well for his future writings. That he could publish what he himself considered potboilers demonstrates how much in demand his writing had become—just as long as it had "Mark Twain" on the title page.

"I wish I could live on offers," he told Rogers. McClure wanted him to edit his own humor magazine. The English humor magazine *Puck* offered him $10,000 a year for "one hour per week" of his editorial judgment. Pond, who had been trying to get Twain back on the lecture circuit under his auspices, offered him another $10,000 for ten nights of lecturing.[10] While initially interested in the offer from McClure, Clemens ultimately turned down all such offers. He would lecture now, if at all, only for free, because only then was it enjoyable.

As Twain approached the end of his long exile abroad, he might have looked back on the road that had led him to world fame and a complete edition of his published works up to that time (though it did not yet include "Hadleyburg"). It had started with the Jumping Frog in a story that wasn't original with him. Like Shakespeare, he had many sources, but his adaptations of the works of others were always original. Twain had come out of the oral tradition of the Old Southwest and proven to be its culmination. But that feat was just the starting point for his greatness as a writer. He turned harmless humor into profound tragedy, always reflecting his times and the nation that had nurtured him. He couldn't have started out from a less promising place than Florida, Missouri, but then Whitman was the son of a drunkard and Dreiser was the twelfth of thirteen children of impoverished parents. These democrats of our literature thrived because they drew from the nutriment of their native soil and humble beginnings. Yet all three employed the American vernacular in literary plots that were sharpened by their sense of competition with world literature. Like Whitman and Dreiser, who objected to European pretentiousness, Mark Twain couldn't have achieved the heights of his humor without the sham of English aristocracy and its American claimants.

In 1900, as he produced fodder for such magazines as *Cosmopolitan,* Twain hardly realized just how remarkable his accomplishment was. When he gave Paul Kester permission to dramatize *Tom Sawyer,* he told him: "Turn the book upside down & inside out if you want. . . . My literary vanities are dead, & nothing that I have written is sacred to me."[11] *Personal Recollections of Joan of Arc* may have been the one exception here, but generally he took a dim view of his work as having served its time and place in a writing career dedicated to making money. From now on, he would rule out not just lecturing for money, but writing literature that catered to the popular view. As he turned inward, he wrote more and more for himself. He would put much of his energy into his autobiography (admittedly written in part for money, since he was sure it would furnish his survivors with a steady income after his death). Most of what he would write but decline to publish would attempt to be directly autobiographical.

Having made arrangements for an osteopath to care for Jean in New York, and receiving Kellgren's release certifying that she was well enough to leave his care, the Clemenses booked passage on the steamer *Minnehaha,* where they secured "promenade quarters." Their ship departed on October 6 and arrived in New York on October 15. They planned to stop at the Everett House for a week or so while they looked for a furnished house in what had become the second-largest city in the world.

50 Exile's Return

The America to which Mark Twain returned was changing as he stepped into the twentieth century. The old assumptions about principle and decency and an ordered universe were giving way ever so steadily to the pragmatic view of a relativistic universe in which the weaker members of the old Social Darwinist world were now seen as cosmic if not yet social victims. The first month of Twain's homecoming saw the publication of Dreiser's *Sister Carrie,* a tale about commonplace people committing unprincipled acts and mostly getting away with it. Howells, who had encouraged other literary naturalists such as Stephen Crane and Frank Norris, flatly told Dreiser that he didn't like *Sister Carrie.* The reason: while Crane's Maggie of *Maggie, A Girl of the Streets* (1893) and Norris's Trina in *McTeague* (1899) are ultimately punished for their behavior, Dreiser's Carrie is not. Her lover Hurstwood dies in a flophouse in the Bowery, but she is spared and even elevated essentially by chance. Dreiser's novel was the harbinger of the twentieth century, a world in which human beings are like leaves in the wind, blown this way or that for no particular reason and according to no particular plan. Just before he left England, Twain wrote in his notebook: "The 20th Century is a stranger to me—I wish it well but my heart is all for my own century. I took 65 years of it, just on a risk, but if I had known as much about it as I know now I would have taken the whole of it."[1]

The Clemens family spent its first few weeks, as it turned out, at the Hotel Earlington on West 27th Street before moving into a furnished house at 14 West 10th Street. (The rental was arranged with the help of Frank Doubleday, whose firm, after accepting Dreiser's *Sister Carrie* without fully consulting its president, was now arranging for its suppression even as it reluctantly published the novel to meet the terms of its contract.) Before the Clemenses could make that move, however, they were summoned to Hartford for the memorial service for Charles Dudley Warner, who had died on October 20, 1900. "The Monday Evening Club," Twain told the Hartford *Courant,* was "assembling in the cemetery," so many of his fellow Nook Farmers had already passed away.[2] He told a reporter present at the wake that his family soon hoped to return to their home, but seeing it once more in the context of another death, the remaining members of the Clemens family presumably decided then and there that they could never return home to Hartford again.

But Hartford wasn't the only home Twain couldn't return to. He had also lost his literary home through an exhaustive series of fragmentary works that would characterize almost the rest of his writing life. In its stead he had now found politics and become an outspoken critic of U.S. foreign policy in the Philippines and of imperialism in general. All the criticism of the human race that had been bottled up in his earlier works now manifested itself in his political harangues in the press. Twain was aghast when Twichell tried to discourage him from publishing "To the Person Sitting in Darkness." "*I* can't understand it!" he told this old and dear friend, the man who officiated at his wedding, who had been his companion for six weeks during the European romp that became the basis for *A Tramp Abroad,* the man who would preside at his funeral. "If you teach your people, as you teach me, to hide their opinions when they believe the flag is being abused and dishonored, . . . how do you answer for it to your conscience?" Livy, too, was apparently uncomfortable with his speaking out, seeing it as simply an extension of the venom she found in the stories of "The Mysterious Stranger." "I've often tried to read it to Livy," he told Twichell, "but she won't have it; it makes her melancholy."[3]

We know that there was a direct connection between the theme of "The Chronicle of Young Satan," which Twain must have gone back to after coming home, and "To the Person Sitting in Darkness." While Little Satan is telling the boys the future, he states that "two centuries from now it will be recognized that all the competent killers are Christian;

then the pagan world will go to school to the Christians: not to acquire his religion, but his guns. The Turk and the Chinaman will buy those, to kill missionaries and converts with." In the essay, he refers to the severe indemnities that Germany demanded of China after the Kaiser had "lost a couple of missionaries in a riot in Shantung." "The Kaiser's claim was paid [$100,000 for every dead missionary, twelve miles of territory, and the construction of a Christian church]; yet it was bad play, for it could not fail to have an evil effect upon Persons Sitting in Darkness." Either this particular essay or those that followed in its wake inspired Livy to join Twichell in trying to moderate, if not silence, his public anger. Twain had published "To My Missionary Critics" in the April number of the *North American Review* in response to public criticism, including the New York *Times'* characterization of his protesting as "the sour visage of an austere moralist."

An angry letter he evidently proposed to publish about a New York writer who had offended him (the details of which have been lost to history) may have triggered Livy's admonition, but her cautionary note to him clearly had a broader application. "Why don't you let the better side of you work?" she pleaded. "Your present attitude will do more harm than good. You go too far, much too far in all you say, & if you write in the same way as you have in this letter people forget the cause for it & remember only the hateful manner in which it was said. . . . There is great & noble work being done, why not sometimes recognize that? Why always dwell on the evil until those who live beside you are crushed to the earth & you seem almost like a monomaniac." Livy dearly loved the man she still called her "Youth," but she hoped, she said, that he would heed her words.[4]

In looking back today on the subsequent century or more of U.S. foreign policy involving protracted combat operations in such places as Vietnam and Iraq, it is not implausible to think that Mark Twain, with those essays and other anti-imperialistic writings, would today be nominated for a Nobel Peace Prize, for he was clearly placing his reputation on the line when he wrote his political pieces that still possess historical insights. Admittedly, he felt the majority of the American people agreed with him, in spite of the carping from the press and the attack from the

American Board of Commissioners for Foreign Missions following the appearance of "To the Person Sitting in Darkness." His friend Howells, who lived nearby at 115 East 16th Street, was earning his own reputation as an anti-imperialist through polemical essays in the "Editor's Easy Chair" of *Harper's* and in the *North American Review.*[5] One of the reasons Twain may have pulled no punches in his condemnation of imperialism at home and abroad was that he was feeling more and more solvent financially. He faltered, however, when it came to the home front—his old home in the South. As noted earlier, when he thought to publish "The United States of Lyncherdom" in 1901, in the middle of an era in which the first generation of blacks born and raised outside the confines of slavery were being murdered by the Ku Klux Klan, he was quickly talked out of it for fear of alienating his southern readership.[6]

This self-censorship extended to other moral questions less compelling. Twain speaks in his autobiography of counseling a British writer who "by the time this chapter reaches print . . . may be less well known to the world than she is now." Elinor Glyn (1864–1943) became a pioneer in producing women's erotic fiction for the mass market. At the time of their meeting, she proposed a novel whose "unstated argument . . . is that the laws of Nature are paramount and properly take precedence [over] the interfering and impertinent restrictions obtruded upon man's life by man's statutes." Glyn sought Mark Twain's support for this post-Victorian theme in literature, but he refused. "I said we were the servants of convention; that we could not subsist, either in a savage or a civilized state, without conventions." In other words, we must "steadfastly" refuse to obey, or write about succumbing to, the laws of nature.[7] He might have added, of course, that she could have written such a novel privately, just as he had been writing but not publishing highly anti-conventional things since just before the turn of the century.

After spending the summer of 1901 in a cabin on Saranac Lake in the Adirondacks—during which Twain left the family for a few weeks in August to accompany Rogers and a number of his influential friends on a cruise on the tycoon's yacht the *Kanawha*—the family rented (for $3,000 a year) the Appleton estate in Riverdale-on-the-Hudson between 248th and 252nd streets, only twenty-five minutes by train from city center. The furnished mansion had fourteen bedrooms on three floors. Across from the beautiful Palisades, the place—Howells jokingly called it Twain's "baronial hall"—had a dining room sixty feet wide and thirty feet long. That fall he extended his political activities by speaking at a dinner sponsored by the opposition to Tammany Hall. His subsequent efforts in this vein may have helped defeat the Tammany candidate for mayor. In October he went (in person this time) to Yale for another honorary degree, this one a Doctor of Letters, which Howells also received at the same ceremony. While touring the campus, he wrote Livy, "a great crowd of students thundered the Yale cry, closing with 'M-a-r-k T-w-a-i-n. Mark *Twain!*' & I took off my hat & bowed."[8]

Before his summer on the lake had ended, Twain had written not only "The United States of Lyncherdom" (the title indicating Twain's fear for America's future international reputation because of the murderous epidemic) but also "A Double-Barreled Detective Story." A rather bland burlesque of the Sherlock Holmes stories that were then at the height of their popularity, it came out in the January and February issues of *Harper's Magazine.* Arthur Conan Doyle's most successful book in the series, *The Hound of the Baskervilles,* was then appearing in the *Strand Magazine* prior to its book publication in 1902. Doyle may have been a particular target of Twain's displeasure because he had defended the Boer War in a highly publicized pamphlet, for which he would subsequently be knighted. To write "A Double-Barreled Detective Story," Twain reached back to his silver-mining days in Nevada for a setting in which a wife beater is pursued by the woman's son, who has the gifts of a bloodhound. This theme, or "barrel," is doubled with a tale of murder in the same mining town in which Sherlock Holmes is accused and almost burned at the stake, like Joan of Arc. Twain even borrowed from his 1862 hoax, "Petrified Man." Holmes, "The Extraordinary Man," is earlier depicted in the same pensive attitude as Twain's petrified man, with his thumb on the side of his nose. The lode that brings the miners together in this detective story is called "The Consolidated Christian Science and Mary Ann." Finally, Twain even took something from his unpublished anti-lynching arsenal in a scene in which the sheriff stops the "lynching" of Sherlock Holmes. In doing so, he sounds like Colonel

Sherburn in *Huckleberry Finn* when the colonel condemns mob violence as well as any sheriff who would allow a mob to take a prisoner out of his custody. "By the statistics," he has the sheriff say, in a clear echo of "The United States of Lyncherdom," "there was a hundred and eighty-two of them drawing sneak pay in America last year." "Magazinable at 20 cents a word," as he bragged to Rogers, "A Double-Barreled Detective Story" also appeared as a twenty-thousand-word book from Harper's in 1902.[9]

One of those influential friends on the *Kanawha* that summer had been former Speaker of the House Thomas B. Reed, who had recently quit Congress after President McKinley promoted the war with Spain. "Czar" Reed, as he had been known on Capitol Hill, would have been one to whom Rogers might have appealed when the Ida Tarbell storm clouds began to gather in *McClure's Magazine.* Rogers did turn to his friend "Mark," since Twain had recently discussed business with the McClure Syndicate. "I send you a clipping from the 'World' relating to the much advertised history of the Standard Oil Company now being prepared for McClure's Magazine," Rogers told him on December 26. "I do not know whether you can be of any service in the matter, but it would be a kindness to Mr. McClure as well as myself if you could suggest to him that some care should be taken to verify statements which may be made through his magazine." Twain agreed a day later, and eventually Ms. Tarbell sat down with Rogers first at his palatial residence at 26 East 57th Street and then in a long series of meetings at his office at 26 Broadway, where Tarbell remembered that she was ushered in and out without anyone else seeing her. Evidently, their "frank" discussions, as Tarbell remembered them in a 1939 memoir, didn't lessen the impact of her success as America's first muckraker. Although Rogers defended the Standard Oil Company without appearing defensive, he was personally concerned about the lingering damage to his reputation from an 1885 indictment against him and two other Standard Oil directors for illegal business practices, even though he had been acquitted. Tarbell found the oil and gas tycoon charming at first but ultimately cunning. Their relationship broke down finally with the publication of one of the *McClure's* articles in her series. The Supreme Court dissolved the Standard Oil

Trust as an illegal monopoly in 1911. It would take another generation and the philanthropy of John D., Jr., to change the negative perception of the Rockefeller dynasty.[10]

Leaving Clara well chaperoned in Riverdale, the rest of the family set out by train for a visit to Elmira in January 1902. On the way, Jean had one of her more severe epileptic attacks. In telling Clara of the ordeal in a letter that night, Twain dwelled not on Jean's condition altogether but the "fagged out" condition of her mother as a result of the attack. This may have been the beginning of his alleged insensitivity or intolerance with regard to his youngest daughter's medical condition, whose worst moments were also social irruptions. "Jean is bad again," he reported to Rogers ten days after the attack. "It is a continuous distress—without a break these 5 years."[11] Twain dealt with his daughters best through Livy, occasionally complaining to her of Clara's talking back to him, and entrusting the supervision of Jean's care more and more to his wife's hands. Livy was the hub that held that wheel together.

Her own health continued the same up-and-down pattern. In Riverdale, Livy was plagued by gout, but otherwise she was well enough for her husband to go on another cruise on the *Kanawha* in March—this time to the Caribbean. Twain took a train to Palm Beach, where he boarded the boat with a crew of friends very similar to the group that had gone out the previous summer—Congressman Reed, Dr. Clarence Rice, Laurence Hutton, and other mutual friends of his and Rogers. He wrote affectionate letters to his wife at every port they touched, but he barely acknowledged Clara and Jean (now twenty-seven and twenty-one), except to say in one letter: "Children! make your mother's days a pleasure to her."[12] Their ship's itinerary included Key West briefly because Rogers had to consult a lawyer there. (The robber baron in him was still active, soon to be involved in the copper war in which he and his partners attempted a monopoly in that metal to match their success in oil.) Twain had touched Key West almost as briefly thirty-four years previously, when his malaria-ridden shipmates had emerged from the Nicaragua Isthmus to take another ship north to New York.

51 Homeless

While Sam was cavorting around the West Indies with Rogers, Livy bought a house with nineteen acres in Tarrytown, New York. She made the $45,000 purchase without consulting her husband, and the house wasn't even big enough for their needs. This impulsive act underscored her sense of homelessness, which had been growing ever since they left their Hartford residence in 1891. The nuclear Clemens family, which had profoundly enjoyed the Nook Farm community of close friends and neighbors for nearly twenty years, had now been on the road for nearly a decade, going from hotel to rented house or villa on a yearly, sometimes monthly, basis. Livy yearned to "settle down" again in a home of their own, as she told Frank Whitmore, who had managed the Hartford house while they were abroad. She had finally given him permission to sell that house in order to pay for the Tarrytown place as well as its planned expansion. They first listed Hartford at $75,000, a bargain, they thought, for what the land, house, and stable had cost them in 1872 (almost $140,000), not to mention the expensive interior renovations made in 1880. After several months they dropped the price to $40,000 and then to $30,000. The quaintly old-fashioned house was finally sold to Richard M. Bissell, an insurance executive, for $28,800 in the spring of 1903.[1] Much of its furniture was sold at auction at the same time.

Sam, who seemingly never expressed disapproval of anything his wife did, was hoping to sell the Hartford house to help pay for the Tarrytown place, on which only a down payment of $2,500 had thus far been made. They found the money elsewhere, including $21,000 in the Guaranty

Trust and some unknown amount in the Lincoln bank, and by selling shares of stock in Union Pacific or U.S. Steel.[2] Encouraged by his Plasmon investment abroad, he had also purchased, earlier in the year, $25,000 worth of stock in the new American Plasmon Company—an investment ultimately undercut by unscrupulous financiers. These renewed financial pressures were pushed into the background by the news that the University of Missouri in Columbia had selected its native son for an honorary LL.D. degree to be awarded at its commencement on June 4. The invitation gave Mark Twain what proved to be his final opportunity to revisit the town that had been the source of his greatest writing. He left New York on May 27 on the thirty-hour train ride to St. Louis, from where he was accompanied by a reporter upriver to Hannibal.

In a charming description of his visit, he told Livy that, after checking into his hotel, he "went & stood in the door of the old house I lived in when I whitewashed the fence 53 years ago; was photographed, with a crowd looking on." He visited the cemetery where his parents and his younger brother Henry were buried and by noon "was driven to the Presbyterian Church & sat on the platform 3½ hours listening to Decoration-Day addresses; made a speech myself." He mentioned meeting Laura Hawkins (now Frazier), the "Becky" of his boyhood infatuation, diplomatically described to his wife as a "schoolmate 62 years ago." That night he attended the high school commencement at the opera house and handed out diplomas to the sixteen graduates, making another speech. Before he closed his letter to Livy, he backed up to mention his Memorial Day speech, in the church again: "I was speaker No. 3, & when I stepped forward the entire house rose; & they applauded so heartily & kept it up so long, that when they finished I had to stand silent a long minute till I could speak without my voice breaking." Afterwards he shook hands with practically everyone in the church that day—his final day in Hannibal.[3] It and the brown river that rolled by it had together made him "Mark Twain."

Happy at the prospect of returning "home" once more, albeit ever so briefly, he hoped that some of his old friends farther out west might meet him halfway in Missouri. He wrote to the Gillis brothers, hoping for some sort of reunion in Columbia. He even sent out feelers to one of his oldest friends, Joe Goodman. "I feel old, but not often," he told his former boss. "But I am persistently old in this . . . Wine & beer do not invite me any more, & it has taken me 5 months to drink one bottle of Scotch whisky, my pet of brews." "But I smoke all day," the sixty-six-year-old confessed, "& I get up twice a-night to do the like."[4] The same day he wrote those letters—May 16, ten days before he left for St. Louis and Hannibal—Livy suffered an asthmatic attack that she and Sam viewed as a heart problem. Actually, it was both, since the coughing and difficulty of breathing during such seizures put a strain on her heart. Today, from the vantage of our smoke-free environments, scholars have already suggested that thirty years of passively inhaling her husband's cigar and pipe smoke was a part of the problem.

In June they took a cottage in York Harbor, Maine, not far from Howells's summer place on Kittery Point. Here the trouble began. Just as Twain was settling down to write—he was working on a story prophetically entitled "Was It Heaven? or Hell?"—Jean suffered another epileptic attack. This was either July 6 or 7. A month later—on August 12, 1902—Livy collapsed from another asthmatic attack that raised her pulse to an alarming rate and gave her heart palpitations. Both she and Sam thought she was dying. He blamed it in part on her worry over Jean, and that feeling perhaps began to color his relationship with his youngest daughter especially later on, with her mother gone, when she needed him the most. For now the focus was entirely on Livy, who was felled by the attack, couldn't breathe easily even after the acute phase had subsided, and was soon surrounded by doctors and specialists, who concluded that she was in a state of "nervous prostration." This led to her isolation from the world and all its possibly disturbing news. It barred Sam from seeing her at all for the next three months, and after that, all day except for three or four minutes. The only family member allowed to see her on an unlimited basis was Clara, who had been in Europe (probably to see Ossip Gabrilowitsch) but arrived home on the day of the attack. Sam and Jean simply excited the patient too much. Clara in effect replaced her mother as head of the household and went about hiring and firing nurses. She even censored her father's letters and advised him on "Was It Heaven? or Hell?"[5]

That story, whose plot he had gotten from Howells, eerily foretold the sickroom drama that actually occurred that summer and fall in York Harbor. Twin maiden aunts Hannah and Hester rigidly consider all lies sinful—black or white, regardless of whether they are told in the service of a higher good. They are tending after a niece sick with typhoid when they discover that her teenage daughter Helen has told a lie. Not knowing that their niece's ailment is contagious and potentially fatal, they force Helen to admit her sin before her bedridden mother. The mother quickly forgives her, but the daughter also becomes ill with typhoid and is taken to her own sickbed. The two aunts finally are forced to lie themselves to protect the mother from the emotional distress of knowing that her child is fatally ill. In real life, Clara had to do the same thing to protect her mother from any form of bad news; this became doubly necessary when in December 1902 Jean, who had been free of her attacks since July, came down with double pneumonia and barely survived the winter.

In the story the daughter dies, her only relief at the end being that she died hallucinating that she lay in her mother's arms even though they were in fact the arms of one of the maiden aunts. When the piece appeared in the December 1902 issue of *Harper's,* Twain received a letter from a reader who said he had gone through a strikingly similar experience, thus reinforcing Twain's long-standing belief in mental telepathy. Yet in this case, he told A.H. Tyson, he hadn't invented most of the plot, including "the dying girl's mistaking the old aunt for her mother. My own dying daughter (26 [*sic*] years old)—blind the previous 3 hours, and out of her mind, rapturously embraced the maid who had tended her from childhood, and died happy thinking she was her mother."[6]

Reflecting on Susy's loss was soon swept aside by events. In September, Livy suffered another asthmatic attack after a "strenuous" massage by the attending osteopath. Twain again feared that she was dying, telling a friend that she was now "only a shadow." The rented cottage could hardly contain the nurses and specialists attending her, and Sam often had to sleep at a next-door neighbor's house. It wasn't until October 16 that his wife could safely travel by train back to Riverdale. The family had come to York Harbor on Rogers' yacht, and there were plans in the making to return that way. But Livy was simply too weak to withstand a sea voyage of any length. Instead, Sam arranged an invalid car to be attached to one of the trains going to Hoboken, from where they took Rogers' yacht up the Hudson to the Riverdale house on October 16.[7]

Sam was again banned from the sickroom in Riverdale, and it wasn't until the end of the year that he was allowed to visit his wife at all. He told Twichell that the interview lasted exactly three minutes and fifty seconds, as timed by "the trained nurse holding the watch in her hand." Except for Clara, who ran errands into town and tried to continue her singing lessons in the city, the Riverdale house became a prison of sorts. Even though Sam wasn't allowed to see Livy, she didn't want him to go too far away from her. Jean continued her recovery from pneumonia in January 1903, when she was able to travel to the sunshine of the South, accompanied by Katy Leary, to complete her convalescence. By that time, Livy had begun to show some improvement. She was allowed to sit up in bed and see her husband for fifteen minutes once a day.[8]

He put his banishment to good use, however. Even before leaving Maine, he had gone back to "Tom Sawyer's Conspiracy," a tale begun in Vienna, in which Jim, now "a free nigger this last year and more," is almost lynched by vigilantes after Tom and Huck start a rumor about an invasion of abolitionists from across the river in Quincy, Illinois. In the wake of all the lynching at the turn of the century and Twain's unpublished essay about it, the old Hannibal days were taking on a darker hue in his mind's eye. This led him back to "The Mysterious Stranger" manuscripts not long after settling back into the Riverdale house. In November 1902 he began the version he titled "No. 44, The Mysterious Stranger," the longest and most nearly complete of the three surviving versions. In it he took the devil's nephew back to Austria, where "The Chronicle of Young Satan" takes place, but now it is 1490 instead of 1702, soon after the invention of printing and two years before Columbus discovered America. The change allowed him to integrate his early memories of working as a printer's devil in Hannibal. In a fan letter, a reader of *The Man That Corrupted Hadleyburg and Other Stories* (1900) got Twain to admit that his recent fiction could be read "between the lines." Twain added that he had nevertheless always tried to restrain himself in this respect, "to keep from breaking my wife's heart, whose contentment I value above the salvation of the human race." We now know just what he restrained in that story: his utter pessimism about the worth of the human race as exemplified in Hadleyburg's nineteen leading citizens.[9]

"The Mysterious Stranger" manuscripts—and the Hadleyburg story with its devious stranger ought to be included among them—evidently put a strain on the couple's relationship. In the fall of 1903 Sam wrote his wife that after much thought, he was "vexed to find that I more believe in the immortality of the soul than misbelieve in it. Is this inborn, instinctive, & ineradicable, indestructible? Perhaps so." Livy replied, expressing gratitude for this unprecedented confession, and wondering why he felt "vexed" at the discovery. "I should think you would be most pleased, now that you believe or do not disbelieve, that there is so much that is interesting to work for." What Livy surely never knew was what her husband penciled on the envelope of her letter, probably after her death: "In the bitterness of death it was G. W.'s chiefest solace that he had never told a lie except this one."[10]

In the December 6, 1902, issue of *Harper's Weekly,* he introduced yet another version of the mysterious stranger in "The Belated Russian Passport." It is the story of a Yale student abroad who is duped into traveling from Berlin to St. Petersburg without a passport or visa, thereby risking twenty years' incarceration in Siberia. The duper is another mysterious actor, this time a Major Jackson, whose refrain is that everybody knows him ("the very dogs know me"), including the Russian authorities who confront the student about his lack of the proper traveling credentials. In 1902, peasant unrest over land reform (which would lead to the unsuccessful 1905 revolution) was in the world news, and Twain, whose anti-czarist philosophy had been evident since *A Connecticut Yankee,* readily sided with the serfs. In the "Passport" story, the cruelty of the Russian ruling class is represented by the looming threat of imprisonment in the subfreezing wastes of Siberia. The piece was one of the seeds for "The Czar's Soliloquy," a severe condemnation of the Russian autocracy that appeared in the March 1905 issue of the *North American Review,* soon after the czar's soldiers had fired upon striking workers in St. Petersburg in January.

Twain set aside, or pigeonholed, "The Mysterious Stranger" manuscripts at regular intervals over eleven years. During those interludes, he worked on shorter pieces, including "The $30,000 Bequest." Appearing in *Harper's Weekly* for December 10, 1904, it resembles "The Man That Corrupted Hadleyburg" with a plot in which the prospect of unearned income ruins the lives of a married couple. In narrating how the imagined bequest warps their lives, Twain may have been reflecting on his own love of money and the fact that he continued to make bad investments. Besides the American Plasmon Company, whose failure would not become apparent for a few more years, he also lost another sixteen thousand dollars in the American Mechanical Cashier Company.

Harper's Weekly printed almost anything and everything Twain gave it. Indeed, he was in a position now—Howells as well—where he could publish just about whatever happened to be on his mind, so long as it did not exceed the tolerance of his audience at the dawn of the twentieth century. When he and Howells had a conversation in which they both condemned a life sentence given to a woman who drowned her baby after having it out of wedlock, Twain published "Why Not Abolish It?" in the *Harper's Weekly* of May 2, 1903. The "It" of the title was the legal age of consent, the point at which a woman could be held personally responsible for her sexual conduct. In the case being discussed, because the woman had reached the age of consent when she conceived the child, she was held responsible for killing it, even though she had been seduced and was unmarried. Arguing that the seducer should have been held responsible for the child's murder, Mark Twain was still primarily concerned with the disastrous effect seduction had on a woman's reputation and—perhaps even more important—that of her family. We will remember the harsh lecture Twain gave to Clara back in 1893 when she was left alone in a room with forty men. He closed his 1903 article by suggesting that he and his readers ("many of us") would want to sign a petition recently circulated for the girl's pardon. Back in his Buffalo days, when he scoffed at the lack of objectivity in jury trials, he may not have been so sensitive to this kind of social issue.

In December 1903 he published "A Dog's Tale," an anti-vivisectionist story with a moral that began: "My father was a St. Bernard, my mother was a collie, but I am a Presbyterian." The story is partly a reminiscence of Twain's mother, who appears as a collie presiding over "dogmatic gatherings" and impressing on the female dog, Aileen, the value of using big words without knowing what they mean. The story also echoes the Hartford days when the Clemens family was young and enjoyed its pets. Aileen, the dog narrator, is sold to a human family and separated from her mother. Her new family's state of innocence is broken by the family patriarch, who savagely kicks the canine narrator when he thinks it has attacked the baby (when in fact it has just saved the child from a burning crib). Later, this unfeeling father, a scientist, allows Aileen's puppy-child to be operated on in a cruel, though supposedly useful, optical experiment, which ultimately kills it.[11]

By the winter of 1903 Livy was getting better, but as Twain told Whitmore, the doctors had ordered her "to some suitable climate in Europe." The family decided to return to Florence, and to pay for that, they rented the Tarrytown house with an option to sell for $35,000. In this case, however, Livy's one known speculation paid off, and they made a profit, eventually selling the house for $52,000—$7,000 above their initial investment. It surely didn't come close to offsetting the loss in Hartford, but then, Twain was simply happy to be rid of the expense of keeping up the Hartford house and paying its enormous taxes. Livy, the doctors pronounced, would be ready for the transatlantic trip by October.[12]

After Livy became too weak to run the Clemens household and Clara needed to get back to her own life, the family hired Isabel V. Lyon, an attractive thirty-four-year-old spinster who lived with her mother in Hartford. She joined the Clemens establishment in November 1902, the Whitmores having recommended her. She had worked for them as a governess. Her main duties for the Clemenses were that of secretary, but after Livy's death she would eventually take over the management of the entire household. The family maintained Lyon's services and took her with them to live in their villa in Florence.

The traveling party—consisting of Sam, Livy, Clara, Jean, Katy, and nurse Margaret Sherry—boarded the steamship *Princess Irene* on October 24 bound for Naples. Because of an eye injury, Isabel Lyon followed with her mother a couple of weeks later. Howells was sorry to see his friend go back to Europe. He told his sister a few days before they left: "Clemens, I suppose, will always live at Florence, hereafter. He goes first for his wife's health, and then because he can't stand the nervous storm and stress here. He takes things intensely hard, and America is too much for him."[13]

52 A Death in Florence

Howells was right. Mark Twain expected to live several more years abroad, most likely in Florence. After the two-week voyage on the *Princess Irene* nearly exhausted Livy and set her back months in her recovery, it became clear that he would never return to America while his wife still lived. The passengers in their first-class accommodations had been "very noisy," and Livy "got but little sleep." No sooner had they reached Italy on November 5 and established themselves in the Villa Reale di Quarto than she suffered "a bad and disabling burn" from carbolic acid, commonly used then as an antiseptic and disinfectant. The very next day she had a major asthma attack—one of "those (breathless) bad turns," the first for "2 or 3 months," as Clemens wrote Rogers.[1]

November in Florence was rainy and foggy. The house was vast and lacked "the home feeling." The first floor was divided into twenty-one rooms for the Clemens party—in a house two hundred feet long. There were several large rooms on the top floor, but they were reserved for the servants, none of whom could speak English. Only Jean could converse with them. Twain found it "unspeakably awkward & harassing," but his frustration manifested itself productively in "Italian without a DICTIONARY," appearing in *Harper's Weekly* for January 1904. "It is almost a fortnight now," he wrote, "that I am domiciled in a mediæval villa in the country, a mile or two from Florence. I cannot speak the language; I am too old now to learn how, also too busy when I am busy, and too indolent when I am not; wherefore, some will imagine that I am having a dull time of it. But it is not so. The 'help' are all natives; they talk Italian to me, I answer in English; I do not understand them, they do not understand me, consequently no harm is done, and everybody is satisfied."

Like the mother collie in "A Dog's Tale," he now used words without knowing their meaning, taking them at random. "I get the word out of the morning paper. I have to use it while it is fresh, for I find that Italian words do not keep in this climate. They fade toward night, and next morning they are gone. But it is no matter; I get a new one out of the paper before breakfast, and thrill the domestics with it while it lasts." This lightheartedness belied the fact that Livy was now a permanent invalid. By December the family was back to seeing her for only five minutes a day at times. When she rallied later that month and the Italian weather (which she had come for) beckoned her outdoors, she stayed on the veranda too long and caught tonsillitis. To make matters worse, the American-born countess who was their landlady made their life a hell, shutting off phones and water at different times, because she was angry about having to live in an apartment over her stable in order to rent her villa. During the course of their stay and beyond, Twain initiated several lawsuits to seek revenge for her treatment of them.[2]

As the tension from Livy's failing health mounted in the Tuscan winter and spring of 1904, Twain kept writing, as he seems always to have done in the face of personal hardship. In May he told Rogers that he was sticking "close to the house." By then visits to Livy's room (only next door to Sam's) were restricted to those five-minute intervals again, with an exception again made for Clara, who was permitted to see her mother one hour a day. It was "deadly lonesome on the days when the pen refuses to go." "It's a whole-day thing, too," he added, "for the girls are as busy as bees, and far away in their corners of this barrack, so we are not likely to meet, except at dinner—for we all breakfast in bed, and I take no luncheon." During that time he wrote "Italian with Grammar," a follow-up to his earlier piece, much resembling his satire on the German language in *A Tramp Abroad*. Published in *Harper's Magazine* in August, it began: "I found that a person of large intelligence could read this beautiful language with considerable facility without a dictionary, but I presently found that to such a person a grammar could be of use at times. It is because, if he does not know the Were's and the Was's and the Maybe's and the Has-beens's apart, confusions and uncertainties can arise. He can get the idea that a thing is going to happen next week when the truth is that it has already happened week before last."[3]

More than the writing, it was the humor that kept him sane during this period, which was surely, except for the death of Susy, the darkest one in his life. When he returned (for an hour a day, as he told Twichell) to "The Mysterious Stranger" stories, the humor in Satan's view of the human race still came across. In one he wrote in January 1904 called "Sold to Satan," a tall, slender, and graceful Satan tells the narrator, "Do you know I have been trading with your poor pathetic race for ages, and you are the first person who has ever been intelligent enough to divine the large commercial value of my make-up." Thinking of stocks and his own investments, Twain has Satan give the narrator a physics lesson about radium, whose power fuels the furnaces of hell. Such an investment in this element will enable the narrator, in partnership with Satan, to make "a killing on the market" once radium is combined with the soon-to-be discovered polonium to give the world its first taste of radioactivity. It is as if Satan were a reflection of Twain himself in his greed to make as many fortunes (or conquests of souls) as possible. And in this way Twain was making fun of himself—of his own human weakness for grandiosity.[4] When we read the indictment in Hamlin Hill's *Mark Twain: God's Fool* (1973) of a man who was banal and acrimonious, a raging Lear in his final decade, we have to remember Twain's intuitive and conscious sense of himself as no better than any other fool claiming membership in the human race.

Not long after the Clemens family arrived in Florence, Orion's wife, Mollie, died. This news was kept from Livy, as was the death that spring of Thomas Bailey Aldrich's son. Any bad news, the doctors feared, could set off another asthmatic attack or provoke her "nervous prostration." Curiously, Twain claimed between 175 and 200 books from his brother's library and had them sent to Susan Crane's home in Elmira for safekeeping. If there was one thing he and Orion had in common, it was their intellectual interest in the world. They were both avid readers and writers. Both brothers wrote autobiographies: Orion's (what there was of it) is no longer extant, but Twain got back to his—a project he had toyed with for more than thirty years—while in Florence, dictating to Isabel Lyon.[5]

Writing his own version of the past was in large part another way to escape the pain of watching his wife grow weaker. The American Plasmon investment also became more troublesome, and by February he was confessing to Rogers that it was "one of those investments of mine that I am ashamed of." His bank account with Rogers had now dwindled to just under twenty-five thousand dollars, less that half of what it had been before he left Europe in 1900. One bright interlude in his life that winter of his discontent was Clara's debut on the concert stage in Florence, which "astonished the house—including me—with the richness and volume of her voice, and with her trained ability to handle it."[6] Clara was a talented singer as well as an accomplished pianist, but apparently her vocal chords were injured by bronchitis or some other throat ailment, for this career ultimately took her nowhere. In any case, even with great talent, it wouldn't have been easy with the iconic Mark Twain as her father. The best she could ultimately do in the face of that competition was to marry an artist.

Olivia Langdon Clemens died on June 5, 1904. She was fifty-eight years old. "We are crushed," Twain told Aldrich in one of the letters he wrote in the next day. Even though it had been obvious that she was fading, her death came as a shock to Twain and his two daughters. It sent Clara into emotional collapse and led to Jean's first attack in thirteen months. Livy had suffered a fatal heart attack at around 9:15 that evening. "She was mercifully spared the awful fate she has been dreading," he told his sister-in-law, "death by strangulation." He recalled going into her room on the night of her death to say good night. Seeing her in good spirits for the first time in a while, he was moved to do something he had seldom done since the death of Susy: "I went up stairs to the piano & broke out into the old Jubilee songs. . . . Jean came straightway & listened—she never did it before. I sang 'Sweet Low, Sweet Chariot,' & the others." Livy, he recalled, told the nurse, "'He is singing a good-night carol for me'—& almost in that moment she passed away."[7]

When he returned to her room to measure the impact of his playing on his wife, he found her sitting up in bed with her head on Katy's shoulder and the nurse on the other side. Clara and Jean were standing at the foot of the bed looking dazed. This at least was Twain's recollection in the days following the death. Many years later, when one of Clara's closest friends and a former actress, Mary Lawton, transcribed Katy Leary's memories of her service in the Clemens family, the story comes down to us a little differently. It suggests that Twain unconsciously conflated the night he played the Negro spirituals for her with the night of her death. Katy recalled that Livy died in her arms without anyone else being present in the room. She also recalled that the singing occurred "a few days before." Whatever the actual sequence of events, Twain evidently spent much of that night alone with the corpse of the woman who had meant the world to him—the woman who had married him when he so desperately needed the social grooming that Mary Fairbanks (having now also died, in 1899) had maternally applied. He would be at sea once again without Livy—for the rest of his days. "I have been down stairs to worship that dear face," he wrote Sue Crane five hours after Livy died, "& for the first time in all these long years it gave no heed."[8]

Epilogue

Mark Twain also died that early June day. Samuel Clemens would live another six years. Unfortunately, it was as an old man lost in the twentieth century. "I am tired & old," he told Howells, "I wish I were with Livy." To his brother-in-law Charley, the person who had first introduced him to his wife of thirty-four years, Clemens described himself as "a man without a country. Wherever Livy was, that was my country. And now she is gone." Clemens and his daughters returned to New York City on the *Prince Oscar* at the end of June and then to Elmira, where Livy would be buried alongside their daughter Susy and infant son, Langdon. At first the remaining Clemens trio clung together even in the absence of the force that had bound them. In preparing to leave Florence, the "trunk-packing" went on for four days—"and Livy not superintending. *That* has never happened before." Even when they had packed up to leave Riverdale in 1903, this matriarch had given "instructions from her bed."[1] After the funeral, whereupon Clemens vowed that he would never witness the lowering into the grave of another he loved, the three spent the summer of 1904 in a cottage next door to Richard Watson Gilder's property in the Berkshire Mountains not far from Lee, Massachusetts. Once Twain established a permanent residence in New York City at 21 Fifth Avenue that fall, however, the final breakup of the remaining family of Samuel Langhorne Clemens began.

One problem was that Clemens, like most fathers in the nineteenth century, had always dealt with his daughters through their mother, or certainly with her help. Another was that his world fame kept him from them, or they from him. Clara, now aged thirty, wanted to establish her own identity as a concert singer; it was hard enough to do that without a famous father always stealing the scene, as he did with a curtain speech after one of her first New England performances, or simply upstaging her by his ubiquity in the press. Clara, as noted, was a better pianist than a contralto, something her father may have come to realize in 1907 when he characterized her various singing performances as "warbling around the country." Jean, almost twenty-four, was weighed down by her medical condition. People in her condition at that time were simply considered unpleasant at best and dangerous at worst. One medical text on the disease described epileptics as "self-willed, obstinate as a rule, easily angered." Although there is a poorly documented incident of Jean's striking Katy Leary in anger, her diaries suggest that she was otherwise a gentle-minded young woman who simply wanted, first, more attention from her father and, second, a love interest of her own. Her medical condition served only to confirm for her father the bitter fact that his daughter was yet another victim of biology. "God Almighty alone is responsible for your temperament, your malady, and all your troubles and sorrows," he told Jean in 1907. "I cannot blame you for them and I do not."[2]

Still another factor in the family's disintegration was Isabel Lyon, who, after Livy's death, tried to take her place. Lyon, the daughter of a Latin and Greek professor at Columbia, had taken her widowed mother to Hartford when she went to work for the Whitmores, before joining the Clemens family in 1902. As her diaries demonstrate, she was an intelligent, observant witness to the family's doings for almost five years after Livy's death. She was also completely devoted to Clemens, whom she christened her "King" and with whom she was vaguely ambitious of becoming queen. In this dream she was probably never directly encouraged by Clemens, who said on several occasions that only one woman had ever possessed his heart, and she was now in the grave.[3] Little by little and almost accidentally, Lyon got into trouble by becoming too deeply involved in the family's affairs and thus wedging or appearing to wedge herself between Clemens and his two daughters, especially Clara, who finally forced her dismissal in 1909. Then there was the matter of whether or not Jean actually needed institutional care (both daughters were hospitalized at times, Jean for epilepsy, Clara for "nervous prostration"), but Twain scholars today still differ over whether Lyon engineered Jean's banishment to a sanitarium simply to get her out of the way. Yet that offense, if indeed she was guilty of it, was a misdemeanor compared to her interfering with Clara and her father's bank account.

The drama of Sam Clemens's life after 1904 clearly devolved into the mock-heroic of daughters and domestics. The ostensible reason for recent scholarly focus on these years is to debate the myth of Mark Twain's geriatric despair following Susy's death in 1896 and Livy's in 1904. Yet few lives end happily; most flicker down to nothing. In 1912 Paine quoted Mark Twain's facetious solution to the problem of old age, probably made in 1908: "If I had been helping the Almighty when He created man, I would have had Him begin at the other end, and start human beings with old age. How much better it would have been to start old and have all the bitterness and blindness of age in the beginning! . . . Think of looking forward to eighteen instead of eighty!"[4] That way life would end simply with the animal spirit—instead of with a body plagued by gout, carbuncles, a heart condition, and what he finally conceded was due to his heavy smoking, "permanent bronchitis." Physically and intellectually, after 1904 Clemens was no match for the domestic intrigue that enveloped him.

Ralph Ashcroft was another wildcard thrown into this mix. A native Englishman, he came to Twain's attention in 1903 as the treasurer of the American Plasmon Company, and he helped to resolve some misunderstandings between Clemens and his fellow investors. Although never a full-time employee of Clemens's, he acted as his business manager and accompanied the writer in 1907 to Oxford, where Twain received an honorary doctorate along with such greats as Auguste Rodin. Like Twain, the French sculptor was obsessed with the concept of the devil as an apt symbol of humanity and spent the greater part of his adult life working on a huge piece entitled *The Gates of Hell.* Ashcroft kept elaborate notes on Clemens's doings in England, and he made himself equally useful to him upon their return. Eventually, Ashcroft and Lyon married, perhaps as a convenience in order to continue serving Clemens or perhaps to protect each other from prosecution, for they soon got into trouble by assuming too much control over the household, persuading or tricking Clemens into signing a sweeping power of attorney that gave them legal control over all his assets. By this time, Clemens could count on twenty-five thousand a year from Harper's in addition to payments for the magazine articles he regularly published. Although Lyon probably spent more of Clemens's money than was authorized on her wardrobe and a nearby cottage in Redding, Connecticut, that he deeded to her, there is little or no evidence that either she or Ashcroft acted against Twain's best interests while in control of his finances. Clara, however, didn't see it that way, and eventually the two were dismissed amidst newspaper accounts of threats to sue and countersue.[5]

A third outsider was Albert Bigelow Paine, who became not only Clemens's authorized biographer in 1906 but also for much of that time his constant companion, especially after the writer moved to "Stormfield," the seventy-six-hundred-square-foot mansion with eighteen rooms in Redding designed as an Italian villa by Howells's son John and built for Clemens in 1908.[6] Paine, a writer for *Harper's Weekly* and later an editor at *St. Nicholas,* a children's magazine (which had published "Tom Sawyer Abroad"), had published a biography of Thomas Nast in 1904, a task that had involved asking Twain for permission to quote his letters to Nast. This biography was probably the accomplishment that most recommended him to Clemens. Paine, who also became one of Twain's frequent billiards partners, vied with Lyon for access to the "King" and to letters that she hoped to edit, but eventually he was the victor when she and Ashcroft were turned out in 1909. Significantly, there is only a single mention of Isabel Lyon in the multivolume biography Paine published in 1912. Paine also became Mark Twain's literary first executor and, along with Clara, kept watch over his documents and manuscripts for another generation, always with an eye to protecting the author's reputation so that his books and posthumous editions would continue to sell. Paine wasted no time getting out his biography, which appeared two years after Twain's death. In fact, he began researching and writing the life while his subject was still alive.

Between 1904 and 1910 Clemens merely acted out the role of Mark Twain, attending countless dinners, taking cruises on Rogers's boat, and making a series of visits to Bermuda with various friends. Practically his every move was reported in the press, and he was instantly recognized wherever he went. This became even truer after 1906, when he started wearing white suits year-round. ("I wore full evening dress of *white broadcloth*—just stunning!" he once wrote his daughter Clara.) That spring, for example, Rogers and Clemens attended a championship billiards match at Madison Square Garden between a Frenchman and an American. As the Frenchman was about to make his shot, the audience gave up a great cheer—which both puzzled and distracted the player, who ultimately lost the match. The applause had been for Mark Twain, who was then leaving the auditorium with Rogers. The *New York Times* reported that "Mark Twain saluted the spectators by throwing kisses to them, and when [the French player] saw this he waved his hand to the retiring humorist and resumed his play."[7]

There were, to be sure, periods of literary clarity during this six-year decline. He wrote "The War Prayer" in 1905 and saw it turned down by *Harper's Bazaar.* "The Czar's Soliloquy" was also written and published in 1905. And starting in 1906 Mark Twain began dictating several hundred thousand words of his "Autobiography," not completed until 1909. As for works of fiction, we know that Twain had written the first twenty-five chapters of "No. 44, The Mysterious Stranger" by the time his wife died in 1904. And we recall that he had in fact worked on chapters 8 through 25 during the winter of 1904. The first-person narrator, August Feldner, is sixteen at the time of the story (slightly older than Huck Finn), telling it while looking back as an old man of indeterminate age. And the village of Eseldorf, judging by some of its inhabitants, is based on Hannibal; indeed, several of them are drawn from people listed in "Villagers of 1840–[5]3." (The good priest, Father Peter, is based on Orion.) Twain returned to the story in the summer of 1905, just after drafting "3,000 Years among the Microbes," whose narrator is actually named Huck. Chapters 26 through 32 of this final version of "The Mysterious Stranger" are cleverly bizarre and indeed anticipate the kind of postmodern fantasies found in the fiction of, say, John Barth. These chapters include a woman transformed into a talking cat, a black minstrel show ("I's Cunnel Bludso's nigger fum Souf C'yarlina"), attacks on Mary Baker Eddy and czarist Russia, and the running of the world's history backwards, the last perhaps owing something to Dante's *Inferno.*

He returned to the manuscript in 1908 to write chapter 33, apparently intended as the penultimate chapter of the book. Here we have the parade of skeletons from the reversal of time ("Among them was the Missing Link") and this final sentence: "Then, all of a sudden 44 waved his hand and we stood in an empty and soundless world." This conclusion was his subtle condemnation of God, but he had marked yet another chapter as the "Conclusion of the Book," chapter 34, which he had written in 1904, just before Livy's death, that stands today as his parting diatribe. Everything, No. 44 tells August, is a dream. "Strange, indeed, that you should not have suspected that your universe and its contents were only dreams . . . because they are so frankly and hysterically insane—like all dreams." Insane most of all, he continues, is "a God who could make good children as easily as bad, yet preferred to make bad ones; who could have made every one of them happy, yet never made a single happy one; who made them prize their bitter life, yet stingily cut it short."[8]

Chapter 34 was indeed pessimistic, but this last literary outburst was also The Joke. Human existence was all a practical joke and a "swindle" that sent Mark Twain out of the world laughing, albeit bitterly.

In 1908—the same year in which he stopped all work on "The Mysterious Stranger"—he suffered yet another of life's swindles in the sudden death by drowning of Sam Moffett at the age of forty-seven, then at the peak of his journalistic career as editor of *Collier's Weekly.* After attending the funeral in August in New York City, Clemens felt faint from what was diagnosed as sunstroke. This loss of a nephew whose professional career he had advised was followed in 1909 by the death of Henry Rogers on May 19. As Clemens reached Grand Central Station from Connecticut on his way to visit Rogers for a few days, Clara greeted him with the sad news. Reporters were there, also. "I am inexpressibly shocked and grieved," he told them. "I do not know just where I will go."[9] The man who, he believed, had helped him more than anyone else had left him. An even bigger blow, however, soon came in the death of his youngest daughter, Jean, on the morning of Christmas Eve 1909, in what most likely turned out to be yet another drowning.

Within hours of getting the horrible news, he began what was first published in *Harper's Monthly* almost a year after his own death, in slightly expurgated form, as "The Death of Jean." Clemens had just returned from his sixth trip to Bermuda. Stormfield was filled with holiday decorations and presents arranged by Jean. That morning, Katy came to his bedroom with the sad announcement "Miss Jean is dead!" She had suffered a grand mal seizure and could not get herself out of the bathtub, where Katy found her. As had been the case with Livy, this ever-faithful and long-serving domestic was on hand to usher yet another of Sam's loved ones out of his life. He had temporarily lost Jean to a series of sanitariums for her epilepsy, but then she had returned to him and even forgiven his failure to look after her personally instead of allowing the "bitch" Lyon to sweep his daughter out of his life. "There are no words," he wrote, "to express how grateful I am that she did not meet her fate in the house of a stranger, but in the loving shelter of her own home." His memorial to her formed the closing chapter of his autobiography. He wrote it during the day of her death and into Christmas Day, visiting the body at intervals the way he had Livy's the night she died in Florence. He finished his tribute the following day as a snowstorm swirled around him. Keeping his vow after Livy's funeral never to attend another family member's burial, he decided to imagine it instead—the way he had had to imagine Susy's more than a decade earlier. He could picture the Langdon homestead in downtown Elmira with Jean's coffin standing where her mother's had, where Susy's had, where he and Livy had stood forty years earlier to be married. "How poor I am," he wrote in this final chapter of his autobiography, "who was once so rich!"[10]

Clara, who had married Ossip Gabrilowitsch on October 6, 1909, in her father's Connecticut house, had departed for Europe only weeks before her sister's death and did not return for Jean's funeral. She would soon return, however, in preparation for another. Her father would suffer a stroke that signaled the increasing danger of his angina. Yet he continued to smoke. And he continued to write. He made his last important contribution to American literature in the fall of 1909, only weeks before Jean's death. Not published until 1962, the year of Clara's death, the work was called *Letters from the Earth*.

It was the final appearance of the Mysterious Stranger, and here the mask fell away to reveal none other than Mark Twain himself. Essentially it is a satire on the whole idea of heaven and the "Bible God." In reality God is revealed to be an idler and possibly a drunk who created His "little toy-world" and then effectively abandoned it. In the narrative, Satan is banished once again by God "for a day" because of his "flexible tongue" that criticizes the Creator. Thrown out into space, Satan decides this time to investigate the earth and report back to his fellow archangels, St. Michael and St. Gabriel. "Man," Satan tells his colleagues, "is at his very very best . . . a sort of low grade nickel-plated angel," yet man blandly refers to himself as the "noblest work of God" and thinks he is God's pet. In fact, man stands in God's eyes below the housefly. There are, of course, Twain's familiar ideas that humans are machines and their despicable conduct is not their fault. Their crimes are merely an imitation of God the Father, who made humanity miserable through accidents, war, and disease.[11]

Twain, as we have seen, had been fascinated with the concept of Satan since childhood. In *Is Shakespeare Dead?*—published as a small book by Harper's in 1909, reluctantly because of its largely unoriginal argument against Shakespeare as the author of the plays—he considered what we knew about Shakespeare to be based on evidence as flimsy as that supporting the case for the existence of Satan. "When I was a Sunday-school scholar something more than sixty years ago," he wrote, "I became interested in Satan, and wanted to find out all I could about him." He eagerly began to ask questions of his teacher, who appeared reluctant to answer them, especially the one about "Eve's calmness" when confronted by a snake. He asked his teacher, quite logically, "if he had ever heard of another woman who, being approached by a serpent, would not excuse herself and break for the nearest timber."[12]

The eleven epistles in *Letters from the Earth* become increasingly angry and bitter as Mark Twain drops the mask of the devil entirely and decides, like his most famous protagonist, to "go to hell." What kept these letters from being published for so long was not the blasphemy (that became more acceptable in literature after the age of Howells and the twentieth century; even Dreiser's *Sister Carrie* was allowed back in circulation in

1907) but his writing openly about human sexuality, especially the capacity of women to desire and to endure more intercourse than men. In his obituaries, he would be celebrated as "a clean-minded man." Yet in Letter VIII he wrote that "during twenty-three days in every month (in the absence of pregnancy), from the time a woman is seven years old till she dies of old age, she is ready for action, and *competent.* As competent as the candlestick is to receive the candle." Imagine the shock his usual censors—his wife and Howells—would have felt at reading about a woman's being "ready for action." One has to ask here whether Clemens wasn't engaging in pornographic fantasies, not simply the scatological humor he had allowed himself in *1601.* His excuse for discussing such issues so frankly is that the woman's sexual drive is simply another human compulsion "commanded by the law of God," but Sam's own loneliness had to be a factor. Whatever its source, this delicate subject matter didn't suit *Letters from the Earth* any better than it did his life and other work.[13]

Samuel Langhorne Clemens died of heart failure on April 21, 1910, at six o'clock in the evening. He had suffered two distinct attacks of angina pectoris in August 1908 and June 1909 and was told to "cut" his smoking down, advice he ignored. He had, however, gladly obeyed his doctors' recommendation to avoid exercise in order to protect his "smoker's heart." The Gabrilowitsches had returned from Europe before the death. Clara—the last of his "fair fleet" of ships—was pregnant, but for some reason—perhaps because of her father's fragile condition—she didn't tell him. But in a deathbed note to her, he indicated that he may have known anyway. "Dear," he wrote in a hand almost indecipherable: "You didn't tell me, but I have found out that you—Well, I . . ." The rest is illegible.[14] He was buried in Elmira beside the rest of his family. Clara lived another fifty-two years, married twice, and died almost a pauper, borrowing money from friends. Her first husband, as noted, became the conductor of the Detroit Symphony. After he died of stomach cancer in 1936, Clara moved to Southern California and, for a time, lived comfortably off the estates of her father and late husband.

In 1944 she married Jacques Samossoud, an unemployed orchestra conductor and friend of Gabrilowitsch. He was also a gambler who eventually spent most of his wife's money at a San Diego racetrack. Clara left the enormous cache of her father's manuscripts and papers to the University of California in 1949 and, before she died in 1962, bequeathed what remained of her assets to Samossoud and (upon Samossoud's death) a second beneficiary, Dr. William E. Seiler, a racetrack associate of Samossoud's who had allegedly provided Clara with drugs.[15] In spite of all the efforts Twain made to insure that his descendents would be financially secure, much of his financial legacy was ultimately shared by two "frauds" whose behavior reminds us of nothing so much as the Duke and the King, two of Twain's most enduring characters.

Clara's daughter, Nina, like Huck Finn, was something of an orphan with parents whose busy lives may have prevented them from having a close relationship with her. During a career in which he associated professionally with such greats as Rachmaninoff and Toscanini, Gabrilowitsch was often absent from home as a guest conductor either in other American cities or abroad. Clara inevitably accompanied him, leaving Nina at home.[16] Born in August 1910, this only child, who may have shared her Russian father's melancholia, graduated from Barnard College in 1934. When Clara died, having earlier settled a one-million-dollar trust on Nina, who was therefore left out of her will, the daughter decided to sue Samossoud (who quickly settled out of court) to secure what she considered her fair share of her mother's estate. She of course had never known her grandfather, but she claimed to have read all his writings. And her grandfather, condemned to look for his grandchildren among his "Angel-fish," only suspected her imminent existence in his final days.[17] Sadly, Nina's life was anything but angelic. She became an alcoholic and a drug addict. She died four years after her mother at age fifty-five, possibly a suicide. Nina was found dead on January 16, 1966, in a Los Angeles motel that she frequented. The *New York Times* reported that several bottles of pills and alcohol were in the room. It also reported that the day before her death Nina told a bartender, "When I die, I want artificial flowers, jitterbug music and a bottle of vodka at my grave."[18] Six months after Nina's death, her stepfather, Samossoud, died and the income from the estate began to flow to Dr. Seiler. What remained of Nina's original million-dollar legacy was divided between the Red Cross and Yale, as per Clara's instructions.

It seems that if Nina did read Mark Twain, the main lesson she picked up was the Mysterious Stranger's revelation that life was a "swindle."

Conversely, Sam Clemens as Mark Twain experienced one of the fullest and most famous lives on record. He suffered, it must be conceded, great personal losses toward the end, but through it all his towering sense of humor and profound empathy seldom failed him for long. His name recognition a century after his death is probably greater than that of most famous Americans living or dead, and equally prominent on the world stage. He was the culmination of a long history of American humor beginning first in New England before the Civil War and developing in the Old Southwest both before and after the war. It was there in the Missouri backwoods of Hannibal that he picked up its ironic angle on the world. In such small towns of the American hinterland, the "stranger" was always mysterious, at least at first, and sometimes a trickster, as in "Jim Smiley and His Jumping Frog." Yet human beings are always easy prey to the stranger because of the greed ingrained in their system. When the parson suggests that his wife, who has been seriously ailing, may get well, Jim Smiley, *before he thought,* wagers that "she don't." Mark Twain's greatest book, and one of the greatest American novels ever written, celebrates and laughs at these human flaws in a series of episodes along the Mississippi River, a stream that cuts through the heart of America. In *Adventures of Huckleberry Finn* we find ourselves looking through the eyes of a young observer who struggles to distinguish between illusion and reality in the world to which his adolescence introduces him. And the difference between what we expect and what we find is, amazingly, at once funny and tragic—from the runaway slave who becomes a conscientious father to Huck to the reprehensible Duke and the King, who ultimately sell Jim down the river. What appeals to us in all of Twain's fiction, even in the parade of skeletons in "The Mysterious Stranger," is both horrible and hilarious—because it is humanity stripped of its pretensions, and ridiculed because of them. We both laugh and cry because, in the words of James M. Cox, this is "the fate of humor."[19] What begins as tragic becomes with enough time humorous, and what at a distance appears funny is up close ultimately tragic, for that is the fate of the human condition.

APPENDIX A Clemens Genealogy

Samuel B. Clemens (1770–1805) Pamela Goggin (1775–1845) Benjamin Lampton (1774–1837) Margaret Montgomery Casey (1783–1817)

John Marshall Clemens (1798–1847) Jane Lampton (1803–1890)

1. Orion Clemens (1825–1897) m. Mary Eleanor (Mollie) Stotts (1834–1904)

Jennie Clemens (1855–1864)

2. Pamela Anne Clemens (1827–1904) m. William A. Moffett (1816–1865)

Annie Moffett (1852–1950) m. Charles L. Webster (1851–1891)

Samuel Erasmus Moffett (1860–1908)

3. Pleasant Hannibal Clemens (1828–1829)

4. Margaret L. Clemens
(1830–1839)

5. Benjamin Clemens
(1832–1842)

6. Samuel Langhorne Clemens (1835–1910) m. Olivia Louise Langdon (1845–1904)

Langdon Clemens
(1870–1872)

Olivia Susan (Susy) Clemens
(1872–1896)

Clara Langdon Clemens (1874–1962) m. Ossip Gabrilowitsch (1878–1936) m. Jacques Samossoud (1894–1966)

Nina Clemens Gabrilowitsch
(1910–1966)

Jane Lampton (Jean) Clemens
(1880–1909)

7. Henry Clemens
(1838–1858)

APPENDIX B Books Published by Charles L. Webster & Company

1885

Grant, Ulysses S *Personal Memoirs of U. S. Grant,* volume 1.
Twain, Mark. *Adventures of Huckleberry Finn.*
———. *The Prince and the Pauper* (originally published in 1881).

1886

Grant, Ulysses S *Personal Memoirs of U. S. Grant,* volume 2.

1887

Cox, Samuel Sullivan. *Diversions of a Diplomat in Turkey.*
Crawford, General Samuel Wylie. *The Genesis of the Civil War: The Story of Sumter, 1860–1861.*
Custer, Elizabeth. *Tenting on the Plains; or, General Custer in Kansas and Texas.*
Hancock, Almira Russell. *Reminiscences of Winfield Scott Hancock.*
McClellan, George Brinton. *McClellan's Own Story: The War for the Union, the Soldiers Who Fought It, the Civilians Who Directed It and His Relations to It and to Them.*
O'Reilly, Father Bernard. *Life of Pope Leo XIII.*
Twain, Mark. *The Prince and the Pauper* (reissue).

1888

Beecher, William C., and Samuel Scoville. *A Biography of Rev. Henry Ward Beecher.*
Burton, Rev. Nathaniel J. *Yale Lectures on Preaching and Other Writings.*
Daggett, Rollin Mallory. *The Legends and Myths of Hawaii.*

Filippini, Alessandro. *The Table: How to Buy Food, How to Cook It, and How to Serve It.*
Kalakaua, David. *The Legends and Myths of Hawaii.*
Library of American Literature, ed. E. C. Stedman, volumes 1–6.
Mark Twain's Library of Humor.
Sheridan, P. H. *Personal Memoirs of P. H. Sheridan, General, United States Army.*
Twain, Mark. *Life on the Mississippi* (reissue).
———. *The Prince and the Pauper* (reissue).
———. *The Stolen White Elephant and Other Stories* (reissue).

1889

Conkling, Alfred R. *The Life and Letters of Roscoe Conkling, Orator, Statesman, Advocate.*
Library of American Literature, ed. E. C. Stedman, volumes 7–10.
Twain, Mark. *A Connecticut Yankee in King Arthur's Court.*

1890

Library of American Literature, ed. E. C. Stedman, volume 11.
Ridenbaugh, Mary Young. *Biography of Ephraim McDowell, M.D.*
Sherman, William T. *Personal Memoirs of General W. T. Sherman,* 2 vols. (reissue of 1875 publication).
Stoddard, William O. *Inside the White House in War Times.*

1891

Bliss, Edgar Janes. *The Peril of Oliver Sargent.*
Byers, S. H. M. *The Happy Isles and Other Poems.*
Crim, Matt (Martha Jane). *Adventures of a Fair Rebel.*
Dahlgren, Madeline Vinton. *Memoirs of John A. Dahlgren.*
Ireland, A. E. *Life of Jane Welsh Carlyle.*
Lucas, Daniel B., and James F. McLaughlin. *Hour-Glass Series.*
Sanford, E. B. *Concise Cyclopedia of Religious Knowledge.*
Scott, Henry W. *Distinguished American Lawyers, with Their Struggles and Triumphs in the Forum.*
Sims, George R. *Tinkletop's Crime.*
"Sixtus." *A Review of Professor Briggs's Inaugural Address* (45-page pamphlet).
Tolstoi, Leo. *Ivan the Fool* (reprint of short story).
Twain, Mark. *Adventures of Huckleberry Finn* (cheap edition).
———. *Facts for Mark Twain's Memory Builder* (11-page pamphlet).

———. *Life on the Mississippi* (reissue).
Ward, Herbert. *My Life with Stanley's Rear Guard.*

1892

Bacheller, Irving. *The Master of Silence.*
Beard, Daniel C. *Moonblight and Six Feet of Romance.* (Beard illustrated a number of the Webster books, including *A Connecticut Yankee.*)
Bigelow, Poultney. *The German Emperor and His Eastern Neighbors.*
———. *Paddles and Politics Down the Danube.*
Columbus, Christopher. *Writings of Christopher Columbus, Descriptive of the Discovery of the New World.*
Crim, Matt (Martha Jane). *In Beaver Cove and Elsewhere.*
Dahlgren, Madeline Vinton. *Chim: His Washington Winter.*
Filippini, Alexander. *One Hundred Ways of Cooking Eggs.*
———. *One Hundred Ways of Cooking Fish.*
Garner, R. L. *The Speech of Monkeys, in Two Parts.*
George, Henry. *A Perplexed Philosopher: Being an Examination of Mr. Herbert Spencer's Various Utterances on the Land Question* (reissue).
———. *Progress and Poverty* (reissue).
Illustrated Catalogue of Charles L. Webster and Co.'s Publications.
Johnston, Richard Malcolm. *Mr. Billy Downs and His Likes.*
Miller, Annie J. *Physical Beauty. How to Obtain and How to Preserve It.*
Pullen, Elisabeth C. *Don Finimondone: Calabrian Sketches.*
Repplier, Agnes. *Essays in Miniature.*
Schmidt, W. *The Flowering Bowl.*
Scollard, Clinton. *Under Summer Skies.*
Sharp, William. *Flower o' the Vine: Romantic Ballads and Sospiri de Roma.*
Springer, William M. *Tariff Reform, the Paramount Issue: Speeches and Writings on the Questions Involved in the Presidential Contest of 1892.*
Tolstoi, Leo. *Life Is Worth Living, and Other Stories.*
Twain, Mark. *The American Claimant.*
———. *Merry Tales.*
———. *The Prince and the Pauper* (cheap edition).
Whitman, Walt. *Autobiographia; or, The Story of a Life.*
———. *Selected Poems.*

1893

Bangs, John K. *Toppleton's Client; or, A Spirit in Exile.*
Benton, Joel. *The Truth about "Protection."*

Brooks, Henry S. *A Catastrophe in Bohemia and Other Stories.*
Crim, Matt. *Elizabeth, Christian Scientist.*
Filippini, Alexander. *One Hundred Desserts.*
Fraipont, Gustave B. *The Art of Sketching.*
George, Henry. *The Condition of Labor: An Open Letter to Pope Leo XIII.*
———. *The Land Question: What It Involves, and How Alone It Can Be Settled.*
———. *The Land Question . . . Property in Land . . . The Condition of Labor* (separately paginated).
Isaacs, Abram S. *Stories from the Rabbis.*
Moffett, Samuel Erasmus. *The Tariff; What It Is and What It Does.*
Scollard, Clinton. *On Sunny Shores.*
Sixtus. *Progressive Protestantism.*
Twain, Mark. *The £1,000,000 Bank-note and Other New Stories.*

1894

Grant, Ulysses S. *Personal Memoirs of U. S. Grant* (cheap edition).
Holdsworth, Annie E. *Joanna Traill, Spinster.*
Twain, Mark. *Tom Sawyer Abroad.*
Waugh, Arthur. *Alfred Lord Tennyson.*

Notes

ABBREVIATIONS

Benson:	Ivan Benson. *Mark Twain's Western Years.* Stanford, CA: Stanford University Press, 1938.
Brashear:	Minnie M. Brashear, *Mark Twain, Son of Missouri.* Chapel Hill: University of North Carolina Press, 1934.
ET&S:	*Early Tales & Sketches.* 2 vols. Edited by Edgar Marquess Branch and Robert H. Hirst. Berkeley: University of California Press, 1979–81.
Fatout:	Paul Fatout. *Mark Twain on the Lecture Circuit.* Bloomington: Indiana University Press, 1960.
FE:	Mark Twain. *Following the Equator.* Hartford: American Publishing Company, 1897.
L:	*Mark Twain's Letters, 1853–1875.* 6 vols. Edited by Edgar Marquess Branch et al. Berkeley: University of California Press, 1988–2002.
Letters:	*Mark Twain's Letters.* 2 vols. Edited by Albert Bigelow Paine. New York: Harper & Brothers, 1917.
LLMT:	*The Love Letters of Mark Twain.* Edited by Dixon Wecter. New York: Harper & Brothers, 1949.
Lorch:	Fred W. Lorch. *The Trouble Begins at Eight: Mark Twain's Lecture Tours.* Ames: Iowa State University Press, 1968.
MT:	Mark Twain (Samuel Langhorne Clemens).
MTA:	*Mark Twain's Autobiography.* 2 vols. Edited by Albert Bigelow Paine. New York: Harper & Brothers, 1924.

MTB:	Albert Bigelow Paine. *Mark Twain: A Biography.* 3 vols. New York: Harper & Brothers, 1912.
MTBus:	Samuel Charles Webster. *Mark Twain, Business Man.* Boston: Little, Brown, 1946.
MTCI:	*Mark Twain: The Complete Interviews.* Edited by Gary Scharnhorst. Tuscaloosa: University of Alabama Press, 2006.
MTE:	*Mark Twain in Eruption.* Edited by Bernard DeVoto. New York: Harper & Sons, 1940.
MTEnt:	*Mark Twain of the* Enterprise. Edited by Henry Nash Smith. Berkeley: University of California Press, 1957.
MTHHR:	*Mark Twain's Correspondence with Henry Huttleston Rogers.* Edited by Lewis Leary. Berkeley: University of California Press, 1969.
MTHL:	*Mark Twain–Howells Letters.* 2 vols. Edited by Henry Nash Smith and William M. Gibson. Cambridge, MA: Harvard University Press, 1960.
MTL:	Alan Gribben. *Mark Twain's Library: A Reconstruction.* 2 vols. Boston: G. K. Hall, 1980.
MTLP:	*Mark Twain's Letters to His Publishers.* Edited by Hamlin Hill. Berkeley: University of California Press, 1967.
MTMF:	*Mark Twain to Mrs. Fairbanks.* Edited by Dixon Wecter. San Marino, CA: Huntington Library, 1949.
MTN:	*Mark Twain's Notebook.* Edited by Albert Bigelow Paine. New York: Harper & Brothers, 1935.
MTP:	Mark Twain Project/Papers. University of California, Berkeley.
MTSpk:	*Mark Twain Speaking.* Edited by Paul Fatout. Iowa City: University of Iowa Press, 1976.
MTTB:	*Mark Twain's Travels with Mr. Brown.* Edited by Franklin Walker and G. Ezra Dane. New York: Alfred A. Knopf, 1940.
MTVC:	Paul Fatout. *Mark Twain in Virginia City.* Bloomington: Indiana University Press, 1964.
N&J:	*Mark Twain's Notebooks & Journals, 1855–1891.* 3 vols. Edited by Frederick Anderson et al. Berkeley: University of California Press, 1975–79.

PROLOGUE

1. "Jane Lampton Clemens," in *Mark Twain's Hannibal, Huck & Tom,* ed. Walter Blair (Berkeley: University of California Press, 1969), 43–53.

2. "Schoolhouse Hill," in *No. 44, Mark Twain's Mysterious Stranger Manuscripts,* ed. William M. Gibson (Berkeley: University of California Press, 1982), 187; and John S. Tuckey, *Mark Twain and Little Satan: The Writings of The Mysterious Stranger* (West Lafayette, IN: Purdue University Studies, 1963), 31.

3. *L,* 1: 322–23.

4. *MTE,* 202–3.

5. Mark Twain to Samuel S. McClure, c. February 1, 1900 (MTP); and Bernard De Voto, *Mark Twain's America* (Boston: Little, Brown, 1932), 238.

6. Emerson, "The Comic," in *Letters and Social Aims* (Boston: Houghton Mifflin, 1884), 151–53.

7. William Dean Howells, *My Mark Twain: Reminiscences and Criticisms* (New York: Harper & Brothers, 1910), 63.

8. "Jane Lampton Clemens," 52.

9. It doubtless started with William Dean Howells's statement in his *My Mark Twain,* in which he recalls that Twain had begun "to amass those evidences against mankind which eventuated with him in his theory of what he called 'the damned human race'" (76).

10. James H. Justus, *Fetching the Old Southwest: Humorous Writing from Longstreet to Twain* (Columbia: University of Missouri Press, 2004), 320.

1. LIFE ON THE SALT RIVER

1. Dixon Wecter, *Sam Clemens of Hannibal* (Boston: Houghton Mifflin, 1952), 6–12; Margaret Sanborn, *Mark Twain: The Bachelor Years* (New York: Doubleday, 1990), 1–11; Ralph Gregory, *Mark Twain's First America: Florida, Missouri, 1835–1840* (privately printed, 1965); and MT, *The American Claimant* (New York: Charles L. Webster & Co., 1892), 23 ("crushed by a log at a smoke-house raising").

2. Rowland Berthoff, *An Unsettled People: Social Order and Disorder in American History* (New York: Harper & Row, 1971), 287; Mark Twain, *Pudd'nhead Wilson and Those Extraordinary Twins,* ed. Sidney E. Berger (New York: W.W. Norton, 1980), 43.

3. *FE,* 2: 18.

4. De Lancey Ferguson, *Mark Twain: Man and Legend* (Indianapolis: Bobbs-Merrill, 1943), 16; and *MTHL* 2: 567.

5. *MTA,* 1: 3. Today a historical marker near the Fentress County Courthouse indicates a spring as "the source of water for early settlers of Jamestown,

including Clemens's parents, who settled on the adjoining property to the north."

6. Wecter, *Sam Clemens,* 33–34.

7. Ralph Gregory, "John A. Quarles: Mark Twain's Ideal Man," *Bulletin of the Missouri Historical Society,* 25 (April 1969), 229–35.

8. *MTA,* 1: 96, 95.

9. Wecter, *Sam Clemens,* 47; Brashear, 48, 44 n. 34.

10. *MTA,* 1: 96–97; and *Adventures of Huckleberry Finn,* ed. Victor Fischer and Lin Salamo (Berkeley: University of California Press, 2003), 288.

11. *MTA,* 1: 100–101.

12. Gregory, *Mark Twain's First America,* 234; *Civil War Dictionary,* ed. Mark M. Boatner III (New York: David McKay, 1959), 355, 669.

13. *Huck Finn and Tom Sawyer among the Indians and Other Unfinished Stories,* ed. Dahlia Armon and Walter Blair (Berkeley: University of California Press, 1989), 208.

14. *Pudd'nhead Wilson and Those Extraordinary Twins,* 8–9.

15. Brashear, 52–53; *MTB,* 96.

16. *Tom Sawyer Abroad, Tom Sawyer, Detective,* ed. John C. Gerber and Terry Firkins (Berkeley: University of California Press, 1980), 155.

2. WINDOW TO THE WEST

1. Dixon Wecter, *Sam Clemens of Hannibal* (Boston: Houghton Mifflin, 1952), 56–57; *Mark Twain's Hannibal, Huck & Tom,* ed. Walter Blair (Berkeley: University of California Press, 1969), 39.

2. MT to Dora Bowen (Goff), June 6, 1900 (University of Texas library).

3. Blair, *Mark Twain's Hannibal,* 35–36.

4. Henry Nash Smith, *Mark Twain: The Development of a Writer* (Cambridge, MA: Harvard University Press, 1962), 128.

5. See *The Innocents Abroad,* chap. 18; *MTA,* 1: 131–32; *Missouri Courier,* May 2, 1850.

6. *MTB,* 2: 63–64; Wecter, *Sam Clemens,* 148; *MTA,* 2: 174; *The Adventures of Tom Sawyer,* ed. John C. Gerber et al. (Berkeley: University of California Press, 1980), 74.

7. *Huck Finn and Tom Sawyer among the Indians,* ed. Dahlia Armon and Walter Blair (Berkeley: University of California Press, 1989), 325; Bernard De Voto, *Mark Twain at Work* (Cambridge, MA: Harvard University Press, 1942), 13.

8. *Huck Finn and Tom Sawyer among the Indians,* 339–40; *MTA,* 1: 131.

9. *L,* 4, 50–53.

10. Larzer Ziff, *Mark Twain* (New York: Oxford University Press, 2004), 4.

3. ORION

1. *MTA,* 1: 124.

2. "Villagers of 1840–3," in *Mark Twain's Hannibal, Huck & Tom,* ed. Walter Blair (Berkeley: University of California Press, 1969), 40.

3. Philip Ashley Fanning, *Mark Twain and Orion Clemens: Brothers, Partners, Strangers* (Tuscaloosa: University of Alabama Press, 2003).

4. Dixon Wecter, *Sam Clemens of Hannibal* (Boston: Houghton Mifflin, 1952), 228.

5. *L,* 1: 14.

6. *Dictionary of American Biography* (New York: Scribner's, 1937), 2: 48–49.

7. Wecter, *Sam Clemens of Hannibal,* 227.

8. *MTHL,* 1: 253.

9. *MTA,* 2: 272–74.

10. Terrell Dempsey, *Searching for Jim: Slavery in Sam Clemens's World* (Columbia: University of Missouri Press, 2003), 78.

11. *MTB,* 2: 270.

12. *MTA,* 1: 89.

4. SOUTHWEST HUMORIST

1. Walter Blair, *Native American Humor* (Chandler Publishing Company, 1960).

2. James H. Justus, *Fetching the Old Southwest: Humorous Writing from Longstreet to Twain* (Columbia: University of Missouri Press, 2004), 188.

3. Justus, *Fetching the Old Southwest,* 231.

4. Edgar Marquess Branch, *The Literary Apprenticeship of Mark Twain* (Urbana: University of Illinois Press, 1950), 9.

5. Dixon Wecter, *Sam Clemens of Hannibal* (Boston: Houghton Mifflin, 1952), 236.

6. *ET&S,* 1: 62.

7. *MTE,* 136–42.

8. *ET&S,* 1: 66–68.

9. *L,* 4: 198–200; Jeffrey Steinbrink, *Getting to Be Mark Twain* (Berkeley: University of California Press, 1991), 137; *ET&S,* 1: 72–77; Wecter, *Sam Clemens of Hannibal,* 249–52; Brashear, 109–16.

10. *ET&S,* 1: 78.

11. Brashear, 122; and "My First Literary Venture," *Galaxy,* 11 (April 1871), 615, reprinted in *Contributions to the "Galaxy," 1868–1871, by Mark Twain,* ed. Bruce R. McElderry, Jr. (Gainesville, FL: Scholars' Facsimiles and Reprints, 1961), 131–32.

12. Brashear, 135–39.

13. *ET&S,* 1: 106–9.

5. TRAMP PRINTER

1. *MTA,* 2: 287–89; *L,* 1: 1–3; MT to Mrs. A. P. Cosgrove, April 11, 1885 (University of Virginia Library), in which he maintained that he kept his promise not to imbibe between ages fifteen and twenty-one.

2. *L,* 1: 9–12; *MTB* 1: 96. I am indebted to Kevin Mac Donnell for the fact of Gray's printing of MT's first book.

3. Horace L. Traubel, *With Walt Whitman in Camden* (Carbondale: University of Southern Illinois Press, 1992), 7: 98.

4. *L,* 1: 19–28.

5. *L,* 1: 12n, 20.

6. *MTA,* 2: 287; *L,* 1: 24n, 28–29, 4.

7. MT to Frank Bliss, August 26, 1901 (University of Texas Library); Ron Powers, *Mark Twain: A Life* (New York: Free Press, 2005), 51.

8. *L,* 1: 28–29, 33, 37–39.

9. *MTA,* 2: 287; *L,* 1: 40–44.

10. Anthony Kennedy, "'Mark Twain' a Poor Typo," *The Inland Printer* 40 (January 1908), 560, as quoted in *L,* 1: 2–3, 5n.

11. *L,* 1: 53n.

12. Fred W. Lorch, "Mark Twain in Iowa," *Iowa Journal of History and Politics* 27 (July 1929), 408–56.

13. *MTB,* 1: 107–12.

14. This view, and indeed the actual existence of Macfarlane as more than a conceit when Twain used the name in his autobiography, has been challenged by later scholars. See Paul Baender, "'Alias Macfarlane': A Revision of Mark Twain Biography," *American Literature* 38 (May 1966), 187–97; and Howard G. Baetzhold, *Mark Twain and John Bull* (Bloomington: Indiana University Press, 1970), 56. For Paine, see *MTB,* 1: 115; *MTA,* 1: 146.

6. CUB PILOT

1. See John Gerber, "Mark Twain's 'Private Campaign,'" *Civil War History* 1 (March 1955), 37–60, which includes the text of "A Private History of a Campaign That Failed."

2. *MTA,* 1: 146.

3. Allan Bates, "Mark Twain and the Mississippi River" (unpublished doctoral diss., University of Chicago, 1968), 3.

4. *MTCI,* 418–25; Dudley R. Hutcherson, "Mark Twain as a Pilot," *American Literature* 12 (November 1940), 353–55; and Edgar Marquess Branch, "Mark Twain: The Pilot and the Writer," *Mark Twain Journal* 23, no. 2 (1985), 29.

5. *L,* 1: 103–5n.

6. *N&J*, 2: 473n.

7. *L*, 1: 385–90.

8. Edgar M. Branch, "Bixby vs. Carroll: New Light on Sam Clemens's Early River Career," *Mark Twain Journal* 30 (Fall 1992), 2–22; Arlin Turner, "Notes on Mark Twain in New Orleans," *McNeese Review* 6 (Spring 1954), 10–22.

9. *MTA* 2: 289; Branch, "Bixby vs. Carroll," 2–3; *L*, 1: 134n.

10. *L*, 1: 62; Branch, "Bixby vs. Carroll," 2.

11. *L*, 1: 71–73; *The Mysterious Stranger*, ed. John S. Tuckey (Berkeley: University of California Press, 1982), 184.

12. *Autobiography of Mark Twain, Including Chapters Now Published for the First Time*, ed. Charles Neider (New York: Harper & Row, 1959), 79.

13. *MTA* 2: 290; Bates, "Mark Twain and the Mississippi River," 113.

14. *N&J*, 2: 555n; and Ernest E. Leisy, "Mark Twain and Isaiah Sellers," *American Literature* 12 (January 1941), 398–405; *MTB* 1: 150 and 3: 1593. For a healthy sampling of the pros and cons on the enduring question of whether Samuel Langhorne Clemens was a successful pilot, see Edgar Marquess Branch, "'Old Times on the Mississippi': Biography and Craftsmanship," *Nineteenth-Century Literature* 45 (June 1990), 73–87; "Mark Twain: The Pilot and the Writer," *Mark Twain Journal* 23, no. 2 (1985), 28–43; Richard Bridgman, *Traveling with Mark Twain* (Berkeley: University of California Press, 1987), 64–69; Horst H. Kruse, *Mark Twain and "Life on the Mississippi"* (Amherst: University of Massachusetts Press, 1981); Raymond P. Ewing, *Mark Twain's Steamboat Years* (Hannibal, MO: Cave Hollow Steamboat Landing, 1981), 45–49; Edgar J. Burde, "Mark Twain: The Writer As Pilot," *Publications of the Modern Language Association* 93 (1978), 878–92; and DeLancey Ferguson, *Mark Twain: Man and Legend* (Indianapolis: Bobbs-Merrill, 1943), 49–53.

15. Bates, "Mark Twain and the Mississippi River," 128, 131–32; *Letters*, 1: 43–44.

7. DEATH ON THE MISSISSIPPI

1. *L*, 1: 85; Edgar Marquess Branch, *Men Call Me Lucky: Mark Twain and the Pennsylvania* (Miami, OH: Friends of the Library Society, 1985). Most of the facts about the tragedy are drawn from this work.

2. *L*, 1: 80.

3. *L*, 5: 42.

4. *L*, 1: 84n.

5. *L*, 1: 84n, 86n.

6. *L*, 1: 270n, 321–22.

8. FETCHING GRANT

1. For the most detailed coverage of this aspect of Twain's life, see John Gerber, "Mark Twain's 'Private Campaign,'" *Civil War History* 1 (March 1955), 37–60; it includes the text of "Private History of a Campaign That Failed," as well as summaries of the other documents. This Collection is updated in *Mark Twain's Civil War,* ed. David Rachels (Lexington: University of Kentucky Press, 2007).

2. *L,* 1: 238, 165.

3. *L,* 1: 259–61.

4. Philip Ashley Fanning, *Mark Twain and Orion Clemens* (Tuscaloosa: University of Alabama Press, 2003); *L,* 4: 171; *MTBus,* 47.

5. *Absalom Grimes, Confederate Mail Runner,* ed. M.M. Quaife (New Haven: Yale University Press, 1926), 3–5; Terrell Dempsey, *Searching for Jim: Slavery in Sam Clemens's World* (Columbia: University of Missouri Press, 2003), 268.

6. *Mark Twain's Letters, 1876–1880: An Electronic Edition,* Mark Twain Project (Berkeley: University of California), 4: 139, 142; *MTHL,* 1: 278–81.

7. J. Stanley Mattson, "Mark Twain on War and Peace: The Missouri Rebel and 'The Campaign That Failed,'" *American Quarterly* 20 (Winter 1968), 783–94.

8. *Absalom Grimes,* 11; *MTSpk,* 106–9. The short speech was published as "Mark Twain's War Experiences" in the *New York Times* of October 7, 1877.

9. Justin Kaplan, *Mr. Clemens and Mark Twain: A Biography* (New York: Simon & Schuster, 1966), 225, 272–77; *Absalom Grimes,* 15–16.

10. *L,* 4: 142, 144. See also Neil Schmitz, "Mark Twain's Civil War: Humor's Reconstructive Writing," in *Cambridge Companion to Mark Twain,* ed. Forrest G. Robinson (Cambridge: Cambridge University Press, 1995), 74–92.

11. *L,* 1: 165.

12. Gerber, "Mark Twain's 'Private Campaign,'" 59.

13. Clara Clemens, *My Father, Mark Twain* (New York: Harper & Brothers, 1931), 292.

14. Jerome Loving, *Walt Whitman: The Song of Himself* (Berkeley: University of California Press, 1999), 265–66.

15. Quoted in Fred W. Lorch, "Mark Twain and the 'Campaign That Failed,'" *American Literature* 12 (January 1941), 454–70.

16. Mark Twain, *Roughing It,* ed. Harriet Elinor Smith and Edgar Marquess Branch (Berkeley: University of California Press, 1993), 574; *MTB,* 1: 170; Lorch, "Mark Twain and the 'Campaign That Failed,'" 460.

9. LIGHTING OUT

1. *L,* 4: 171.

2. Mark Twain, *Roughing It,* ed. Harriet Elinor Smith and Edgar Marquess Branch (Berkeley: University of California Press, 1993), 33.

3. Noah Brooks, "Mark Twain in California," *Century* 57 (November 1898), 97.

4. *Roughing It,* 67.

5. *Roughing It,* 77, 80, 88.

6. *Roughing It,* 591–92.

7. *Roughing It,* 88, 93.

8. *Roughing It,* 99, 115, 844–46.

9. *Roughing It,* 127; James C. McNutt, "Mark Twain and the American Indian: Earthly Realism and Heavenly Idealism," *American Indian Quarterly* 4 (August 1978), 223–242; Helen L. Harris, "Mark Twain's Response to the Native American," *American Literature* 46 (January 1975), 495–505; Lynn W. Denton, "Mark Twain and the American Indian," *Mark Twain Journal* 16 (Winter 1971–72), 1–3; Louis J. Budd, *Mark Twain: Social Philosopher* (Bloomington: Indiana University Press, 1962), 67.

10. *L,* 1: 132.

11. Effie Mona Mack, *Mark Twain in Nevada* (New York: Charles Scribner's Sons, 1947), 74.

12. Mack, *Mark Twain in Nevada,* 77.

13. *L,* 1: 145.

10. A MILLIONAIRE FOR TEN DAYS

1. Effie Mona Mack, *Mark Twain in Nevada* (New York: Charles Scribner's Sons, 1947), 13–23.

2. Mark Twain, *Roughing It,* ed. Harriet Elinor Smith and Edgar Marquess Branch (Berkeley: University of California Press, 1993), 147.

3. *L,* 1: 129.

4. *L,* 1: 129n, 130; *Roughing It,* 197, 174.

5. *Roughing It,* 175.

6. Quoted in *MTVC,* 20.

7. *L,* 1: 245.

8. *Roughing It,* 211–19; *L,* 4: 23n. See also Everett Emerson, "Smoking and Health: The Case of Samuel L. Clemens," *New England Quarterly* 70 (1997), 548–66.

9. *L,* 1: 156–57; 165. The Great Landslide Case was a hoax in which the new U.S. attorney for Nevada Territory, called "Buncombe" in chapter 34 of *Roughing It,* was duped into arguing the case of a rancher whose land had allegedly been covered by his neighbor's ranch during a spring thaw in the hilly precincts of Washoe (Dick Hyde's "ranch was situated just in the edge of the valley, and . . . [Tom] Morgan's ranch, fences, cabins, cattle, barns and everything [slid] down on top of *his* ranch and exactly covered up every single vestige of his property, to the depth of about thirty-eight feet"). The greenhorn U.S. attorney, who con-

sidered himself "a lawyer of parts, and . . . very much wanted an opportunity to manifest it," lost the case when the presiding judge ruled against Hyde, saying that plaintiff had "been deprived of his ranch by the visitation of God! And from this decision there is no appeal."

10. *Roughing It*, 230–31, 233.

11. *MTB*, 3: 1648–50. See also *Mark Twain's Fables of Man*, ed. John S. Tuckey (Berkeley: University of California Press, 1972), 158–59.

12. *L*, 1: 193.

13. *L*, 1: 240n.

14. Michael J. Phillips, "Mark Twain's Partner," *Saturday Evening Post* 193 (September 11, 1920), 22–23, 69–70, 73–74. The title of Higbie's only partly published manuscript, obviously intended to take advantage of Mark Twain's fame, is "A Little Experience in Nevada and Surrounding Country, in the Early Sixties, Leading Up to My Acquaintance with Samuel L. Clemens, 'Mark Twain'" (MTP).

11. "MARK TWAIN"

1. *L*, 1: 238; *ET&S*, 1: 389–91; *MTB*, 1: 205; Benson, 54. See also Robert E. Stewart, "Mark Twain's Return from Aurora," *Nevada Historical Society Quarterly* 51 (Summer 2008), 127–39.

2. Effie Mona Mack, *Mark Twain in Nevada* (New York: Charles Scribner's Sons, 1947), 183.

3. Benson, 69; Andrew Hoffman, *Inventing Mark Twain: The Lives of Samuel Langhorne Clemens* (New York: William Morrow, 1997), 76.

4. Ronald M. James, *The Roar and the Silence: A History of Virginia City and the Comstock Lode* (Reno and Las Vegas: University of Nevada Press, 1998), 31–32.

5. Van Wyck Brooks, *The Ordeal of Mark Twain* (New York: E. P. Dutton, 1920).

6. *L*, 1: 242.

7. *ET&S*, 1: 155–59.

8. *ET&S*, 1: 173.

9. *MTB*, 1: 216.

10. *MTEnt*, 47–54. I wish to thank Robert H. Hirst for assistance in determining the facts about the illustration.

11. *L*, 1: 244.

12. *L*, 1: 255.

13. *ET&S*, 1: 320–21; Benson, 91; and Mack, *Mark Twain in Nevada*, 195.

14. Benson, 105.

12. GOVERNOR OF THE THIRD HOUSE

1. *MTVC,* 147–49.
2. *MTVC,* 156–67; Benson, 94–96.
3. Bernard De Voto, *Mark Twain's America* (Boston: Little, Brown, 1932), 138.
4. *MTB,* 1: 243–44; Benson, 100.
5. *MTEnt,* 25–26.
6. *L,* 1: 287–90.
7. *L,* 1: 287n, 289.
8. *L,* 1: 291–95n.
9. *MTB,* 1: 250–52; *MTEnt,* 24–30; *MTA,* 1: 354–60.
10. *MTA,* 1: 360; John C. Gerber, "Mark Twain's 'Private Campaign,'" *Civil War History* 1 (March 1955), 37–60.

13. THE JUMPING FROG

1. *MTE,* 257–58.
2. *Clemens of the* Call: *Mark Twain in San Francisco,* ed. Edgar Marquess Branch (Berkeley: University of California Press, 1969), 41, 23–24.
3. *Walt Whitman: The Correspondence,* ed. Edwin Haviland Miller (New York: New York University Press, 1961), 2: 81–82n, 97–98.
4. William R. Gillis, *Memories of Mark Twain and Steve Gillis* (Sonora, CA: Banner Press, 1924), 40.
5. Benson, 122–23.
6. *MTHL,* 1: 147.
7. *ET&S,* 2: 86–93.
8. *The Adventures of Tom Sawyer,* ed. John C. Gerber et al. (Berkeley: University of California Press, 1980), 233; *L,* 1: 315.
9. *ET&S,* 2: 134.
10. Leonard Keen Hirshberg, M.D., *What You Ought to Know about Your Baby* (New York: Butterick Publications, 1910), 21.
11. *L,* 1: 322, 325n.
12. *L,* 1: 327.
13. Quoted in *ET&S,* 2: 272.
14. *ET&S,* 2: 284.
15. *MTE,* 200–203.

14. VANDAL ABROAD

1. This was the subtitle by which it is now much better known; the original main title in the *Californian* is "The Christmas Fireside for Good Little Boys and

Girls. By Grandfather Twain." The others are in chronological order: "Answers to Correspondents," cobbled together from several such columns first published in the *Californian* on May 27 and June 10, 17, and 24; "'After' Jenkins," first published as "The Pioneers' Ball," *Enterprise,* November 19 or 21, 1865; "Among the Spirits," a conflation of "Among the Spiritualists," *Enterprise,* January 26 or 27, 1866, and "'Mark Twain' among the Spirits," *Enterprise,* February 4, 1866; "Among the Fenians," first published as "Bearding the Fenian in His Lair," *Enterprise,* January 30 or 31, 1866; "A Complaint about Correspondents, Dated in San Francisco," first published as "An Open Letter to the American People," New York *Weekly Review,* February 17, 1866; and "Brief Biographical Sketch of George Washington," first published as "A New Biography of Washington," and "Remarkable Instances of Presence of Mind," first published as "Presence of Mind," both in the *Enterprise,* sometime between February 25 and 28, 1866. I am indebted to Robert H. Hirst, general editor of the Mark Twain Project, for much of this information.

2. "The Turning Point of My Life," in *What Is Man? and Other Philosophical Essays,* ed. Paul Baender (Berkeley: University of California Press, 1973), 528; *Mark Twain's Letters from Hawaii,* ed. A. Grove Day (New York: Appleton-Century, 1966), 53.

3. "An Inquiry about Insurances" was first published as "How, for Instance?" in the New York *Weekly Review* of September 29, 1866; "Origin of Illustrious Men" appeared under the same title in the *Californian,* also on September 29; and "Concerning Chambermaids" was first published in the *Weekly Review* as "Depart, Ye Accursed!" on December 15, 1866.

4. *Mark Twain's Letters from Hawaii,* 6, 33.

5. *Mark Twain's Letters from Hawaii,* 260.

6. *Mark Twain's Letters from Hawaii,* 112.

7. Andrew Hoffman, *Inventing Mark Twain: The Lives of Samuel Langhorne Clemens* (New York: William Morrow, 1997), 104–5; *N&J,* 1: 189; and *L,* 1: 145.

8. *Mark Twain's Letters from Hawaii,* 27, 31, 279, 282.

9. R. Kent Rasmussen, *Mark Twain: A to Z* (New York: Oxford University Press, 1995), 49–50; Walter Francis Frear, *Mark Twain and Hawaii* (Chicago: Lakeside Press, 1947), 95; "Forty-three Days in an Open Boat," *Harper's* 34 (December 1866), 104–13.

10. *L,* 1: 343–44.

11. Mark Twain, *Roughing It,* ed. Harriet Elinor Smith and Edgar Marquess Branch (Berkeley: University of California Press, 1993), 371.

12. *N&J,* 1: 234; *L,* 1: 359.

13. *L,* 1: 353, 355n.

15. WILD HUMORIST OF THE PACIFIC SLOPE

1. *MTSpk,* xv.

2. *MTSpk,* 5; Mark Twain, *Roughing It,* ed. Harriet Elinor Smith and Edgar Marquess Branch (Berkeley: University of California Press, 1993), 533.

3. *MTB,* 3: 1601–4; Lorch, 47; Walter Francis Frear, *Mark Twain and Hawaii* (Chicago: Lakesides Press, 1947), 447.

4. *Mark Twain's Speeches,* ed. Albert Bigelow Paine (New York: Harper & Row, 1923), ix.

5. Lorch, 26–27.

6. It is not altogether clear whether he gave his Sandwich Islands lecture in Dayton, Nevada, on November 8, 1866; see *L,* 1: 362n, 365. This date is not included in Frear, *Mark Twain and Hawaii,* 422.

7. *L,* 1: 364–65.

8. *Alta California,* December 15, 1866, quoted in Lorch, 49–50.

9. *MTTB,* 25.

10. *MTTB,* 34–35.

11. *N&J,* 1: 239; *MTTB,* 41.

12. *N&J,* 1: 269–80.

13. *MTTB,* 70, 73–74.

16. WESTERNER IN THE EAST

1. *MTTB,* 83.

2. *MTHL* 1: 329 n. 2.

3. *N&J,* 1: 109; *L,* 2: 48–49, 57.

4. *MTTB,* 111.

5. *MTTB,* 111–16; *L,* 2: 16.

6. *MTTB,* 122–26.

7. *L,* 2: 19n; Albert von Frank, *An Emerson Chronology* (Boston: G.K. Hall, 1994), 430; *Letters of Ralph Waldo Emerson,* ed. Ralph L. Rusk (New York: Columbia University Press, 1939; repr., 1966), 500n.

8. James Elliot Cabot, *A Memoir of Ralph Waldo Emerson* (Boston: Houghton, Mifflin and Company, 1893), 2: 796.

9. *L,* 2: 29.

10. *MTA,* 2: 352; *MTB,* 1: 312; Frank Fuller, "Utah's War Governor Talks of Many Famous Men," New York *Times,* October 1, 1911; Fatout, 77; "Frank Fuller and My First New York Lecture," in *Who Is Mark Twain?* ed. Robert H. Hirst (New York: HarperCollins, 2009), 8–9.

11. This was the reason Fuller gave for Nye's absence that night, but its accuracy is challenged by the fact that Fuller told the *New York Times* (see note 10,

above) that Nye had called Clemens "a damned Secessionist" during a reunion of the two former governors in 1892, whereas James Warren Nye died in 1876; see Robert E. Stewart, "Mark Twain's Return from Aurora," *Nevada Historical Society Quarterly* 51 (Summer 2008), 137.

12. *MTA*, 2: 355.

13. *L*, 2: 49–50, 52, 60; *MTTB*, 248.

17. PILGRIMS ON THE LOOSE

1. *L*, 2: 64.

2. Charles J. Langdon to Mrs. Jervis Langdon, June 9, August 21 and 22, 1867, all in MTP.

3. *L*, 2: 192n.

4. Quoted in Robert H. Hirst, "The Making of *The Innocents Abroad*" (doctoral diss., University of California, Berkeley, 1975), 94–95.

5. Quoted in Hirst, "The Making of *The Innocents Abroad*," 58.

6. *L*, 2: 392–97.

7. *L*, 2: 202.

8. Van Wyck Brooks, *The Ordeal of Mark Twain* (New York: E. P. Hutton, 1920), 258.

9. Elisha Bliss to MT, August 4, 1869, MTP; Hirst, "The Making of *The Innocents Abroad*," 252, 475 n. 3.

18. LOVE IN A LOCKET

1. *L*, 2: 101–2, 105n.

2. *L*, 2: 103–5, 399–406.

3. *L*, 2: 107n.

4. *L*, 2: 109–10.

5. *L*, 2: 116–17, 111–12.

6. *MTE*, 147–48; *L*, 2: 119–20.

7. *L*, 2: 133–34.

8. Michael Horigan, *Elmira: Death Camp of the North* (Mechanicsburg, PA: Stackpole Books, 2002); K. Patrick Ober, *Mark Twain and Medicine* (Columbia: University of Missouri Press, 2003), 125; Mrs. Thomas Bailey Aldrich [Lilian Woodman], *Crowding Memories* (Boston: Houghton Mifflin, 1920), 151–54; MT to Poultney Bigelow, March 22, 1899, Library of Poultney Bigelow, Bigelow Homestead, Malden-on-Hudson, NY.

9. *L*, 3: 320–21; *MTA*, 2: 110, 103–5; the full transcript of Twain's letter to Charles Warren Stoddard of August 25, 1869, is in MTP.

10. *L*, 2: 144–46n.

11. *L*, 2: 155–59.

19. THE INNOCENT AT HOME

1. This recovered letter restores parts not included in the truncated version in the University of California Press edition. The full transcript made from the original letter (now lost) was recently acquired from the estate of Albert Bigelow Paine and is available at the MTP. The mystery woman may be "Pauline," originally of Cleveland; see Frank Fuller's 1912 letters to Albert Bigelow Paine, excerpted in *L,* 2: 115n.

2. *L,* 2: 202.

3. *L,* 2: 206; Richard B. Sewall, *Life of Emily Dickinson* (New York: Farrar, Strauss and Giroux, 1974), 2: 444–50; Jerome Loving, *Emily Dickinson: The Poet on the Second Story* (New York: Cambridge University Press, 1986), 84–85; *ET&S,* 2: 536–37.

4. *L,* 2: 207.

5. See Leon T. Dickinson, "Mark Twain's Revisions in Writing *The Innocents Abroad,*" *American Literature* 19 (May 1947), 139–57.

6. "The Holy Land Excursion Letter No. 46," San Francisco *Alta,* March 15, 1868, reprinted in Daniel Morley McKeithan, *Traveling with the Innocents Abroad: Mark Twain's Original Reports from Europe and the Holy Land* (Norman: University of Oklahoma Press, 1958), 272–77. Twain recycled essentially the same catalog of nineteenth-century inventions in both his 1889 birthday letter to Walt Whitman and "Queen Victoria's Jubilee" (1897).

7. *L,* 2: 232–33n.

8. *MTA,* 1: 238; *L,* 2: 241.

9. *MTB,* 1: 367–68. See also *L,* 2: 242–44.

10. *L,* 2: 250; *MTBus,* 101–2.

11. *L,* 2: 283.

12. *L,* 2: 286–87n, 284–86.

13. *L,* 2: 318.

14. *L,* 2: 353–56n.

15. *L,* 3: 82.

16. *MTE,* 155.

17. *L,* 3: 440, 267, 404.

18. *L,* 3: 195, 270, 288n.

19. *L,* 4: 338–39n; *MTB,* 386n; *L,* 3: 291, 294; 2: 349; 3: 298.

20. FALSE START IN BUFFALO

1. *L,* 2: 267.

2. Leah A. Strong, *Joseph Hopkins Twichell: Mark Twain's Friend and Pastor* (Athens: University of Georgia Press, 1966), 64; *Civil War Letters of Joseph Hopkins*

Twichell: A Chaplain's Story, ed. Peter Messent and Steve Courtney (Athens: University of Georgia Press, 2006), 1–14, 125–26. See also Steve Courtney, *Joseph Hopkins Twichell: The Life and Times of Mark Twain's Closest Friend* (Athens: University of Georgia Press, 2008).

3. The record of their religious differences comes mainly from Howells and Paine. The counterargument that they did not really differ on this subject can point only to the fact that Twain and his family, who never formally joined the Asylum Hill Church, nevertheless participated in its services and social activities while they lived in Hartford. See William Dean Howells, *My Mark Twain* (New York: Harper & Brothers, 1910), 32–33; *MTB,* 631–32; and Strong, *Joseph Hopkins Twichell,* 91–108.

4. *Mark Twain at the Buffalo* Express, ed. Joseph B. McCullough and Janice McIntire-Strasburg (DeKalb: Northern Illinois University Press, 2000), 5.

5. *L,* 3: 303–7.

6. *Mark Twain at the Buffalo* Express, 19.

7. *L,* 3: 361n.

8. *MTB,* 1: 424. Mentioning the fork stabbing, Paine states that medical authorities called cancer blood poisoning then. The MTP holds a note from Riley to Clemens dated May 16, 1872, stating he was caught in "a simple contest between Cancer and Constitution"; see *L,* 5: 189n, and Justin Kaplan, *Mr. Clemens and Mark Twain* (New York: Simon & Schuster, 1966), 128. See also Paul Baender, "Mark Twain and the Byron Scandal," *American Literature* 30 (January 1959), 467–85.

9. *L,* 4: 424–26; *Contributions to the* Galaxy, *1868–1871, by Mark Twain,* ed. Bruce R. McElderry, Jr. (Gainesville, FL: Scholars' Facsimiles & Reprints, 1961), 90–91; *Mark Twain at the Buffalo* Express, 243–46. See also *Roughing It,* ed. Harriet Elinor Smith and Edgar Marquess Branch (Berkeley: University of California Press, 1993), 33, 701–2.

10. For a probing study of Twain's development as a writer during his Buffalo period, see Jeffrey Steinbrink, *Getting to Be Mark Twain* (Berkeley: University of California Press, 1991).

11. *Mark Twain at the Buffalo* Express, 204–6. See also Paul Fatout, "Mark Twain Litigant," *American Literature* 31 (March 1959), 31–43.

12. *L,* 4: 50.

13. *L,* 4: 108n, 182n.

14. Walter Blair, *Mark Twain & Huck Finn* (Berkeley: University of California Press, 1960), 64–66.

15. *Contributions to the Galaxy,* 50.

16. *Contributions to the Galaxy,* xv; *Mark Twain at the Buffalo* Express, 269.

17. *L,* 4: 338n, 365.

21. BACK ON THE LECTURE CIRCUIT

1. *L*, 4: 176n, 392, 99, 40; 5: 55–56n.

2. *L*, 4: 269, 378–79; *Roughing It*, ed. Harriet Elinor Smith and Edgar Marquess Branch (Berkeley: University of California Press, 1993), 840–41.

3. *L*, 4: 469–70, 517, 484–86.

4. *L*, 4: 561–63; Lorch, 121.

5. *LLMT*, 161, 163–64; *L*, 4: 491, 499, 506.

6. *L*, 5: 2n.

7. *L*, 5: 15, 43–44.

8. *L*, 5: 46, 49n.

9. Richard B. Sewall, *Life of Emily Dickinson* (New York: Farrar, Straus & Giroux, 1974), 1: 115n; *L*, 5: 83, 93n.

10. *L*, 5: 98–101. When Sue Crane documented Langdon's last days for Paine in 1911, she noted that "Mr. Clemens was often inclined to blame himself unjustly" (*MTA*, 2: 230–31).

22. HOME IN HARTFORD

1. R. Kent Rasmussen, *Mark Twain: A to Z* (New York: Oxford University Press, 1995), 176.

2. Kenneth R. Andrews, *Nook Farm: Mark Twain's Hartford Circle* (Cambridge, MA: Harvard University Press, 1950); Wilson H. Faude, *The Renaissance of Mark Twain's House* (Larchmont, NY: Queens House, 1978), 11; Van Wyck Brooks, *The Ordeal of Mark Twain* (New York: E. P. Dutton, 1920).

3. For an excellent summary of the Stowe-Byron controversy, see Philip McFarland, *Loves of Harriet Beecher Stowe* (New York: Grove Press, 2007), 174–94.

4. Susan Goodman and Carl Dawson, *William Dean Howells: A Writer's Life* (Berkeley: University of California Press, 2005), 148–98. See also Howells's statement in *My Mark Twain* (New York: Harper and Brothers, 1910): "Emerson, Longfellow, Lowell, Holmes—I knew them all and all the rest of our sages, poets, seers, critics, humorists; they were like one another and like other literary men; but Clemens was sole, incomparable, the Lincoln of our literature" (101).

5. DeLancey Ferguson, *Mark Twain: Man and Legend* (Indianapolis: Bobbs-Merrill Company, 1947), 165–66; Howells, *My Mark Twain*, 138–39; Mrs. Thomas Bailey Aldrich [Lilian Woodman], *Crowding Memories* (Boston: Houghton Mifflin, 1920), 128–32.

6. *L*, 4: 316; 5: 105; *MTE*, 272–80. See also "Mark Twain in Sydney: A Further Interview" (*MTCI*, 202), where MT puns that Harte "has no heart, except his name."

7. *L*, 3: 120.

8. "Mark Twain on His Travels," San Francisco *Alta California*, dateline Febru-

ary 1, published March 3, 1868, 1. Clemens said he was writing on January 25 in his first paragraph on Hartford.

9. Justin Kaplan, *Mr. Clemens and Mark Twain: A Biography* (New York: Simon & Schuster, 1966), 183, 181; Rasmussen, *Mark Twain: A to Z*, 362.

10. *MTMF*, 252; "A Family Sketch" (James S. Copley Library, La Jolla, CA).

23. SEQUEL TO A SUCCESS

1. Henry Nash Smith, *Mark Twain: The Development of a Writer* (Cambridge, MA: Harvard University Press, 1962), 52.

2. Jeffrey Steinbrink, *Getting to Be Mark Twain* (Berkeley: University of California Press, 1991), 131; *L*, 4: 105.

3. *Roughing It*, ed. Harriet Elinor Smith and Edgar Marquess Branch (Berkeley: University of California Press, 1993), xxiv, 321, 313–15, 321, 361, 365–66, 440, 528, 531, 731.

4. See *Mark Twain's Letters from Hawaii*, ed. A. Grove Day (New York: Appleton-Century, 1966), 112; chapter 14.

5. Edgar Lee Masters, *Mark Twain, A Portrait* (New York: Scribner's, 1938), 218; *MTE*, 240.

6. Walter Francis Frear, *Mark Twain and Hawaii* (Chicago: Lakeside Press, 1947), 388–89.

7. *Roughing It*, 739n.

24. A BOOK ABOUT THE ENGLISH

1. *L*, 5: 159, 205.

2. *L*, 6: 546; London *Times*, May 5, 1910, p. 12.

3. For a more benign if not altogether reliable characterization of the Clemens-Hotten relationship, see Dewey Ganzel, "Samuel Clemens and John Camden Hotten," *The Library*, 20 (1965), 230–42. See also *ET&S*, 1: 586–607.

4. *L*, 5: 215–16.

5. Franklin Walker, *San Francisco's Literary Frontier* (New York: Knopf, 1939), 273, also quoted in John W. Crowley, *The Mask of Fiction: Essays on W. D. Howells* (Amherst: University of Massachusetts Press, 1989), 64. For Stoddard and Whitman, see Horace Traubel, *With Walt Whitman in Camden* (New York: Mitchell Kennerley, 1914), 3: 444–45; *Walt Whitman: The Correspondence*, ed. Edwin Haviland Miller (New York: New York University Press, 1961), 2: 97–98; and Clara Barrus, *Whitman and Burroughs, Comrades* (Boston: Houghton Mifflin, 1931), 48.

6. Roger Austen, *Genteel Pagan: The Double Life of Charles Warren Stoddard*, ed. John W. Crowley (Amherst: University of Massachusetts Press, 1991), 57–58, 65.

7. *MTHL*, 1: 154.

8. Lorch, 146–51; Charles Warren Stoddard, *Exits and Entrances* (Boston: Lothrop Publishing Company, 1903), 70; *MTHL,* 1: 154.

9. *L,* 5: 456n.

10. Mark Twain, *Following the Equator* (1897; repr., New York: Harper & Brothers, 1925), 1: 139.

25. COLONEL SELLERS

1. *MTB,* 476–77.

2. Bryant Morey French, *Mark Twain and the Gilded Age* (Dallas: Southern Methodist University Press, 1965), 175–76; Arlin Turner, "James Lampton, Mark Twain's Model for Colonel Sellers," *Modern Language Notes* 70 (December 1955), 592–94.

3. Edgar Lee Masters, *Mark Twain: A Portrait* (New York: Charles Scribner's Sons, 1938), 109; French, *Mark Twain and the Gilded Age,* 87, 131, 96.

4. *L,* 5: 367; French, *Mark Twain and the Gilded Age,* 292n.

5. *MTB,* 1: 518.

6. *L,* 6: 129n; Jerry Wayne Thomason, "*Colonel Sellers:* The Story of His Play" (doctoral diss., University of Missouri, 1991), 67 (original of letter in the Stowe-Day Library, Hartford, CT).

7. Quoted in Thomason, "*Colonel Sellers*: The Story of His Play," 95.

8. *L,* 6: 267–73.

9. French, *Mark Twain and the Gilded Age,* 242.

10. "A Play from Saml L. Clemens: Colonel Sellers," ed. Jerry Thomason and Tom Quirk, *Missouri Review* 18, no. 3 (1995), 109–51.

11. *L,* 4: 167–69; Thomason, "*Colonel Sellers:* The Story of His Play," 128.

12. Thomason, "*Colonel Sellers:* The Story of His Play," 133, 141, 147; Mary Lawton, *A Lifetime with Mark Twain: The Memories of Katy Leary* (New York: Harcourt, Brace, 1925), 349; MT to Joseph E. Hinds or Samuel S. Hinds, September 1894, and MT to Joseph E. Hinds, September 1894 (photocopies in MTP, courtesy of George J. Houle).

26. MISSISSIPPI MEMORIES

1. *L,* 6: 55n.

2. See Shelley Fisher Fishkin, *Was Huck Black? Mark Twain and American Voices* (New York: Oxford University Press, 1993), 13–40.

3. *L,* 6: 262–63.

4. Allan Bates, "Mark Twain and the Mississippi River," (doctoral diss., University of Chicago, 1968); Walter Blair, *Mark Twain and Huck Finn* (Berkeley: University of California Press, 1960), 36–37; *L,* 1: 329, 331n; 4: 499.

5. Alan Trachtenberg, *The Incorporation of America: Culture and Society in the Gilded Age* (New York: Hill and Wang, 1982).

6. *L,* 4: 402, 410.

7. MT to Dora Bowen (Goff), June 6, 1900 (University of Texas Library).

8. *Adventures of Huckleberry Finn, Tom Sawyer's Comrade,* ed. Victor Fischer and Lin Salamo (Berkeley: University of California Press, 2003), 408n. For the argument in favor of including the raft episode in *Huckleberry Finn,* see, for example, Peter G. Bridler, "The Raft Episode in *Huckleberry Finn,*" *Modern Fiction Studies* 14 (Spring 1968), 11–20.

27. THE RILEY BOOK

1. William Dean Howells, *My Mark Twain* (New York: Harper & Brothers, 1910), 125. Twain had accepted a two-thousand-dollar advance for the diamond book that he used to support Riley's trip to Africa. Later, when Bliss's son Frank tried to steal *A Tramp Abroad* for his own newly formed publishing company, Elisha Bliss insisted that *A Tramp Abroad* be used at the American Publishing Company to fulfill the 1870 contract. But in a conciliatory effort to win back Twain to his own company, he allowed *Tom Sawyer* to fulfill the earlier contract. See *N&J,* 2: 291n; and Mark Twain to Elisha Bliss, Jr., March 6, 1879 (photocopy in MTP, courtesy of Nick Karanovich).

2. For an analysis of Irving's most famous tale, see Jerome Loving, *Lost in the Customhouse: Authorship in the American Renaissance* (Iowa City: University of Iowa Press, 1993), 3–18. For a spirited defense of *Tom Sawyer* as a book intended for children, see John Seelye's introduction to the Penguin edition of the novel, *Mark Twain: The Adventures of Tom Sawyer* (New York: Penguin, 1986).

3. Quoted in *Civil War Letters of George Washington Whitman,* ed. Jerome M. Loving (Durham, NC: Duke University Press, 1975), 8.

4. "The Lessons of the Hour," in *Frederick Douglass Reader,* ed. William L. Andrews (New York: Oxford University Press, 1996), 356.

5. *L,* 6: 503; *MTHL,* 1: 122; *Huck Finn and Tom Sawyer among the Indians,* ed. Dahlia Armon and Walter Blair (Berkeley: University of California Press for the Bancroft Library, 1989), 265–66.

6. Bernard DeVoto, *Mark Twain at Work* (Cambridge, MA: Harvard University Press, 1942), 5–6; *The Adventures of Tom Sawyer,* ed. John C. Gerber et al. (Berkeley: University of California Press, 1980), 7–8.

7. *MTHL,* 1: 110–11, 121–22; *L,* 6: 595n.

8. *MTHL,* 1: 111; *The Adventures of Tom Sawyer,* 18–21.

9. *MTLP,* 106–7.

10. See *L,* 6: 596n4, for a counterargument to this speculation.

11. *MTCI,* 1, 4–7.

28. BANNED IN BOSTON

1. Donald Hoffmann, *Mark Twain in Paradise: His Voyages to Bermuda* (Columbia: University of Missouri Press, 2006), 26.

2. *MTE,* 320; and G[eorge] P[arsons] L[athrop], "The Whittier Dinner," New York *Evening Post,* December 19, 1877.

3. Henry Nash Smith, "That Hideous Mistake of Poor Clemens's," *Harvard Library Bulletin* 9 (Spring 1955), 145–80.

4. *L,* 6: 317–20.

5. Bernard DeVoto, *Mark Twain's America* (Boston: Little, Brown, 1932), 195.

6. *Mark Twain's Own Autobiography: The Chapters from the North American Review,* ed. Michael J. Kiskis (Madison: University of Wisconsin Press, 1990), 234–36.

7. William H. Bishop, *Detmold; A Romance* (Boston: Houghton, Osgood, and Company, 1879), 175, 159. The novel was serialized in the *Atlantic Monthly* in 1877–78. See also Jerome Loving, "Twain's Whittier Birthday Speech and Howells," *The Howellsian* 8 (Fall 2005), 6–9.

8. *MTHL,* 1: 213, 215; *MTMF,* 217; and "Mark Twain in 1906: An Edition of Selected Extracts from Isabel V. Lyon's Journal," ed. Laurie Lentz, *Resources for American Literary Study* 11 (Spring 1981), 32.

9. Quoted in Smith, "That Hideous Mistake," 147, 167; see also a more recent analysis of the speech and its fallout in Harold K. Bush, "The Mythic Struggle between East and West: Mark Twain's Speech at Whittier's 70th Birthday Celebration and W. D. Howells's *A Chance Acquaintance," American Literary Realism* 27, no. 2 (1995), 53–73.

10. Smith, "That Hideous Mistake," 165–66.

11. William Dean Howells, *My Mark Twain* (New York: Harper & Brothers, 1910), 63.

12. Smith, "That Hideous Mistake," 176–77 (holograph in Yale University Library).

29. THE INNOCENT ABROAD AGAIN

1. Jean Webster McKinney Family Papers, Vassar College Library.

2. *The Adventures of Tom Sawyer,* ed. John C. Gerber et al. (Berkeley: University of California Press, 1980), 22–25; *Adventures of Huckleberry Finn,* ed. Victor Fischer and Lin Salamo (Berkeley: University of California Press, 2003), 549–61.

3. *MTMF,* 219.

4. *Letters,* 1: 319–20.

5. MT to Orion Clemens, February 21, 1878; MT to Jane Lampton Clemens, February 23, 1878 (MTP).

6. MT to David Gray, April 10, 1878 (Franklin D. Roosevelt Library, Hyde Park, NY).

7. *MTHL*, 1: 220–21, 223n; *MTB*, 617–18.

8. Jerome Loving, *Walt Whitman's Champion: William Douglas O'Connor* (College Station: Texas A&M University Press, 1978), 110–11, 115–19.

9. *MTSpk*, 116–19.

10. *MTCI*, 14; *N&J*, 2: 268–70; *MTE*, 305–9.

11. *N&J*, 2: 42, 123n.

12. *A Tramp Abroad*, ed. Robert Gray Bruce and Hamlin Hill (New York: Penguin Books, 1997), xxii–xxiv.

13. *N&J*, 2: 81–82.

14. *A Tramp Abroad*, 28, 38.

15. *N&J*, 2: 113n.

16. *A Tramp Abroad*, 162–64.

17. *A Tramp Abroad*, 80; *Adventures of Huckleberry Finn*, 158.

18. *A Tramp Abroad*, 12–13.

30. DOWN AND OUT IN PARIS AND LONDON

1. Olivia L. Clemens to Samuel E. Moffett, March 9, 1879 (MTP), quoted in *N&J*, 2: 292n.

2. MT to Joseph H. Twichell, September 9 [1879] (Yale University Library), printed without date in *Letters*, 1: 338.

3. MT to Bayard Taylor, December 14, 1878 (Cornell University Library); [Bayard Taylor], "American vs. English Criticism," New York *Tribune*, April 12, 1876.

4. *N&J*, 2: 308–9, 316

5. *N&J*, 2: 324–26.

6. *N&J*, 2: 294–95.

7. *MTB*, 2: 646; N&J, 2: 339, 486.

8. "Mr. Darwin's *Descent of Man* had been in print five or six years, and the storm of indignation raised by it was still raging in pulpits and periodicals," Twain wrote in "A Monument to Adam" in a July 1903 issue of *Harper's Weekly*. "In tracing the genesis of the human race back to its sources, Mr. Darwin had left Adam out altogether. We had monkeys, and 'missing links,' and plenty of other kinds of ancestors, but no Adam. Jesting with Mr. [Thomas K.] Beecher and other friends in Elmira, I said there seemed to be a likelihood that the world would discard Adam and accept the monkey, and that in the course of time Adam's very name would be forgotten in the earth; therefore this calamity ought to be averted; a monument would accomplish this, and Elmira ought not to waste this honorable opportunity to do Adam a favor and herself a credit."

9. *MTCI*, 22–27; MT to Daniel Slote, September 4, 1879 (photocopy in MTP, courtesy of Heritage Book Shop, April 27, 1994); "Unconscious Plagiarism," in *Mark Twain's Speeches* (New York: Oxford University Press, 1996), 56–58.

31. ASSOCIATIONS NEW AND OLD

1. Frederick Anderson and Hamlin Hill, "How Samuel Clemens Became Mark Twain's Publisher," *Proof* 2 (1972), 118–19.

2. Carl J. Webber, *The Rise and Fall of James R. Osgood* (Waterville, ME: Colby College Press, 1959), 176–82.

3. Charles L. Webster to MT, May 5, 1881 (MTP); *MTMF*, 247–50.

4. *Walt Whitman: The Correspondence*, ed. Edwin Haviland Miller (New York: New York University Press, 1964), 3: 224; and Jerome Loving, *Walt Whitman's Champion: William Douglas O'Connor* (College Station: Texas A&M University Press, 1978), 125n.

5. Ed Folsom and Jerome Loving, "Mark Twain: 'The Walt Whitman Controversy,'" *Virginia Quarterly Review* 83 (Spring 2007), 123–38.

6. *N&J*, 2: 486, 510n; Edgar M. Branch, "'The Babes in the Wood': Artemus Ward's 'Double Health' to Mark Twain," *Publications of the Modern Language Association* 93 (October 1978), 972 n. 64; *L*, 5: 222–26n.

32. RETURN TO THE RIVER AND THE LECTURE CIRCUIT

1. *N&J*, 2: 527, 531, 533.

2. *N&J*, 2: 547.

3. See Horace E. Bixby, "How the Boy Became a Pilot and the Pilot a Humorist," *New Orleans Times-Democrat*, May 7, 1882.

4. Eric Sundquist, "Realism and Regionalism," in *Columbia Literary History of the United States*, ed. Emory Elliott (New York: Columbia University Press, 1988), 514; James Kinney, "Race in the New South: Joel Chandler Harris's 'Free Joe and the Rest of the World,'" *American Literary Realism* 33, no. 3 (2001), 244. See also Guy A. Cardwell, *Twins of Genius* (East Lansing: Michigan State University Press, 1953); and Arlin Turner, *Mark Twain and George W. Cable: The Record of a Literary Friendship* (East Lansing: Michigan State University Press, 1960).

5. *LLMT*, 212.

6. Arlin Turner, "Notes on Mark Twain in New Orleans," *McNeese Review* 6 (Spring 1954), 10–22.

7. *N&J*, 2: 489–91.

8. *N&J*, 2: 567–69.

9. MT to James R. Osgood [June 11, 1882] (MTP; courtesy of Todd M. Axelrod); *MTBus*, 207.

10. R. Kent Rasmussen, *Mark Twain: A to Z* (New York: Oxford University Press, 1995), 445; *MTHL,* 1: 435–36; *N&J,* 3: 19n.

11. *Personal Memoirs of U.S. Grant,* ed. E.B. Long (New York: Da Capo, 1982), 20. Another possibility for "G.G." is George Griffin. As the Clemens butler, he was chief of all the other servants and in charge of household security. For example, he locked up the silverware every night to protect it from domestic pilfering. See *Adventures of Huckleberry Finn,* ed. Victor Fischer and Lin Salamo (Berkeley: University of California Press, 2002), 376.

12. *N&J,* 3: 29n.

13. *N&J,* 3: 60n.

14. *N&J,* 3: 83.

15. Arlin Turner, *George W. Cable: A Biography* (Durham, NC: Duke University Press, 1956), 160–93.

16. Lang's essay also appeared in *The Critic* 16 (July 25, 1891), 45–46, where he compared *Huckleberry Finn* to the *Odyssey*; see Roger Asselineau, *The Literary Reputation of Mark Twain from 1910 to 1950* (Paris: Librairie Marcel Didier, 1954), 70.

17. Lorch, 168; Turner, *George W. Cable,* 176.

18. "Cable and Twain: The Author and the Humorist Arrive in the City Today," St. Louis *Post-Dispatch,* January 9, 1885 (in *MTCI,* 70–72).

19. MT to Olivia Langdon Clemens, February 3 and 8, 1885 (MTP).

33. MARK TWAIN AND THE PHUNNY PHELLOWS

1. Walter Blair, *Native American Humor* (Chandler Publishing Company, 1960), 147n; MT to David Gray, June 10, 1880, quoted in *Roughing It,* ed. Harriet Elinor Smith and Edgar Marquess Branch (Berkeley: University of California Press, 1993), 797.

2. Blair, *Native American Humor,* 109.

3. Walter Blair and Hamlin Hill, *America's Humor from Poor Richard to Doonesbury* (New York: Oxford University Press, 1978), 263–64.

4. Alan Trachtenberg, *The Incorporation of America: Culture and Society in the Gilded Age* (New York: Hill & Wang, 1982), 23.

34. WEBSTER AND PAIGE

1. Pamela A. Moffett to MT, July 10, 1887 (MTP), quoted in Charles H. Gold, *Hatching Ruin, or Mark Twain's Road to Bankruptcy* (Columbia: University of Missouri Press, 2003), 115.

2. "Invented a Typesetting Machine: Joseph [*sic*] W. Paige, Who Has Been Sued for $950,000 for Breach of Promise," Chicago *Daily Tribune,* June 11, 1892.

3. MT to Orion Clemens, July 1, 1889, quoted in *MTLP,* 1; *MTA,* 1: 78.

4. Kenneth Sanderson, "The Books of Charles L. Webster & Co.," unpublished paper dated August 16, 1979 (MTP). Interestingly, in the appendix to *The American Claimant,* one of the later books included in the Webster & Company list, Twain alluded to O'Connor's description of weather in the posthumously published "The Brazen Android," *Atlantic Monthly* 62 (April 1891), 433–54.

5. Albert Bigelow Paine's comments in the margin of the typescript for Twain's autobiographical dictation for May 29, 1906 (MTP), quoted in Gold, *Hatching Ruin,* 64.

6. *N&J,* 3: 201n.

7. Pamela A. Moffett to Samuel E. Moffett, April 17, 1881 (MTP), quoted in Gold, *Hatching Ruin,* 80; MT to Charles L. Webster, July 27, 1885 (Vassar College Library).

8. Justin Kaplan, *Mr. Clemens and Mark Twain* (New York: Simon & Schuster, 1966), 282.

9. *N&J,* 3: 288.

10. *N&J,* 3: 288–89, 202n, 218n; *MTLP,* 195–96, 255n, 269n. For Higbie, see also chapter 10, note 14.

11. Fred A. Hall to MT, September 17, 1888, quoted in *N&J,* 3: 304.

12. Gold, *Hatching Ruin,* 131; MT to Pamela Ann Moffett, July 1, 1889 (MTP).

13. MT to Pamela Ann Moffett, June 7, 1897, quoted in Gold, *Hatching Ruin,* 154.

14. *MTHHR,* 66.

15. MT to Orion Clemens, February 25, 1891 (MTP).

35. A ROMANCE OF THE WHITE CONSCIENCE

1. *Adventures of Huckleberry Finn,* ed. Victor Fischer and Lin Salamo (Berkeley: University of California Press, 2003), 445, 743.

2. Along this line, see Louis J. Budd, "A 'Nobler Roman Aspect' of *Adventures of Huckleberry Finn,*" in *One Hundred Years of Huckleberry Finn: The Boy, His Book, and American Culture,* ed. Robert Sattlemeyer and J. Donald Crowley (Columbia: University of Missouri Press, 1985), 26–40.

3. Samuel E. Moffett, "Mark Twain, Humorist, Man of Letters and Champion of the Right," *The Pilgrim* (Battle Creek, MI), September 1903, pp. 6–8; Clara L. Clemens to Samuel E. Moffett [October–December 1902] (MTP).

4. *N&J,* 3: 538, 343.

5. *MTL,* 2: 666.

6. "I was named Langhorne from a valued friend of my father, but he was not a relative, but a comrade of my father's youth in Virginia. I merely served by my name as a remembrance of that loved and lost comradeship of a vanished day" (MT to W.H. Langhorne, August 1–17, 1892 [MTP], published in the London *Times,* May 5, 1910).

7. *N&J*, 3: 383n, 389n. Arnold's essay "Civilisation in the United States" appeared in the April number of *Nineteenth Century* for 1888 and was reprinted in the New York *Evening Post* of April 9, 1888. To his credit, Arnold also described Grant as "a man of sterling good-sense as well as of the firmest resolution; a man withal, humane, simple, modest; . . . never boastful where he himself was concerned, and where his nation was concerned seldom boastful."

8. MT to Francis E. Bliss, August 26, September 8, 1901 (University of Texas Library); "Only a Nigger," in *Mark Twain at the Buffalo* Express, ed. Joseph B. McCullough and Janice McIntire-Strasburg (DeKalb: Northern Illinois University Press, 2000), 22–23.

9. Tom Quirk, *Mark Twain and Human Nature* (Columbia: University of Missouri Press, 2007), 157.

10. R. Kent Rasmussen, *Mark Twain: A to Z* (New York: Oxford University Press, 1995), 280.

36. PUBLISHING GRANT

1. *MTE*, 170, 175.

2. William S. McFeely, *Grant: A Biography* (New York: W.W. Norton, 1982), 490, 492.

3. *Who Is Mark Twain?* ed. Robert H. Hirst (New York: HarperCollins, 2009), 27.

4. MT to Olivia Susan (Susy) Clemens, November 23, 1884 (MTP).

5. *MTE*, 170–74.

6. *MTE*, 175–78; *MTA*, 1: 37.

7. *MTA*, 1: 48.

8. *MTA*, 1: 49–51.

9. *MTA*, 1: 55–56; MT to Boston *Herald*, July 6, 1885 (MTP).

10. MT to Karl Gerhardt, July 6, 1885 (Yale University Library); MT to Edward H. House, July 21, 1885 (University of Virginia Library).

11. *Who Is Mark Twain?* 27–28

12. *Personal Memoirs of U.S. Grant*, ed. E.B. Long (Cleveland: World Publishing Company, 1952), vii; *Who Is Mark Twain?* 27.

13. *The Prince and the Pauper* reissues were actually made up of sheets from the original publication by James R. Osgood and Company, reissued with new inserted title pages under the imprint of Charles L. Webster & Company.

14. The reprint of *Life on the Mississippi* was a reissue of Osgood sheets with a new Webster & Company title page.

37. BROODING IN KING ARTHUR'S COURT

1. Quoted in *A Connecticut Yankee in King Arthur's Court*, ed. Bernard Stein, with an introduction by Henry Nash Smith (Berkeley: University of California Press, 1979), 27.

2. James M. Cox, "'*A Connecticut Yankee in King Arthur's Court*': The Machinery of Self-Preservation," *Yale Review* 50 (1960), 89–102. See also James M. Cox, *Mark Twain: The Fate of Humor* (Princeton, NJ: Princeton University Press, 1966), 207.

3. *MTL,* 1: 447–48; MT to Olivia Susan Clemens, February 8, 1885 (University of Virginia Library); *MTMF,* 257–58; Howard G. Baetzhold, "'The Autobiography of Sir Robert Smith of Camelot': Mark Twain's Original Plan for *A Connecticut Yankee*," *American Literature* 32 (January 1961), 456–61.

4. *N&J,* 3: 398, 401, 293; Howard G. Baetzhold, *Mark Twain and John Bull: The British Connection* (Bloomington: Indiana University Press, 1970), 107–13.

5. Baetzhold, *Mark Twain and John Bull,* 135.

6. Susan Goodman and Carl Dawson, *William Dean Howells: A Writer's Life* (Berkeley: University of California Press, 2005), 280–81.

7. Paul J. Carter, Jr., "Mark Twain and the American Labor Movement," *New England Quarterly* 30 (September 1957), 383–88.

38. PROGRESS AND POVERTY

1. Mark Twain, *The American Claimant* (New York: Charles L. Webster & Co., 1892), 97. Clemens actually quoted from his own speech, "The American Press," written in 1888 for the Society of the Army of the Cumberland but never delivered (MTP).

2. *MTHL,* 2: 595.

3. MT to Orion Clemens, December 8, 1887 (Vassar College Library). See also Alan Gribben, "Autobiography as Property: Mark Twain and His Legend," in *The Mythologizing of Mark Twain,* ed. Sara de Saussure Davis and Philip D. Beidler (Tuscaloosa: University of Alabama Press, 1984), 39–55.

4. *Camden's Compliment to Walt Whitman,* ed. Horace Traubel (Philadelphia: David McKay, 1889), 64–65 (letter dated May 24, 1889, in Beinecke Library, Yale University).

5. *MTHL,* 2: 628n.

6. MT to Timothy Dwight, letter published in the Hartford *Courant,* June 29, 1888.

7. MT to Charles H. Clark, July 2, 1888 (MTP).

8. MT to Orion Clemens, July 2, 1888; MT to Olivia Lewis Langdon, December 1, 1888 (MTP).

9. On February 2, 1890, he told Daniel Frohman in a letter he may not have mailed: "Do not make any foreign contracts. I cannot consent to have this amazing burlesque played in England . . . if you had allowed me to see the manuscript in time, this stuff would not have gone on the stage" (St. John's Seminary, Camarillo, CA).

10. Takashima Mariko, "Not Twain, But Twichell: The Hartford Support System of Edward House's Japanese Students," *Mark Twain Studies* 2 (October 2006), 142–57; MT to Dean Sage, February 5, 1890 (James S. Copley Library, La Jolla, California). See also MT to Edward H. House, March 19, 1889 (University of Virginia Library); and Paul Fatout, "Mark Twain, Litigant," *American Literature,* 31 (March 1959), 30–45.

11. MT to Hamlin Garland, March 23, 1889 (University of Southern California Library); MT to Pamela A. Moffett, July 1, 1889 (MTP).

12. MT to Olivia Susan Clemens, July 16, 1889 (MTP); Andrew Hoffman, *Inventing Mark Twain: The Lives of Samuel Langhorne Clemens* (New York: William Morrow, 1997), 367; *Papa: An Intimate Biography of Mark Twain by Susy Clemens,* ed. Charles Neider (New York: Doubleday, 1985), 15; Karen Lystra, *Dangerous Intimacy: The Untold Story of Mark Twain's Final Years* (Berkeley: University of California Press, 2004), 16.

13. Olivia L. Clemens and MT to Georgina Sullivan Jones, January 23–25, 1891 (MTP); *Susy and Mark Twain,* ed. Edith Colgate Salsbury (New York: Harper & Row, 1965), 283.

14. *Papa,* 131; *Susy and Mark Twain,* 286–88.

15. *MTMF,* 265–66; *Susy and Mark Twain,* 284.

39. EUROPE ON ONLY DOLLARS A DAY

1. For texts of the *Sun* essays as they were syndicated in the Chicago *Tribune,* see Barbara Schmidt's website at www.twainquotes.com/newspapercollections.html.

2. MT to Olivia L. Clemens, September 28, 1891 (transcribed from manuscript, courtesy of Christie's, MTP).

3. MT to Orion Clemens, June 28, 1892 (MTP).

4. Clara Clemens, *My Father, Mark Twain* (New York: Harper & Brothers, 1931), 64.

5. MT to Charles J. Langdon, August 7, 1892 (MTP).

6. *MTLP,* 318–19.

7. *LLMT,* 265; MT to Susan L. Crane, September 18, 1892 (MTP).

8. MT to Susan L. Crane, September 30, 1892 (MTP); Olivia Susan Clemens to Louise Brownell [October 14, 1892] (Hamilton College Library); MT to Clara L. Clemens, November 10, 1892 (MTP).

9. *MTLP,* 321; MT to Chatto and Windus, November 10, 1892 (Albert A. and Henry W.S. Berg Collection, New York Public Library); MT to Chatto and Windus, October 13, 1892 (University of Louisville Library); MT to Frederick J. Hall, December 2, 1892 (MTP); *MTLP,* 328.

10. MT to unidentified, June 25, 1895 (University of Texas Library).

11. *MTLP,* 328, 337.

12. *MTLP,* 344, 354–55, 359; Ron Powers, *Mark Twain: A Life* (New York: Free Press, 2005), 543.

13. J. Henry Harper, *I Remember* (New York: Harper & Brothers, 1934), 134–35.

40. A DREAM SOLD DOWN THE RIVER

1. See Eric J. Sundquist, "Mark Twain and Homer Plessy," in *Mark Twain: A Collection of Critical Essays,* ed. Eric J. Sundquist (Edgewood Cliffs, NJ: Prentice-Hall, 1994), 169–83.

2. Theodore Dreiser, "Nigger Jeff," *Ainslee's* 8 (November 1901), 366–66; Arthur Henry, *Nicholas Blood, Candidate* (New York: Oliver Dodd, 1890), 32.

3. *MTLP,* 359.

4. Mark Twain, *Pudd'nhead Wilson and Those Extraordinary Twins,* ed. Sidney E. Berger (New York: W. W. Norton, 1980), 9.

5. *Pudd'nhead Wilson,* 70, 40, 39, 71.

6. *Pudd'nhead Wilson,* 124.

7. *Pudd'nhead Wilson,* 114, 8. For Hawthorne, see Jerome Loving, *Lost in the Customhouse: Authorship in the American Renaissance* (Iowa City: University of Iowa Press, 1993), 19–34.

8. *Pudd'nhead Wilson,* 11, 114.

41. FAMILY MATTERS

1. *MTMF,* 268–70; 336; MT to Olivia L. Clemens, April 4, 1893 (MTP); Olivia Susan Clemens to Louise Brownell [April 1893] (Hamilton College Library).

2. Olivia Susan Clemens to Louise Brownell [March 5, 1893, March 1893] (Hamilton College Library).

3. MT to Clara L. Clemens, January 21, 1893 (MTP); Olivia Susan Clemens to Louise Brownell [April 3, 1893] (Hamilton College Library); "In Defense of Harriet Shelley," in *How to Tell a Story and Other Essays* (New York: Oxford University Press, 1996), 15.

4. MT to Susan L. Crane, March 19, 1893 (Mark Twain House, Hartford, CT).

5. MT to Olivia L. Clemens, April 4, 1893 (MTP); *MTE,* 312.

6. MT to Susan L. Crane, April 23, 1893 (MTP); Erik Larson, *The Devil in the White City* (New York: Random House, 2003).

7. MT to Orion Clemens, April 26, 1893; MT to Pamela A. Moffett, April 26, 1893 (MTP); *MTLP,* 343.

8. MT to Susan L. Crane, August 20, 1893 (MTP); Olivia Susan Clemens to Louise Brownell [September 3 and November 8, 1893] (Hamilton College Library).

9. *LLMT,* 267–68; *MTHL,* 2: 653.

42. A FRIEND AT STANDARD OIL

1. Justin Kaplan, *Mr. Clemens and Mark Twain* (New York: Simon & Schuster, 1966), 383–85, 321.

2. MT to Olivia L. Clemens, October 18, 1893 (transcribed from manuscript, courtesy of Christie's, New York [MTP]); *LLMT,* 269–70.

3. *MTHHR,* 11; *LLMT,* 280.

4. *LLMT,* 287.

5. J. Henry Harper, *I Remember* (New York: Harper & Brothers, 1934), 137–39; James J. Corbett, *The Roar of the Crowd* (New York: G. P. Putnam's Sons, 1925), 328; *MTB,* 2: 973–74.

6. MT to Olivia L. Clemens, January 27–30, 1894 (MTP).

7. MT to Olivia L. Clemens, February 15, 1894 (MTP).

8. *L,* 3: 303–7, 333–34; Orion Clemens to MT, February 2, 1894 (MTP).

9. Samuel E. Moffett, "Henry Huttleston Rogers," *Cosmopolitan* (September 1902), 532–35.

10. MT to Olivia L. Clemens, February 11–13, 1894 (MTP).

11. MT to Olivia L. Clemens, February 20, 1894; MT to Pamela A. Moffett, February 25, 1894; MT to Olivia L. Clemens, March 1, 1894 (MTP).

12. MT to Olivia L. Clemens, April 22, 1894 (MTP); *LLMT,* 301–2.

13. MT to Frederick J. Hall, June 1, 1894 (University of Virginia Library). See also *MTLP,* 363–66.

43. BROKEN TWIGS AND FOUND CANOES

1. MT to Olivia L. Clemens, May 16, 1894 (transcript read against the manuscript, courtesy of Sotheby's, New York [MTP]); Mark Twain, "Fenimore Cooper's Literary Offenses," *North American Review* 161 (July 1895), 1–12; Bernard DeVoto, "Fenimore Cooper's Further Literary Offenses," *New England Quarterly* 19 (September 1946), 291–301; "Cooper's Prose Style," in *Mark Twain: Letters from the Earth,* ed. Bernard De Voto (New York: Harper & Row, 1962), 135–45; MT to Richard Watson Gilder, April 29, 1898 (Pierpont Morgan Library).

2. Partially contained in MT to Olivia L. Clemens, December 20, 1893 (MTP); see also Clara Clemens, *My Father, Mark Twain* (New York: Harper & Brothers, 1931), 132–34, where the passage is slightly misquoted.

3. Wayne Franklin, *James Fenimore Cooper: The Early Years* (New Haven, CT: Yale University Press, 2007), xviii.

4. *Percy Bysshe Shelley: Complete Poems* (New York: Book of the Month Club, 1993), 259.

5. Allen Walker Read, "The Membership in Proposed American Academies," *American Literature* 7 (May 1935), 145–65.

6. MT to Olivia L. Clemens, August 9, 1894 (MTP).

7. Olivia Susan Clemens to Louise Brownell [July 29, 1894] (Hamilton College Library); also printed but misdated in *Papa: An Intimate Biography of Mark Twain by Susy Clemens,* ed. Charles Neider (New York: Doubleday, 1985), 23–29; MT to William Dean Howells, September 14, 1894 (Huntington Library).

44. BACK HOME AND OVERLAND

1. *MTB,* 2: 989; MT to Franklin G. Whitmore, October 7, 1894 (MTP); MT to Francis E. Bliss, October 13, 1894 (collection of Donald T. Bliss, facsimile in MTP); *MTHHR,* 80.

2. *MTB,* 2: 991; *MTHHR,* 108.

3. MT to Franklin G. Whitmore, January 8, 1895 (Mark Twain House, Hartford, CT); *MTHHR,* 117–19.

4. *LLMT,* 312.

5. *MTB,* 1: 81–82.

6. San Francisco *Examiner,* August 17, 1895, quoted in *Overland with Mark Twain: James B. Pond's Photographs and Journal of the North American Lecture Tour of 1895,* ed. Alan Gribben and Nick Karanovich (Elmira, NY: Center for Mark Twain Studies at Quarry Farm, 1992), viii.

7. Clara Clemens, *My Father, Mark Twain* (New York: Harper & Brothers, 1931), 136.

8. *MTHHR,* 171; *Overland with Mark Twain,* 3.

9. *MTCI,* 185.

10. This warm feeling was apparently not reciprocated. After they parted in Victoria, Twain told Rogers—in one of several complaints about his lecture agent—that Pond "hasn't any sand or any intelligence or judgment. I must make no contract with him to platform me through America next year if I can do better" (*MTHHR,* 188).

45. LOST IN THE BRITISH EMPIRE

1. *MTCI,* 242.

2. *MTCI,* 190–92.

3. Fatout, 241, 265; *MTCI,* 240.

4. *MTCI,* 201; *FE,* 1: 9–10.

5. Lorch, 200–201; *MTCI,* 249–51, 263–64; *FE,* 2: 319.

6. *FE,* 2: 300–301, 18–19.

7. MT to Samuel E. Moffett, November 10, 1895 (MTP); *MTCI,* 250.

8. *FE,* 2: 262; *MTHHR,* 215, 223.

9. *LLMT,* 316; MT to Olivia Susan Clemens, February 7, 1896 (MTP); MT to Franklin G. Whitmore, April 5, 1896 (Mark Twain House, Hartford, CT).

10. *MTHL,* 2: 690.

11. *FE,* 2: 381–82.

12. MT to James B. Pond, August 10, 1896 (Henry W. and Albert A. Berg Collection, New York Public Library); MT to Andrew Chatto, August 11, 1896 (MTP); Peter Messent, "Mark Twain in Guildford," *Mark Twain Journal* 36 (Fall 1998), 26–29; MT to Anna Goodenough, August 14, 1896 (Mark Twain Museum, Hannibal, MO); MT to Mrs. Armstrong, August 18, 1896 (facsimile in Henry Sotheran Ltd. catalogs, February 14, 1998, item 14, in MTP).

13. *LLMT,* 321, 323.

14. Clara Clemens, *My Father, Mark Twain* (New York: Harper & Brothers, 1931), 171.

46. MARK TWAIN'S DAUGHTER

1. *MTB,* 2: 1023; *MTN,* 320.

2. *MTB,* 2: 1023; *MTN,* 321, 318–19; *LLMT,* 319.

3. *MTHHR,* 235; *LLMT,* 320, 325.

4. Olivia Susan Clemens to Louise Brownell [November 13, 1892 and October 2, 1891] (Hamilton College Library).

5. *Letters,* 636; *MTN,* 320.

6. *MTA,* 2: 39–40.

7. *LLMT,* 322.

8. *MTHL,* 2: 663.

9. MT to Orion and Mary E. Clemens, [c. October 1, 1896] (MTP, Scrapbook 20).

10. *MTHHR,* 238, 253–55; MT to Eleanor V. Hutton, November 26, 1896 (Princeton University Library); *MTLL,* 328; MT to Pamela A. Moffett, January 7, 1897 (MTP).

11. MT to Joseph H. Twichell, January 19, 1997 (Yale University Library).

12. MT to James R. Clemens, June 3, 1897 (Mark Twain House, Hartford, CT); MT to Frank Fuller, June 3, 1897 (transcript only, University of Wisconsin Library); MT to James G. Bennett, June 24, 1897 (Middlebury College Library); *MTHHR,* 285–88.

13. *MTHL,* 2: 669n.

47. CITY OF DREAMS

1. *MTHL,* 2: 670.

2. Carl Dolmetsch, *"Our Famous Guest": Mark Twain in Vienna* (Athens: University of Georgia Press, 1992).

3. Clara Clemens, *My Father, Mark Twain* (New York: Harper & Brothers, 1931), 190–92.

4. Clemens, *My Father, Mark Twain*, 188–89; Dolmetsch, *"Our Famous Guest,"* 146–47.

5. *MTHHR*, 360; *MFMT*, 208.

6. John S. Tuckey, *Mark Twain and Little Satan: The Writings of The Mysterious Stranger* (West Lafayette, IN: Purdue University Studies, 1963), 26; *MTN*, 256; "Conversations with Satan," in *Who Is Mark Twain?* ed. Robert H. Hirst (New York: HarperCollins, 2009), 31–32.

7. *Is He Dead? A Comedy in Three Acts*, ed. Shelley Fisher Fishkin (Berkeley: University of California Press, 2003), 152, 173, passim; *MTHHR*, 358–62; John Lahr, "Devil May Care: Resurrections in Conor McPherson and Mark Twain," *New Yorker* (December 17, 2007), 98–100.

8. MT to Heinrich Obersteiner, October 5, 1897, quoted in Dometsch, *"Our Famous Guest,"* 202–3.

9. "Stirring Times in Austria," in *The Man That Corrupted Hadleyburg and Other Stories and Essays* (New York: Oxford University Press, 1996), 285, 316.

10. Albert Speer, *Inside the Third Reich* (New York: Macmillan, 1970), 98; William L. Shirer, *The Rise and the Fall of the Third Reich* (New York: Simon and Schuster, 1960), 24. For Twain's authorial interest in the Dreyfus Affair, see his letters to Chatto and Windus (University of Virginia Library) and to J. Henry Harper (University of Illinois Library), both penned on February 8, 1898.

11. Shelley Fisher Fishkin, "Mark Twain and the Jews," *Arizona Quarterly* 61 (Spring 2005), 137–66; "Concerning the Jews," in *The Man That Corrupted Hadleyburg*, 264–66, 269–71, 274–76, 281–83; and Jerome Loving, *The Last Titan: A Life of Theodore Dreiser* (Berkeley: University of California Press, 2005), 367–71.

12. "Concerning the Jews," 278–79.

13. Fishkin, "Concerning the Jews," 253–54; "Jane Lampton Clemens," in *Mark Twain's Hannibal, Huck & Tom*, ed. Walter Blair (Berkeley: University of California Press, 1969), 44–45; *Letters*, 2: 818.

14. MT to Franklin G. Whitmore, December 11, 1897 (MTP); *MTHHR*, 308.

48. WINTER FANTASIES

1. Mark Twain to Francis D. Finlay, April 25, 1900 (University of Wisconsin Library); *L*, 5: 487–88. Twain had met Finlay in 1873 while visiting Ireland; he was the owner of the Belfast *Whig*.

2. MT to Frank Bliss, November 4, 1897 (MTP and Yale University Library); *MTHHR*, 305.

3. *MTHL*, 2: 658–59.

4. Carl Dolmetsch, *"Our Famous Guest": Mark Twain in Vienna* (Athens: University of Georgia Press, 1992), 266–70.

5. Notebook entry for August 10, 1898, quoted in Dolmetsch, *"Our Famous Guest,"* 278.

6. *No. 44, Mark Twain's Mysterious Stranger Manuscripts,* ed. William M. Gibson (Berkeley: University of California Press, 1982), 49–51.

7. *No. 44, Mark Twain's Mysterious Stranger Manuscripts,* 72–73.

8. John S. Tuckey, *Mark Twain and Little Satan: The Writings of the Mysterious Stranger* (West Lafayette: Purdue University Studies, 1963), 37.

9. *The Man That Corrupted Hadleyburg and Other Stories and Essays* (New York: Oxford University Press, 1996), 32–33, 47; *MTHHR,* 382n, 384.

10. *MTHHR,* 355.

11. *No. 44, Mark Twain's Mysterious Stranger Manuscripts,* 190.

12. *MTHL,* 2: 679.

13. *No. 44, Mark Twain's Mysterious Stranger Manuscripts,* 166.

14. *MTHL,* 2: 683; *MTB,* 2: 1094.

15. MT to Poultney Bigelow, December 19, 1898 (Library of Poultney Bigelow, Bigelow Homestead, Malden-on-Hudson, NY); MT to James R. Clemens, March 5, 1899 (Mark Twain House, Hartford, CT); *MTHL,* 2: 683; Caroline Thomas Harnsberger, *Mark Twain's Clara* (Evanston, IL: Press of Ward Schori, 1982), 30; MT to Charles Dudley Warner, February 15, 1899 (University of Virginia Library).

16. MT to Samuel E. Moffett, September 15, 1899 (MTP); *Correspondence of William James,* ed. Ignas K. Skrupkelis and Elizabeth M. Berkeley (Charlottesville: University of Virginia Press, 2001), 9: 595–96; Robert D. Richardson, *William James: In the Maelstrom of American Modernism* (Boston: Houghton Mifflin, 2006), 388; *MTHHR,* 409. For Kellgren, see also K. Patrick Ober, *Mark Twain and Medicine* (Columbia: University of Missouri Press, 2003), 153–68.

49. WEARY SOJOURNERS

1. MT to Susan L. Crane, December 22, 1899 (MTP); *MTHHR,* 425–26, 430.

2. *MTHHR,* 424; *MTHL,* 2: 715–16; Mark Twain, *Following the Equator* (New York: Harper & Brothers, 1897), 2: 300–301; *Letters,* 2: 694.

3. MT to C. F. Moberly Bell, July [9], 1900 (MTP); MT, "To the Person Sitting in Darkness," in *Following the Equator and Anti-imperialist Essays* (New York: Oxford University Press, 1996), 2.

4. Orion Clemens to MT, December 5, 1887 (MTP); MT to Orion Clemens, December 8, 1887 (Vassar College Library). Articles by Samuel E. Moffett, other than the *Pilgrim* essay of 1903 (see chapter 35, n. 3), include "Mark Twain: A Biographical Sketch," *McClure's Magazine* 13 (October 1899), 523–29; and "Mark Twain, Doctor of Letters," *Review of Reviews* 36 (August 1907), 167–68.

5. MT to Samuel E. Moffett, July 28, 1900 (MTP); *MTHHR,* 446–47n.

6. Hamlin Hill, *Mark Twain: God's Fool* (New York: Harper & Row, 1973), xxvii, 260–61; MT to Samuel E. Moffett, July 29, 1900 (MTP).

7. MT to T. Douglass Murray, June 7, 1900 (Oxford University Library).

8. MT to Joseph H. Twichell, June 22, 1900 (Yale University Library).

9. Mark Twain, *Christian Science* (New York: Oxford University Press, 1996), 9.

10. *MTHHR*, 449.

11. MT to Paul Kester, March 24, 1900 (Division of Rare Books and Manuscripts, New York Public Library).

50. EXILE'S RETURN

1. *MTN*, 372.

2. Hartford *Courant*, 26 October 1900; *MTCI*, 369.

3. *Letters*, 2: 704–6.

4. *Mark Twain's Mysterious Stranger Manuscripts*, ed. William M. Gibson (Berkeley: University of California Press, 1969), 137; "To the Person Sitting in Darkness," in *Following the Equator and Anti-imperialist Essays* (New York: Oxford University Press, 1996), 5–6; *New York Times*, February 7, 1901; *LLMT*, 333.

5. William M. Gibson, "Mark Twain and Howells, Anti-Imperialists," *New England Quarterly* 20 (December 1947), 435–70.

6. For recent commentary on "The United States of Lyncherdom" as well as its text in *Europe and Elsewhere*, ed. Albert Bigelow Paine (New York: Harper & Brothers, 1923), re-edited to replace the bowdlerized version in Paine's edition, see L. Terry Oggel, "Speaking Out about Race: 'The United States of Lyncherdom' Clemens Really Wrote"; Mark Twain, "The United States of Lyncherdom"; and Louis J. Budd, "Afterword: Mark Twain and the Sense of Racism," *Prospects: An Annual in American Cultural Studies* 25 (2000), 115–58.

7. *MTE*, 312–19.

8. *MTHL*, 2: 732n; *LLMT*, 330.

9. "A Double-Barreled Detective Story," in *The $30,000 Bequest and Other Stories* (New York: Oxford University Press, 1996), 490–91, 504, 522; *MTHHR*, 469–70.

10. *MTHHR*, 478–79n; Ida M. Tarbell, *All in the Day's Work: An Autobiography* (New York: Macmillan, 1939), 211–30.

11. *LLMT*, 331–32; *MTHHR*, 480.

12. *LLMT*, 335.

51. HOMELESS

1. *MTHHR*, 484; MT to Franklin G. Whitmore, June 14, 1902, October 18, 1902, and May 18, 1903 (MTP).

2. *MTHHR*, 484.

3. *LLMT,* 338.

4. MT to William R. Gillis, May 16, 1902; MT to Joseph T. Goodman, May 16, 1902 (MTP).

5. *MTHL,* 2: 758n; MT to Frederick A. Duneka, September 15, 1902 (Berg Collection, New York Public Library); MT to Joseph H. Twichell, September 30, 1902 (Yale University Library).

6. MT to A.H. Tyson, December 5, 1902, in *Mark Twain: The Letter Writer,* ed. Cyril Clemens (Boston: Meador, 1932), 108.

7. MT to John Y.W. McAlister, September 23, 1902 (University of Virginia Library); *MTHHR,* 506n, 508, *MTHL,* 2: 747n.

8. MT to Joseph H. Twichell, December 31, 1902 (Yale University Library); MT to Franklin G. Whitmore, January 16, 1903 (MTP); MT to Thomas Bailey Aldrich, January 23, 1903 (Harvard University Library).

9. Carl Thalbitzer to MT, November 13, 1902; MT to Carl Thalbitzer, November 26, 1902 (courtesy of Brita Thalbitzer Hartz; facsimile in MTP).

10. *LLMT,* 344–46.

11. "A Dog's Tale" was published in a pamphlet in 1903 by the National Anti-Vivisection Society; Harper's also published it as a dollar book in 1904.

12. MT to Franklin G. Whitmore, January 16, 1903 (MTP).

13. *MTHL,* 2: 774n.

52. A DEATH IN FLORENCE

1. MT to Mary Mapes Dodge, December 18, 1903 (University of Dayton Library); *MTHHR,* 541–42.

2. MT to John Y.W. MacAlister, November 17, 1903 (University of Virginia Library); *MTHL,* 2: 775; "Italian without a Master," *Harper's Weekly* 48 (January 1904), 18–19; *MTHHR,* 546; Mary Lawton, *A Lifetime with Mark Twain* (New York: Harcourt, Brace & Company, 1925), 223.

3. *MTHHR,* 566; "Italian with Grammar," *Harper's Monthly Magazine* 109 (August 1904), 397–400.

4. *Letters,* 2: 749. "Sold to Satan" was not published until 1923, when it was included in *Europe and Elsewhere* (New York: Harper & Brothers, 1923), 326–38.

5. MT to Susan L. Crane, February 15, 1904 (MTP); *MTHL,* 2: 778.

6. *MTHHR,* 557–58, 567, 561–62.

7. MT to Thomas Bailey Aldrich, June 6, 1904 (Harvard University Library); MT to Susan L. Crane, June 6, 1904 (MTP); MT to Charles J. Langdon, June 8, 1904 (Mark Twain House, Hartford, CT); *MTHHR,* 570–71.

8. Lawton, *A Lifetime with Mark Twain,* 227–29; MT to Susan L. Crane, June 6, 1906 (MTP).

EPILOGUE

1. *MTHL*, 2: 785; MT to Charles J. Langdon, June 19, 1904 (Mark Twain House, Hartford, CT).

2. Karen Lystra, *Dangerous Intimacy: The Untold Story of Mark Twain's Final Years* (Berkeley: University of California Press, 2004), 50. See MT to Jean Clemens, November 6, 1906, and February 21, 1907 (MTP), for Twain's view of his daughter's singing ability and for Clara's fear of being eclipsed in public by her famous father ("She wouldn't be publicly connected with me, but is going to stand or fall on her own merits"). For his comment to Jean about her epilepsy, see MT to Jean Clemens, June 1907 (Mark Twain House, Hartford, CT), transcribed in Ralph W. Ashcroft to J. B. Stanchfield, July 30, 1909 (Ashcroft-Lyon Manuscript, MTP). For the view that Jean actively struck other individuals, see Laura Skandera Trombley, "'She Wanted to Kill': Jean Clemens and Postical Psychosis," *American Literary Realism* 37 (2005), 225–37.

3. Perhaps Clemens's most emphatic rejection of Lyon as a possible mate appears in his unpublished account of the entire Ashcroft-Lyon matter, cast in the form of a letter to Howells, now in the MTP: "Howells, you knew Mrs. Clemens, from the fall of 1871 until her death in 1904, & I wonder if you are able to believe I could ever find a person who would seem to me to be her match, & thus be moved to marry again? Would it occur to you that if I found such a person it might, would or could be Miss Lyon? . . . Miss Lyon compares with her as a buzzard compares with a dove. (I say this with apologies to the buzzard.)" (MS p. 393).

4. Quoted in William Lyon Phelps, *Autobiography with Letters* (New York: Oxford University Press, 1939), 965. Phelps was obviously remembering what Paine quoted Clemens as saying in 1908 (*MTB*, 3: 1440).

5. For the most detailed and comprehensive treatment of the Ashroft-Lyon affair, see Lystra's *Dangerous Intimacy* and Hamlin Hill's *Mark Twain: God's Fool* (New York: Harper & Brothers, 1973). See also the unpublished account in the MTP. Lystra points out that Lyon may have been duplicitous in spending funds to renovate a Connecticut cottage Clemens gave her (185).

6. See Kevin Mac Donnell, "Stormfield: A Virtual Tour," *Mark Twain Journal* 44 (Spring–Fall 2006), 1–68.

7. MT to Clara L. Clemens, March 5, 1907 (photocopy of the MS courtesy of Nick Karanovich, MTP); Journal of Isabel V. Lyon for April 9 or 10, 1906 (University of Texas Library).

8. *Mark Twain's Mysterious Stranger Manuscripts*, ed. William M. Gibson (Berkeley: University of California Press, 1969), 403–5; John S. Tuckey, *Mark Twain and Little Satan* (West Lafayette, IN: Purdue University Studies, 1963), 76.

9. *MTHHR*, 651, 657, 648.

10. Mark Twain, "The Death of Jean," *Harper's Monthly Magazine* 122 (January 1911), 210–15; Lystra, *Dangerous Intimacy,* 255, 258, 249.

11. Mark Twain, *Letters from the Earth,* ed. Bernard De Voto (New York: Harper & Row, 1962), 7.

12. Mark Twain, *1601 and Is Shakespeare Dead?* (New York: Oxford University Press, 1996), 20–21. He wrote Jean on March 3, 1909 (MTP), that he was "having a good time all by myself dictating to the stenographer (Autobiography) a long day-after-day scoff at everybody who is ignorant enough & stupid enough to go on believing Shakespeare ever wrote a play or a poem in his life."

13. Twain, *Letters from the Earth,* 40.

14. MT to William R. Coe, June 27, 1909 (Mark Twain House, Hartford, CT); MT to Clara L. Clemens, February 21 (MTP) and April 21, 1910 (University of Virginia Library).

15. Caroline Thomas Harnsberger, *Mark Twain's Clara* (Evanston, IL: Press of Ward Schori, 1982), 147; Andrew Hoffman, *Inventing Mark Twain: The Lives of Samuel Langhorne Clemens* (New York: William Morrow, 1997), 503.

16. Clara Clemens, *My Husband Gabrilowitsch* (New York: Harper & Brothers, 1938), 31, 84, 173, 190, 193.

17. In his extreme loneliness, Clemens cultivated, beginning in 1908, a relationship with a number of girls between the ages of ten and fifteen whom he dubbed his "Angel-fish." They formed his "Aquarium" or club. These girls were often invited to stay with Clemens and Isabel Lyon for a week or more. Their mothers were fully informed of their visits and assured (and granted) proper supervision for their daughters during the visits. The club began with five or six young people and eventually reached the number of twelve. In several letters, Clemens shared his delight with these young people with both his daughters, and the Aquarium became so popular with those in the writer's New York social circle that even adult women pretended to want to become members. In a letter to Dorothy Quick, one of the earliest Angel-fish, he told her that the wife of dramatist Daniel Frohman "has been trying to get into our Aquarium, & I wouldn't let her. . . . She was dressed for 12 years, & had pink ribbons at the back of her neck & looked about 14 years old; so I admitted her as an angel-fish. . . . There are lots of lady candidates." (MT to Dorothy Quick, May 12, 1908 [MTP]). See also Dorothy Quick, *Mark Twain & Me* (Norman: University of Oklahoma Press, 1961); and Barbara Schmidt, "Mark Twain's Angel-fish and Other Young Women of Interest" (www.twainquotes.com/angelfish/angelfish.html).

18. MT to Clara L. Clemens, April 21, 1910 (University of Virginia Library); and "Nina Clemens Gabrilowitsch, 55, Twain's Last Direct Heir, Dies," New York *Times,* January 19, 1966.

19. James M. Cox, *Mark Twain: The Fate of Humor* (Princeton, NJ: Princeton University Press, 1966).

Index

Works by Twain appear at the end of the index.

WORKS BY MARK TWAIN

Text: 10/14 Palatino
Display: Univers Condensed 47, Bauer Bodoni, Palatino
Compositor: BookMatters, Berkeley
Printer and Binder: Thomson-Shore, Inc.